The Continuous
and the Discrete

The Continuous and the Discrete

*Ancient Physical Theories
from a Contemporary Perspective*

MICHAEL J. WHITE

CLARENDON PRESS · OXFORD

1992

Oxford University Press, Walton Street, Oxford OX2 6DP
Oxford New York Toronto
Delhi Bombay Calcutta Madras Karachi
Petaling Jaya Singapore Hong Kong Tokyo
Nairobi Dar es Salaam Cape Town
Melbourne Auckland
and associated companies in
Berlin Ibadan

Oxford is a trade mark of Oxford University Press

Published in the United States
by Oxford University Press, New York

British Library Cataloguing in Publication Data
Data available

Library of Congress Cataloging in Publication Data
White, Michael J., 1948–
The continuous and the discrete: ancient physical theories from a
contemporary perspective / Michael J. White.
p. cm.
Includes bibliographical references and index.
1. Science—Philosophy—Mathematical models. 2. Aristotle—
Contributions in metaphysics. 3. Metaphysics—Mathematical models.
4. Mathematics—Philosophy. 5. Philosophy, Ancient. I. Title.
Q175.W569 1992   501—dc20   91–28127
ISBN 0-19-823952-1

Typeset by Joshua Associates Ltd, Oxford
Printed in Great Britain by
Biddles Ltd, Guildford & King's Lynn

Preface and Apologia

This book consists of an analysis of three ancient conceptions or 'models' of spatial magnitude, time, and motion: an Aristotelian, a quantum, and a Stoic model. This characterization, I realize, requires its own apologia. Although the nature and extent of the influence of Aristotle on subsequent Hellenistic thought—philosophical and scientific—is a matter of dispute, I am not particularly concerned with that historical issue here. Rather, my aim is to analyse in some detail Aristotle's account of spatial magnitude, time, and motion, and then to examine two Hellenistic conceptions of these basic physical phenomena as conceptual alternatives to the Aristotelian model. I am aware of the lack of parallelism with respect to my designation of the three models. Although I am uncomfortable about this fact, there seemed no easy way to avoid the situation. There is no simple descriptive tag, analogous to 'quantum', for the Aristotelian and Stoic models. And versions of the quantum theory can be associated not only with the Epicurean tradition but also with the 'Dialectical' philosopher Diodorus Cronus, who was a contemporary of Epicurus.

The Aristotelian model receives the most space (roughly the first half of the book) largely because we have much more hard information about it than we do about the other two models. At one level, the Aristotelian model looks very familiar: spatial magnitude, time, and motion have the formal, structural properties of infinite divisibility and continuity. In other words, these phenomena are 'continua' in one sense of this term. Although Aristotle does not have the mathematical apparatus (e.g. the mathematical concept of a function) capable of rigorously expressing these properties in a contemporary form, he does possess the basic formal, structural *ideas*. And in some cases his own apparatus is sophisticated enough that it is possible to show that what Aristotle had in mind is closely related to contemporary accounts of certain properties of spatial magnitude, time, and motion. For example, with respect to a stretch of local motion, the continuity of the function from time elapsed to distance traversed (since the beginning of the motion) can be fairly rigorously deduced from Aristotle's principles of relative speed.

At another level, however, Aristotle's analysis and a standard contemporary analysis of continua part ways. For Aristotle, a fundamental ontological principle is that what is infinitely divisible and continuous cannot be constituted from what is, in an intuitive sense, discrete. Thus, for example, points, which are intuitively discrete, cannot constitute a line; and, in general, continua of dimension n cannot be conceived as sets of limit entities of dimension $n - 1$. It is only in the latter part of the nineteenth century that the development of set theory made attractive such an ontology of continua. In the case of Aristotle, however, the ontology of continua seems to be inextricably wedded to his metaphysical notion of *dunamis* or potentiality, particularly as he employs this concept in his account of infinite divisibility.

One might say that the Aristotelian model, discussed in Part I of this book, represents an application to the physical world of the standard, ancient geometrical conception of extended magnitude. The Hellenistic alternatives to this model discussed in Part II are ungeometrical conceptions of spatial magnitude, time, and motion. The quantum model is an attempt to reduce the geometrical idea of a *megethos* (magnitude) to the arithmetical idea of a *plēthos* (collection) of discrete units. On the other hand, the Stoic model, according to the interpretation of it that I develop, emphasizes the idea of *megethos* at the expense of the idea of a *plēthos* of units. While infinite divisibility is retained in the Stoic model, geometrical-limit entities are eliminated from the physical world in favour of small regions of fuzziness or indeterminacy. The result is a picture in which body blends insensibly into body and motion blends insensibly into rest, without a sharp discrimination among individual things in the world. Both quantum and Stoic models involve a refusal to conceive the physical world in terms of the developing standard ('Euclidean') geometry of antiquity.

Having presented, by way of foreword, some general idea of the content of this study, I turn to the apologia. My subtitle, *Ancient Physical Theories from a Contemporary Perspective*, indicates the methodological orientation of this book. The book may not please, I fear, two prospective groups of readers: those who insist upon taking their history of thought neat, without adulteration by any contemporary philosophical or scientific concerns, and those who are interested only in philosophical or scientific issues in their contemporary, state-of-the-art shape, without adulteration by any developmental, historical concerns. I am most certainly interested in what Aristotle, Diodorus Cronus, the Epicureans, and the Stoics said (and thought) about spatial magnitude, time, and motion. But I am also interested in what they said and thought from the perspective of later developments in mathematics, physics, and the philosophy of science.

A basic conviction underlying my approach, which I shall now try to make quite explicit, is that history of philosophical or scientific thought that is entirely 'Baconian'—that is, merely the collection of textual and historical data and its meticulous classification—is seldom of great *philosophical* or scientific—as opposed to philological—interest. In expressing this conviction, I do not mean to condescend to such philological or historical collection and classification of data. It can be highly useful—perhaps even more so than in the natural sciences. Those of us whose interests (or abilities) may lie in other directions cannot be too grateful to those who undertake such exacting research. Indeed, I remain convinced of the value of methodological pluralism in the history of philosophy.

There seems to me to be a proper place—indeed, a necessary place— for the sort of analysis and hypothesis formation that may not always flow directly, as it were, from the historical and textual data. Consequently, I have not been timid in developing conjectural plausible stories about the historical material with which I am concerned. Also, I have not hesitated to attempt to relate this material, when it has seemed to me useful and appropriate to do so, to issues pertaining to the methodology of mathematics and the physical sciences that arose later in the development of these disciplines. Some may consider my approach to be 'history of *possible* philosophy' rather than history of philosophy. In response, I would maintain that the creative but prudent pursuit of the history of possible philosophy can deepen our philosophical understanding not only of the 'history of *actual* philosophy'—in so far as it is historically recoverable—but also of contemporary philosophical and scientific developments. One way of achieving an understanding of a certain 'model' or doctrine (and its alternatives) is the exploration of ways in which such models *might* have been developed, particularly within the general intellectual constraints of the doctrine or model's own historical period. Of course, it is not for me to say whether, in what follows, I have always been 'creative but prudent' in the application of my method. But the method has been deliberately chosen. And I have attempted to be scrupulous in indicating where, in my view, one of my plausible stories outreaches the historical evidence.

An obvious pitfall of my approach is anachronism. I should like to make a distinction between anachronism that is pernicious and anachronism that is not. The use of contemporary analytical tools does not always, in my view, constitute pernicious anachronism. Nor does the attempt to place a historical philosophical (or scientific) discussion within the conceptual context of later, perhaps more sophisticated, developments. Indeed, I suspect that a degree of anachronism is necessary for achieving the deepest level of *one* kind of understanding of historical philosophical and scientific material. That is, understanding material of this sort requires that it be interpreted in terms of a contemporary philosophical or technical idiom. On the other hand, I certainly recognize the existence of pernicious anachronism. But I doubt that there is an algorithm, at least any very simple algorithm, for distinguishing it from the non-pernicious variety. Consequently, I can offer no guarantee that I have always avoided the pitfall that I have sought to avoid.

Nor can I assure the reader that the following text is neither difficult nor technical. The idea that a book in a so-called humanistic (as opposed to scientific) discipline should make minimal demands with respect to readers' intellectual effort and educational background is a notion—often implicit, sometimes explicit, in critical discussions of such works—that I find curious. Although this issue is perhaps worthy of further discussion, I shall not here indulge the temptation to say more about it. My topic is, I believe, intrinsically 'technical', in some common but harmless sense of that term. Some previous acquaintance with fundamental concepts of mathematics and physics and with the history of ancient physical thought should certainly prove most useful to the reader. The text presupposes practically nothing, however, from modern (Newtonian) or contemporary (relativistic or quantum) physics. More use is made of the contemporary discipline of mathematics than of that of physics. But few mathematical concepts will be encountered that are more advanced than those found in a first-year university calculus course. And, I hope, such concepts are explained in a way that will be comprehensible to those whose formal encounter with mathematics does not constitute the subject-matter of recent (or perhaps particularly fond) memory.

Logical and mathematical symbolism has also been kept to a minimum. Where it does occur, its general import can, I hope, usually be gleaned from its immediate environment. In those cases where something is encountered that may strike a reader as forbidding, I invite that reader—borrowing a colleague's phrase—to 'hum' the offending formula. Likely as not, the general sense of the passage will not be lost.

M. J. W.

Tempe, Arizona
August 1990

Acknowledgements

I find that the setting-down of acknowledgements is one of the very few pleasures to be derived from the ultimate stages of preparing a manuscript for publication. I have received many varieties of assistance from many persons throughout all stages of work on this project. I wish to express my gratitude to all such persons—especially those who may not be mentioned by name in these acknowledgements.

Much of the writing of the manuscript was done during the academic year 1988-9, during the tenure of a Fellowship at the National Humanities Center in Research Triangle Park, North Carolina. The Center and its staff provided an almost idyllic setting for a project such as mine. I am grateful to all the staff, particularly Dr Kent Mullikan, Acting Director during my tenure, and to the other Fellows resident during my stay—the 'Class of 1988-9'. I was especially honoured to be the recipient of one of the two initial Fellowships funded by the Delta Delta Delta sorority. I should also like to thank Arizona State University and its College of Liberal Arts and Sciences for the sabbatical leave during which I was resident at the Center. Also warmly remembered is the hospitality, intellectual and otherwise, of three historians of ancient philosophy, Drs Michael Ferejohn and Paul Vander Waerdt of Duke University and Dr David O'Connor of the University of Notre Dame.

I am grateful to Oxford University Press and its Delegates for their willingness to publish a work that does not fit very neatly into either of the categories of history of ancient philosophy or history and philosophy of science. My special thanks are extended to a reader for OUP, Dr David Bostock of Merton College, Oxford, for supplying detailed, insightful, and eminently useful criticism of my manuscript. Deficiencies of various sorts doubtless remain in the present text. But these deficiencies are at least an order of magnitude less than would have been the case in the absence of Dr Bostock's supererogatory good offices.

Finally, I wish to thank the journals *Apeiron* and *Greek, Roman, and*

Byzantine Studies for permission to use material that overlaps to a degree articles that I have previously published: 'Aristotle on "Time" and "A Time"', *Apeiron: A Journal for Ancient Philosophy and Science*, 22: 3 (1989), 207–24 (by permission of Academic Printing and Publishing); 'What to Say to a Geometer', *Greek, Roman, and Byzantine Studies*, 30: 2 (1989), 297–311. I am also grateful to Sarah Waterlow Broadie for permission to quote from her monograph *Nature, Change, and Agency in Aristotle's 'Physics'* (Oxford, 1982).

Contents

Figures

PART I
Spatial Magnitude, Time, and Motion:
An Aristotelian Model

Introduction to Part I

The mathematician Hermann Weyl, in a wonderfully aphoristic and often quoted remark, claimed that

the objective world simply *is*, it does not *happen*. Only to the gaze of my consciousness, crawling upward along the life line of my body, does a section of this world come to life as a fleeting image in space which continuously changes in time.[1]

Weyl's remark was made within the context of a discussion of contemporary relativistic physics. From that perspective it has received both criticism and support. In antiquity, Aristotle was a consistent and determined opponent of the ontological model of the physical world undergirding the remark. In Part I of this study I shall closely examine both Aristotle's analysis of the physical properties of spatial magnitude, time, and locomotion, and the metaphysical view undergirding this analysis. At the heart of Aristotle's metaphysical view is a conception of 'happening'—'motion' or process (*kinēsis*)—as a fundamental ontological category.

What does the conception of process as fundamental ontological category amount to? This is a question that I hope can be answered, at least with respect to Aristotle, as a result of the examination to be undertaken in Part I. As a beginning, however, I should make clear that such a conception of process amounts to more, for Aristotle, than the affirmation of the reality of change, in one sense of change. In chastising Max Black for what he takes to be a misunderstanding of Weyl, Adolf Grünbaum writes:

but contrary to Black, Weyl's claim that the time of inanimate nature is devoid of *happening* in the sense of *becoming* is not at all tantamount to the Eleatic doctrine that *change* is an illusion of the human mind! It is of the essence of the relativistic account of the inanimate world as embodied in the Minkowski representation that there is change in the sense that different kind of events can (do) occur at different times: the attributes and relations of an object

---

[1] *Philosophy of Mathematics and Natural Science* (Princeton, NJ, 1949), 116.

associated with any given world-line may be different at different times (e.g. its world-line may intersect with different world-lines at different times).[2]

Aristotle certainly wishes to affirm, in opposition to Eleatic monism, the reality of change in Grünbaum's sense: he contends that it is a fundamental physical fact that things are different (i.e. objects have different properties and stand in different relations) at different times. However, I shall argue that he is equally committed to the reality of process or becoming, in precisely the sense of becoming in which it is *contrasted* with change by Grünbaum in the preceding passage.

The import of Aristotle's commitment to process (*kinēsis*) I shall attempt to work out in some detail in the following pages. In brief, however, there is both a physical (or, perhaps more properly, physical/ mathematical) dimension and a metaphysical dimension to this commitment. The physical dimension finds expression in Aristotle's conception of the *continuity* of (at least some forms of) change. It is fair to say, I think, that in this respect the Aristotelian conception of change, particularly change with respect to position, has become the standard, dominant Western conception. On the other hand, the meta-physics undergirding Aristotle's commitment to process enjoyed a long period of ascendancy. But, particularly since the late nineteenth century, the Aristotelian *metaphysical* conception of process has not represented the standard or dominant view. This Aristotelian ontology of motion can most easily be characterized negatively: it opposes the *ontological reduction* of process to (a series of) states of affairs or full actualizations (*energeiai*). This sort of reduction is, from the Aristotel-ian perspective, a special case of the ontological reduction of poten-tialities (*dunameis*) to such states of affairs.

While it is quite indisputable that, according to Aristotle, the fully actualized states of affairs in which potentialities *for those states of affairs* (normally) issue enjoy both a logical/conceptual and an ontological *priority* with respect to those potentialities, I do not believe that Aristotle holds the stronger view that it is possible to reduce potentialities to such fully actualized states of affairs in our scientific analysis of the physical world.[3] For example, the contemporary 'at-at'

---

[2] *Philosophical Problems of Space and Time*, 2nd edn. (Dordrecht and Boston, 1973), 327.

[3] I do not here attempt to defend this more general claim. When the claim is more precisely delimited than here, it becomes obvious that it can be expressed in a variety of weaker and stronger forms. According to one fairly strong interpretation the claim would entail the denial of what Frank Lewis has called the principle of Full Necessitation: 'Where finality [an account or explanation in terms of formal/final *aitia*] obtains, there

analysis of motion—about which I shall have more to say—is reduction-istic in a way objectionable to Aristotle. The locomotion of a body is analysed as a series of states of affairs, i.e. a linearly ordered set of positions of the body with respect to a linearly ordered set of temporal instants at which the body is held to occupy those positions (with some general constraints on the properties of the function from the temporal instants to the instantaneous positions of the body).

The fact that Aristotle's ontology of motion does not agree with the standard contemporary view tends, I believe, to obscure the interest (and subtlety) of his physical analysis of spatial magnitude, time, and motion. I shall be devoting considerable attention in Part I to what might be termed Aristotle's rational kinematics or formal, structural analysis of these magnitudes. Furthermore, I shall argue that, although many of Aristotle's arguments against a reductionist ontology of process are not, by contemporary mathematical and scientific lights, successful, it does not follow from this fact that the development of Newtonian physics and the mathematics of the calculus in the seven-teenth and eighteenth centuries *commits* us to an anti-Aristotelian, reductionist ontology of process.[4] In fact, it is only the full develop-ment, in the late nineteenth century, of the point-set analysis of continuous magnitudes that makes such an ontology of process attrac-tive.

The phrase 'Aristotelian physics' is, I conjecture, most likely to provoke one of the following two psychological associations in the generally informed contemporary reader. One picture commonly associated with the phrase is a cosmological picture of a bounded universe with its unmoved-mover teleological 'generating plant', sys-tem of concentric celestial spheres, and sharp distinction between sup-ralunary and sublunary regions. The other usual connotation of the phrase is that of an erstwhile predominant but now (since the sixteenth or seventeenth century) discredited approach to the study of nature—a 'physics' that (i) overemphasized the 'qualitative' aspects of the natural world (particularly the more striking sense qualities issuing

---

exists a chain of material/efficient causes that fully necessitates *exactly the same product* governed by the formal/final cause' ('Teleology and Material/Efficient Causes in Aristotle', *Pacific Philosophical Quarterly* 69: 1 (1988), 55). See also D. Charles, 'Aristotle on Hypothetical Necessity and Irreducibility,' ibid. 1–53.

[4] The degree to which an Aristotelian, non-reductionistic ontology of motion can accommodate useful concepts (e.g. instantaneous velocity) supplied to classical mechanics by the mathematics of the differential and integral calculus is a topic that I shall explore in Ch. 4.

from our interaction with this world), (ii) underemphasized mensuration and the mathematical analysis of quantitative aspects of this world, and (iii) appealed to such dubious explanatory principles as occult essences and final causes.

However, when we examine the contents of the work of Aristotle traditionally referred to as the *Physica* (or, in Greek, *Phusikē akroasis*, 'physical [or natural] discourse'), it is clear that, after a general historical introduction, the bulk of it consists of conceptual examination of process (with an emphasis on locomotion) and of various allied concepts that, Aristotle believes, must necessarily enter into an analysis of process or motion: time, place, void, spatial extension or magnitude (*megethos*), infinity. Indeed, in *Phys*. 3. 4 Aristotle characterizes the 'science pertaining to nature' as being concerned with spatial magnitude (*megethos*), motion or process (*kinēsis*), and time (*chronos*) (202^{b}30–1).[5] In what follows I shall be concerned with Aristotle's physics in this fairly specific sense. His rational kinematics or analysis of process (particularly locomotion) and his analysis of the closely allied concepts of spatial magnitude and time will occupy centre stage. There is a clear sense in which Aristotle's physics, so understood, is not mathematical: we do not find the *Physics* chock-full of mathematical equations; nor do we find in it much in the way of *dynamics*, an attempt to determine precise mathematical relations among the motion of a body and such concepts as its mass and the forces impressed on it. None the less, we do find detailed, rigorous analysis of the formal, structural features of motion, time, and spatial magnitude. Rather than attempting to specify an abstract account of what I mean by 'formal, structural features', I hope to develop a more detailed sense of this concept in the ensuing discussion. I turn first to Aristotle's formal, structural analysis of physical continua such as spatial magnitude and local motion, and then turn to the metaphysical underpinnings of his analysis of these continua.

---

[5] I shall cite, in the text, quotations from Aristotle using the standard Bekker pagination.

1

Aristotle: The Formal Analysis of Spatial Magnitude and Locomotion

Aristotle, no less than the contemporary physicist, assumes that any rigorous investigation of motion—at least in the special case of *locomotion* or motion with respect to place—will also involve an investigation of time and spatial magnitude. Just as contemporary scientific and philosophical thought typically attributes to space, time, or space-time properties of some Cartesian power of the field of real numbers (e.g. density and continuity), so Aristotle's conception of these magnitudes is developed—as I argue in Chapter 4—on the basis of his understanding of the mathematical (geometrical) science of his day.

In this chapter, I shall concentrate on Aristotle's formal, structural analysis of spatial magnitude and locomotion. What I mean by 'formal, structural analysis' will emerge in the following discussion. In brief, it is an analysis of spatial magnitude and motion in terms of their *geometrical* or *topological* properties. Although this analysis is not entirely 'metaphysically neutral', it can to a certain extent be separated from the more obviously metaphysical features of Aristotle's discussion of spatial magnitude, time, and motion. Doing so seems to me to be valuable as an aid both to understanding Aristotle's contributions to the formal analysis of continuous magnitudes and to clarifying the relation between Aristotle's formal analysis and the metaphysics that he develops to undergird that analysis.

SPATIAL MAGNITUDE

Aristotle regards the formal, structural properties of time and locomotion as being derived from the structural properties of spatial extension or magnitude. For example, in *Phys*. 4. 11 he comments that

since what is moved is moved from something to something and every spatial magnitude is continuous, motion follows magnitude in this regard: for it is on account of the magnitude's being continuous that the motion is continuous, and on account of the motion's [being continuous] that the time is. (219ª10–13)

What Aristotle means by 'continuity' (*sunecheia*) will be discussed in detail later in this chapter. However, one property that Aristotle considers continuity to *imply* is infinite divisibility: 'it is clear that everything that is continuous is divisible to what is itself always divisible' (*Phys*. 6. 1. 231ᵇ15–16). In the *Physics* and in *On generation and corruption* (hereafter abbreviated *GC*), Aristotle develops several arguments to the effect that what is continuous is infinitely divisible in the following strong sense of this phrase: what is continuous cannot be partitioned (i.e. divided into parts that are mutually disjoint—none 'overlaps' any other—and that are jointly exhaustive—none of the original whole is 'left out') in such a way that any of these resultant parts is itself indivisible (*adiaireton*). Although his arguments for infinite divisibility in this sense are not unrelated, there are some interesting and significant differences among them.

A Metrical Argument Against the Constitution of Continua from Points

One sort of indivisible, in Aristotle's view, has 'zero measure': it is a point having no quantity or size (*to poson*).[1] One argument, in its simplest form, that a magnitude cannot be constituted of such punctal indivisibles is summarized by Aristotle's remark in *GC* 1. 2: 'it is absurd that a magnitude should be constituted from non-magnitudes' (316ᵇ5).

Brian Skyrms has argued that this comment implicitly appeals to a principle that is crucial to contemporary formulations of what has come to be known as 'Zeno's paradox of measure'. According to this principle, variously termed complete additivity, ultra-additivity, or super-additivity, if a magnitude is partitioned into a class of parts, then the 'size' or measure of the whole original magnitude must equal the sum of the measures ('sizes') of all the parts. According to Skyrms, the present application of the principle is the following: although Aristotle has, as we shall see, reasons for denying that a magnitude could be partitioned into an infinitely large collection of punctal parts, he is committed to the propositions that *if* (perhaps *per impossibile*) such a partition could be effected, the size of each point would have to be nil,

---

[1] See e.g. *Phys*. 6. 1. 231ª25–26.

and irrespective of the number of times nil is added to nil, the sum cannot be anything other than nil.

Although the standard contemporary mathematical conception of continuous magnitudes denies the complete additivity principle, 'this', as Skyrms comments, 'does not appear to be a line that was taken in ancient times'.[2] I am inclined to think that Skyrms is indeed correct that *denial* of a complete additivity principle was not a 'line that was taken in ancient times' but that this claim is correct largely because of the lack of adequate means in antiquity for *formulating* anything like the principle.

A necessary (but not sufficient) condition of explicitly formulating the principle is the capacity for extending the notion of addition to cases involving an infinite number of addenda. In cases where a denumerable collection of addenda (i.e. a collection that can be put into one-to-one correspondence with the natural numbers) is involved, this extension is now standardly effected using the limit concept. The sum S of a denumerably infinite series of addenda, $s_1 + s_2 + \ldots + s_n + \ldots$, is the limit (if there is such a limit) of the denumerably infinite sequence $\{t_n\}$, where each term t_n in the sequence is the sum of the first n s_is. To take a simple Zenonian example, $S = 1/2 + 1/4 + 1/8 \ldots$ will be the limit of the infinite sequence $\{(2^n - 1)/2^n\} = 1/2, 3/4, 7/8, 15/16, \ldots$, which is 1.

By the lights of contemporary, Cantorian mathematics, however, the cardinality of the points in any continuous region is greater than the cardinality of the set of natural numbers. So, for *complete* additivity, i.e. a form of additivity principle that would be applicable to points in a continuous region, a further extension of the notion of addition is required. As Massey, Grünbaum,[3] Skyrms, *et al.* have noted, such an extension is mathematically possible. For example, Skyrms employs the following generalized account of 'sum', applicable to non-denumerable as well as denumerable collections of addenda:

Let S be an infinite set of magnitudes, and let S^* be the set of *finite* sums of magnitudes in S. A real number is an *upper bound* for S^* if and only if it is greater than or equal to every member of S^*. Let the *sum* of S be defined as the

---

[2] 'Zeno's Paradox of Measure', in R. S. Cohen and L. Laudan (eds.), *Physics, Philosophy and Psychoanalysis: Essays in Honor of A. Grünbaum* (Dordrecht, 1983), 227.

[3] See Grünbaum, *Philosophical Problems of Space and Time*, ch. 6, 'The Resolution of Zeno's Metrical Paradox of Extension for the Mathematical Continua of Space and Time', 158–76; see also Appendix, 808–21. See also G. Massey, 'Panel Discussion of Grünbaum's Philosophy of Science', *Philosophy of Science*, 36 (1969), 337.

least upper bound [that is, the real number r such that, for every upper bound r' of S^*, $r \leqslant r'$] of S^* if a real least upper bound exists, and as infinity otherwise.[4]

Although the definition of a measure possessing such a strong additivity property is mathematically possible, it would yield consequences that are paradoxical in a manner reminiscent of Zeno. For, if zero measure is assigned to the points (more properly, to the singleton sets of points) in a continuous region, the measure of the region itself would then be zero. But if some positive finite real number r is the measure of each singleton of a point, then, by Archimedes' axiom[5], the measure of the region would be infinite.

There is very little evidence that Aristotle would have recognized any such extension of the concept of addition to cases where there are infinite addenda. However, a *necessary condition* of the extension of addition to cases of denumerably infinite addenda is noted by Aristotle in *Phys*. 3. 6:

> The infinite by addition is in a sense the same as that by division, but in a finite magnitude the infinite by addition occurs in a way inverse to that by division; for as that magnitude is seen being divided to infinity, the sum of the parts taken appears to tend toward something definite [*to hōrismenon*]. For if, in a finite magnitude, one takes a definite part and then from what remains keeps on taking a part, not equal to the first part but always using the same ratio, he will not traverse the original finite magnitude; but if he is to so increase the ratio that the parts taken are always equal, he will traverse it, because every finite magnitude is exhausted by any definite magnitude. Thus it is in this and not in any other way that the infinite exists, namely, potentially and by reduction [*epi kathairesei*]. (206^b3–13)[6]

What Aristotle in this passage notices is the following: if one begins with a magnitude, say of unit measure, and successively divides it in a geometrical progression, always taking the same ratio of the remainder, and if one *simultaneously* performs the inverse operation of adding the parts one has *thus far* 'divided off', then the sum of the parts that one has thus far divided, as one carries on with the inverse processes of dividing and summing, 'tend[s] toward something

---

[4] Skyrms, 'Zeno's Paradox', 227.

[5] The so-called axiom/postulate of Archimedes (or of Eudoxus) will receive intensive scrutiny in Ch. 4. One commonly encountered version of it is the following: for any magnitudes x, y such that $0 < x < y$, there is some natural number (positive integer) n such that x added to itself n times exceeds y.

[6] I have here used the translation of Hippocrates G. Apostle, *Aristotle's Physics* (Grinnell, Ia., 1969), 54. Unless explicitly noted, translations are my own.

definite', a limit. For example, in the case of Zeno's Dichotomy, if one takes 1/2 of the whole, then 1/2 of the remainder (1/2 of 1/2), and then 1/2 of the 'new' remainder (1/2 of 1/49), etc., and sums what one has thus far divided off as one is dividing it, the sum 'tends toward something definite', i.e. the whole, as the inverse processes are indefinitely continued. Although he recognizes that the inverse processes of division and addition are 'infinitely extendable' in the sense of indefinitely continuable—one can always take the division and correlative summation a step beyond any finite division/summation— he scrupulously avoids conceiving the infinitely extendable divisions as constituting anything like a complete totality. It is thus also unlikely that it would have occurred to Aristotle to *identify* the limit or 'something definite' to which the *finite* sums of divisions/additions converge (a fact of which Aristotle is fully aware) as an 'infinite sum' of the measures of these divided parts.

Aristotle's strongly 'constructive' conception of infinity precludes his making the move from (*a*) the recognition that an indefinitely extendable series of addenda tends toward a limit to (*b*) the identification of the 'sum' of such a series with the limit. According to Aristotle, 'the infinite is that of which, with respect to quantity, it is always possible to take something beyond what has been taken' (*Phys*. 3. 6. 207^{a}7–8). That is, Aristotle's notion of the infinite is tied to a process that can be thought of as consisting in a series of discrete 'stages' or 'steps'—either a process of addition (*prosthesis*) of a unit or quantity to other such units/quantities or a process of the division (*diairesis*) of some original, fixed quantity into subquantities. Such a process can, in principle, always be carried a step beyond any determinate (i.e. finite) number of steps. 'The infinite', in this sense, Aristotle contrasts with what is 'complete and whole' (*teleion kai holon*) (207^{a}10). Consequently, his conception of infinity precludes his entertaining anything like a principle of perfect additivity in the sense in which this concept is employed by Massey, Grünbaum, Skyrms, *et al*. For the intelligibility of such a principle has as a necessary condition the intelligibility of the notion of a 'sum' of an infinite collection of addenda. And the intelligibility of the notion of such an infinite 'sum' depends, in turn, on treating the infinite collection of addenda as a 'whole' or totality, a 'completed' collection of addenda like any finite collection of addenda but simply of greater cardinality.

So not only historical facts about the development of mathematics but theoretical considerations concerning his analysis of infinity militate against Aristotle's assumption of something like a general principle of complete additivity to ground his claim that, if a continuous magnitude were constituted of punctal parts with no size, then (absurdly) the magnitude itself would have no size. It is none the less arguable that the *per impossibile* context in which the issue arises in *GC* 1. 2—his assumption at 316^a ff. that a magnitude could be divided completely (*pantēi*) in such a way that it is partitioned into points—leads him to accept implicitly a special case of the principle where there is an infinity of addenda (because of the infinity of points required by the *per impossibile* assumption), each of nil size, the sum of which must be nil.

One of the principal arguments that Aristotle gives in *GC* 1. 2 begins at 316^{a}30:

Similarly were it to consist of points, it would not have quantity. For when the points were touching and together and there was one magnitude, they did not make the whole larger: when it was divided into two or more parts, the whole was neither less nor greater than before. So that if all the points were combined, they would not make any magnitude.   (316^{a}30–5)

This argument is obviously compact, even crabbed; furthermore, it presupposes, I believe, quite a bit of Aristotelian doctrine concerning points. Aristotle's conception of points is 'constructive' in the sense that they are always conceived in terms of continuous magnitudes rather than vice versa: they are the terminations or limits (*perata*) of line-segments or the loci of potential divisions of such a line or the juncture of two line-segments joined end on end. Although there are some subtle and significant nuances of signification, the following terms are all used by Aristotle to designate points: *stigmē* ('speck', a common mathematical term), *sēmeion* ('position', a term also used mathematically), *tomē* ('cut'), *diairesis* ('division'), and *aphē* ('contact'). Of course, lines themselves are limits or divisions of surfaces, while surfaces are limits/divisions of bodies.[7]

According to Aristotle's account in *Meta*. 3. 5, when bodies come into contact, their limits or boundaries, which were two in number before contact, become one in number at contact; while if a continuous body capable of being divided is in fact divided, the previously *potential* boundary between the parts, which is conceived as one in number before division, becomes two in number when actual division occurs. As Aristotle puts it, 'so that [a boundary] does not exist but has

---

[7] See *Meta*. 11. 2. 1060^{b}12 ff.

perished when [bodies] have been joined together, and when they have been divided [boundaries] exist that formerly did not' (1002ᵇ2–3). This singular conception of the creation and destruction of points and other limit entities without any accompanying *process* of generation or destruction, according to Aristotle's account, is fundamental to his conception of the continuity of spatial magnitude, time, and (local) motion; as such, it will receive further consideration later. However, its role in the argument of the *GC* 1. 2 passage quoted above seems to be the following: the gain of a boundary—a point, if we consider just one dimension—in the case of the division of a continuous magnitude into two parts, and the loss of a boundary/point in the case of joining together of two magnitudes into a continuous whole, does not cause a difference between the sum of the quantities of the two parts of the continuous whole and the total quantity of the continuous whole in its undivided state. Aristotle then apparently proceeds to generalize inductively: the 'addition' or 'subtraction' of points considered as limits of continuous parts of a continuous whole does not affect the quantity or measure of the sum of the measure of the parts versus the measure of the whole; that is, when we divide a continuous whole we gain an additional point (the potential single point of division has become two points, the respective limits of the two pieces), but the measure of the whole is no less than the sum of the measures of the parts; consequently, the 'composition' of a body out of points could not yield a body with any positive measure or size since the loss or gain of an *individual* point does not affect the (sum of the) measure(s) of the continuous magnitudes to which such a point is added or subtracted.[8]

One could, of course, claim that implicit in this inductive generalization is a principle of complete additivity. But I think that the following principle of non-supervenience of positive measure more perspicuously captures Aristotle's intentions:

N-SM. Each partition of a continuous magnitude having positive measure or size into proper parts yields parts the sums of whose measures are all non-nil.[9]

---

[8] Cf. *Meta*. 3. 4. 1001ᵇ13–14: 'e.g. a plane [segment] and line [segment] in one sense make what they are added to greater [sc. when added 'end to end' in the case of line-segments and 'side to side' in the case of plane segments] but in another sense [sc. in the dimension in which they are assumed to be without extension], they do not. But a point and a [dimensionless] unit do so in no sense.'

[9] Cf. *Phys*. 6. 2. 232ᵃ23: 'every magnitude is divisible into magnitudes.'

I dub this principle a non-supervenience principle because it says, in effect, that, if one is to attribute positive size to a body, its parts must have *some* positive size irrespective of the way we divide it up. In other words, according to the principle, positive magnitude cannot mysteriously 'supervene' when we have 'synthesized' enough parts, each having zero magnitude. As we shall see, Aristotle holds (and clearly states) an analogous non-supervenience principle for the property of continuity. Although both non-supervenience principles hold considerable intuitive appeal, they are squarely at odds with standard contemporary mathematical analysis.

In *GC* 1. 2 Aristotle suggests that the preceding sort of argument for the metrical impossibility of a magnitude's being constituted from points without magnitude might incline one to accept indivisible *quanta*, 'indivisible bodies or magnitudes' (316^{b}16). But, as Aristotle also there notes, he has other arguments that this alternative hypothesis 'turns out to be no less impossible'. Some of these arguments will be considered in Chapter 5 of this study, which is devoted to an examination of the ancient quantum or atomistic alternative to the Aristotelian conception of spatial magnitude, time, and locomotion. However, I shall now examine what I take to be another argument, more topological than measure-theoretic in nature, that he adduces in *GC* 1. 2 against the possibility of an actual or 'completed' resolution of a magnitude into points.

Another Argument Against the Constitution of Continua from Points

A difficult passage in which Aristotle seems to set forth a different sort of argument occurs in *GC* 1. 2:

Since it is not the case that point is contiguous [*echomenē*] to point, divisibility throughout [*pantēi*] of magnitudes is possible in one sense but not in another. When such division is postulated, it seems that there is a point both at any place [*opēioun*] and at every place [*pantēi*], so that it is necessary that the magnitude be divided to nothing. For [it seems that] there is a point at every place so that [the magnitude] is constituted of 'contacts' [*haphōn*] or points. But divisibility throughout is possible only in the sense that there is a single point at any place—and all points taken singly [are at some place]; but there is not more than one at any place (because they are not successively ordered [*epheksēs*]), so that it is not divisible throughout. For, then, if it is divisible at the mid-point, it will be divisible at a contiguous point. But it is not: position is not contiguous with position nor point with point. Thus for division and composition.

The following propositions pertaining to this argument seem to be (relatively) clear: (i) Aristotle allows as legitimate a sense of 'divisibility throughout' or 'complete divisibility' according to which there is no position at which a magnitude cannot be *potentially* divided; (ii) he holds that a stronger sense of 'divisibility throughout', according to which a magnitude could be divided at *every* place (*pantēi*), is illegitimate because of the fact that no point or 'position' is contiguous to any other such point. What is most unclear, as commentators have realized, is the reasoning Aristotle implicitly relies on to support (ii), the claim that the lack of contiguity or successive ordering of points precludes *actual* complete division (division *everywhere*).

This argument has been discussed in detail by Fred Miller. Miller's interpretation, in brief, is the following. Since point is not contiguous to point in a (continuous) magnitude, it will be the case, at any finite stage in a process of division, that there is a remaining interval of magnitude between any two points of division thus far made; and this remaining interval is capable of being further divided. To quote Miller,

In conclusion, a magnitude can be 'divided everywhere' only by a process in which a subsection is divided into further subsections. There is never a stage at which the division is completed and the line consists exclusively of unextended constituents. For an actually existing point necessarily presupposes the existence of extended magnitudes which have been divided.[10]

As Miller remarks, his interpretation of the argument assumes that Aristotle 'relies upon his own "constructivist" conception of a point as an accidental feature of extended magnitudes undergoing operations'.[11] Miller's attractive interpretation warrants, in my view, further consideration. Two elements of his account probably should be distinguished. And a question that arises is whether these elements are invoked by Aristotle as implicit *premises* of the argument. The first element is Aristotle's own 'constructive' account of infinite division, i.e. his conception of infinite division as a process that can, in principle, proceed beyond *any* actual (finite) stage of division and that can never actually be completed. Given this conception of infinite division, Aristotle has a rather simple argument at his disposal against the supposition of the everywhere-divisibility or divisibility-throughout of extended magnitude: since extended magnitude is infinitely divisible,

[10] F. D. Miller, Jr., 'Aristotle against the Atomists', in N. Kretzmann (ed.), *Infinity and Continuity in Ancient and Medieval Thought* (Ithaca, NY, and London, 1982), 100.
[11] Ibid.

division of the magnitude can always (at each finite stage) be taken a step further and, consequently, the magnitude cannot actually be divided into an infinite number of constituents. On the assumption that there is an infinite number of 'potential divisions' (points) in a magnitude—and the fact that point is not contiguous to point would serve as a statement of the infinite divisibility of magnitude, in this sense—it follows that the magnitude could not actually be resolved into nothing but points. That is, to quote Miller, 'there is never a stage at which the division is completed'.[12] If this is all that Aristotle had in mind, however, it is not crucial to the argument that the 'terminal elements' of such a division be points. For, consider the division characterizing (one version of) the Zenonian Dichotomy: successive division of the unit magnitude into the subsections [0,1/2], [1/2,3/4], [3/4,7/8], etc. *ad infinitum*. This division can always be carried a step further (than any finite step) and thus, in Aristotle's view, cannot be conceived as *actually* completed. But the elements into which the division resolves the unit magnitude *are* successive and contiguous (and, in fact, continuous) according to the definitions of these concepts given in *Phys*. 5. 3.

The second element in Miller's interpretation is, I take it, what underlies his comment concerning Aristotle's '"constructivist" conception of a point as an accidental feature of extended magnitudes undergoing operations'. I interpret the upshot of this remark, as well as several others made by Miller, to be the following. According to Aristotle's conception, a point is either the 'locus of a potential division of a *magnitude*' or a 'terminus (end-point) of a magnitude after the actual division of a given magnitude into smaller *magnitudes*'. Either way, the existence of points presupposes the existence of magnitudes (or potentially divided 'submagnitudes') of which the points are the (potential or actual) limits. Consequently, there is a conceptual incoherence in the idea that a magnitude could be divided throughout in the sense that it could be resolved into *nothing but* points (more specifically, into points but no magnitudes). As Aristotle has said earlier in *GC* 2. 1, 'A contact is always a contact of two things; that is, there is something beyond the contact or division or point' (316[b]6–7).

It is worth noting that this argument is simply an argument against a magnitude's being resolved into nothing but points. On the assumption (made by Philoponus in his commentary on 316[b]6–7[13] and

---

[12] Ibid.

[13] Philoponus, *In Aristotelis libros de generatione et corruptione commentaria*, ed. H. Vitelli, Commentaria in Aristotelem Graeca (hereafter, CAG), 14: 2 (Berlin, 1897), 32.

explicitly argued for in several places by Aristotle) that the 'some-things' that are touching or contiguous and the 'contact' of which is a point cannot *themselves* be points, the argument does not depend upon the non-successive or non-discrete ordering of points in a magnitude. Points have to be points *of* things that are not themselves points. Con-strued in this way, the argument is equally effective against the assumption that a magnitude could be resolved into a collection of points that are ordered discretely or successively (*epheksēs*).

Aristotle's argument as interpreted by Miller seems to resolve itself into separate arguments. Given his conception of the only-potential-not-actual nature of infinite divisibility, Aristotle can argue that a division of an extended magnitude into *any* infinite collection of con-stituents (e.g. points) cannot actually be completed and, hence, that the magnitude is not divisible throughout in the strong (point every-where, no undivided magnitudes remaining) sense. Or, given his con-ception of a point as a (potential) locus of a division of a magnitude or as a contact of the two 'somethings' (which are not themselves points) resulting from such a division and then reunited, he can argue that a division of an extended magnitude into a collection of constituents containing points and nothing else is impossible and, hence, that the magnitude is not divisible throughout in the same 'strong' sense. Not only do we have two arguments; neither seems to require that the ele-ments into which a process of infinite division resolves the magnitude should *not* be contiguous with each other. Of course, in Aristotle's view, at every stage in a process of infinite division there is a magni-tude left to be divided and, consequently, at no stage are two points either contiguous with or in succession (*epheksēs*) to each other;[14] and there is additionally a conceptual absurdity in supposing that two points could be contiguous (although it is not quite so clear that there is an altogether similar absurdity in the assumption that they could be in succession).

It seems that Aristotle's argument (or arguments), particularly the role played in the argument by the premiss concerning the non-contiguous ordering of points, is considerably less than pellucid. One possibility is that Aristotle is not assuming as *premisses* either his

---

[14] The fact that there is a point in the sense of *potential* division between any two such points—even if such a division has not *actually* been made—seems to be regarded by Aristotle as sufficient to exclude the 2 points' being in succession on the grounds that there is something of the same kind, the point in the sense of potential division, between them.

'constructive' conception of infinite division or his conception of points as (potential or actual) termini/limits of something (e.g. magnitudes) other than points. It may be that, rather than *assuming* his full-blown doctrine of infinity, which precludes such a completed actual infinite division, Aristotle is here attempting an indirect proof of it. I believe that Miller also entertains this possibility in his discussion of the argument. 'Aristotle's reasoning'—i.e. his reasoning that in a process of division subsections *of magnitude* must necessarily remain—could be evaded, Miller suggests (pp. 98-9),

only if, at some state, subsections were divisible not into still smaller subsections but into something else altogether, viz., unextended points. In order to rule out this alternative, Aristotle adds the sentence at 317ᵃ10-12: 'For, if it is divisible at the centre (*kata to meson*) it will also be divisible at the adjoining point; but (this cannot be the case), for there is no location adjoining location or point adjoining point, but this is division and combination.' The use of *kata to meson* at 317ᵃ10 implies that Aristotle is envisaging a division which is a stage in the recursive process of division *kata to meson* by which the magnitude is divided up. Aristotle denies that the magnitude could consist of point-like locations or be divided up into points, because neither of these can be 'adjoining' (*echomenē*) or 'in succession' (*ephexēs*).

The suggestion is that, since the points in a continuous magnitude are not 'adjoining' or *discretely* ordered, it is impossible that the magnitude be divided into 'nothing but points', i.e. be conceived as a collection of points with no undivided magnitudes remaining 'intact'. But *why* might Aristotle have thought this? There seem to me to be two possible lines of reasoning that could underlie this assumption. The first is that it is only with a discrete ordering of points in a finite interval[15] that one could actually effect a 'complete division' in a *finite* number of steps—'slice' the magnitude into singletons of points or 'punctal bits' no two of which remain joined. But the fact that points are not discretely ordered means that one cannot, in a finite number of steps, complete the division. So this line of reasoning *does* implicitly appeal to Aristotle's 'constructive' notion of an infinite process as one that is essentially not completable, because, at any finite stage, it can always be continued.

According to another possible line of reasoning, which I suspect is more likely to have been what Aristotle had in mind, the fact that

[15] Actually, a strong, 'second order' property, which may be regarded as a form of discreteness, is required: every subset of linearly ordered points in the finite, bounded interval must have both a first and a last element.

points do not occur in succession, i.e. are not discretely ordered, means that there must *necessarily* remain 'undivided' magnitude 'between' points. Aristotle may have thought that it is possible to *argue* successfully for this claim—to argue that such a completed infinite division is impossible. Assume, for the sake of *reductio*, that a 'completed' infinite division of a magnitude into nothing but points has been effected; but then, because a point is not contiguous (or in succession) to point, there must be undivided magnitudes remaining, which contradicts the *reductio* assumption. Although Philoponus' commentary is not much help, he seems to interpret the core of Aristotle's argument in something like this way: 'since it is not possible that point is contiguous to point, this given point [e.g. the mid-point] and the division at this point are also a joining together of magnitudes (*sunthesis megethōn*)'.[16] The question remains, however, as to how Aristotle might have derived this conclusion—that undivided magnitudes would remain even after a supposed 'complete' infinite division—from the premiss of the non-contiguity of points.

The following represents an argument, which perhaps would have been plausible by Aristotle's standards, even if fallacious from the contemporary logical and mathematical perspective. Suppose that a 'complete' division of a unit magnitude has been effected and consider, as Aristotle does, the mid-point (*meson*). Since no point is contiguous or in succession to any other point, the following principle must hold:

P1. For each point p before the mid-point m, there is some finite positive quantity ϵ such that the distance between p and m is at least ϵ.

Aristotle may have concluded on the basis of P1 that, since the principle is true of *every* point before m, there must be *some* undivided magnitude with m as its 'right' terminus. This conclusion, however, could be plausibly supported only by the truth of

P2. There is some finite positive quantity ϵ such that, for each point p before mid-point m, the distance between p and m is at least ϵ.

So, according to this analysis, the argument would implicitly involve an illicit quantifier shift. P1 says (quite correctly, from the contemporary perspective) that for *each* point before the mid-point m, *there is some* finite positive distance between it and m. Reversing the order of universal and existential quantifiers, P2 says (incorrectly, from the

---

[16] Philoponus, *In de gen. et corr.*, 41. 12–13.

contemporary perspective) that there is some finite positive distance such that *m* is at least that far from each and every point before it.

If P2 were true, it would (absurdly) leave an undivided magnitude after a supposed 'complete' infinite division of the original unit magnitude and the *reductio* would be successful. But P2 would follow from P1 only if the 'limit' (least upper bound) of the collection of points before *m* were itself some point *p* before *m*. But, by contemporary lights, it is not; the least upper bound of this set of points is *m* itself.

Cast in this 'measure-theoretic' way, the fallacy may look rather simple-minded. It should be remembered, however, that quantifier-shift fallacies are extraordinarily easy to commit, particularly when arguments are formulated without the aid of the notation of predicate logic. Yet I believe that there are more subtle, 'proto-topological' considerations that might have made the distinction between P1 and P2 very difficult for Aristotle to fathom. According to contemporary analysis, if the unit interval is bisected at the mid-point, what results are two sub-intervals. If the mid-point itself is put into the 'right' interval, the 'left' interval will be 'open on the right', i.e. it will not contain a least upper bound.

Aristotle, however, does not seem to recognize such open (or half-open) intervals of magnitude. As we saw, his view is that the actual bisection of an interval results in *two distinct points*, a limit or terminus of each sub-interval, where there was formerly one 'position' (*sēmeion*). And if the sub-intervals are joined, the two distinct termini become one *sēmeion*. This view of bisection[17] probably derives from a rather 'visual' or 'physical' conception of the process of bisection. For, if we take a (supposedly continuous) physical object and cut it into two pieces, it would seem strange to say that one piece contains its limit (at the place of bisection) but that the other piece does not contain such a limit—that the end where it has been cut, although obviously limited, does not *contain* its terminus in the way that the other piece does.

For Aristotle to distinguish P1 and P2, he needs to be able to conceive the unit magnitude as being bisected at the mid-point *m* in such a way that the collection of points before *m* is 'open'—has no terminus or last member. But his notion of an *actual* bipartition of a magnitude seems to preclude his doing so. Even such a stalwart exponent of the reasonableness of the standard contemporary mathematical analysis of continuous magnitudes as Adolf Grünbaum

---

[17] *Meta*. 3. 5. 1002ª32–4.

admits that the 'attempt to form a *visual* picture of the *open end* of a finite space interval' is 'misguided' and, indeed, impossible.[18] And this seems to be part of Aristotle's problem. But the problem goes a bit deeper, I think. Suppose that we do conceive of all the points before the mid-point *m* as a densely ordered totality, itself not containing an upper bound (i.e. as a 'right-open' interval) followed by *m*. We hold—as did Aristotle—that between *m* and any point *p* in this collection there is some finite distance. But what is the distance between *m* and the *totality* of these points? If this question is admitted to be well-formed, the answer would have to be 'zero'. On a little reflection, this answer seems quite strange. For it may suggest that it is at least logically possible for, say, the punctal centre of gravity of a moving body to be nil distance from *m* (having traversed the totality of points prior to *m*) without actually having arrived at *m* (since *m* is not itself one of the points in the collection of points prior to it).[19] But there is no point distinct from *m* that is nil distance from *m*; hence, there is no punctal location for the centre of gravity of a body which has traversed all the points prior to *m* but which has not arrived at *m*.

The upshot is that, for Aristotle to support a distinction between P1 and P2, he needs some concepts, in particular, the (proto)topological concepts of a linearly but densely ordered set of points 'constituting' a finite but right-open interval, that would not readily be accessible to or accepted by him. And without such machinery to support the distinction, it would be very easy for him to move from the claim that mid-point *m* is separated from *each* point by some finite quantity of magnitude (since *m* is not contiguous or in succession to any other point) to the following conclusions: (*a*) *m* is separated from *all* points by some finite quantity of magnitude; (*b*) it is thus (absurdly) the case that a *completed* infinite division of a magnitude would leave residual magnitudes.

Irrespective of the faithfulness to Aristotle's intentions of this last interpretation of his argument in *GC* 1. 2, the interpretation does, I

---

[18] *Modern Science and Zeno's Paradoxes* (London, 1967) 88.

[19] Obviously analogous is the claim that, if one can treat as a totality what Gregory Vlastos has called the Z-runs in Zeno's Dichotomy (the run that places the runner at the mid-point of a unit interval, the run that places him at the mid-point of the remaining distance, the run that places him at the mid-point of the 'next' remaining distance, etc., *ad infinitum*), then it seems to be logically possible for the runner to be zero distance from the endpoint (by having completed all the Z-runs) without traversing the endpoint (because the endpoint is not a point arrived at by *any* Z-run). Whether this a reasonable moral to draw from the standard contemporary mathematical analysis of the Dichotomy will be discussed in Ch. 4.

believe, point up a noteworthy aspect of Aristotle's conception of continuous magnitudes. There is a sense in which Aristotle is quite willing to admit the 'density' of points in a (one-dimensional) continuous magnitude. Since a 'line is always between points' (*Phys.* 6. 1. 231ᵇ9), it is always theoretically *possible* to divide this line and mark a third point between the two. I refer to this notion as '*distributive density*'. Note that distributive density, as I am using the concept, does not postulate an 'actually infinite' collection of discrete elements, linearly ordered in such a way that between any two there is a third, distinct element (and hence an infinite number of distinct elements). I refer to a linear array of an actually infinite collection of intuitively 'discrete' elements, such that between any two elements there is a third element, as '*collective density*'. There is no indication that Aristotle ever conceives a (one-dimensional) continuous magnitude as constituted by a collectively dense array of points. One suspects that the very notion of collective density would not be considered a coherent notion by Aristotle. Because of the density of the ordering, no such element could 'adjoin' or 'touch' any other such element. Our visual imagination then presents a problem: is it not the case that, since one such element does not adjoin/touch any other such element, either (*a*) there will have to be 'undivided stretches' of magnitude between such elements or (*b*) there will have to be 'gaps' of some sort between them? In either case we seem to have somehow lost the supposed conception of the continuous magnitude as constituted from *nothing but* a set of densely ordered discrete elements. The problem is that our visual imagination demands to know how an element is related to 'the very next' such element: Does it abut it? Or overlap it? Or is there an intervening gap?[20] But the density of the supposed ordering of elements means that this demand is misplaced: what our visual imagination demands cannot, on pain of contradiction, be supplied. Another argument that Aristotle develops in the *Physics* against the constitution of what is continuous from indivisible

---

[20] Such an argument against the constitution of a line from a linear collection of points is given by Sextus Empiricus, *Adversus mathematicos* (hereafter, *M*), 9. 386 ff. The two options considered by Sextus are that the points touch (*haptetai*) one another (either part to part or whole to whole) or that they are interrupted by gaps (*topois mesolabeitai*). But neither of these options is possible if the line is to be constituted of points (and nothing but points). Again, of course, from the contemporary perspective this disjunction is not exhaustive: it does not consider a *dense* (and Dedekind-continuous) linear ordering of points, a possibility that, as I have claimed, it is almost impossible (visually) to *imagine*.

elements, to which we next turn, seems to have some such intuitive considerations as its point of departure.

A Prototopological Argument Against the Constitution of Continua from Indivisibles

In *Phys*. 6. 1 Aristotle produces an argument with the conclusion that 'it is impossible that something that is continuous (*suneches*) should be constituted from indivisibles (*adiaireton*), e.g. a line from points if the line is continuous but the point indivisible' (231ª24–6). His argument for this claim proceeds as follows:

Neither is it the case that the extremities [*eschata*] of points are one (for it is not possible that one part of an indivisible is an extremity and another something else) nor is it the case that [indivisibles'] extremities are together [*hama*] (since it is not the case that there is any extremity of what has no parts since an extremity and that of which it is an extremity are different). But it would be necessary for the points out of which what is continuous is formed to be continuous with and touching one another. (And the same reasoning applies to all indivisibles.) Indivisibles could not be continuous because of the reasoning just set forth. Everything touches [*haptetai*] either whole to whole or part to part or part to whole. Since the indivisible is without parts, it is necessary that it touch whole to whole. But what touches whole to whole will not constitute what is continuous. For the continuous has distinct parts, and may be divided into these, which are thus different and separate in place.

This argument depends on several concepts defined by him in *Phys*. 5. 3. Consequently, before examining the structure of the argument, I shall need to say something about these definitions.

The definitions, I think, initially seem fairly clear and straight-forward:

(1) 'I say that those things are *together* [*hama*] with respect to place that are in one primary place and those things *separate* [*chōris*] that are in different places;

(2) [I say that those things] *are touching* [or *in contact*: *haptesthai*] of which the edges [*akra*] are together'. (226ᵇ21–3)

(3) 'A thing is *successive* or *in succession* [*ephekses*] of which, being after an entity in position or form or some other definite way, there is nothing of the same kind between it and that to which it is successive'. (226ᵇ34–227ª1)

(4) 'Something is contiguous [*echomenon*] [to something] that is successive to and touches [it]'. (227ª6)

(5) 'I say that something is *continuous* [*suneches*], which is a kind of being contiguous, whenever the limit of both things at which they touch becomes one and the same and, as the word implies, they are 'stuck together' [*sunechetai*]. But this is not possible if the extremities are two. It is clear from this definition that continuity pertains to those things from which there naturally results a sort of unity in virtue of their contact [*kata tēn sunapsin*]'. (227ª10–15)

David Furley has discussed the attempts of the ancient commentators to deal with a deep-seated problem in these definitions.[21] The problem centres on Aristotle's definition of touching, a concept that is then employed in the definitions of 'contiguity' and 'continuity'. According to Aristotle, two things touch the edges or extremities of which are 'together'; and what is 'together in place' is in one and the same primary place. The problem is created by Aristotle's long discussion of place in *Phys*. 4. 1–5, the denouement of which seems to be that 'the first motionless boundary of what contains [a thing], this is [its] place' (212ª20–1). However, according to Aristotle, 'not everything that exists exists in a place, but only movable body' (212ª28–9). Since 'edges', boundaries, or limits are not movable bodies, they cannot essentially (*kath' hauto*) have or be in places. So what are we to make of Aristotle's account of two things touching in terms of their edges being 'together' and, hence, in 'one and the same primary place'?

As Furley notes, the commentators seem to take one of two tacks in attempting to answer this question. One is represented by Alexander of Aphrodisias (*apud* Simplicius) and consists of the following elements: (*a*) he claims that Aristotle in *Phys*. 5. 3 is defining 'together' *only* in the sense of 'together in place' and that when, in the same chapter, he defines 'to touch' in terms of extremities being together, he is *not* using 'together' in this sense of 'together in place' but in some other sense; (*b*) where Aristotle elsewhere (*Phys*. 4. 4. 211ª33–4) characterizes the extremities of things that touch as being 'in the same' (*en tōi autōi*), Alexander does not read the phrase as elliptical for 'in the same place'; (*c*) rather, he interprets Aristotle's claims about the extremities of things that are touching as being 'together' and 'in the same' in terms of what seems to be a geometrical, intransitive use of the verb *epharmozein*, 'to fit onto' or 'to coincide with'.[22]

---

[21] 'The Greek Commentators' Treatment of Aristotle's Theory of the Continuous', in Kretzmann (ed.), *Infinity and Continuity*, 17–36.

[22] Alexander of Aphrodisias *apud* Simplicius, *In Aristotelis physicorum libros commentaria*, ed. H. Diels, in CAG 9 (Berlin, 1882), 569–70; CAG 10 (Berlin, 1895), 868–

Simplicius' tack seems to be to rest content with the claim that, while Aristotle means 'in the same *place*' at 211ᵃ33-4 and also means, in *Phys*. 5. 3, to assert that the extremities of touching bodies are 'together' in the sense of 'together with respect to place', he must be understood as claiming that they are in the same place incidentally or accidentally (*kata sumbebēkos*), since extremities (considered as limits or surfaces) do not essentially (*kath' hauto*) have a place.[23]

I am inclined to agree with Furley that the account of Alexander (and Philoponus) 'appears to go in the right direction'[24] in the sense of faithfulness to what *should have been* Aristotle's ultimate intentions. But as exegesis of the text it appears strained. On Alexander's account, Aristotle's definition in *Phys*. 5. 3 of 'together with respect to place' would not be relevant to the immediately following definition of 'to touch' in terms of 'together'. On the other hand, Furley dismisses Simplicius'

tentative solution, that he [Aristotle] meant 'in the same place *incidentally*'. . . . When Aristotle said that the parts of a body could be said to be in place incidentally, he meant that we could give an account of where they are by talking about the place of the whole body. But the place of the whole body, according to Aristotle, is the inner surface of the containing body: what a body is in contact with, in other words, *is* its place. If Aristotle wanted to use the concept of place in his definition of *in contact*, he should have said that two things are in contact if each is part of the place of the other, not that their extremities are in the same place.[25]

If we modify the last sentence to read 'two things are in contact if part of the surface of one is part of the place of the other',[26] we have one of

71. If an excerpt from Philoponus' commentary on *Phys*. 5 (*Excerpta Paris. in Physicorum*, 791. 21-7) represents his own view, then he apparently adopted the same interpretation as Alexander.

²³ Simplicius, *In phys*., CAG 9, 568-9; ibid., CAG 10, 870-1.

²⁴ Furley, 'The Greek Commentators', 25.

²⁵ Ibid.

²⁶ It is not clear that a reciprocal relation always holds: that is, that we should say that 'two things are in contact if part of the surface of each is part of the place of the other'. Consider a sealed container filled with some substance (e.g. a cask of wine). Clearly, the wine *A* is in contact with (is contiguous with) the cask *B*. And *if A* has a place 'of its own', its place is clearly the inner surface of *B*. But, it seems that, according to Aristotle's account of place, the place of *B* will not include the outer surface of the wine that it *contains* but must be the inner surface of whatever it is contained in (e.g. the surrounding air and the ground on which it sits). It is not clear to me, however, that Aristotle intends to claim that something contained in a movable vessel has a place of its own. For a discussion of the difference between Aristotle's conception of place as presented in the *Physics* and an earlier view alluded to in the *Categories* (according to which place seems

two plausible ways of dealing with the place(s) of things that touch and, hence, are contiguous. However, there is another approach, which seems just as plausible, and which allows us to make better sense of Simplicius' 'tentative solution'. According to this approach, if *A* and *B* touch and are contiguous, they are 'topologically one'. That is, they do not then actually have separate places, but only do so potentially. As long as they are in contact, 'they' have as a place, the 'immovable inner surface' of what contains *their union*. Hence, since *A* and *B* share the same place, i.e. the place of their union, their extremities are in the same place 'incidentally' (*kata sumbebēkos*).

Although this latter approach might be made to work if kept charitably imprecise, it is unlikely to be what Aristotle *meant* in saying that two things touch if their edges are together in (the same) place. To begin with, it seems to be Aristotle's view that, although parts of what is continuous individually have places only potentially, parts which are 'separate but in contact' have places actually (*kat' energeian*).[27] Furthermore, according to the preceding account, the fact that *A* and *B* touch and are (essentially) in the same place entails that *all* the surface, edges, or extremities of *A* are (incidentally) in the same place as *all* the surface, edges, or extremities of *B*. But it seems exceedingly likely that Aristotle is saying of things that touch only that the edges *at which they touch* are 'together in (the same) place'.

The principal source of difficulty here, I suspect, is that Aristotle implicitly appeals to a 'pre-analytical' concept of place in his definitions in *Phys*. 5. 3. Unfortunately, his considered, 'analytical' concept—an interesting concept but one that is replete with difficulties—simply cannot be made to serve satisfactorily in this context.

Before I return to the argument in *Phys*. 6. 1 that what is continuous cannot be constituted from indivisibles, it is necessary to address one further (and, from the perspective of this section, more fundamental) difficulty with respect to the definitions of *Phys*. 5. 3. The difficulty pertains to the relation between Aristotle's concepts of what is continuous (*to suneches*) and what is contiguous (*to echomenon*). Aristotle defines the contiguity of *A* and *B* in terms of *A* and *B* being successive and touching (i.e. being in contact). He then distinguishes continuity as a species of contiguity: things are continuous when the

to be identified with the extension (*diastēma*) of a body), see H. Mendell, 'Topoi on Topos: The Development of Aristotle's Concept of Place', *Phronesis*, 33: 2 (1987), 206–31.

[27] *Phys*. 4. 5. 212b4–6.

'limits of both at which they touch become one and the same'. He adds—rather more helpfully, I believe—that 'continuity pertains to those things from which there naturally results a sort of unity in virtue of their contact'. Furley characterizes the problem to which I alluded: 'Aristotle wanted to distinguish things *in contact* from *continuous* things by claiming that the former have extremities "in the same [place]" and the latter have extremities that are "one".'[28] But it is not at all clear what this difference amounts to. As Furley notes, the problem led Alexander to comment that

the limit of both, with respect to things touching [whose limits] coincide, becomes one on account of there not being an interval at that place. But with respect to things that are continuous, even the one is destroyed; for things are continuous of which there is no intermediate boundary in actuality (*energeiai*).[29]

Furley objects that

the cost of [Alexander's] move is that a body or line can no longer be regarded as continuous as soon as an intermediate point is mentioned or even considered. There is a continuous line let us say, from Trenton to New York. . . . The mention of Princeton Junction actualizes the intermediate point and thus transforms continuity into contact.[30]

Although Alexander's understanding of the distinction, interpreted quite literally, may in fact entail such a conclusion, it is clearly a conclusion that neither he nor Aristotle would want to accept. There is for Aristotle, I suspect, no *topological* distinction between parts that are contiguous and parts that are continuous. Rather, continuity pertains to what is homeomerous,[31] while contiguity pertains to parts which are spatially joined but essentially different. Furley seems to me to be correct in his claim that

When [Aristotle] discusses things that are continuous, he thinks primarily of homogeneous natural substances, such as air or water, The distinction between *in contact* and *continuous* is primarily to distinguish a case such as the junction of the upper surface of the sea with the lower surface of the air from the junction of two bodies of water.[32]

Consider a container half-full of liquid *A* that has 'floating' on top of it another appropriate liquid *B* of less specific gravity. Here, according to

---

[28] Furley, 'The Greek Commentators', 23.

[29] Alexander *apud* Simplicius, *In phys.*, CAG 9, 570. 4–7.

[30] Furley, 'The Greek Commentators', 24.

[31] At least once (*Phys*. 4. 5. 212^{b}5), Aristotle uses the term *homoiomeres* in connection with continuity.

[32] Furley, 'The Greek Commentators', 30.

Aristotle, the upper surface of A and the lower surface of B coincide, and we might say that they are one 'in number' or, better, 'topologically one'.[33] However, since A and B are readily distinguishable, their respective surfaces are different 'in *logos*', as Aristotle would say. Now, suppose that we siphon off liquid B and replace it with the same volume of liquid A. Here, the portion of liquid A added on top is continuous, in Aristotle's sense, with the portion of liquid A in the bottom of the container. Although Aristotle speaks of the surfaces of the two portions of A as becoming 'one', Alexander (for fairly obvious reasons) comments that there is 'no intermediate boundary in actuality'. That is, once we have replaced the top layer of liquid B by an equivalent amount of liquid A (the *same* liquid as that constituting the bottom layer), we have a boundary between the top and bottom portions only *potentially*. Aristotle describes this situation—arguably in somewhat misleading terms—in terms of the 'limits of both parts, at which they touch, becoming one and the same'. But his following comment, that 'continuity pertains to those things from which there results a *natural* unity in virtue of their contact', tends to suggest that this is the sort of situation he had in mind.

Once the liquid B has been replaced by an equal volume of A, the *topological* relation between the 'top' and 'bottom' parts—although they are now, arguably, only *potential* parts—is exactly the same as the relation between the (actual) parts when a layer of B occupied the place of the present 'upper layer' of A. My conclusion is that, for Aristotle, there is no *topological* distinction between contiguity and continuity.[34]

We now, at long last, return to Aristotle's argument from *Phys*. 6. 1, which we quoted at the beginning of this section, that what is continuous cannot be constituted of indivisibles. The argument is fairly

[33] This, I think, is the answer to Furley's question 'How could the surface of the sea be one with the surface of the air?'

[34] The essential topological or geometrical identity of contiguity and continuity is recognized by Sextus Empiricus in an argument at *Adversus mathematicos* 3 (*Adversus geometras*), 61 ff. There Sextus argues that since, in the case of two distinct but geometrically contiguous bodies, the surfaces of the bodies are (partly) coincidental, every such geometrical juxtaposition (*parathesis*) of bodies should result in the unification (*henōsis*) of the bodies. E.g. it should in such a case be just as likely that, when we separate the bodies thus juxtaposed, they come apart at some *different* place as at exactly the place where they were juxtaposed. What this argument shows is that, if the distinction between contiguity and continuity that we have been talking about is not a topological or geometrical distinction, the intuitive distinction should be retained and must then be drawn in some other way.

straightforward. Suppose that what is continuous is constituted of indivisible units of some sort (e.g. points). Then each indivisible either (*a*) would have to be continuous with some other indivisible or (*b*) would have to be in contact with (*haptomenon*, 'touch') some other indivisible. Here a relatively minor problem develops. Why *either* 'would have to be continuous with' *or* 'would have to touch'? Although in *Phys.* 5. 3 Aristotle has defined 'touches' in terms of the coincidence of boundaries or edges, the structure of this argument indicates that he is here appealing to a broader sense of the term: to coincide at the limits *or* to coincide in any [proper or improper] part. In other words, touching is here to be understood as comprehending something like the notion of overlapping, in part or whole. However, since indivisibles—because of the very fact that they are indivisible—do not have either extremities or proper parts, the only possibility is that two such indivisibles would touch (i.e. overlap) 'whole to whole'. But in this case, the indivisibles could not constitute spatially distinguishable parts of what is continuous, which is absurd.

Possible responses that an advocate of indivisible quanta could make to this argument will be discussed in Chapter 5. At present, I want to point out that at the very core of the argument is a principle of non-supervenience of continuity analogous to the principle of non-supervenience of positive measure that I earlier attributed to Aristotle:

N-SC. Each partition of a continuous magnitude into proper parts yields parts each of which is pairwise continuous with at least one other part.

In other words, Aristotle clearly maintains that, since (so he claims) no indivisible can be continuous with (or partially overlap) any other indivisible, no body constituted of such indivisibles could be a continuum. Although this non-supervenience principle has considerable intuitive appeal, it is, interestingly enough, the most objectionable element in Aristotle's argument from the perspective of standard contemporary topology. For, from the topological perspective, continuity is a thoroughly supervenient property. A point-set can be a continuum; but when it is partitioned into the singletons of its points, *all* of these singletons are pairwise discontinuous (that is, *none* of the pairwise unions of such singletons is a continuous set).[35]

[35] See my 'On Continuity: Aristotle versus Topology?', *History and Philosophy of Logic*, 9 (1988), 1–12.

These two non-supervenience principles, the principles of the non-supervenience of positive measure and of the non-supervenience of continuity, are central to Aristotle's conception of the basic structural properties of spatial magnitude or extension. At places Aristotle seems to identify continuity with infinite divisibility. At *Phys*. 3. 7. 207^{b}16–17, for example, he comments that 'what is continuous is in each case divisible to infinity', and at *Phys*. 6. 2. 232^{b}24–5 he gives what almost seems to be an alternative definition—alternative, that is, to the definition given in *Phys*. 5. 3—of continuity: 'I call continuous that which is, in each case, divisible to [parts] that are continuous.' But in *Phys*. 6. 1 Aristotle makes it clear that he regards this infinite divisibility as a consequence of the definition of continuity given in *Phys*. 5. 3 and the use made of that definition in the argument of *Phys*. 6. 1 that we have been examining.

It is also clear that every divisible is divisible, in each case, to [parts] that are divisible. If it were divisible to indivisibles, then an indivisible will be touching an indivisible [which Aristotle claims to have shown to be impossible]; for the extremities of things that are continuous with one another are one and touch. (231^{b}15–18)

In effect, Aristotle's non-supervenience principles support a strong or 'foundationless' form of infinite divisibility for spatial magnitude or extension. Since a partition of a spatially extended magnitude into points having zero measure would violate the first principle of non-supervenience of positive measure N-SM, the parts of any such partition must have some positive measure. And by the second principle of non-supervenience of continuity N-SC and Aristotle's argument in *Phys*. 6. 1, the parts of any such partition cannot be atomic or indivisible. Consequently, Aristotle seems to conclude that any such partition must yield parts each of which itself has the properties of being continuous and of having positive 'size' or measure and each of which, consequently, can itself be partitioned only into parts that, individually, are continuous and have positive measure. In moving from coarser partitions (one constituted of 'larger parts') to finer partitions, one never arrives at a 'foundation level' in the sense of a *finest* such partition.

Underlying Aristotle's conception of spatial magnitude is his consistent opposition to any attempt to 'resolve' such continuous quantities into discrete units. Aristotle is steadfastly opposed, as we have seen, to the 'analysis' of a linear magnitude into a set of points. Similarly, there is no temptation on his part to conceive, say, a hemisphere as a 'sum' of a 'stack' of two-dimensional circles, starting with the base of the hemisphere and, remaining parallel to the base, decreasing in radius to limit zero as the 'stack' of circles approaches the top of the hemisphere. In general, 'number' (*arithmos*) and 'magnitude' (*megethos*) are opposed concepts for Aristotle. For example, in *Phys.* 3. 7 he claims that

> it is correctly said in the case of number that, with respect to the least, there is a limit but with respect to the greater it is always possible to exceed any multiplicity; but in the case of magnitudes the contrary is true: with respect to the less, it is possible to surpass any magnitude, but with respect to the greater, there is no unlimited magnitude. (207ᵇ1–5)

Aristotle's view of *number* can be summarized in terms of a variation on the aphorism attributed to the nineteenth-century mathematician Leopold Kronecker: 'God made the integers; everything else is a matter of *magnitude*, not *number*.'[36] The tendency of contemporary mathematics, of course, has been to break down this opposition between number and magnitude by, as it were, arithmetizing magnitude and, consequently, facilitating the treatment of continuous magnitudes as constituted of indivisible elements (e.g. sets of points) that are in a certain intuitive sense 'discrete'. It then becomes possible to 'reconstitute' the properties of continuous magnitudes using these indivisibles. Such a procedure (to be discussed in detail in Chapter 4) may suggest an ultimately 'atomistic' ontology of magnitude very much at odds with the Aristotelian dictum that 'every magnitude is divisible into magnitudes (for it has been shown that it is impossible that what is continuous should be constituted of indivisibles [*ex eks atomōn*], and every magnitude is continuous' (*Phys.* 6. 2. 232ᵃ23–5). Magnitudes are constituted only of smaller magnitudes without any ultimate atomistic 'foundation': consequently there remains, according to Aristotle, a radical discontinuity between *numerable* 'groups', 'sets', or multiplicities (*plēthē*) and *measurable* magnitudes (*megethē*). As we shall see, Aristotle maintains this view with respect not only to spatial magnitude but also to the 'magnitudes' of time and locomotion.

---

[36] Kronecker's actual aphorism is 'God made the integers; everything else is the construction of man'.

LOCOMOTION

According to a classical modern classification, the science of mechanics is divided into three parts: statics, kinetics (or dynamics, in one sense of this term), and kinematics. Statics deals with the forces acting on and within a body or system of bodies at rest. Kinetics (dynamics) is concerned with the relation between the motion of a body (system of bodies), the forces acting on the body (system of bodies), and their mass (masses). Finally, kinematics deals with motion of bodies *without reference to* either their masses or the forces acting on them. That is, kinematics is the study of the geometrically or topologically *possible* motion of a body or system of bodies.

In this section, I shall be concerned with what might be called the rational kinematics in Aristotle's *Physics*. As an aside, I might add that there really is nothing that could count as statics and very little that could qualify as kinetics to be found in the work.[37] However, when we turn to rational kinematics, we find in the *Physics* a good deal of material that might reasonably be included under this rubric. If considered from a sufficiently broad perspective, the Aristotelian conception of what is geometrically possible with respect to local motion is very similar to what might be termed the classical modern conception of what is geometrically possible with respect to local motion. At the heart of Aristotle's conception is the idea that locomotion comes in 'smooth chunks', i.e. episodes that are, in some sense, *continuous*. This idea is also central to what I am calling the 'classical modern conception' of kinematics.

Where the Aristotelian and classical modern conceptions differ is in their *ontology* of the continuous. The classical modern conception, as I understand it here, appeals to a point-set ontology of the continuous. That is, a continuous n-dimensional magnitude is conceived as a set of $(n-1)$-dimensional entities. In the particular case of a linear or 1-dimensional magnitude (e.g. a lapse of time, a linear spatial interval), the magnitude is conceived as a set of points. Such a set will be a non-

---

[37] What there is by way of rational kinetics is not very satisfactory from the contemporary perspective. It consists mainly of *Phys*. 7. 5, in which Aristotle argues (with some qualifications) that 'force' or *dunamis* required to move a body is directly proportional to its magnitude or 'mass', directly proportional to distance traversed, and indirectly proportional to time elapsed. That is, *dunamis* is something like momentum, in the Newtonian sense, or cumulative determination of motion. I discuss this passage from the *Physics* at greater length in Ch. 4.

denumerably infinite, linearly ordered collection of points satisfying certain other requirements. For our purposes, the most important of these are density and Dedekind continuity. The set of points is dense if and only if between (i.e. 'between', in terms of the linear ordering) any two points there is a third distinct point. In order to define Dedekind continuity, it is necessary to define a 'cut'. A cut is a partition of the set of points into two disjoint, non-empty subsets such that each of the members in the 'first' subset precedes (in terms of the linear ordering) each of the members of the 'second' subset. The linearly ordered, dense set is Dedekind-continuous if and only if, for each cut, either (i) the 'first' subset determined by the cut has a last ('terminal') point but the second subset does not have a first ('initial') point or (ii) the 'second' subset has an initial point but the 'first' subset does *not* have a terminal point.[38] Dedekind continuity constitutes the standard contemporary account of continuity for 1-dimensional magnitudes. It is significant that this notion of continuity presupposes a point-set analysis according to which (a) there is an *actual* infinity of the set of points constituting the continuous magnitude in question and (b) this set of points is characterized by what I, in the last section, termed 'collective density': a linear array of an actually infinite set of discrete elements such that no element (uniquely) succeeds or precedes any other element.

Aristotle, however, does not accept the point-set ontology of continuous magnitudes. What is continuous can be divided into or can be constituted of only parts that are themselves continuous. This 'foundationless' ontology of continuous intervals of distance (and of continuous 'stretches' or 'lapses' of time) is grounded in the non-supervenience principles of measure and of continuity (N-SM and N-SC, respectively) enunciated in the last section. Viewed in more 'metaphysical' terms, the foundationless ontology holds that what are ontologically fundamental are positive intervals of continuous distance (or spatial magnitude) and positive intervals or 'lapses' of time. Spatial points, positions, or *loci* have less reality than continuous intervals or distances of magnitude; they are analysed in terms of ('constructed' from) potential or actual divisions of spatial magnitude or distance.

---

[38] There is a 3rd requirement that is necessary for a linearly ordered set to have the order type (λ) of the real numbers: the non-denumerably infinite, linearly ordered set must have a denumerably infinite subset *dense in it*. This requirement is so directly dependent upon Cantorian mathematics that we shall not be further concerned with it here.

And 'nows' or temporal instants are analysed in terms of potential or actual divisions of time.

Aristotle accepts a similar foundationless ontology for local motion. What are ontologically fundamental are continuous episodes of local motion; and local motion can be divided into or constituted of *only* smaller continuous episodes of local motion. Local motion is *not* constituted of 'freeze-frame slices' of motion or the 'instantaneous positions' of the moving body. Such punctal divisions of motion, which have a lesser degree of reality than the continuous episodes of motion, are analysed in terms of potential terminations of motion. In the following section, we shall examine Aristotle's kinematics of local motion. Particularly in the sixth book of the *Physics*, he derives some fundamental kinematic characteristics of motion. Although these characteristics are also ascribed to motion by standard contemporary kinematic analysis, their 'ontological basis' is quite different in the case of Aristotle.

Continuity, 'Jumps', and Pauses: The Rational Kinematics of *Physics* 6

The Greek term *sunecheia* and the English 'continuity', and their respective cognates, have a variety of interrelated senses. Perhaps Aristotle's most technical account occurs at *Phys*. 5. 3. 227^{a}10–15, in a passage which I quoted in the last section. There, continuity (sense (*a*)) is distinguished as a species of contiguity (*to echomenon*) according to which there are only *potential* 'divisions' of the continuous thing: when we imagine such a division or 'cut', the limit (*peras*) at which the division is imagined is the common limit of both sections at which they are 'stuck together' (*sunechētai*), as Aristotle says (227^{a}12). As we saw, Aristotle sometimes recognizes infinite divisibility, or the property of 'always being divisible to what is divisible' (*Phys*. 6. 2. 232^{b}25), as a *consequence* of continuity as defined in *Phys*. 5. 3. However, he sometimes—as in *Phys*. 6. 2—treats 'being infinitely divisible' as a distinct definition (sense (*b*)) of 'continuity'.

Continuity in both senses applies most directly and obviously to spatial magnitudes, e.g. to lines or to two- or three-dimensional spatial areas (and the substances 'filling' them). But the extension of continuity in either sense to *kinēsis*, even in the special sense of locomotion, is more problematic. If such an extension seems entirely natural from the contemporary perspective, this naturalness is largely due, I suspect, to the fact that our intellectual imagination is accustomed to the graphic representation of locomotion, to its representation as a line on a position/time or distance/time co-ordinate system. It is perhaps salutary to remember, however, that we have no evidence that Aristotle or his contemporaries had the benefit of such a visual representation of motion. As applied to (local) motion, the two senses of continuity amount to the following: (*a*) if a continuous motion is bipartitioned at a now, this now is the common limit of the two parts or segments of motion in the sense of the *terminus ad quem* of the temporally prior segment of motion and the *terminus a quo*[39] of the temporally posterior segment of motion; (*b*) a continuous motion is 'infinitely divisible' or, more properly, always divisible into continuous segments of motion or 'kinetic segments' that are themselves divisible into continuous kinetic segments.

What underlies both senses of continuity is the idea that a continuous *kinēsis* is *unitary* in the sense of not having any temporally defined constituent segments that are characterizable in any way other than as stretches of being-in-motion. As Aristotle puts it in *Phys*. 6. 4,

> For let *Γ* be the whole stretch of being-in-motion. Then with respect to half the motion, the corresponding stretch of being-in-motion will be less than the whole stretch, and again with respect to half of the half [the corresponding stretch of being-in-motion will be less than that corresponding to half the motion], and similarly in all succeeding cases. By successively laying down the stretch of being-in-motion corresponding to each of the motions—say, that corresponding to *ΔΓ* and to *ΓE*—it is possible to argue that the whole [stretch of being-in-motion] corresponds to the whole [motion]. If each stretch of being-in-motion is understood as corresponding to each ['segment' of the motion], the whole will be continuous. (235ª25–34)

I have in this passage translated the present (imperfective), middle articular infinitive *to kineisthai* as 'stretch of being-in-motion'. As Ross notes, it is not very clear what the distinction, introduced by Aristotle earlier in this chapter, between *to kineisthai* and *kinēsis* amounts to. Ross suggests that 'by the *kinēsis* Aristotle means a certain movement considered as capable of being undergone by a variety of subjects, by *to kineisthai* the historical undergoing of the movement by some individual subject'.[40] This may well be part of the story. But I suspect that Aristotle may also be utilizing the imperfectivity of the articular infinitive. 'Motion' in English can function either as a count noun or as

[39] Aristotle's *to eis ti* and *to ek tinos*, respectively; see e.g. *Phys*. 6. 8. 239ª23–4.
[40] W. D. Ross, *Aristotle's Physics: A Revised Text with Introduction and Commentary* (Oxford, 1936), 647.

a mass noun; it is the former fact that allows us to speak of 'a motion', 'the motion', and 'one, two, several, few, or many motions', the latter that allows us to speak of more or less motion (without an article). *Kinēsis* also functions sometimes as a count noun. And it is arguable that Aristotle holds that a 'real' (as opposed to a 'dummy')[41] count noun presupposes some principle of 'natural individuation' of its referents. I conjecture that at least part of the import of Aristotle's use of *to kineisthai* is to invoke the 'mass sense' of motion—that is, to connote 'stretches of being-in-motion' of arbitrary temporal duration without 'natural', intrinsic principles of individuation, such as *actual* 'starting state'/ *terminus a quo* and 'ending state'/ *terminus ad quem*. A *stretch* of being-in-motion is thus individuated by reference either to a complete, 'natural' *kinēsis*, with actual *termini a quo* and *ad quem*, or to 'segments' (e.g. half, half of a half) of such a *kinēsis*.

Both conceptions of continuity are intended by Aristotle, I believe, to capture the intuitive notions of homogeneity and smoothness that he associates with the continuity of *kinēsis*. I shall argue that these notions of homogeneity and smoothness do not amount to quite the same thing. In the case of sense (a) of continuity, suppose that we are trying to ascertain whether a body's motion from position Δ (*terminus a quo*) to position E (*terminus ad quem*) is continuous. Let us further consider an intermediate position Γ, through which the body moves in transition from Δ to E. Continuity of the local motion of the body requires that, if we 'segment' the body's motion ΔE into $\Delta\Gamma$ and ΓE, there should be a now or temporal instant that is the common limit of the body's motion segments $\Delta\Gamma$ and ΓE; i.e. there should be a common now that is paired with the *terminus ad quem* of segment $\Delta\Gamma$ and the *terminus a quo* of the segment ΓE. However, if there is no such common now but, rather, what Aristotle in *Phys*. 8. 7 terms a *chronos metaxu* ((interval of) time in between), the motion from Δ to E cannot be continuous. In discussing changes that cannot belong to the same subject at the same time (e.g. contradictory or contrary changes), Aristotle in *Phys*. 8. 7 asserts that in such a case 'the change [to opposites] will not be continuous, but there will be an interval of time between them' (261^b6–7). Later he adds that the changes in question

---

[41] By a 'dummy' count noun, I mean a noun phrase of the form 'chunk (piece, bit, cup, sample, handful) of A' where A is a mass noun. Despite the fact that such noun phrases behave grammatically as count nouns, it does not follow that the stuff A is naturally individuated into discrete units in the way that, e.g. human beings, pine trees, and amoebae are so individuated.

do not have to be contraries, etc., 'so long as there occurs an interval of time in between; for thus it is not possible that the change be continuous' (262^{b}13–14).

Similarly, the force of Aristotle's sense (*b*) of continuity as applied to motion, i.e. the requirement that such motion be always 'divisible with respect to time' (*Phys*. 6. 4. 235^{a}13), is to insure the homogeneity of motion. A *kinēsis*, according to this requirement, is constituted of nothing other than kinetic segments. In the special case of locomotion, such a kinetic segment might be characterized, initially, in terms of a temporal interval $t_i t_j$ ($t_i \neq t_j$) during which the moving body traverses a spatial interval $s_i s_j$ ($s_i \neq s_j$). In other words, a *continuous* motion will contain no temporally defined segments that are 'non-kinetic', e.g. temporal periods of *stasis* or rest. The two senses of continuity may be encapsulated in a third non-supervenience principle to which Aristotle subscribes, a principle of the temporal non-supervenience of *kinēsis*:

TN-SK. Each temporal partition of a continuous motion into kinetic proper segments[42] of motion yields segments each of which is continuous with at least one other kinetic segment of the partition in the following sense: there is a common now/temporal instant that is paired with the *terminus a quo* of one of the kinetic segments and the *terminus ad quem* of the other segment.

A question of some interest, to which I return later, is whether Aristotle considers (or should consider) these kinetic segments of motions to be themselves, individually, motions. The non-supervenience principle TN-SK seems to capture adequately the intuitive notion that motion should be homogeneous. One sort of phenomenon that precludes the continuity of movement from, say, position Δ to position E is what might be called 'pauses' of the body anywhere along the way. TN-SK rules out such pauses: if the motion from Δ to E is to be continuous, then any temporal interval between the temporal limits of the body's departure from Δ and its arrival at E must be an interval during which the body is traversing a divisible spatial magnitude.

[42] In the case of locomotion, a kinetic segment of motion may be thought of as the pair of a (non-zero) interval s of distance or spatial magnitude traversed by a body in a (non-zero) temporal interval t satisfying the following conditions: (i) for each sub-interval s'' of each sub-interval s' of s, there is a sub-interval t'' in which s'' is traversed, and t'' is a sub-interval of a sub-interval t' of t in which the body traverses sub-interval s'; (ii) for each sub-interval t'' of each sub-interval t' of t, there is a sub-interval s'' which is traversed in t'', and s'' is a sub-interval of a sub-interval s' of s, which is traversed by the body in sub-interval t'.

However, what Aristotle calls *kinēmata* (translated 'starts' by Hardie and Gaye, 'impulses' by Apostle), what Ross and Sorabji both refer to as 'jerks', and what I call 'jumps',[43] also seem to violate the intuitive idea of smoothness of motion that Aristotle (and we) associate with its continuity; and, as we shall later see, it is not clear that the homogeneity of motion as I have characterized it (encapsulated by TN-SK) rules out such jumps. Motion by a jump is described by Aristotle as traversal of a distance 'by something which is not in the process of moving (*ti mē kinoumenon*) having completed a movement (*kekinēsthai*)' (*Phys*. 6. 1. 232[a]9).

What does the presence and absence of jumps amount to? A plausible contemporary explication seems to me to be the following: (i) the continuity (in the contemporary mathematical sense) of a function from the sub-intervals of a total distance traversed since the inception of motion by a body to the sub-intervals of time that have elapsed since the inception of its motion rules out pauses by the body that has traversed the total distance in question; (ii) the continuity of a function from the sub-intervals of a total time elapsed since the inception of motion by a body to the sub-intervals of distance traversed by the body since the inception of its motion rules out jumps by the body that has moved during the total time in question. The continuity of a type (ii) function at a time *t* can be characterized in a rather complicated (but, I hope, intelligible) way:

Let *S* be the set of sub-intervals of distance traversed by a body moving some total distance and *T* be the set of sub-intervals of time that it takes the body to move each of the sub-distances in *S*. Let f(*t*) = *s* designate the time *t* that it takes the body to traverse subdistance *s*, for each *t* ∈ *T*, *s* ∈ *S*. The members of *S* and the members of *T* are both linearly ordered by 'natural' metrics; hence, arbitrarily ordered subsets (intervals) can be defined on them. Then, for every positive interval *ε* in *S* that is centred at sub-distance *s* = f(*t*), there is a corresponding positive interval δ that is centred on *t* such that the following condition (CONT) obtains: for any time lapse *t'* since the inception of motion (i.e. any *t'* ∈ *T*) that falls

---

[43] I use 'jumps' rather than 'jerks' here because the latter term perhaps suggests not only the sort of spatial discontinuity of motion in which a spatial interval or distance is traversed with no lapse of time but also a temporal discontinuity in the form of pauses or periods of rests interlarded between such spatial discontinuities. It is (conceptually and mathematically) possible, however, to have such jumps or spatial discontinuities of motion that involve no pauses.

within the interval δ, the distance s' traversed by the body during that t' (i.e. $s' = f(t')$) falls within the interval ϵ.

The type (ii) function f is continuous if the preceding condition CONT holds for each $t \in T$. Expressed yet more informally (and roughly), the continuity of function f of type (ii) amounts to the requirement that, for every interval of distance traversed by a moving body, there must be a corresponding positive interval of time such that, in each lesser sub-interval of time, the body traverses a lesser sub-interval of distance. According to this contemporary explication, then, the Aristotelian requirement that a continuously moving body should not *have moved* without *having been in the process of moving* (i.e. that it should not have moved by any jumps) is tantamount to the requirement that, for every interval the body traverses, there is a positive interval of time such that in less time the body traverses less distance. More precisely, the requirement is tantamount to a requirement of the continuity (in the contemporary mathematical sense) of a function f of type (ii), i.e. a function f from sub-intervals of time elapsed (since inception of motion) to sub-intervals of distance traversed in those times.

Although Aristotle does not have the technical, mathematical tools at his disposal to state this continuity property of motion in what would now be recognized as an acceptably rigorous and precise form, there is an important sense in which he possesses the concept. In *Phys.* 6. 2, he proceeds to spell out what we would consider to be some of the consequences of the continuity of locomotion for the notion of relative speed:

(1) in an equal time, the faster traverses a distance greater than that traversed by the slower (232^a31);

(2) in less time, the faster traverses a distance greater than that traversed by the slower (232^a32, 232^b4–5);

(3) in less time, the faster traverses a distance equal to that traversed by the slower (232^b5–6, 232^b19–20, 232^b30–1).

(4) Aristotle also implicitly appeals to the assumption of the continuity (at least in the infinite-divisibility sense (b)) of degrees of speed and the lack of an upper bound of degrees of speed—the assumption that there is no fastest speed.

As he says,

Since every motion is in an interval of time, and in every interval of time it is possible to be moved, and everything that is moved can be moved faster and slower, in every interval of time it is possible for there to be a faster being-moved and a slower being-moved.   (232^{b}20-3)

The second chapter of Book 6 of the *Physics* may seem to be little more than an extended (and vicious) *petitio*. For Aristotle apparently, at 232^{b}20-233^{a}12, uses the preceding principles (1)-(4) of relative speed and of the divisibility/unboundedness of degrees of speed to argue for the continuity of spatial magnitude and time (in the infinite-divisibility sense (*b*) of continuity). But it might with some justification be maintained that the plausibility of Aristotle's account of speed depends upon the continuity (infinite-divisibility) of spatial magnitude and time. I believe, however, that the strategy of argument in this chapter is dialectical, in Aristotle's sense of this term.[44] He explicitly identifies his conception of speed, or at least principles (1)-(3) of relative speed, as part of a definition that 'some' give (232^{a}27). So the argument is that some 'common conceptions' (*endoxa*) entail the sense (*b*) continuity of time and spatial extension; and so, if we deny this continuity, the price to be paid will be that the *endoxa* can no longer be retained.

These *endoxa* pertaining to speed also turn out to be sufficient to derive the continuity (in the contemporary mathematical sense) of our function (ii) above—a function from the set T of sub-intervals of a time during which a body is moving to the set S of sub-intervals of a distance traversed by the body during that time. Suppose that we consider a moving body A and define a function f of type (ii) from sub-intervals of time elapsed to sub-intervals of distance traversed since the inception of its motion. Let us select an arbitrary sub-interval t of time; then body A will traverse sub-interval s of distance in time t: i.e. f(t) = s. According to Aristotle's principles (1) and (4), any interval ϵ on the set of sub-distances traversed by the body A can be defined 'on the right end' by such an arbitrary sub-distance s traversed by body A and 'on the left end' by the sub-distance s' traversed by a body B (moving at an appropriately slower speed) in the same time t in which body A traversed s. Now consider the time lapse t' in which A traverses s'. By principle (3) this time lapse t' is less than t. So t' and t define a positive interval δ on the set T of sub-intervals of time that have lapsed since the inception of A's motion. Now consider any time lapse

---

[44] By dialectical argumentation, in Aristotle's sense, I mean argumentation that begins with premises held by one's opponents in argument or premises commonly held, whether by the 'many' or the 'learned few'. In the present case, Aristotle may be using premises of the latter sort.

t'' since the inception of A's motion (i.e. any $t'' \in T$) in this interval δ. By principles (3) and (4), t'' can be represented as the time lapse necessary for a body C moving appropriately slower than A and faster than B to traverse distance s'. It then follows from (1) that the distance s'' traversed by body A when time t'' has elapsed is greater than s'. Suppose, however, that s'' is greater than or equal to s. Since t'', the time lapse required for A to traverse distance s'', is (*ex hypothesi*) less than t, the sub-interval of time required for A to traverse s, it follows from principles (2) and (3) that A is faster than itself. Since it seems reasonable to assume that Aristotle would have accepted the irreflexivity of the faster-than relation, we have a contradiction and can conclude by *reductio* that s'' is less than s. Hence, $s' < s'' < s$; i.e. s'' falls within the interval ϵ (see Fig. 1). This proof can be generalized for *any* sub-interval t of time since the inception of motion of a given body A.

The upshot of this rather convoluted proof is that the contemporary mathematical conception of the continuity of a function f from sub-intervals of time elapsed since the inception of motion of a body to sub-intervals of distance traversed in those times *follows* from Aristotle's principles of speed. That is, were one to define, relative to a moving body, such a function f from the set T of sub-intervals of time elapsed since its inception of motion to the set S of sub-intervals of distance traversed since its inception of motion, Aristotle's principles of relative speed entail that f would obey the continuity constraint CONT previously stated.

I have set forth this proof in fairly tedious detail because it seems to me to be an unusually clear example of a situation in which a philosopher, although clearly not possessing the contemporary conception of continuity of a function (or the idea of a function *simpliciter*, for that matter), *does* possess not only the rudimentary idea underlying the contemporary conception but also a technical apparatus of his own precise enough to yield a fairly rigorous derivation of the contemporary conception.

Is movement that is discontinuous in the sense of involving jumps also necessarily discontinuous in the sense of involving pauses? As we shall see directly, the short answer to this question is 'no'. However, it is perhaps plausible to claim that movement that is *radically* discontinuous in the sense of being constituted of *nothing but* jumps—displacements, which do not require any lapse of time, of a body from one position to a finitely distant position—would also have to involve

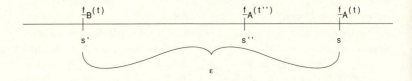

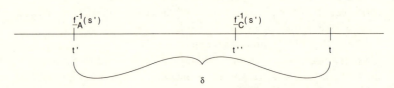

F IG . 1. The Continuity of Function from Time Elapsed to Distance Traversed

Let T be the set of times (temporal intervals) elapsed and S be the set of distances traversed since the inception of motion of 3 bodies, A, B, and C, which began moving simultaneously and move at constant but unequal speeds. A moves at the fastest speed, B moves at an 'appropriate' slowest speed, and C at an 'appropriate' intermediate speed. Let the motion of the 3 bodies be represented by 3 functions, f_A, f_B, and f_C, respectively, all with T as domain and S as range. We shall demonstrate the continuity of the function f_A at arbitrary argument (time lapse) t. By Aristotle's principles, any interval ϵ on S can be defined 'on the right' by a distance s traversed by A in time-interval t and 'on the left' by a distance s' which is the distance traversed by the appropriately slowest body B in the same time t that it takes A to traverse s $(f_B(f_A^{-1}(s)) = f_B(t))$. By Aristotle's principles, the time t' it takes A to traverse this distance s' is less than the time t it takes the slowest body B to traverse the same distance $(f_A^{-1}(s') = t' < t)$. So (t, t') defines a non-null interval δ on T (corresponding to ϵ). Consider any $t'' \in \delta$. By Aristotle's principles, let $t'' = f_C^{-1}(s')$ for the body C moving appropriately faster than B and slower than A. It follows by Aristotle's principles that $s' < f_A(t'') = s'' < s$, and thus that $f_A(t'') \in \epsilon$. (This procedure can be carried out for arbitrary interval ϵ 'on the right' of $f_A(t)$ as well.) So f_A is continuous at t. The argument then can be generalized for any $t \in T$.

pauses or finite periods of rest. However, the nature of such radical discontinuity of motion is a more complicated matter than it first seems, and will receive further attention in Chapter 5's discussion of the quantum model of spatial magnitude, time, and motion. The radical discontinuity of motion is the object of Aristotle's criticism in the first chapter of *Physics* 6, where he closely associates it with an atomistic or quantum conception of spatial magnitude and time. So it is not surprising to find Aristotle in this chapter associating pauses with jumps, as at 232ᵃ12ff., where he argues that a body, when it has moved over a distance $AB\Gamma$ by means of traversing by jumps the constituent *atomic* intervals of distance A, B and Γ, has also been at rest at each of these constituent intervals. The anti-atomic polemic of *Phys*. 6. 1 will also be discussed in Chapter 5. My present purpose is to explore the way in which it is possible for motion to be discontinuous in the sense of containing jumps but not pauses.

Suppose that the world were constructed in such a way that, as a body moving continuously approaches each hour of time elapsed since the beginning of its motion, it finds itself not at a location the distance of which from its starting-point is that which would be expected if its continuous motion were to continue (i.e. the 'limit' of this motion), but, rather, at some location 1 km. beyond that location. In such a world, continuous motion of whatever speed is, as it were, rewarded by a bonus kilometre at the end of each hour of continuous motion. The graph of a type (ii) function—a function from times elapsed to distances traversed—of such a motion is presented in Fig. 2. There is an intuitive, pictorial sense in which the graph is discontinuous at the points with 1-hour, 2-hour, etc. time abscissas ('x coordinates') and 3-km., 6-km. ordinates ('y coordinates'), respectively. And, in fact, the type (ii) function from time elapsed to distance traversed is discontinuous as the points $x = 1, = 2$, etc.[45]

While each gap in the graph has a particular point defining it 'on the right', there is not any such point 'on the left' of each gap, a fact represented by the right parenthesis, signifying that the preceding line-segment is right open. That is, there is no last time lapse (at which the moving body has traversed a distance of less than 2 km.) prior to the time lapse of an hour, at which it has traversed a distance of 3 km. The consequence is that, despite these discontinuities (jumps), there is a sense in which the motion is 'homogeneous': there is no *temporal interval* during which the body does not traverse some distance, and if t' is a proper sub-interval of temporal interval t, the body traverses in t' a distance s' that is a proper sub-interval of the distance s it traverses in t. Furthermore, such a motion satisfies the principle of the temporal non-supervenience of *kinēsis* (TN-SK) previously stated. Yet

---

[45] There is an interval $\epsilon > 0$ centred on $y = 3$ km. for which there is no interval $\delta > 0$ of time elapsed such that, for every $t \in \delta$, $f(t) \in \epsilon$.

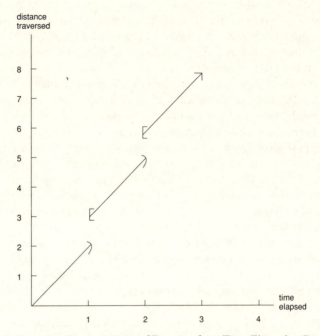

F ı g. 2. 'Jumps' as Discontinuities of Function from Time Elapsed to Distance Traversed

Square brackets indicate that there is a 'now' or instant of arrival at the distances of 3, 6, etc. km from origin of motion. Rounded brackets indicate that there is no immediately preceding distance traversed or instant at which it is traversed prior to these arrivals.

there does seem to be a sense in which the body whose motion is graphed in Fig. 2 can be said to have completed a movement (*kekinēsthai*) across a distance of 1 km. from its position at *t* = 1 hour without *having been in the process of moving* (*kineisthai*) through that distance. (For the representation of pauses as discontinuities in the function from the distances traversed by a particular moving body to the times taken to traverse these distances, see Fig. 3.)

What Aristotle seems to require is a principle of the *spatial*, as well as the temporal, non-supervenience of (local) *kinēsis*:

SN-SK. Each spatial partition of a continuous motion into kinetic proper segments[46] of motion yields segments each of which is

---

[46] For the account of a kinetic segment of motion see n. 42 above.

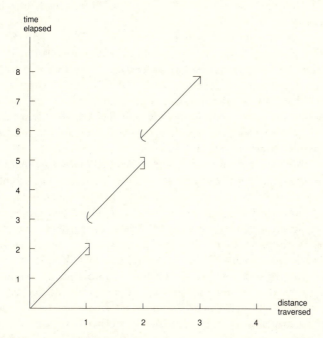

F I G. 3. Pauses as Discontinuities of Function from Distance Traversed to Time Elapsed

Square brackets indicate that there is a 'now'/instant at which the body arrives at a position a given distance from origin of motion. Rounded brackets indicate that there is no initial instant at which the body has departed from a position a given distance from origin.

continuous with at least one other kinetic segment of the partition in the following sense: there is a common spatial point that is paired with the *terminus a quo* of one of the kinetic segments and the *terminus ad quem* of the other segment.

Our representation of discontinuous motion in Fig. 2 violates this non-supervenience principle. For example, a spatially defined partition of that motion that would yield the kinetic segments corresponding to the distances traversed of [0,2) and [3,5) violates the principle because (since the intervening interval [2,3) cannot qualify, according to our definition, as a kinetic segment of the motion) the right limit (*terminus ad quem*) of the first kinetic segment, which is 2, does not correspond with the left limit (*terminus a quo*) of the 'next' kinetic segment, which is 3.

The kinetic non-supervenience principles TN-SK and SN-SK together guarantee that a continuous local motion is constituted only of kinetic segments of motion, which can be informally characterized as paired intervals of distances and times (temporal stretches or lapses) that can be 'decomposed' into paired *sub-intervals* of the respective intervals. That is, SN-SK and TN-SK are 'Aristotelian' principles corresponding, respectively, to the continuity of a function f from sub-intervals of time lapsed to sub-intervals of distance traversed and of the inverse f^{-1} of that function. TN-SK guarantees that non-kinetic-segment *temporal* intervals (pauses) do not get inserted into a continuous motion; SN-SK guarantees that non-kinetic-segment *spatial* intervals (jumps) do not get inserted. These two principles, I believe, lie at the conceptual centre of Aristotle's treatment of motion. Their function, however, is quite different. The temporal non-supervenience principle TN-SK serves to individuate kinetic activity in the cosmos, to sort out that kinetic activity into unitary, continuous temporal stretches of motion. Pauses or periods of *stasis* do occur, and, in general, such non-kinetic temporal stretches serve to bound temporal stretches of *kinēsis*. Aristotle has other informal criteria of individuation for *kinēseis*, even of local motions; but, as we shall later see, he seems to assume (incorrectly, from the contemporary perspective) that such criteria agree with this notion of the individuation of motions, according to which an individual motion is temporally bounded by pauses (at least if its subject exists both before the inception of and after the termination of the motion in question).

The spatial non-supervenience principle SN-SK holds quite generally, however. While Aristotle certainly recognizes that pauses do occur in the cosmos, he seems to hold that jumps, at least in the case of locomotion, do not. It is only when a body does not pause but moves continuously that in less time it traverses less distance and, consequently, satisfies TN-SK. But, as Aristotle indicates (*Phys*. 6. 2), it is true 'universally (*haplōs*) that for a body to traverse a (closed interval) proper sub-distance of a (closed interval) spatial magnitude, it must take the body less time than it takes it to traverse the whole (closed interval) distance. In other words, the spatial non-supervenience of motion principle SN-SK holds generally, in Aristotle's view. Jumps, in which a body traverses a distance without traversing its sub-distances in less time than it traversed the whole, simply do not occur.

Motion and Rest at an Instant

Although the sorts of continuity explicated in the preceding section lie at the conceptual centre of Aristotle's kinematics, the postulation of the sorts of continuity encapsulated by the two principles of non-supervenience of motion certainly does not resolve all the perplexities concerning motion that exercise Aristotle. A perplexity not thus resolved pertains to the status of nows (*ta nun*) or temporal instants with respect to motion and rest.

One consequence of the continuity of motion is that 'nothing is moving in a now' (*Phys*. 6. 3. 234ª24), in the sense that a now or instant cannot temporally define a kinetic segment. Recall that a kinetic segment of the motion of a body is a pair of 'infinitely divisible' spatial and temporal intervals (intuitively, the distance traversed by the body in that time) for which it is the case that every temporal sub-interval represents the temporal component of a kinetic sub-segment (i.e. is paired with a sub-interval of the spatial component of the original kinetic segment) *and* every spatial sub-interval represents the spatial component of a kinetic sub-segment (i.e. is paired with a sub-interval of the temporal component of the original kinetic segment). Clearly, a temporal point, being a limit of temporal lapse rather than a temporal lapse, can never be the temporal component of a kinetic segment—a body never traverses any distance during a now because there is no '*during* a now'. It is not surprising to find Aristotle, who, as we saw, develops in *Phys*. 6. 2 the notion of the continuity of motion in terms of principles of relative speed, making this point concerning motion and points in *Phys*. 6. 3 in terms of relative speed:

If this is the case [sc. that there is motion in a now], it is possible to move faster and slower. Let there be a now *N*, then, and let the faster traverse [the distance] *AB* in it. Therefore, the slower will in the same time traverse less distance than *AB*, say *AΓ* [Principle 1 of relative speed]. Since the slower will have traversed *AΓ* in the whole now, the faster will have traversed [*AΓ*] in less time than this [Principle 3] so that the now will have been divided, but it was indivisible. Consequently, it is not possible to move in a now. (234ª24–31)

Aristotle proceeds, in concluding the chapter, to argue that it is also the case that nothing rests at a temporal point. Here it is clear that his view does not depend on his earlier account of continuous motion. He adduces three considerations in support of his view. The first is metaphysical: the natural capacity for rest with respect to a now implies the natural capacity for motion with respect to a now; but the latter capacity does not exist (234^{a}31–4). The second consideration is a logical elaboration of the first: if there were a natural capacity for motion and rest at a temporal point, it would be necessary to attribute both capacities—and, inconsistently, both their actualizations—to the now that is a common 'extremity' of a stretch of motion and of a stretch of rest (234^{a}34–^{b}5). The last consideration is linguistic/conceptual: rest, according to our conception of it, implies a temporal lapse or sameness now and before; but there is no before/after 'in' a temporal point (234^{b}5–7).

It might seem that Aristotle's conception of the status of temporal points or instants with respect to motion and rest is unequivocally set forth in the preceding claims and his succinct summary at the end of *Phys*. 6. 3: 'therefore it is necessary that what is moving is moving and what is resting is resting in [an interval of] time' (234^{b}8–9). Unfortunately, however, the matter is not so simple. Other passages (in *Phys*. 6. 5 and 8. 8) in which Aristotle discusses the *terminus ad quem* of continuous change suggest that a body can have a property F (e.g. be in a position P) 'at a now'. Sorabji has interpreted these passages as presenting a view that is a second strand in Aristotle's kinematics, a line of thought to be distinguished from the 'better known' strand, i.e. the view that there can be neither motion nor rest at an instant.[47] I shall argue that Aristotle's considered view is that, in the case of locomotion, the property of a body A's *actually* being at a position P at an instant *t* implies A's resting at P for a time-interval which contains the punctal *t*.

The issue of the *terminus* of *kinēsis* arises, of course, in the case of a non-eternal continuous motion; and the paradigm that Aristotle seems to have in mind is locomotion. So what we have is a body A which is at rest for a period of time in position S, and then continuously moves to position F, where it rests for a period of time. Perhaps because of the teleological character of the Greek system of verb aspect and, of course, the teleological character of Aristotle's conception of motion, it is the latter *terminus ad quem*, the *telos* or completion of the motion, that receives most of his attention. The continuity of time in sense (*a*), which requires that contiguous parts of what is continuous share a common boundary, guarantees, as Aristotle puts it in *Phys*. 8. 8, that there be a 'point common to both periods, the former [continuous

[47] Sorabji, 'Aristotle on the Instant of Change', *The Aristotelian Society*, supplementary vol. 50 (1976), 69–89.

motion *to* position F, in our example] and the latter [rest *at* position F], that is the same in number' (263^b12–13). He immediately adds two qualifications. First, this temporal instant is not logically (*logōi*) the same: it is the beginning of the posterior time-interval but the completion of the prior interval (263^b13–14). Second, he adds a sentence (263^b14–15) paraphrased by Ross as 'the thing is in it [i.e. in the temporal instant in question] qualified only by the quality which it has in the subsequent period'.[48]

The latter claim clearly seems intended by Aristotle to hold only where the prior period temporally demarcates a *kinēsis* (or kinetic segment) and the latter a pause or period of *stasis*. He gives essentially the same argument for it in *Phys*. 6. 5 and 8. 8: the completion, *telos*, or *terminus ad quem* of a continuous motion is temporally paired with this limit point; the completion or *telos* of a *kinēsis* is connoted by a stative-perfective verbal form, which entails the possession of the property or obtaining of the state of affairs that supervenes on the completion of the *kinēsis*. For example, '*gegone* (Φ)' or 'it has become (F)' entails '*esti* (Φ)' or 'it is (F)'; and '*ephthartai* (Φ)' or 'it has ceased to be (F)' entails '*ouk esti* (Φ)' or 'it is not (F)'.[49] Therefore, at the limit point temporally marking the *terminus ad quem* of a continuous *kinēsis*, the body that has undergone the *kinēsis* in question must be said to possess the property or be in the state supervening on the completion of the *kinēsis*. There is good reason, given the way the system of Greek verb aspect works and the continuity of time, spatial magnitude, and motion, to regard the two premisses of this argument as true. But is the argument valid? This question is not easy to answer. In attempting an answer, it seems important to note an ambiguity in the notion of a 'first time' when something has changed or completed a change (*metabeblēke*). One sense connotes the *terminus ad quem* in the sense of temporal limit between the temporal stretch of motion or continuous change 'on the left' and the ensuing temporal stretch of *stasis* (state of possessing property F or being in state G) 'on the right'. That there should be such a limit point follows from the continuity of time and of (temporally bounded) continuous motion; and Aristotle has no real problem (in *Phys*. 6. 5) establishing the existence of such a limit and that it is 'indivisible' (punctal, in fact, given the continuity of time). But it is not clear that such a limit point is 'the first time with respect to which it is true to say that something has changed'. It does seem to be

---

[48] Ross, *Aristotle's Physics*, 714.
[49] See *Phys*. 6. 5. 235^b27–9, 8. 8. 263^b21–6.

the case, as Aristotle argues in 6. 5, that one cannot say *prior* to such a limit that something A has changed; for then it would be true to say at the same time that A has both changed (completed a change to B) and is changing (in the process of changing to B), which Aristotle takes to be a *reductio* on the assumption (235^b20-6).

However, if one considers the *intervals* of time with this temporal point as 'left' limit (i.e. intervals at which it is true to say that A has changed to B and, consequently, now is B), it follows from the continuity of time that there is no *first interval* at which it is true to say that A has changed to and now is B. For example, there is no first temporal *interval* with respect to which it is true that A has moved to position P *and* now is at rest at P). In *Phys*. 6. 5 Aristotle considers the sense of 'that in which something has first changed' which connotes 'that in which something first *began* to change'. It seems that, when he there argues that there is no such beginning of continuous change, his argument depends upon understanding such a temporal beginning of change as a time at which we can truly say 'motion *has been* occurring'. In effect, the complex argument that Aristotle proceeds to give has the following structure: a time at which it is true to say that motion *has been occurring* must be either a time *interval* corresponding to what we have been calling a kinetic segment or a punctal now corresponding to the *terminus ad quem* ('right bound') of such a segment. On either alternative, there will not be a first such time.[50]

---

[50] Suppose there is such a beginning of motion, signified as $A\Delta$ by Aristotle. If $A\Delta$ is indivisible, either there would be an immediately preceding time at which the thing has not moved (which is impossible because nows are not contiguous—or in succession) or $A\Delta$ itself is the right bound of a period ΓA of rest. But then (because we are assuming motion to *have occurred* with respect to $A\Delta$ and because it thus follows—because $A\Delta$ is indivisible—that motion *has occurred* with respect to A) we are entitled (by the argument of *Phys*. 6. 3. 234^a32-$^b4$) to infer that, since the body can be in motion with respect to A, it can be in rest with respect to A, and since A is also by assumption a part of the period ΓA in which the body *is* actually at rest, it must be at rest at A as well. But since Δ is indivisible, it must be at rest with respect to $A\Delta$. Thus, it will 'at the same time [*terminus* of $A\Delta$] have [immediately before] been at rest and have changed' (236^a19), which is impossible. Finally, if $A\Delta$ is divisible, the thing will have changed with respect to the whole interval (and hence, there will be proper sub-interval $A\Delta$ ' (such that Δ ' is 'to the left' of Δ) in which the thing has changed. So $A\Delta$ will not be the *first* such interval in which the thing will have changed. Or the thing will not have changed with respect to all of $A\Delta$ but only with respect to a proper part of it, for which reason again $A\Delta$ will not be a *first* time of change. It is clear that a crucial assumption of this argument is that motion *has occurred* with respect to $A\Delta$. Thus, one 'candidate' for $A\Delta$ that would vitiate Aristotle's argument is ruled out from the beginning: the now or punctal limit serving as the common bound of a temporal stretch of *stasis* from an ensuing, contiguous temporal stretch of motion.

Following this strategy—which Aristotle employs to argue that there is no first time of change—one *could* also claim that there is no first time in which something *has completed a change* or, in other words, no first time of *stasis*. Although there is a punctal limit that bounds a continuous change 'on the right' and also bounds the ensuing, contiguous period of *stasis* 'on the left', the first time at which it is true to say that something *has changed* must be some time *after* the process of change is completed. But such a time will be either an interval of time that has as its 'left bound' the punctal now marking the *terminus* of the process, or the 'right bound' of such an interval. On either alternative, there is no first such time after the process of change is terminated (because of the continuity/infinite divisibility of time). Alternatively, one could deny the truth of the entailment ('it has become *F*' ⇒ 'it is *F*'): while allowing the truth of the *premiss* 'it has become *F*' at the punctal temporal *terminus* of the process of becoming F, one might none the less maintain that the entailment holds only with respect to intervals of time because it is only with respect to intervals of time that the conclusion 'it is *F*' can be true.

Aristotle, however, seems to see a close connection between the perfective achievements connoted by the 'perfect' verb forms he uses and the punctal temporal limits (*termini ad quem*) of continuous changes. He is perhaps particularly successful in evoking this connection in an interesting sentence in *Phys*. 8. 8: 'it is clear, then, that if [*Δ*] was becoming [white] in the whole time [interval] *A*, it is not possible that the time in which it has become and was becoming is greater than all the time in which it was becoming only' (264^{a}4–6). If the total time in which it has become (*gegone*) *and* was (continuously) becoming (*egigneto*) is no more than the time in which it was (continuously) becoming (sc. the time it was becoming *without* having become), one of two situations must obtain: (*a*) there must be an interval or 'lapse' of time during which it is *both* continuously becoming (*F*) and it has become (*F*); (*b*) the achievement of having become (*F*) is to be temporally demarcated by the 'now' serving as the 'right' limit of the temporal stretch of becoming (*F*). Since alternative (*a*) is ruled out by considerations from *Phys*. 6. 5 (what has already become *F* or has arrived at position *P* would still be becoming *F* or moving to *P* when it has 'got there', so to speak), we are left with (*b*). And, it is worth noting that (*b*) nicely accords with a technical claim that Aristotle makes about what is continuous that was discussed earlier in this chapter: the 'addition' or 'subtraction' of a boundary point from continuous magnitudes does not affect the (sum of the) 'bulk' or size of the magnitude(s) in question. Aristotle's conclusion appears to be that something has achieved the *telos* of a continuous motion, e.g. has become *F* or has arrived at position *P*, at the now or temporal instant that temporally bounds that continuous motion 'on the right' and, in this sense, is the motion's temporal *terminus ad quem*.

This conclusion agrees, I suspect, as much with English usage as it does Greek. We can also see, I believe, the linguistic basis of Aristotle's refusal to treat the punctal temporal limit marking the beginning of a continuous change in the same way that he treats the punctal temporal limit marking the termination of such a change. For Aristotle equates the beginning of change with a first time in which it is true to say that change *has begun*. In view of the continuity of change, to say that change has begun is to say that some has been going on. And in view of the continuity of time, there is no *first* time in which change has been going on; no change has been going on at the punctal terminus marking the inception of change, so it cannot be the beginning of change. But Aristotle equates the inception of the state attendant on the completion of change with a first time at which it is true to say that something *has changed* or that the change *has been completed*. It is arguable that, in this case, there is such a first time of the state attendant upon the completion of change, namely, the temporal punctal limit that bounds 'on the right' the stretch of continuous change and 'on the left' the ensuing stretch of time in which the subject of change is no longer changing but, rather, is in the state of having changed.

Understood narrowly, this conception of its being true 'at a now' that something has changed is perfectly consistent with Aristotle's claim that there is neither motion nor rest at a temporal instant. As Aristotle has implied in *Phys*. 6. 8, it is possible for something to have arrived at position *P* at a now *t* and, thus, there is a sense in which it is possible for it to *be* at *P* at a now *t*; but it does not follow that it is possible to *rest* at *P* for/at a now *t*. To rest (*ēremein*), for Aristotle, is to remain (*menein*); and for something to remain requires the lapse of time.

Sorabji, I believe, is in essential agreement with the preceding interpretation:

For although [Aristotle] denies that things can *change* or *remain* in the same state at an instant, he concedes that there are many other things that can be true of them at an instant. He is quite prepared to allow that what is moving can be at a point (VIII 8, 262ª30; ᵇ20), or level with something (VI 8, 239ª35–ᵇ3) at an instant. As regards other kinds of change, the object that is changing colour can be white at an instant (VIII 8, 263ᵇ20; 23), or the white have perished and non-white have come into being at an instant (VI 5, 235ᵇ32–236ª7; VI 6, 237ª14–15). In allowing something to *be* white at an instant, he is not allowing that it could *remain* white, or *rest* in the white state, at an instant.[51]

He none the less sees a contrast between 'two strands of thought in Aristotle about the process of transition involved in the four genuine kinds of change. Sometimes he argues that a thing cannot be changing or resting at any instant. But sometimes he argues or implies, in conformity with our view about continuous changes, that there cannot be a first instant at which a thing is changing, nor a last instant of not having reached its terminal state'.[52] In view of the prior quotation, why does Sorabji find *two* strands rather than one coherent view in the *Physics'* treatment of motion/rest with respect to temporal instants? I suspect that the answer is that Sorabji sees in his 'second strand' (i.e. Aristotle's discussion of the issues of the first and last instants of continuous motion and his concession that 'there are many other things that can be true of [things] at an instant') a 'wedge' for the admission of the notion of motion at an instant, a notion that Aristotle's 'first strand of thought' explicitly denies. Sorabji, following G. E. L. Owen, sees Aristotle's explicit exclusion of any concept of motion at an instant as a flaw in his rational kinematics. I return to this particular issue in Chapter 4. A concern which I address in the following chapter is whether Aristotle's apparent concession that a body can have a position at an instant creates a 'metaphysical' difficulty concerning the unity or 'identity conditions' for a motion. I shall argue that his concession does create such a difficulty, but that he attempts to resolve the difficulty in Book 8 of the *Physics*.

THREE KINEMATIC MISTAKES: AN ANALYSIS

In this chapter we have examined, first, Aristotle's discussion of the formal, structural properties of spatial magnitude and, then, his account of the formal, structural properties of local motion. Working with an *ontology* of what is continuous that is very different from

[51] Sorabji, 'Aristotle on the Instant of Change', 82.
[52] Ibid. 85.

standard contemporary point-set ontology, Aristotle develops a rational kinematics that looks very familiar—i.e. a rational kinematics that is quite similar to the standard contemporary account. In this section I shall consider some kinematic claims made by Aristotle that are, from the contemporary perspective, mistakes. It is, I think, useful to concentrate on these mistakes as salient illustrations of just where Aristotle's kinematic analysis and the standard contemporary analysis part ways. Part of what lies behind this divergence, of course, is the fact that neither Aristotle nor the ancient geometers had the sophisticated mathematical tools for dealing with continuous magnitudes, the development of which depended on the 'algebraization' of geometry. But I shall suggest that part of the story also is the difference between basic ontological conceptions of what is continuous.

Reversed Rectilinear Motion

In *Phys*. 8. 8 we find Aristotle 'refining' (i.e. correcting) certain aspects of the kinematic analysis of *Phys*. 6. He argues in *Phys*. 8. 8 that a body moving continuously from position S (spatial *terminus a quo*) to position *F* (spatial *terminus ad quem*) neither has come to be at (*gegonenai*) nor has departed from (*apogegonenai, apelēluthenai*) any intermediate (*meson*) position *B*.

One might expect Aristotle to argue as follows: since a continuously moving body does not pause or 'stand' (*stēnai*) at any of the places it traverses that are strictly between its *actual* spatial *termini a quo* and *ad quem*, it neither has come to be at nor has departed from any of these places. However, we do not seem to find the sort of 'ordinary-language' argument that we might expect concerning the connection between a continuously moving body's not pausing, resting, or standing at a *meson* position and its neither arriving at nor departing from such a position: viz., the argument that the concepts of 'having arrived at' and 'having departed from' imply a period of *stasis* in between. Rather, Aristotle's argument in this chapter seems to be just the converse. It is *because* the 'having arrived at a given position' and the 'having departed from that same position' cannot be temporally coincidental that we are assured of the existence of a period of *stasis* in between the 'having arrived at …' and the 'having departed from …': 'For it is impossible that the body *A* has simultaneously arrived at and departed from *B*; for [these must have occurred] at different points of time. Therefore there will be [an interval of] time in between, so that A will have rested at B' ($262^{a}32-^{b}3$). Later Aristotle states his reason for refusing to allow that the 'having come to be at' and the 'having departed from' a position could be simultaneous: 'And [a body] has not simultaneously come to be at $\varDelta$ and departed from $\varDelta$; for then it would simultaneously be there and not be there at the same now' ($262^{b}26-8$). Aristotle seems to be interpreting the 'having come to be (*gegonenai*) at B at instant t' as implying 'being at B at instant t' and the 'having departed from (*apelēluthenai*) B at t' as implying '*not* being at B at t'. In other words, 'having departed from' connotes or implies 'being some distance away from'. So far so good. But Aristotle apparently proceeds to infer from the impossibility of a moving body's simultaneously having come to be at and having departed from a particular position that if a body *actually* does both come to be at and depart from a position, there must be two distinct instants or temporal points, an earlier instant t_1 at which the body has come to be (*gegonen*) at B, and a later instant t_2 at which it has departed from (*apelēluthon*) B. So, in the interval between (*en mesōi*), it must rest at B.

It is arguable that this conclusion would follow if there were a *unique* t_2, a unique (first) instant of having departed from a position in the sense of a first instant of being away from that position.[53] But, of course, Aristotle has argued back in *Phys*. 6 that there is no first time of having departed from a position in this sense. This problem leads Sorabji to doubt whether Aristotle has a 'firm grasp' of the continuity of change, according to which 'there cannot be a first instant at which a thing is changing, nor a first instant at which it has left its initial state, nor a last instant of not having reached its terminal state':

For in *Phys*. VIII 8, $262^{a}31-^{b}3$; $^{b}21-263^{a}3$, he appears to contradict it, by assuming that when a moving object reverses direction, there is a first instant of having left the point of reversal. At least, this is the assumption which he seems to require for his conclusion, which is that the reversing object must spend a period of time at the point of reversal.[54]

It certainly seems to be the case that Aristotle made such a mistake; but, in view of his generally 'firm grasp' on the concept of continuous motion, his doing so constitutes a most puzzling blunder. I suspect that his error—for so it must be termed—is rather more subtle than it may at first seem. It is true that, for Aristotle, each of the nows when the

---

[53] I should like to thank Prof. Richard McKirihan for helpful discussion concerning Aristotle's mistake here.

[54] Sorabji, 'Aristotle on the Instant of Change', 85.

continuously moving body can truly be said to have departed from a
meson position B (in the sense of being some distance 'past' it) is 'after'
the now when the body can be said to have arrived at B. From *our*
perspective, it seems correct to say that *all* such points of time are
temporally posterior to the now t at which the body has arrived at B.
If we are not careful, we might be tempted to assume that, since all
such points are (collectively) after t, all such points must be 'separated
from t' (i.e. after t) by some interval of time. Such an interval would
have to be an interval of time at which the body is resting at B. The
fallacy can be characterized as that of illegitimate quantifier shift: from

> (A) for each time t$'$ at which it is true that a body *has departed* from
> B, there is some interval ϵ of time such that t$'$ is later than the time
> t when the body has come to be at B by at least ϵ,

we (in effect) inferred

> (B) there is some interval of time ϵ such that, for each time t' at
> which it is true that a body *has departed* from B, t$'$ is later than the
> time t when the body arrived at B by at least ϵ.

Quantifier-shift fallacies, to which Aristotle is prone, are of course
easier to see and avoid if one has been schooled in first-order predicate
logic. But it may seem that this particular instance of the fallacy is one
that Aristotle *should* have seen. The key question is why he does not
seem to recognize that the time t at which the body has come to be
(*gegonen*) at B is the limit not only of the 'stretch of time on the left'
during which the body is in the process of moving to B but also the
limit of the 'stretch of time on the right' during which the body is in
the process of moving away from B. Were Aristotle clearly to recognize this fact, it seems that he could recognize that t, while not a time
at which the body *has* departed from (*apelēluthon*) B, is the 'left
temporal limit' of this state of affairs (i.e. the body's having departed
from, and, hence, being some distance away from B). But he then,
surely, would recognize that there is no 'time in between' at which the
body must rest at B.

Why, then, does Aristotle fail to see that the 'right temporal limit' t
of the state of affairs of the body's *not yet being at B* is also the 'left
temporal limit' of the state of affairs of the body's *having departed from
B*? I suspect that part of the answer is that he does not conceive of t as
the common limit of two sets of dense and Dedekind-continuous
temporal instants: the set of 'prior' times, representing instantaneous
positions of the body *before* it occupies position B, and the set of

'posterior' times, representing instantaneous positions of the body *after* it occupies position *B*. Rather, *t* would have to be the common limit of two continuous 'stretches' of time, the 'prior' stretch character-ized by the state of affairs of 'being on the way *towards B*' and the 'posterior' stretch characterized by the state of affairs of 'having departed *from B*'.

In *Phys*. 8. 8. 263^{b}9 ff. Aristotle is concerned with the problem of characterizing the common limit of two contiguous stretches of time. While he admits that such a limit or point (*sēmeion*) 'is common to both [temporal intervals], the former and the later, and is one and the same in number' (263^{b}12–13), a choice must be made with respect to the 'fact of the matter' (*tōi pragmati*). Consider the common limit or temporal *sēmeion t* of two contiguous temporal intervals, the former characterized by the *kinēsis* of something's becoming (and, hence, not yet being) white and the later by the *energeia* of the thing's having become (and, hence, being) white. With respect to the 'fact of the matter', Aristotle says, the thing cannot both 'be becoming' (and, hence, not yet actually be) white at *t* and 'have become' (and, hence, actually be) white at *t*. Aristotle decides that, in such a case, *t* belongs to the *later* interval 'with respect to the fact of the matter': that is, it is true to say that the thing *has become* (and, hence, is) white at *t*. It was *becoming* white at all of the prior interval *except* the limit *t* of that interval. Although he does not discuss the mirror-image case (of a thing's being in a state during an earlier temporal interval and then being in a process of change in a contiguous, later temporal interval), it seems fairly clear that Aristotle would want to place the common limit in the earlier, 'stative' temporal interval 'with respect to the fact of the matter'. For, as we saw earlier in this chapter, the view forcefully stated in *Physics* 6 is that there is no 'beginning of motion/change' in the sense of an initial time at which something can be said to *have* moved/changed.

Now, if a common limit of two contiguous temporal intervals must always belong to either one or the other 'with respect to the fact of the matter', the present case poses a problem. For the earlier interval is characterized by the *kinēsis* of 'moving toward *B*' and the (supposedly) contiguous later interval is characterized by the *kinēsis* of 'having departed from/moving away from *B*'. By Aristotle's own principles, a supposed common limit point *t* could not belong either to the earlier temporal interval or to the later temporal interval 'with respect to the fact of the matter'. That is, *t* can neither be a time at which it is true to say that the body is 'moving toward B' nor a time at which it is true to say that the body 'has departed from/is moving away from B'. Aristotle's resolution of the problem, I suggest, is to maintain that where there is *actual kinēsis* of coming-to-be at B and an *actual kinēsis* of departing from B, there must be a period of rest at B in between. When this temporal interval of *stasis* is 'inserted', Aristotle's problem of where to put common limit points is solved. I say 'points' because, of course, there are two such points now. There is a temporal *sēmeion* t that is common to the kinetic period C at which the body is coming-to-be-at/moving-toward B and the succeeding static period S at which it rests at B. t belongs to the later static period S 'with respect to the fact of the matter'. And there is a temporal *sēmeion* t' that is common to the static period S during which the body is at rest at B and the successive kinetic period D at which the body is departing-from/moving-away-from B. t' belongs to the earlier static period S 'with respect to the fact of the matter'.

We see no difficulty in identifying t and t' because this temporal point simply marks one instantaneous position (of the continuously moving body at B) among a dense and Dedekind-continuous infinity of other times, viz., those marking instantaneous positions of the continuously moving body *prior* to its instantaneous presence at B and those *posterior* to its instantaneous presence at B. But Aristotle does not decompose continuous motion into an infinity of instantaneous positions of the moving body. He evidently holds that a common limit point of two successive, contiguous temporal stretches of *kinēsis* or *energeia / stasis* must 'essentially' or 'with respect to the fact of the matter' be characterized in terms of one or the other of these processes or states. But when the two contiguous temporal stretches are both *kinēseis*, the supposedly common limit point cannot plausibly be characterized as 'essentially' or 'with respect to the fact of the matter' belonging to *either*. Aristotle thus comes to two conclusions. (i) When there is an *actual kinēsis* of coming-to-be or arriving at a position B followed by an *actual kinēsis* of moving-away-from or departing from B, these *kinēseis* cannot be contiguous; there must be a period of *stasis* inserted in between. (ii) When we conceptually distinguish a *meson* or intermediate position B 'within' a body's continuous motion from actual *terminus a quo* to actual *terminus ad quem*, the body does not *actually* arrive at and depart from B; however, according to Aristotle, it is at B 'at a cut of time and not for a [period of] time'

(262^{b}20–1), and B is really only a *potential* position of the moving body, not an actual one (262^{b}31–2).

The preceding analysis is certainly different from the contemporary point-set analysis, and, from the contemporary perspective, it is unnecessarily complicated. But it is not clear that there is anything kinematically 'mistaken' about it. The mistake occurs when Aristotle applies his analysis to reversed rectilinear direction. His argument is that in such a case we do have an actual *kinēsis* of moving-toward/arriving-at the position of reversal of motion and an actual *kinēsis* of moving-away-from/departing from this position. Intuitively, we have *two* discrete continuous motions in the case of something continuously moving from a starting position to a position $\varDelta$, where it reverses direction and moves continuously back to its starting position. Aristotle says that in such a case the moving body uses the turning position $\varDelta$ both as a *terminus ad quem* and as a *terminus a quo* (262^{b}24–5), and adds that (unlike the case of a continuously moving body traversing an arbitrary intermediate (*meson*) potential stopping-place) 'it is necessary that [the body] reach the goal as something *actually* existent, not merely potentially' (262^{b}30–1). Consequently, the body both actually has come to be at and actually has departed from $\varDelta$. Hence, by the preceding analysis that we have just discussed, Aristotle comes to the conclusion (incorrect, from the contemporary perspective) that a body undergoing reversed rectilinear motion must have paused (rested some *interval* of time) at the position $\varDelta$ of reversal of motion.

We see here the influence of Aristotle's ontology of motion on his kinematic analysis. Since Aristotle tends to individuate (non-eternal) local motions in terms of their *termini a quo* and *ad quem*, he here 'sees' two discrete motions that are 'in succession' (*ephekses*). The position at which the motion is reversed 'stands out' in a way that other positions that might be attributed to the body during its motion (as 'potential' but not actual *termini*) do not. In fact, the turning position $\varDelta$ seems to introduce some intuitive sort of discontinuity into the motion, dividing it into two, as it were. But we have seen why Aristotle might think, in view of his relation of temporal limit points to the temporal stretches of *kinēsis* and *stasis* that they limit, that there must be a pause inserted here. Aristotle also holds that the only way local motion (of a given body) can be rendered *actually* discontinuous is by the insertion of a pause.

Aristotle's assumption that the only possible way of introducing a discontinuity into motion is through the insertion of a pause seems to be too restrictive, from the contemporary kinematic perspective. But *is* there, from the contemporary perspective, a discontinuity in reversed rectilinear motion with respect to which the reversal is effected at a temporal instant? The function from time elapsed to distance traversed (considered as a scalar quantity)[55] certainly can be—and would standardly be considered to be—continuous at a temporal point t_0 of reversal of direction. If there is a discontinuity to be found, it evidently will pertain to an 'abrupt' change in or 'jump' of direction, rather than a 'jump' with respect to some notion of the 'magnitude' of motion. So the search for discontinuity might point in the direction of the first derivative of distance with respect to time, i.e. velocity, considered as a vector quantity. That is, velocity takes into account direction as well as 'speed', considered a scalar quantity.

Of course, it is logically impossible for 'speed' or the scalar constituent of velocity to be a *constant* positive magnitude throughout such an interval of reversed rectilinear motion: the body could not logically have both a velocity of $\mathbf{A} = (x,y)$ and a velocity of $-\mathbf{A} = (-x,-y)$ at the temporal point t_0 of reversal of motion. So, on the assumption of 'constant speed', it is logically necessary that there be a discontinuity of velocity at t_0.[56] Since he does not mention any constancy of speed qualification, I assume that Aristotle holds that there must be a discontinuity of motion at the position of reversal even in cases where the body gradually (continuously) slows to zero during a period of time as it approaches the position of reversal and continuously speeds up for a period of time after it departs from the position.

In such a case, however, the standard contemporary vectorial account of velocity detects no discontinuity at t_0. But this fact is simply a consequence of a convention concerning the way in which a vector is used to represent velocity. What we are concerned with is the representation of 'instantaneous velocity' as a vector function from real numbers (representing temporal instants) to plane vectors (representing velocity at a temporal instant). Plane vectors, in turn, can be represented by 'arrows' or directed line-segments in a Cartesian coordinate plane. And an 'untransported' vector or vector in standard

---

[55] A scalar quantity, as opposed to a vector quantity, represents only magnitude, prescinding from any considerations of direction or orientation.

[56] I am here leaving aside dynamical considerations ruling out the possibility of constant velocity at every time t during which the body is moving except t_0.

position (with origin point $(0,0)$) can be represented by the x and y coordinates of its tip.

With respect to the continuity of velocity in the case of instantaneous reversed rectilinear motion, the important convention in vectorial representation of velocity is that whereby the scalar magnitude, or 'speed' component is represented by the length of the vector and the directional component by the inclination of the vector in the plane. Since the continuity of a vector function such as the one we are concerned with is defined in terms of the *length* of the difference of vectors, the function turns out to be continuous at t_0 so long as the speed of the body is continuously decreasing to zero through a period of time as the body approaches the turning-point and continuously increasing through a period of time as the body moves away from the point. This fact can perhaps be most easily comprehended intuitively by visualizing an arrow in the plane as continuously 'shrinking' in length to the 'zero vector' (the point $(0,0)$) and then continuously 'growing' in length in the opposite direction. More formally: for any interval ϵ centred on the zero vector (an interval in the range set of vector functions and represented by the 'absolute value' of the length between tips of vectors pointing in the opposite directions), there will be a *temporal* interval δ (an interval in the domain set of vector functions) such that, for any temporal instant within δ, the tip of the vector assigned by the function to t (i.e. the instantaneous velocity of the body at t) will fall within the interval ϵ.

It can plausibly be argued, I believe, that the continuity of velocity in this situation is preserved because of the way in which the directional constituent of velocity is standardly represented. There remains a sense, however, in which there is an intuitive discontinuity in the direction of the moving object: there is a 'jump' in the direction of the object in the sense that it 'abruptly' reverses directions without assuming any of the intermediate directions.

I have presented this material concerning vectorial representation of instantaneous velocity—admittedly, a concept that we have no reason to believe that Aristotle himself ever came close to developing[57]—with a fair amount of detail because I believe that there is at least one 'moral' of some significance to be gleaned from it. It seems that the fact that classical mechanics sees no kinematic discontinuity in the case of reversed rectilinear motion whereas Aristotle does see a

---

[57] The relation between Aristotelian kinematics and classical modern concepts of mechanics, such as instantaneous velocity, will be explored further in Chap. 4.

discontinuity is due to a mathematical convention—a useful and entirely 'appropriate' convention, but still a convention. This convention represents velocity in such a way that a 'jump' in direction—a change in direction that does not involve the moving body's assuming all of the 'intermediate' directions[58]—does not necessarily imply a 'jump' or discontinuity in velocity. As it happens, this convention 'submerges' what may seem to some to be the intuitive discontinuity in the case of 'abrupt' reversal of direction. It is such an intuitive discontinuity that Aristotle sees and to which Sorabji is pointing when (in discussing the instantaneous reversal of motion of a ball 'travelling vertically upwards' and then vertically downward) he comments that 'we could not say that its motion had one direction rather than the opposite direction at that instant'.[59]

It is not clear that there is an 'objective error' in the fact that Aristotle sees a discontinuity in reversed rectilinear motion. Rather, his error lies in his assumption that the only source of discontinuity in nature must be pauses. Consequently, he is too ready to believe that, because he detects a discontinuity in *direction* of motion at the position of reversal, the body must pause there.

A Continuously Moving Body Can Take Only a Finite Time to Traverse a Finite Distance

A second kinematic claim that some have judged, from the contemporary perspective, to be a blunder, is Aristotle's claim (with supporting argument) in *Phys*. 6. 7 that 'it is impossible in a infinite time to effect a limited (or finite: *peperasmenēn*) motion' (237^b24–5). Later in the chapter, he makes the correlative claim that a distance infinite in extent cannot be traversed in a finite time (238^a20 ff.). Aristotle is talking about continuous motion, primarily locomotion, it seems; and he has no difficulty in establishing the former claim (on which I shall concentrate in what follows) for the case where the speed of the moving body is constant, i.e. the case in which the body moves *isotachōs*. An assumption of Aristotle's entire discussion is that we are dealing with a situation in which, supposedly, a finite distance

---

[58] The notion of a continuum (dense, Dedekind-continuous linear ordering) of directions between any 2 directions is, of course, itself somewhat problematic because of the distinction (when just 2 dimensions are considered) between clockwise betweenness and counter-clockwise betweenness.

[59] Sorabji, 'Aristotle on the Instant of Change', 73.

s is traversed 'in an infinite time' by a continuously moving body but in which no proper part of this distance *s* is traversed 'in an infinite time'.

In order to deal with the special case of constant speed, however, he needs only the assumption that there is *some* proper part *s′* of the distance *s* that is traversed in a finite time. He can then make use of a form of Eudoxus' axiom (sometimes called Archimedes' axiom): for all reals *s* > *s′* > 0, there is some natural number *n* such that *s′* added to itself *n* times equals or exceeds *s*.[60] Then, because of the constancy of speed, the complete distance *s* will be traversed in a time less than or equal to the (finite) time it takes the body to traverse *s′* multiplied by *n*, and this obviously will be a finite amount of time.

The problem arises, from the contemporary perspective, when Aristotle attempts to generalize his claim to continuous motion over some finite distance *without* assuming constancy of velocity or speed. The kernel of Aristotle's argument is the following. On the assumption that it takes the moving body an infinite time to traverse *only* the whole of a finite distance *AB*, and not an infinite time to traverse any proper 'initial segment' (segment actually traversed 'starting from the beginning'), any sub-segment of any initial segment will be traversed in *some* finite time, irrespective of alteration in the velocity of the continuously moving body. Select a sub-segment *AE* of *AB* that will 'measure' (*katametrēsei*) *AB*—i.e. a sub-segment *AE* for which it is the case that there is some natural number *n* such that *AB* = *n*(*AE*). Since it is *only* the whole *AB* and not any part that is traversed in an infinite time, each of these *n* segments, each equal in length to *AE*, will be traversed in a finite time—although each will not necessarily be traversed in the *same* finite time. Consequently, the finite sum (sum of *n* addenda) of these individually finite times will be a finite time, equal to the time required to traverse *AB*. So the time taken to traverse the finite whole *AB* then must be finite. QED

A reasonable contemporary reaction to this argument is to hurriedly

---

[60] The axiom is involved in the assumption of the existence of a smaller magnitude or 'motion' that 'will measure the whole' (*katametrēsei tēn holēn*). It is perhaps clearer in Aristotle's other, parallel discussion of the special case of constant velocity at *Phys.* 6. 2. 233ᵃ31 ff. that what he means here by 'measuring the whole' is the capacity of the smaller magnitude to 'exhaust' the larger in the following sense: the smaller added to itself some finite number of times either equals or exceeds the larger. Perhaps the clearest statement of the axiom in the *Physics* is found at *Phys.* 3. 6. 206ᵇ11–12; 'every finite [magnitude] is exhausted [or taken up, *anaireisthai*] by any definite [magnitude] whatsoever.'

remove the 'QED'. Wilbur Knorr provides a particularly lucid illustration of this reaction:

> [Aristotle] there [in our passage in *Physics* 6] allows for a more general situation, covering not only the case of uniform motion but also the cases in which the motion may be accelerating or decelerating. In this he commits a plain error, however. In subdividing the given distance into equal parts, he assumes that the time required for traversing each such part—while not necessarily equal to the time for any other part, since the motion is now nonuniform—is nevertheless finite. His justification, if it can be called such, is that the time for traversing the part cannot be infinite, and he has assumed the whole time is infinite, and the time for traversing the part must be less than that for the whole. . . . In the present case, having admitted nonuniform motion, we might easily construct a decelerating motion which requires some fixed time to traverse each successively diminishing part of the distance; then the time to traverse the whole would indeed be infinite.[61]

Although, as we shall see, his reaction to Aristotle's claim is rather more sympathetic than that of Knorr, Hippocrates Apostle also notes the apparent counter-example provided by a continuously moving body the instantaneous velocity of which asymptotically approaches zero:

> But, one may ask, if $v = 10e^{-t}$, where v is the speed in miles per hour and t is the time [lapsed—since the beginning of motion], would it not take an infinite time to traverse 10 miles, seeing that $\int_0^\infty 10e^{-t}dt = 10$?[62]

Expressed more informally, the situation that Knorr and Apostle have in mind is one in which the velocity of a body is continuously approaching zero without ever 'actually' (i.e. after a finite lapse of time) stopping. And the velocity is decreasing in such a way that the body is continuously traversing some finite spatial interval *AB* (in the particular example of Apostle, one with a length of 10 miles) without ever actually (i.e. in a finite time) reaching the end-point of the interval (i.e. without ever actually *having* traversed the interval in question).

Where, if anywhere, does Aristotle's argument go wrong? Knorr suggests that it is in the thesis (which Aristotle seems to hold as axiomatic for continuous motion) that 'the time for traversing the part must be less than that for the whole'. I suspect that what Knorr has in mind is the fact that (e.g.) in Apostle's example, it would also take the

---

[61] W. R. Knorr, 'Infinity and Continuity: The Interaction of Mathematics and Philosophy in Antiquity', in Kretzmann (ed.), *Infinity and Continuity*, 118–19.

[62] Apostle, *Aristotle's Physics*, 294.

body 'an infinite amount of time' to traverse the *second* half of the 10-mile distance—and, indeed, any proper sub-segment including all of the points 'on the right'. However, for *initial segments*, i.e. for any *closed* interval actually traversed by the moving body, Aristotle's 'axiom' holds: the time taken by a continuously moving body to traverse a closed interval will be greater than the time taken to traverse any proper closed sub-segment of it.

Indeed, an analogous argument in *De caelo* 1. 6 makes the role of this sort of assumption yet more explicit.[63] In the *De caelo* passage Aristotle argues that an infinitely extended body cannot have finite weight (*to baros*). There he uses proportion theory in the following way. Suppose an infinitely extended body *AB* has finite weight *Γ*. Subtract from *AB* a finite quantity *BΔ* having weight *E*. Although Aristotle considers the case where *E* and *Γ* are incommensurable (*asummetra*), that case obviously works if his argument for the case where *Γ* is some exact multiple *n* of *E* works. 'If quantities or magnitudes are proportional to weights' (*ei toinun analogon ta megethē tois baresi*—273[b]3), then the total weight *Γ* should be 'exhausted' by *n* quantities each having the (finite) weight *E* (i.e. the weight of the finite quantity *BΔ*). Even if the weight of *AB* is unevenly distributed, there will always be enough of it to constitute a 'piece' of it having a weight equal to *E*, for each of *n* weights equal to *E* and summing to *Γ* (the total weight of *AB*). But if it is only the whole of *AB* that is an infinite magnitude having a finite weight, each of the *n* magnitudes (each having finite weight *E*) must be finite in extent (magnitude, volume). Hence, the finite (*n*-termed) sum of these magnitudes, each of which is of finite extent, must be of finite extent. On the assumption

---

[63] I should like to thank Prof. Henry Mendell for pointing out to me the fact that the argument in the *De caelo* passage is rather more complete than the analogous argument in *Phys.* 6. 7, and for subsequent discussion of the 2 arguments. This is not to say, however, that Prof. Mendell endorses my account of the arguments. If I understand him correctly, Mendell holds that Aristotle makes, in these 2 passages, a simple (and fairly egregious) mistake in the application of proportion theory. That is, Aristotle employs something like the following identity: finite part *BΔ* of infinitely extended magnitude *AB*/infinitely extended magnitude *AB* = finite weight *E* of finite part *BΔ* of magnitude *AB*/finite weight *Γ* of infinitely extended magnitude *AB*. Aristotle then concludes that the denominator *Γ* of the ratio on the right side of the identity *cannot* be finite. Of course, if we assume a homogeneous density for infinitely extended body *AB*, this use of proportion theory would be correct. But Aristotle does not want his argument limited to such a case. And I think that there are indications that he realizes that a somewhat more complicated argument is needed if he wishes to apply the argument to cases of non-homogeneous density (and, analogously, to cases of non-uniform speed in the *Physics* passage).

that the magnitude (extent, volume) stands in a ratio to the weight, this finite sum of finite magnitudes must 'exhaust' the infinite magnitude AB, which is a contradiction. Symbolically, we have

$$AB/\Gamma = (B\Delta + \Delta Z + \ldots + \Lambda A)/(E_1 + E_2 + \ldots + E_n).$$

Aristotle's quite legitimate point is that, if each of the addenda contained in the numerator of the ratio on the right side of the identity is finite, then AB must be finite as well. For AB to be infinite, at least one of these addenda must be infinite. This means that, no matter how large we make n (as long as it is finite), and no matter how small we make each of the equally weighted E_is (as long as each is non-null), there must be an infinite magnitude having that small weight, if the 'whole' AB is to be an infinite magnitude having a finite weight. I suspect that Aristotle would find this state of affairs, which violates his implicit assumption that it is *only* the 'whole' of the infinite AB and no infinite proper part of it that has finite weight, conceptually unacceptable.[64]

An entirely analogous situation obtains with respect to Aristotle's argument in *Phys*. 6. 7 and the counter-example to it that we were considering. If we divide the 10-mile distance AB into n *equal* sub-distances, then no matter how large n is and how short each of the n sub-distances is, it will take the continuously moving body we have imagined an infinite amount of time to traverse the 'last' of these sub-distances, although only a finite time to traverse each of the preceding $n - 1$ sub-distances. Does this make conceptual (as well as mathematical) sense? I believe that the answer is 'yes' for the following reason. To say that the body takes an infinite amount of time to traverse the 10-mile distance AB is just to say that it *never* does, in fact, traverse AB. But if it never traverses AB, it seems correct to say that it never traverses the *last* 1/4 (or $1/n$, for any $n > 1$) of AB.

In effect, the counter-example postulates a situation in which the

[64] Of course, Aristotle's argument unquestionably holds if the magnitude is 'homogeneously dense'. The case we are imagining is one where, say, the magnitude becomes continuously less dense as we move away from some locus where it is most dense. Such a case is, I think, best described as follows. We can never *actually* get enough of the material to obtain the weight Γ, although the weight of the magnitude 'approaches' Γ as we take larger and larger amounts of it 'without limit'. This means that, as we move further and further away from the most dense locus of the stuff to less and less dense loci, for *any* positive weight whatsoever constituting the 'last nth fractional part of the total weight Γ', it is impossible to get enough of that stuff to make up this last nth fractional part of Γ. See the analogous account, in the text below, of the case of asymptotically decreasing speed.

body actually traverses all the 10-mile interval *AB* except the 10-mile 'boundary' point itself. That is, according to the contemporary analysis, it is true that, for each and every point 'before' the 10-mile point, that point is traversed in a finite time, but false that there is a finite time in which each and every point before the 10-mile point is traversed. We see Aristotle confronted with a dense right-open interval (all the points in the interval traversed by the body in a *finite* interval of time) versus its 'missing' limit (which is not traversed in any finite interval of time). Apostle's succinct analysis of this situation seems to me to be right-minded:

Logically, then, Aristotle is still right in saying that no finite line (and such a line must have limits as its ends and not be an open interval on one end) can be traversed in an infinite time, but we cannot be sure whether or not he was aware of decreasing speeds which would prevent an object from surpassing a given length in an infinite [read: *any* finite] time.[65]

Indeed, I suspect that Aristotle would detect another intuitive discontinuity in our imagined situation, in which a body moves continuously toward a spatial *telos* or *terminus ad quem* without ever actually arriving there. If we consider any arbitrary distance s_0 *actually* traversed in a time t_0, it is true that when we consider an infinite sequence $\{s_n\}$ of distances $s_i < s_0$, which are also actually traversed and which converge to s_0 as a limit, the corresponding sequence $\{t_n\}$ of times $t_i < t_0$, which it takes to traverse each s_i, converges to t_0. However, at $s = 10$, there is not a similar convergence: sequences $\{s_n\}$ of distances $s_i < s = 10$ actually traversed *do* converge to $s = 10$: but there is no value to which the corresponding sequences $\{t_n\}$ of times, which it takes to traverse each of *these* s_i, converge. They do not converge to 'infinity' (∞) because '∞' is not a number of any sort; and 'convergence to a limit' is defined, first, for real numbers and, then by extension for vectors, complex numbers, etc.[66]

This sort of intuitive discontinuity—which I have attempted to specify more precisely using mathematical notions obviously not

---

[65] Apostle, *Aristotle's Physics*, 294.

[66] I refer here to what I take to be the traditional, classical understanding of ∞. However, in some contemporary treatments of real analysis, $+ \infty$ and $- \infty$ are 'added as points' (though not, generally, as *numbers*) to the real line. One result is pointed out by Behnke and Grauert: 'But we must note that a sequence can now be convergent, namely to $+ \infty$ (or $- \infty$), even though it was called divergent before (e.g. the sequence of natural numbers)' (H. Behnke and H. Grauert, 'Points at Infinity', in H. Behnke, F. Bachmann, K. Fladt, and W. Süss (eds.), *Fundamentals of Mathematics*, iii (Cambridge, Mass., and London, 1974), 256).

available to Aristotle—is circumvented in the standard contemporary mathematical analysis simply because, when we consider the inverse of the function from times elapsed to distances traversed, the distance s = 10 is not a member of the domain of this inverse function (although each and every distance $s < 10$ is a member of the domain). Hence, the question of a discontinuity of the inverse function at the point $s = 10$ cannot arise. This fact suggests, I believe, that present even in the standard contemporary analysis is the implication that the moving body in our purported counter-example does not 'actually' attain the *terminus ad quem* $s = 10$.

Of course, there remains Apostle's just observation concerning the difficulty of deciding whether Aristotle would have recognized 'decreasing speeds which would prevent an object from surpassing a given length' in a finite time. One argument that he *should* have recognized such a phenomenon goes as follows. He was certainly familiar with Zeno's Dichotomy, in which the sub-intervals [0,1/2], [1/2,3/4], [3/4,7/8], etc. are traversed in correspondingly decreasing intervals of time. Surely, it would be a small conceptual move to a conception of decelerating motion—as described by Apostle and Knorr above—for which each such interval is traversed in the *same* amount of time. Having made this conceptual move, Aristotle could appeal to Eudoxus' axiom in order to obtain the conclusion that the time needed to traverse all such sub intervals would surpass any finite duration of time.[67]

One can only guess, of course, what Aristotle's reaction to such an argument would be. But perhaps one relevant consideration is the following. It is fairly obvious that the speed of a body moving in this manner approaches zero as its limit without actually stopping. A metaphysical problem that Aristotle would have with this situation is that it postulates a continuous change toward a definite *terminus ad quem* that does not, in fact, attain that *terminus*. But Aristotle's 'teleo-logical' metaphysics of motion suggests, at the very least, that motion necessarily involves the attainment of some *telos*.

What is perhaps a more fundamental problem centres on the fact that we here again encounter, as the body approaches the 'terminal' distance $s = 10$, a right-open interval of distances. We have previously discussed the problems that Aristotle would have with such a mathematical concept. In the present case, however, the

---

[67] This argument is due to my colleague at the National Humanities Center, David Copp.

problem would be acute with respect to the right-open interval of distance [0,10) supposedly traversed by the body 'in an infinite time'. Apostle seems to me correct in his claim that 'for Aristotle a[n] ... interval without a limit has as little existence as a body without a surface'.[68] As we shall see in Chapter 4, there is little evidence that Aristotle (or ancient mathematicians in general) regarded an interval of magnitude—for example, the distance that Zeno's Dichotomy purports to show cannot be traversed—as the union of an infinite sequence of sub-intervals. Nor did they regard the 'measure' (length) of such a spatial (or temporal) interval as the 'sum' of the infinite sequence of lengths of an infinite sequence of sub-intervals. Of course, it is precisely these identities that permit the preceding argument to the effect that, with appropriate deceleration, an infinite time is required to traverse the interval (= 'all the sub-intervals').

What Is Indivisible Cannot Move 'in itself' (kath' hauto)

The final kinematic 'mistake' that I shall consider is not, I think, obviously a mistake. However, Aristotle's discussion of the motion of an indivisible body nicely illustrates how different his ontology of continuous motion is from the standard contemporary 'at–at' ontology. The 'at–at' ontology of motion *identifies* the continuous motion of a body with a (non-denumerably) infinite set of instantaneous positions of the body. These positions are linearly ordered in terms of the 'natural' temporal ordering of the instants at which the body occupies them. In order for the motion in question to be continuous, this linear ordering of instantaneous positions must be dense and Dedekind-continuous. Because of the fact that a moving body has positive size, each instantaneous position will have an infinite number of other positions overlapping it in either the 'prior' temporal direction or the 'posterior' temporal direction. And, if a position is not the actual *terminus a quo* or *terminus ad quem*, it will have an infinite number of positions overlapping it in each of *both* 'directions'. This way of conceiving the motion of the body readily admits of a 'simplification'. If we are concerned only with the 'path' of the body's motion and not with its size or mass, we can easily identify its motion with a dense and Dedekind-continuous linear set of *points*, e.g. the spatial *loci* of the body's (punctal) centre of gravity at each instant of its motion.

[68] Apostle, *Aristotle's Physics*, 294.

At the beginning of *Phys.* 6. 4, and again in *Phys.* 6. 10, Aristotle produces arguments against the possibility of *per se* motion by something that is indivisible, arguments that from this contemporary perspective do not seem very cogent. Aristotle certainly admits that (*a*) physical bodies, extended in three dimensions, can and do move, and that (*b*) such bodies have 'features' that are indivisible in one or more dimensions—e.g. surfaces or 'leading edges' in the direction of motion or punctal centres of gravity. He concludes that indivisibles do indeed move, but only 'incidentally' (*kata sumbebēkos*) (*Phys.* 6. 10240^{b}9–10).

His primary argument for the impossibility of *per se* motion by something that is indivisible is given at *Phys.* 6. 4. 234^{b}10–20; and essentially the same argument is repeated at *Phys.* 6. 10. 240^{b}19–31. The argument is the following: For the *kinēsis* of mov*ing* or chang*ing* (*to kineisthai, to metaballein*) to occur there must be an *interval* of time [*t, t'*] *during* which the moving body is partly in initial *locus* (or state) *AB* and partly in a distinct *locus BΓ* (or state), gradually (continuously) occupying less and less of *AB* and more and more of *BΓ*. But an *indivisible* body cannot be *partly* in one locus/state and *partly* in a distinct one. For example, in the particular case of local motion, an indivisible body cannot be partly in one place (the initial one from which it departs) and partly in a contiguous place of the same magnitude. Therefore, an indivisible can never undergo the *kinēsis* of motion, i.e. *be* mov*ing*. Aristotle's conception of the *kinēsis* of an extended body in terms of its gradually occupying more and more of a contiguous or adjacent spatial area or *locus* of the same size leads to his statement of an 'axiom' of motion at *Phys.* 6. 10. 241^{a}8–9: 'it is impossible that any thing that is moving traverse [a distance] greater than itself before [traversing a distance] equal to or less than itself.' Aristotle uses this principle to argue that a point (*stigmē*) cannot move (except, of course, 'incidentally'). Since a point is indivisible, it cannot traverse any distance *less* that itself. Hence it can never be in the *process* of moving to a supposed contiguous punctal *locus*. But, of course, there is no contiguous punctal *locus*: for it is not the case that a line is constituted out of points (ordered discretely or successively— *ephekses*), and it is not the case that 'a point, always moving a distance equal [to itself], will measure out (*katametrēsei*) each line' (241^{a}12–13). In effect, Aristotle has concluded that there is not *any (particular)* distance—e.g. an adjacent punctal *locus*—that a point must *first* traverse before traversing any greater distance.

Aristotle interprets this consequence as a *reductio* of the supposition that a point is capable of *per se* motion. The consequence does not constitute such a *reductio* from the contemporary perspective. The ontology of motion, I submit, is at the heart of this disagreement. According to the at–at ontology of motion, the 'moving' of a body consists in its instantaneously occupying a dense and Dedekind-continuous linear array of positions. It is an entirely trivial extrapolation to consider an analogous array of *points*, e.g. the positions of the punctal centre of gravity of the body; for what is punctal can be attributed position in an appropriate three-dimensional coordinate-system just as easily as what is extended in three dimensions can.

From the contemporary perspective, it is a great temptation to assume that Aristotle 'really' (or, at least 'implicitly') has the same ontological conception of local motion. For example, in the *kinēsis* of a body's moving, Aristotle conceives it as 'first' moving into a place contiguous with its beginning position (*locus a quo*), then as moving into the *next* contiguous place, etc., until it reaches its actual *locus ad quem*, the place where it comes to rest. But, as we have seen, Aristotle is well aware that there is no 'beginning' to the process of moving into the 'first' place contiguous with its *locus a quo*, in the sense of first *possible* stopping-position next to the actual position of the body before it begins to move. We are apt to equate this awareness on Aristotle's part with the recognition by him of the fact that the linear array of instantaneous positions into which the body's motion is analysed is densely ordered. But Aristotle does *not* analyse local motion into instantaneous positions; and he gives evidence of holding that the notion of an *actually* infinite, *actually* dense linear array of discrete (i.e. distinct) objects is an incoherent notion.

A principle implicit in Aristotle's discussion constitutes a very geometrical conception of motion:

(AP) any distance traversed by any body can be represented as being measured out by some part of the body (and, indeed, by any of an infinite number of parts of the body in a 'harmless', Aristotelian sense of 'infinite'). *Katametrein* ('measure out') is here used in its typical geometrical sense: some part of the body measures the whole distance traversed by the body, if the part is an *aliquot* part of the whole distance, i.e. if the whole distance is an integral multiple of the part.[69]

---

[69] See e.g. the use of *katametrein* in Euclid, Book 5, def. 1 and Book 7, deff. 3 and 4.

So Aristotle apparently conceives the *kinēsis* of continuous motion in terms of the whole or some part of a body occupying more and more of an adjacent, contiguous space of the same size as the whole or part, and then—without pause—occupying more and more of a contiguous space of the same size, etc. until the body reaches its actual *terminus ad quem*, where it does pause. This principle rules out motion by a point. *No* distance supposedly traversed by a moving point can be represented as an integral multiple of the magnitude of the point—nor, of course, as an integral multiple of the magnitude of any part of the (indivisible) point.

(AP), together with Aristotle's geometrical conception of the infinite divisibility of time and spatial magnitude or distance and his conception of the continuity of motion (which rules out jumps and pauses), yields a perfectly satisfactory account of the continuous local motion of bodies *extended* at least in the direction of motion. But the account embodies a very different ontology of motion from the at-at ontology, which analyses local motion into a dense and Dedekind-continuous linear array of instantaneous positions of the moving body. We see in Aristotle's stricture against *per se* motion of a point a manifestation of this difference in ontology of motion. The following chapter will further explore various metaphysical features of Aristotle's discussion of time and of local motion, as well as the relation between these metaphysical features and the formal, structural properties of continuous magnitudes that we have just examined.

2

Aristotle on Time and Locomotion: Physics and Metaphysics

The previous chapter was devoted principally to the consideration of Aristotle's conception of the formal, structural properties of continua— in particular, continuous intervals of spatial magnitude or distance and continuous episodes of local motion. But we noted the difference between Aristotle's interval-based ontology of what is continuous and a standard contemporary point-set ontology. The former part of the chapter emphasized the fact that, in some very fundamental respects, Aristotle's kinematic analysis agrees closely with the standard contemporary kinematic conception of local motion. But in the discussion of Aristotle's kinematic 'mistakes' at the conclusion of the chapter, we explored some of Aristotle's departures from contemporary kinematics; and I claimed that these differences may, in part, be attributed to the different ontologies undergirding the Aristotelian and the standard contemporary kinematic analyses of motion.

I propose to examine in this chapter the more metaphysical aspects of Aristotle's accounts of time and of *kinēsis*. In the last chapter I said relatively little about Aristotle's conception of the formal, structural properties of time. There was little need for such a discussion because Aristotle's conception of the structural features of time seems to mirror his (geometrical) conception of the structural features of spatial extension (in one dimension) or distance. That is, temporal instants or 'nows' (*ta nun*) are conceived as temporal *points*. Such instants are thought of as limits of and as potential or actual divisions of stretches/ intervals of time—when Aristotle uses the term *chronos* ('time') he is almost invariably thinking of a *stretch* of time. Intervals of time are 'infinitely divisible' in Aristotle's 'potential' or 'constructive' sense of infinite divisibility, in the same geometrical way that intervals of spatial magnitude or distance are. Temporal instants possess the same dis- tributive density that points possess: any two instants are separated by a (finitely long) stretch of time, and it is always theoretically possible to 'mark off' a third instant within this interval, distinct from its two limit instants. But, in Aristotle's view, a stretch of time is not *constituted* of a dense and Dedekind-continuous linear array of instants. His ontology of time is that of 'foundationless' intervals: each such interval is constituted of nothing but similarly divisible sub-intervals, of which there is no 'foundation' or finest partition. In the following section of this chapter I pursue the Aristotelian metaphysics of time a bit further, distinguishing a topological and a metrical component of his account of time in the last part of Book 4 of the *Physics*.

I then turn to Aristotle's metaphysical analysis of local motion. In this section the two main topics will be the formulaic metaphysical account of *kinēsis* presented in *Phys*. 3. 1 and the Aristotelian identity conditions for local motions. With respect to the latter issue, I suggest that problems implicit in Aristotle's discussion of motion in Book 6 of the *Physics* get resolved, at least to some degree, by a modification introduced in Book 8.

TIME

The conception of time developed by Aristotle in the fourth book of the *Physics* has, I shall argue, two partially distinct components. One component may be termed 'topological': the notion of linear temporal extension in general or the temporal dimension of change or *kinēsis*. The other component may be termed 'metrical': the notion of '*a* time', i.e. a unit of temporal measurement characterized by Aristotle's formal definition at *Phys*. 4. 11. $219^{b}1$ of time as 'a number of motion (*kinēseōs*) with respect to the prior and the posterior'.[1] This metrical notion presupposes, I think, certain features of the topological notion. Although I believe that it is unlikely that Aristotle clearly distinguished these two components of his conception of time, the two components are present in his discussion. Sorting them out seems to me to be an important step in coming to understand what Aristotle has to say concerning time. However, I shall conclude my examination with the suggestion that the metrical and topological components of Aristotle's

---

[1] I emphasize the fact that my distinction between *time* (the temporal dimension of motion or temporal extension, in general) and *a time* (a finite, bounded measure of temporal extension, or a particular token of this type) is a conceptual distinction, not a linguistic one. It is not, so far as I can tell, precisely marked by Aristotle's use or lack of use of the Greek article or of some pronoun such as *hode*.

conception of time are 'synthesized' in his notion of what might be called *Ur-zeit*, the 'fundamental or primitive time' defined, principally, by the periodic motion of the heavenly bodies.

The Number of Motion with Respect to the Prior and the Posterior

Aristotle's formal account of time can, I suggest, be made more intelligible if we understand him to be giving an account of '*a time*'. The import of this suggestion will, I trust, emerge in the following discussion. To begin with, of course, Aristotle sees a very close connection between 'process' or motion (primarily locomotion, it seems) and time. Since time is not to be identified with motion, it must be some feature of motion. (219^a9–10) It is clear that a conception of time as an ontologically independent 'container' of process is quite foreign to Aristotle's thought;[2] rather, time, or times, are in some way ontologically dependent on things in process. The question, as he realizes, is 'in *what* way?'

The beginning of Aristotle's answer to this question is almost certain to strike the contemporary reader as misguided. After claiming (219^a10–13) that one of the principal formal properties he attributes to time, viz., its continuity, is dependent upon the continuity of (loco)motion, which, in turn, is dependent upon the continuity of magnitude (*megethos*), he proceeds to suggest (219^a14–19) that the prior (*to proteron*) and the posterior (*to husteron*) in time are dependent upon the prior and posterior in motion, which, in turn, are dependent upon the prior and posterior in place 'and there in virtue of relative position (*entautha men dē tēi thesei*)' (219^a15–16).[3] Hussey believes that 'the prior and posterior' (*to proteron kai husteron*) 'was a technical term in the Academy and that it denoted something that could be present only in an ordered series',[4] and I think that there is some likelihood that Aristotle is here using the term to mean something like 'directed linear manifold' or 'directed linear dimension'. Then Aristotle is

---

[2] Newton contrasts 'absolute, true, and mathematical time' (which 'of itself, and from its own nature, flows equably without relation to anything external') to 'relative, apparent, and common time' (which is 'some sensible and external ... measure of duration by the means of motion, which is commonly used instead of true time' (*Mathematical Principles of Natural Philosophy*, trans. A. Motte, ed. F. Cajori (Berkeley, Calif., 1946), 6). Aristotle accepts only the concept of what Newton terms 'relative, apparent, and common time'.

[3] The meaning of this apparent qualification of 'in place' is not clear.

[4] E. Hussey, *Aristotle's Physics: Books III and IV* (Oxford, 1983), 146–7.

claiming, in general, that we have, first, directed linear dimensionality with respect to place, and, dependent on that, directed linear dimensionality with respect to motion, and, dependent on that, directed linear dimensionality with respect to time.

An obvious problem is that the directed spatial path or trajectory of a moving body seems to be dependent on the actual motion of the moving body rather than vice versa. As Hussey puts it, '"the before and after in place" ought to be something intrinsic to the places, in advance of any change',[5] and 'ought to be something present . . . along a path of change, independently of any change's actually occurring'.[6] Aristotle's teleological conception of process, including the process of loco-motion, may be relevant here. For Aristotle holds that, with respect to the natural motion of an earthen object, a place nearer the centre of the universe (where the 'bulk' of earth is) is posterior to a place further from the centre of the universe.[7] That is, he seems to view this relation of priority/posteriority among places as constituting an explanation of the natural motion of an earthen body from the further to the nearer place rather than merely describing this natural motion. As he has said in *Phys*. 4. 1, places seem to differ 'not only in relative position (*tēi thesei*) but also in potency' ($208^{b}21$–2). Whether this conception of the 'metaphysical priority' of the ordering of places with respect to the 'direction' of motion is tenable or not for natural motion, it seems extremely doubtful whether it could be extended to 'violent' (i.e. unnatural) motion.

Another possibility, however—which arises in view of the fact that epistemic considerations figure so largely in *Phys*. 4. 11—is that Aristotle's point is merely an epistemic one: we *identify* the continuous local motion of a body by means of a conceptually or experientially ordered, linear spatial path/trajectory, beginning with the concept or experience of the spatial position that is the locomotion's actual *terminus a quo* and ending with our conception/experience of the spatial position that is its *terminus ad quem*. That is, essential to our conception of locomotion is the concept or experience of a directed

---

[5] Ibid. 147

[6] Ibid. 149.

[7] Of course, '*natural* place' is an Aristotelian notion replete with difficulties beyond those connected with his account of place, in general. For a discussion of these difficulties, together with an attractive account of the content of the notion, see P. K. Machamer, 'Aristotle on Natural Place and Natural Motion', *Isis*, 69: 248 (1978), 377–87.

and linear spatial path originating with one position and terminating in another.[8]

Whatever the precise relation between priority/posteriority of place or position and priority/posteriority of motion, it is clear that at the heart of Aristotle's conception of time is a very close epistemic relationship between time and motion:

we distinguish [*gnōrizomen*] a time when we delimit a motion, delimiting [the motion] by a prior and a posterior; and then we say that a time has elapsed, when we have grasped by sensation the prior and posterior in a motion. We delimit them by understanding them to be distinct and that there is something different from them in between. When we think of the extremes as different from the middle, and the mind says that there are two nows, one prior and the other posterior, then we say that this is a time. For what is limited by a now seems to be a time (and let this be assumed). When we perceive the now as one—and not as the prior and posterior in motion—or when we perceive it as the same [limit] of a prior [interval] and of a posterior, it does not seem to be the case that any time has elapsed because there is no motion. But when there is a prior and a posterior, then we say there is a time. For a time is this: the number of a motion with respect to the prior and the posterior. (219ª22–ᵇ2)

If Aristotle means to give an account of time in what might be called the abstract, general, 'mass noun' sense—i.e. an account of the temporal dimension of motion in general—the more or less formal definition with which he concludes this passage does not make much sense. But as an account of '*a* time' it has more to be said for it.[9]

---

[8] This claim does not vitiate, I think, the argument of Corish to the effect that, in attempting to derive a temporal ordering from a 'pre-temporal' before/after relation defined on spatial locations and (derivatively) on motions (motion stages?), Aristotle produces a *petitio* by implicitly conceiving the before/after relation as temporal. (He associates the relata of the before/after relation with 'nows'.) See D. Corish, 'Aristotle's Attempted Derivation of Temporal Order from That of Movement and Space', *Phronesis*, 3 (1976), 241–51. My point is that Aristotle may mean, merely, (*a*) that necessary to the *recognition* of direction of time (temporal order) is a recognition of an experiential direction or order with respect to motion, and (*b*) that necessary to the *recognition* of such a direction/order with respect to motion is recognition of an experientially directed or ordered spatial path. But the necessity of discerning temporal order through an experientially ordered direction of motion stages surely does not require that that experiential order/direction of motion be non-temporal. While (*a*) seems to me to be a plausible thesis, (*b*) seems to me to be less so. For it seems possible to claim that a temporal ordering can also be recognized through an experiential ordering of 'stages' of *other* sorts of change—not just locomotion.

[9] In the 'Corollary [to his commentary on Aristotle's *Physics*] concerning Time', Simplicius reports that Strato of Lampsacus (Theophrastus' successor as Peripatetic scholarch) 'does not agree that time is number of motion, because number is discrete (*diōrismenon*) quantity, but motion and time are continuous, and what is continuous is

Aristotle's view seems to be that *a* time is an interval of motion that is
(*a*) limited or bounded both in the prior and in the posterior 'direction'
and (*b*) considered as a quantitative unit by which motion can be
measured. The conditions are not unrelated: it seems clear that (*a*),
the boundedness condition of 'a time' (which Aristotle takes some

not numerable (*arithmēton*)' (Simplicius, *In phys.*, CAG 9, 789). Strato's objection seems
to be a pointed, impeccably Aristotelian one. Is there any Aristotelian answer to it? I
believe that it is based on a misunderstanding: he is thinking of Aristotle's definition as
pertaining to time in the generic, mass-noun sense, i.e. to temporal extension in general.
A time, on the other hand, defines first a unit (*monas*) of time in terms of motion,
multiples of which do indeed represent stretches of time as numerable. Contemporary
commentators have also noted Aristotle's not infrequent conflation, in *Phys.* 4, of
number and measure See e.g. P. F. Conen, *Die Zeittheorie des Aristoteles* (Munich, 1964); J.
Annas, 'Aristotle, Number and Time', *Philosophical Quarterly*, 25: 99 (1975), 97–113. I
believe that Annas is quite correct that in saying 'what [Aristotle] wants to emphasize is
something common to both of them [counting and measuring], namely the fact that a
unit is involved' (103). I also believe, however, that Aristotle sees counting as appealing
to units in the sense of discrete and, in some sense, natural individuals, the identity
conditions for which are somehow part of the nature of what one is counting. Since
measuring is taken to be applicable to what is continuous and infinitely divisible 'in its
own nature', a unit of measure has to be supplied by something related to the continuous
medius that is regarded as *kath' hauto* numerable or countable, e.g. successive transits of
heavenly bodies past fixed spatial points, successive placements of a rigid rod across a
spatial interval. A principal theme of Annas's paper is that a certain tension (as well as
some ambiguities and peculiarities) in Aristotle's discussion of time in *Phys.* 4 is
generated by his conflation of 'two ways of looking at time: that deriving from the
arguments of *Physics* Z and relating time as a continuum to the other continua of motion
and magnitude, and that deriving from the ideas in *Metaphysics* I and finding expression
in the thesis that time is a number' (113). I suggest that these 'two ways of looking at
time' are closely correlated with, respectively, my notion of time (the topological, mass-
noun notion of the temporal dimension of motion) and my notion of a time (the metrical,
count-noun notion of a temporal unit, or multiplicity of such units). It is also perhaps
worth noting an important point made by Annas pertaining to Aristotle's remarks, in
Phys. 4. 14, concerning the relation between (*a*) time and soul (*psuchē*). In effect, Annas
points out that Aristotle's remarks may be construed simply as his noting that the definition of a metric on time and the use of this metric in measuring periods of time are
psychic activities. Elaborating on this point, I should maintain that, although Aristotle's
remarks may perhaps imply a sort of idealism with respect to the notion *a time* (i.e. a
temporal *metric*), it is far from obvious that they imply any thoroughgoing metaphysical
idealism with respect to *time*, the temporal dimension of *kinēsis*. In fact, Aristotle speaks
of the possibility of the existence of *kinēsis* without *psuchē* (223ª27–8) and proceeds to
claim that 'the before and after exist in *kinēsis*; these *qua* numerable exist as time'
(223ª28–9). I take the import of this remark to be as follows. If *kinēsis* can exist apart
from *psuchē*, so can the 'before and after' (*proteron kai husteron*), which is (are?) constitu-
tive of *time*, in the sense of the temporal dimension of motion. However, the notion of
a time involves this temporal dimension *qua* numerable—that is, it involves the definition
of a unit of time on the temporal continuum (by means of a motion-type) and the
counting of multiples of this unit (i.e. multiples of tokens of the motion-type). But the
definition of a temporal unit and counting by means of the unit are both psychic
activities.

pains to emphasize) is a necessary condition of (*b*), a time's being a 'number'—a unit or multiple of units of measure.

In the following chapter, *Phys*. 4. 12, Aristotle develops several corollaries of this account of a time.

(i) A time is neither quick nor slow. Rather, it is many or few in so far as a time is conceived in terms of multiples of a given unit of motion (e.g. many years or few years); or it is long or short in so far as many or few instances of a given unit are thought of as continuously joined 'end to end' (220ᵃ32–ᵇ5).

(ii) There is a certain reciprocity of measurement between a time and a motion since 'they are delimited by one another' (220ᵇ16). A time measures a motion in so far as the motion's 'extent' can be represented as a multiple of some given time or temporal unit. Conversely, a motion measures a time in so far as a time *qua* unit of time is defined in terms of a motion. Aristotle appeals to an analogy here. We know the magnitude of a group of horses (what is numbered: *to arithmēton*) by determining their number (*arithmos*); but the unit of measure, one horse, is determined by the nature of what is measured. The magnitude of the collection is ten *horses*, not five tons of glue or twenty horse-hair sofas, etc.

(iii) Finally, Aristotle's conception of a time as a motion or quantity of motion that can be used as a unit of measure is quite explicitly stated:

Since a time is a measure of motion and of being moved, it measures a motion by delimiting a given motion that measures out the whole [motion]—just as a cubit [arm and hand's length: *pēkus*] [measures] length by delimiting a given magnitude [i.e. the magnitude of a forearm and hand] that measures out the whole [length]. (220ᵇ32–221ᵃ4)

Although Aristotle's definition in *Phys*. 4. 11 and the corollaries to it that Aristotle proceeds to distinguish pertain to *a time*, i.e. a unit or plurality of units of temporal extension, he is also concerned with *time*, i.e. temporal extension in general or the continuous manifold of time, apparently linear and without beginning or end. It is not obvious, I think, to what extent Aristotle realizes that he is dealing with two separate matters here.

Time without the article, that is, time in the sense of temporal extension in general, involves the idea of a universal continuous linear order defined in terms of the concepts of simultaneity, priority, and posteriority. This is the component of Aristotle's conception of time that I have termed 'topological'. Although his formal account of 'a time'—and, I think, the bulk of the discussion of time found in the fourth book of the *Physics*—pertains to a *metrical* conception of time, there are several significant points of interaction between the two concepts. One such point of interaction occurs in *Phys*. 4. 14. Aristotle raises the question of whether, since a time is a number of a motion and there can be distinct simultaneous motions, there can be distinct simultaneous times. He evidently thinks that an affirmative answer to this question would be quite implausible; so he decides that there is 'the same time of motions that are simultaneously limited' (223^{b}6–7).

This decision, commonsensical as it is, represents a modification of Aristotle's original definition of 'a time'. What Aristotle has, in effect, done is to modify his original definition of 'a time' so that it now amounts to the following: a time is a 'number' of an *equivalence class*[10] of motions that have simultaneous 'prior' limits and simultaneous 'posterior' limits, that is, a time is an equivalence class of simultaneous motions considered as a (potential or actual) quantitative measure of motion. This modification of the original definition of the metrical conception of 'a time' appeals to a central notion, viz., simultaneity, of what is arguably the more fundamental topological conception of 'universal time' as a continuous linear order.

The metrical conception of 'a time' upon which Aristotle focuses is inherently a type-concept, as opposed to a token-concept. That is, a time, or unit of motion considered as a *measure of motion*, seems to be the sort of thing that *has* individual instances. And these instances need not be simultaneous. That is, the idea of time as 'number' takes us from the perspective of motion tokens to that of motion types, since a motion token can only 'number' (measure) itself or motions contemporaneous with it. In some cases, however, such metrical time locutions *do* connote motion tokens: particular instances of the 'unit' or of multiples of such a unit. Thus, although a friend and I took *the same time*, two years, to write our books, we did not write our books in *the same two-year period*. A difficult question, consequently, arises

---

[10] An equivalence class is a class of entities each of which stands in an equivalence relation to each of the members in the class. An equivalence relation is a relation that is reflexive, symmetrical, and transitive. Such a relation partitions a class of entities (temporal intervals, in the present case) into subclasses that are equivalence classes: these classes are pairwise disjoint and jointly exhaustive of the original class; that is, each member of the original class falls into precisely one of the subclasses. In the present case, the equivalence relation is that of being *completely* simultaneous. If 2 temporal intervals partially overlap, or if one is a proper part of the other, they are not completely simultaneous.

concerning the identity conditions for Aristotle's conception of 'a time'. As we have seen, Aristotle holds that if motion *A* and motion *B* are quantitatively indistinguishable in the sense of having simultaneous 'prior' and simultaneous 'posterior' limits, there is 'one and the same' time of both. What if motion *A* and motion *B* are tokens of the same motion type but not simultaneous? Is there then 'one and the same' time of both or different times?

In the course of his discussion Aristotle makes several comments on this issue. The first is in *Phys.* 4. 13:

Is it the same time or different that occurs again? It is clear that as the motion is, so is the time. For if one and the same motion [again] comes to be at some time, one and the same time will [again] occur. If not, then it will not. (222ᵃ30–3)

Aristotle does not really answer the question in this passage: for the issue of whether it is 'one and the same motion' that recurs is dependent upon whether he is conceiving the motion as type or as token. He perhaps comes closer to giving an answer in *Phys.* 4. 14. There he remarks, almost in passing, that times—apparently quantitatively indistinguishable times—that are *not* simultaneous are the same 'in species' (*eidei*) (223ᵇ4). The idea seems to be that, since we are unwilling to say that two tokens of the same motion type that are not simultaneous are *numerically* identical—even when they are 'inherently' indistinguishable, e.g. two instances of solar motion between autumnal and vernal equinoxes—we therefore should not say that the 'times' of two such motions are numerically the same.

Earlier (*Phys.* 4. 12. 220ᵇ5 ff.) in his discussion of time, Aristotle has given what seems to be a rather more ambiguous account, but one which Ross interprets in terms of the later distinction between numerical and specific identity that he sees in the passage at 223ᵇ4 just quoted. Aristotle says that change which has occurred and change which is going to occur are (*ipso facto*) different (220ᵇ7–8), and proceeds to comment that 'a time is a number—not that with which we number but that which is numbered; this [what is numbered] occurs either earlier or later [before or after] and is thus always different. For the nows are different' (220ᵇ8–10). Here Aristotle appears to be talking about motion *tokens*, which are what are numbered and do not do the numbering, and the identity of which is defined by their 'position' relative to the before–after relation of the directed, linear temporal continuum.[11] But a few lines later he says, 'Yet, just as it is possible for a *kinēsis* to be one and the same again and again, so also for a time, e.g. a year or spring or autumn' (220[b]12–14). Here, what Aristotle says makes sense if he is understood as speaking of motion *types* and the temporal interval defined by such a type. Such entities are quite properly said to 'recur', since they are not individuated by their position in the linear temporal continuum. Ross attempts to resolve the apparent inconsistency of these two remarks by maintaining that 'When Aristotle says that the same movement, or time, may recur, he must be understood to be speaking of specific, not numerical identity.'[12]

This ambiguity concerning identity conditions for times—which Aristotle (according to Ross's interpretation) attempts to mitigate by appeal to a distinction between being specifically the same and being numerically the same—is rooted in the type/token distinction as applied to motions. Although Aristotle already has admitted, in effect, that although a time is defined in terms of motion, there is a sense in which it is not individuated by a particular motion token: a particular motion token is *sufficient* to delimit a given period of time, but it is not *necessary* to use that motion to delimit it, since there may be entirely contemporaneous motions capable of doing so. That is, although there may be numerically distinct simultaneous motions, they share 'one and the same' time. Why is the situation different in the case of tokens of the same motion type that are not simultaneous? The answer is to be found in the distinction between the topological 'time', a continuous, directed linear manifold, and the metrical 'a time', a quantitative unit or measure of motion.

There is, as we have seen, a sense of 'a time' or 'stretch of time' according to which it is conceived as a token, as an *individual* interval in a continuous linear manifold. One such time obviously cannot be 'one and the same' with a prior, posterior, or even *partially* overlapping interval. And when Aristotle speaks of times as being differentiated

[11] I wish to thank Paul Vander Waerdt and David O'Connor for drawing my attention to an alternative interpretation: they suggest the possibility that Aristotle's view is that even the times shared by (entirely) contemporaneous motions are only the same in species or kind (*eidei*), and not *numerically* the same. Although I think that Aristotle's text, particularly the discussion in *Phys*. 4. 14, permits this interpretation, I am inclined to reject it. The earlier discussion at *Phys*. 4. 12. 220[b]5 ff. suggests that what *numerically* individuates times is their relative position in the linear temporal continuum (i.e. within time in the mass-noun sense); and, of course, different motions can have the same temporal position.

[12] Ross, *Aristotle's Physics*, 605.

(solely) by the before–after relation, he is clearly thinking of 'a time' in terms of (the simultaneity equivalence class of) a motion token. But it seems that such a time, i.e. an individual interval or equivalence class of a motion token, which is partly defined by its particular location in the linear temporal continuum, would be ill-fitted to serve as a quantitative unit or measure of motion. For it cannot be 'temporally transported' so as to measure any motion not contemporaneous with it. In this respect, it will be noted, there is a disanalogy between time and space. A quantitative unit of spatial magnitude even in the token sense, that is, an *individual* unit (e.g. this particular metre stick or this particular arm and hand) is, in some cases, spatially transportable and, hence, is usable as a measure.[13] Consequently, it appears that if a time as defined by Aristotle is to be usable as a measure, it must be not an individual interval occupying a particular position in a linear continuum (i.e, a token) but a type of such a token. That is, a time in *this* sense is a unit (or some multiple of units) of motion that is regarded as being quantitatively, if not numerically, repeatable. The adoption of a given motion type as a temporal unit involves an assumption of isochronism or self-congruence (conventional, according to Grünbaum[14]) concerning the *tokens* of such a motion type. Aristotle seems to make such an isochronism assumption concerning the circular motions of the heavens; a unit of such motion is thus, for him, pre-eminently 'a time': 'an equable [*homalēs*] circular motion is especially a measure because its number is most distinguishable. Neither alteration nor increase nor coming-to-be is equable, but the [heavenly] circuit is' ($223^{b}19$–21).

According to the preceding account, Aristotle's conception of the relation between a motion and a time is tacitly shifted in the direction of greater generality. From the original connection between a time and a particular motion token, he moves to a connection between a time and the equivalence class of all motions simultaneous to a particular motion token: all these motions share *the same time*. However, if a time is to be a *number* or *measure* of motion, another shift is needed: in

---

[13] A philosopher such as Reichenbach (or Grünbaum) will emphasize, however, that the distinction I am here drawing does not entail that the definition of a spatial metric is any less a matter of convention ('coordinative definition', for Reichenbach) than is the definition of a temporal metric. From such a point of view, analogous to the *definitional* equality of the tokens of a certain periodic motion type is the *definitional* rigidity of physical bodies that might be used to define a spatial metric. See H. Reichenbach, *The Philosophy of Space and Time*, trans. M. Reichenbach and J. Freund (New York, 1958).

[14] *Philosophical Problems of Space and Time*, 450 ff.

order for a time to measure/number a motion, a time must be a multiple of some motion *type*—a certain multiple of the apparent diurnal or annual movement of the sun, or of the apparent movement of a fixed star between two successive transits over the meridian, or (anachronistically) of the period of a pendulum, or of the vibration of a caesium atom. It is not clear, I think, to what extent Aristotle realizes that the dialectic of his account of a time requires this last shift to (multiples of) a motion type. The uncertainty about the conditions rendering motions (and hence times) 'one and the same' reflects his lack of clarity on this score, I believe. But his concern that the motion defining a time be *homalēs* (even, equable, or isochronous) is at least an indirect indication of a focus on motion type. For it is only consideration of more than one instance or token of a motion type that can lead to the question of whether the motion is isochronous or equable.

But what does the attribute of *homalotēs*, equability or isochronism, mean for Aristotle? The 'pre-analytical' answer is likely to be something like the following. Particular tokens of the given motion type 'take the same amount of time to occur'. Once one has fixed upon a motion type as defining a unit of time, i.e. once one has chosen a standard of a time, this pre-analytical account of equability is applicable to *other* motion types: it makes sense to ask with respect to more than one token of *some other motion type* whether they 'took the same time' to transpire. But, from the Aristotelian perspective, it does not seem that equability, in this pre-analytical sense, is applicable to the motion type chosen to *define* a time. For Aristotle does not have the Newtonian conception of 'absolute, true, and mathematical time, [which] of itself, and from its own nature, flows equably' with which to contrast 'relative, apparent, and common time, [which] is some sensible and external (whether accurate or inequable) measure of duration by the means of motion'.[15] The closest that Aristotle can come to isochronism in the sense of the 'equal duration' of tokens of the motion type used to *define* a time is the relative sense of agreement with the results obtained when *other* standards of a temporal unit are employed: if with respect to the temporal measurement of arbitrary motions, two different motion types, each used to define a unit of measure, tend to yield the same (proportionally invariant) results, tokens of each of these motion types may be said to be of 'equal

---

[15] Newton, *Principles*, ed. Cajori, 6.

duration' with respect to other tokens of the same type in this relative sense.

But such agreement among standards does not eliminate, for a theory of time such as that of Aristotle, the conventionality of the postulate of the equal duration of tokens of the motion type(s) selected as defining a (unit of) time.[16] In fact, at one place Aristotle indicates some recognition of this fact: in *Meta*. 10. 1, he comments that 'they postulate [*hupotithentai*] that the motion of the heavens is equable [*homalēn*] and the most quick, and with respect to it they judge the others' (1053[b]11–12). And in *Phys*. 4. 14 he also remarks that since time 'is measured by circular motion [of heavenly bodies]', 'nothing else in addition to the measure is observed in what is measured; rather, the whole is simply a multiplicity of measures' (223[b]33–224[a]2).[17]

I believe, however, that the primary signification of *homalēs* for Aristotle is not some assumption (conventional or otherwise) of isochronism in the contemporary sense—a *per se* equability or equal duration of tokens of a motion type (e.g. celestial motion) used to define a time. In attributing *homalotēs* to circular celestial motion, Aristotle means, I think, primarily to indicate that such motion is 'even' or 'smooth' in the sense of 'uninterrupted'. That is, the end of one 'period' of such a motion is the beginning of another; so the motion is continuous, in Aristotle's sense, with no interruption or pause between its periods. Aristotle says (*Phys*. 4. 14. 223[b]20–1) that while (qualitative) alteration, growth or augmentation, and coming-to-be are not *homaleis*, locomotion (and here he clearly means the circular, celestial locomotion of which he has been speaking) is. I believe that Ross is correct in suggesting that the reason why Aristotle says that these sorts of *kinēsis* are not 'equable' has to do with Aristotle's doctrine that tokens of such motions are necessarily separated by pauses: 'all kinds of *kinēsis* other than circular motion move between opposite termini and involve a pause at each terminus before movement begins in the opposite direction.'[18]

---

[16] See Reichenbach, *The Philosophy of Space and Time*: 'If we consider the revolutions of the earth to have equal duration, we do this because they represent *periods of the same type*. The same principle is involved if we say that the periods of a pendulum are equally long. The counting of periods is the first and most natural type of time measurement' (114). 'A solution is obtained only when we apply our previous results about spatial congruence and introduce the concept of a *coordinative definition* into the measurement of time. The equality of successive time-intervals is not a matter of *knowledge* but a matter of definition' (116).   [17] See the note on the text here in Ross, *Aristotle's Physics*, 612–13.

[18] Ibid. 612.

To sum up, then, it seems that Aristotle's formal account of 'a time' is essentially metrical: a time is some multiple of a motion, regarded as a type or temporally repeatable unit of measure. But underlying this account is the essentially topological conception of 'time'—temporal extension in general—to which I now turn.

The *Nunc Fluens* and the Linear Temporal Continuum

In using the term 'topological conception' for one component of Aristotle's discussion of time, I mean roughly what I take Waterlow to mean by the phrase 'dimension of physical process'.[19] I have suggested that 'time' in this sense does not really amount to the same thing as 'a time' in the metrical sense, which is formally defined by Aristotle in *Phys.* 4. 11 and which we have been discussing. The principal purpose of this section is to elucidate the nature of the topological component of Aristotle's conception of time and the relation of this component to the metrical component of his conception. In the preceding section, I have used some such phrase as 'continuous and directed linear order' in connection with the topological component; and, indeed, there is some evidence in Aristotle's discussion pointing toward a fairly straightforward topological conception of time as a continuous, directed 'line', without beginning or end (although, of course, a 'line' that is ontologically dependent upon the *kinēseis* of the cosmos). However, there is another conception, which might by courtesy be called 'topological', that also figures largely in Aristotle's discussion. It is the conception of the *nunc fluens* or token-reflexive 'now' as a 'generator' of an (apparently continuous and linear) past 'out of' a future that is, in some important ways, not symmetrical to the past.[20]

These two topological conceptions of time—that of the flowing now generating a temporal 'trajectory' and that of time as a continuous, directed line—seem to be rooted in two senses that Aristotle attaches to the substantive *to nun* ('the (a) now'). These two senses, which have been noted by many commentators, are aptly characterized by

---

[19] S. Waterlow, 'Instants of Motion in Aristotle's *Physics VI*', *Archiv für Geschichte der Philosophie*, 65: 2 (1983), 134.

[20] The following discussion is influenced by an insightful paper by S. Waterlow, which I commend to the attention of the reader: 'Aristotle's Now', *Philosophical Quarterly*, 34: 135 (1984), 104–28.

Waterlow as 'two disparate concepts—one of them, as the word implies, that of the temporal present, as opposed to past or future, the other the concept of an instant: a durationless point or position of time, as opposed to a measurable period'.[21] The second sense of *to nun* is most intimately connected with the more 'straightforward' topo-logical conception of the temporal dimension as a directed linear continuum. In view of the earlier discussion of spatial magnitude, it is scarcely necessary to point out that this Aristotelian conception of time as a linear continuum is not the contemporary, point-set conception of a dense and linearly ordered set of *ta nun*, 'instants' or temporal points, satisfying the additional Dedekind continuity condition (i.e. the condition that any cut' of the set of points must be such that either the prior subset of points has a temporally last point or the posterior subset has a first point but not both). Although Aristotle sometimes seems to conceive the temporal dimension in terms of an analogy with a line, he does not hold, as we saw in the last chapter, that a line (or any interval of magnitude) is constituted of points. So also, neither temporal dimension in general nor any 'time', in the sense of interval locatable 'within' that dimension, is constituted of nows.

Waterlow comments that the 'Aristotelian "Now" . . . emerge[s] as a highly theoretical concept developed with no other end in view than to meet certain problems to do with temporal order and continuity'.[22] With respect to Aristotle's conception of the now as a temporal instant, anyway, this suggestion seems to me to be correct. This conception of the now is obviously developed in analogy to Aristotle's of the point in linear extension; indeed, Aristotle sometimes employs the same terminology, e.g. *tomē* ('cut') and '*sēmeion*' ('position'), in referring to a now in this sense. And this indivisible, punctal now fulfils analogous functions that might be termed 'theoretical': (i) such a punctal now must serve as the common boundary of two successive intervals or stretches of time if time is to be continuous, according to Aristotle's formal account of continuity; (ii) two such punctal nows must serve as prior and posterior limits of, and thus define, a stretch/interval (in the token sense) of the temporal continuum. In view of (ii), punctal nows enter into the definition of the metrical 'a time': the nows delimit, 'in the prior and posterior directions', particular tokens of the

[21] Ibid. 104.
[22] Ibid. 108.

motion type used as a unit of time and thus enable us to consider the
class of motions *contemporaneous* with each such token.

Another corollary of (ii) is noted by Aristotle. In *Phys*. 4. 11 he
remarks that

a time is a number, not as of the same point, because it is the beginning of [one
interval] and end [of another, succeeding interval], but rather as the extremities
of a line [segment]. (220ᵃ14–16)

Aristotle's contention seems to be that, for defining a temporal interval
or distance, two distinct nows are required. A *single*, supposedly
'flowing now', which is continuously 'adding' to the past while it is
'subtracting' from the future, cannot serve to define a metric on time
or, it seems, even a linear ordering with respect to time. In order for a
single, flowing now to do so, we should have to conceive it as
successively marking out two distinct temporal *positions*; but these
positions are simply nows in the other, 'static' sense—punctal positions
or limits in a continuous linear continuum. Multiple *ta nun* or nows,
which can serve as limits of temporal intervals and which, therefore, in
some sense enjoy ontological parity, are needed. Once multiple nows
are thus introduced, something approaching a relativistic conception
of the past and future is not far away. Just as there is an infinite number
of points at which we can bisect a line, each point serving as the
common boundary of prior and posterior parts of the line, so also any
to nun partitions time into two parts and serves as the common
boundary of those two parts: the past *relative to that to nun* and the
future *relative to that to nun*. What Waterlow calls the 'unique present' in
the sense of *absolutely* unique present begins to fade away. *Each* 'cut'
or 'division' of continuous time is uniquely 'present' and the unique
indivisible and punctal juncture of past and present. But each such *to
nun* is uniquely present *from its own perspective* and the unique juncture
of *its own* past and *its own* future.

What this description suggests, of course, is a conception of the
temporal dimension according to which what is primary are stretches/
intervals of time definable on a linear continuum. Consequently, a derivative 'primacy' is assigned to the temporally stable or determinate
McTaggart B-series relations of simultaneity, priority, and posteriority
defined on the punctal limits of such intervals. And I believe that there
are tendencies toward this sort of view discernible in Aristotle's
discussion. However, it must be admitted that in the same discussion
there are also tendencies toward a very different view. There has been

much discussion of whether Aristotle's account of time is more appropriately interpreted in terms of the McTaggart B-series conception or in terms of the McTaggart A-series notions of past, present, and future, with the connotation of temporal 'flow' that is often attached to the so-called A-series conception.[23] In this matter I am inclined to agree with Sorabji, who holds that although Aristotle does not have a 'clear sense of the difference between static and flowing terminology', he none the less 'does not consider the flowing terminology inessential'[24] to his account of time.

But in what way, precisely, the A-series picture of flow enters into Aristotle's conception of time is a question that is difficult to answer. What appears to be an important departure from a 'straightforward' B-series conception of the temporal dimension occurs in connection with Aristotle's account, in *Phys.* 4. 14, of the prior (*to proteron*) and the posterior (*to husteron*). The standard B-series account of this relation would take it to be a 'primitive' two-place relation between temporal moments or instants (in Aristotle's case, between the two limits of any possible bounded stretch or interval of time). The relation would be a temporally stable one; that is, if, for any two such instants t_1 and t_2, it is *ever* the case that t_1 is prior (posterior) to t_2, it is *always* the case that this relation obtains. However, Aristotle gives what appears to be an

---

[23] The B-series conception, according to which the basis of temporality lies in the temporal relation of before/simultaneous with/after, is typically connected with a conception of time as a stable ordering of some sort. For it is assumed that this relation is temporally stable: i.e. if A is before (simultaneous with, after) B, then A either atemporally or omnitemporally stands in that relation to B. However, this assumption about the temporal ordering relation can, within the context of certain sorts of semantic models, consistently be denied. See e.g. my *Agency and Integrality: Philosophical Themes in the Ancient Discussions of Determinism and Responsibility* (Dordrecht, 1985), 192–203. The A-series, which takes the notions of past, present, and future as fundamental, is typically connected with the idea of 'temporal flow' because these notions do not yield temporally stable propositions. That is, it is not the case that from the sometime truth of 'it is (was, will be) the case that A' we can infer either atemporal or omnitemporal truth of 'it is (was, will be) the case that A'. It seems clear, however, that given a certain sort of semantic model for the tenses (one which ultimately relies on the B-series relation, interpreted as temporally stable), A-series notions can be interpreted without any connotation of flow. So it seems to me that the notions of supposedly dynamic versus static conceptions of time have little to do with McTaggart's original distinction between A-series and B-series. For more on all of this in relation to Aristotle, see N. Kretzmann, 'Aristotle on the Instant of Change', in *Proceedings of the Aristotelian Society*, supplementary vol. 50 (1976), 91–114; F. D. Miller, Jr., 'Aristotle on the Reality of Time', *Archiv für Geschichte der Philosophie*, 56 (1974), 132–55; R. Sorabji, *Time, Creation and the Continuum* (London and Ithaca, N.Y, 1983), 46–51.

[24] Sorabji, *Time, Creation and the Continuum*, 50.

account of the temporal priority/posteriority relation that makes it a three-place relation:

the prior is applied in a contrary manner with respect to past time and future time: in the case of the past, we say that the prior is further from the now and posterior nearer; but in the case of the future, the prior is nearer and the posterior further. (223^{a}8–13)

Waterlow comments that, in the *Physics'* discussion of time, Aristotle 'assembles his conceptual ingredients for the sole purpose of explaining time *sub specie mensurabilitatis'*.[25] And it does seem that there is a distinctively metrical flavour to the terms that seem to be functioning as *explanantia* in the preceding quotation, viz., 'further' (*porrōteron*) and 'nearer' (*enguteron*), as well as the term '*apostasis*' ('distance' or 'separation'), which Aristotle uses to describe the relation of what is prior or posterior to the now. From the contemporary perspective, one might expect to find the priority/posteriority relation introduced, along with simultaneity, as a 'primitive' topological relation, and *then* a metric superimposed, so to speak. Aristotle, however, seems to begin with concepts of simultaneity, past, and future, proceed to a metrical account of 'a time', and then return to define priority and posteriority by appeal to the implicitly metrical notions of further and nearer. However, it is clear that there is a sense in which the metrical component is not essential to the account of the prior and the posterior as relative to *to nun*. Aristotle could have made an entirely analogous point in terms of a non-metrical three-place relation of betweenness: 'in the case of the past, we say that the posterior is between the prior and the now; but in the case of the future, it is the prior that is between the posterior and the now.'[26]

Neither the metrical nor the topological version of Aristotle's claim can serve, without some supplementation, as an adequate definition of the priority/posteriority relation, however. For the account says nothing about the priority/posteriority relation between past and future points, relative to a now. Perhaps it is best simply to fill in, as an assumption to which Aristotle could not have objected, that any limit

[25] Waterlow, 'Aristotle's Now', 111.

[26] One reason why Aristotle proceeded as he did may be that, since he regards temporal points or nows as limits of temporal intervals, he would have held that the relation of betweenness must itself be dependent upon a conception of nearer and further (shortness and length of temporal intervals): t_0 is between t_1 and t_2 just in case both t_0 is nearer t_1 than t_2 is and t_0 is nearer t_2 than t_1 is.

of a temporal interval in the past direction is prior to any limit of a temporal interval in the future direction.[27]

Even if we supply Aristotle with this natural assumption, the account still constitutes a 'strange conception of temporal order', as Waterlow puts it.[28] A large part of this strangeness, of course, is due to the fact that Aristotle seems to make the temporal priority/posteriority relation a three-place relation, relativizing it to the 'now'. Waterlow considers the issue of possible motivation for this move in detail. As an initial consideration, she notes (a) that, with respect to place, some such relativization of a priority/posteriority relation seems necessary (i.e. in order to speak of place A as prior to place B, we need to relativize the claim, for example, to some 'starting place' $C-A$ is prior to B if you take C as starting place); and (b) that Aristotle exhibits a predilection (which we have previously noted) for claiming that what one can say about time derives from what one can say about motion, which in turn derives from what one can say about spatial magnitude. However, Waterlow also notes that, if time is considered in analogy to a directed line and the priority/posteriority relation as definable on the limits of possible bounded intervals on that line, Aristotle's rationale for preserving this point of analogy between spatial and temporal priority/posteriority would not seem to be very compelling:

However, that seems a feeble reason for saying the same of time, since in this case the order is the same as from every temporal point of view. And anyway Aristotle can surely preserve what he finds important about the parallel without slavishly repeating all the same features on both levels.[29]

Waterlow's point, of course, is that, given the 'line conception' of time, relativizing the relation of t_1 is prior (posterior) to t_2 by adding 'with respect to or from the perspective of t_0' seems to amount to a totally

[27] The inadequacy of Aristotle's triadic account of the before/after relation, without such a supplementation, is also noted in Denis Corish, 'Aristotle on Temporal Order: "Now", "Before", and "After,"' *Isis*, 69: 246 (1978), 68–74. Corish also gives an account of the motivation behind Aristotle's 'peculiar' triadic account in terms of his misguided attempt to attribute a pre-temporal before/after ordering to motion (stages) and then to derive a temporal version of the ordering from the pre-temporal version. Corish argues that, in view of Aristotle's methodology, it is not obvious that every movement is in time and that, in order to ensure that it is, Aristotle adds the third argument place, always to be filled in by the explicitly temporal now to the before/after relation. Of course, according to Corish, this complication is ultimately pointless, because the supposedly pre-temporal ordering of motions (motion stages) must really be an implicitly temporal ordering anyway.

[28] Waterlow, 'Aristotle's Now', 115.

[29] Ibid. 117.

superfluous logical complication since if such a relation obtains relative to any time t_i, it obtains relative to every time t_j.

Aristotle's rather baroque account of the priority/posteriority relation with respect to time is well motivated only if, again to use Waterlow's words, he has some compelling reason to think of the past and future as 'two distinct temporal orders'.[30] Such a distinction of temporal orders is not established simply by appeal to a one common conception of the *nunc fluens*. According to this conception, the now 'moves' from past to future in the way that the crest of a sine wave moves through a medium or a spotlight plays down a (dense and continuous) line of chorus girls. As Waterlow comments, such similes fail because they suggest 'that time is a sort of line whose points [chorus girls] lie in an order which can be conceived independently'[31] of the 'designation' of any point as 'now' (spotlighting of any particular chorus girl).

But in what sense, then, do the past and future constitute 'distinct temporal orders'? If I understand aright her suggestion, Waterlow answers this question as follows. Although the token-reflexive now is a '*principle* of temporal order', it does not, *qua* temporally present, *belong* to either the past or future temporal order defined in terms of it. Rather, the now so conceived represents a 'gap' (although, apparently, an instantaneous or punctal one) that is 'an eternal barrier to the uniting of the orders'[32] of past and future.

It is fairly easy to see the now, according to this account, fulfilling its Aristotelian function as a 'division' (*diairesis*) of time; but it perhaps is not so easy to see how it fulfils its further Aristotelian function of 'joining or making continuous past and future time' (*Phys*. 4. 13. 222ª10–20). Here Waterlow does not appeal to Aristotle's technical notion of continuity, but to the picture according to which 'the Now entraps what was a member of the future series and releases what was Now to join the past series'. In other words, the now continuously 'moves', in an orderly fashion, what is 'most prior' in the future temporal order and makes it 'most posterior' in the past temporal order. Of course, in the process, 'it' falls into a temporary— indeed, instantaneous—'breach', since what is present is not a member of either series. But, according to Waterlow, 'the breach is always occurring, and is always destined to be healed'.[33]

---

[30] Ibid. 122.   [31] Ibid. 124.
[32] Ibid. 125.   [33] Ibid. 126.

I shall not comment upon Waterlow's thesis of the 'missing now' except to note that the textual evidence for Aristotle's belief that the token-reflexive now should be excluded from the temporal order does not seem to be conclusive. A more fundamental issue, it seems to me, is the symmetry between the past and future that Waterlow's model evidently assumes. According to the model, everything that ends up in the past temporal order was once in the future temporal order; in the fullness of time, it was 'peeled off' the 'bottom (most prior position) of the future stack' and placed on the 'top (most posterior position) of the past stack'. This picture does not entirely do justice, I think, to Aristotle's notion of the now as a *generator* of time, in the way that the motion of a body generates a trajectory or the 'flow' of a geometrical point generates a line, to use some Aristotelian similes. Waterlow's model would have the moving body following along a predetermined trajectory and the point tracing out a pre-existent line (with the slight complication of the 'gap' introduced by the now/moving object/point).

The key to Aristotle's reluctance to think of past and future as a single temporal order, I submit, is his notion of the relative necessity or 'fixedness' of the past (and present), as opposed to the relative contingency or indeterminacy of the future.[34] In connection with the present topic, I suggest that its upshot is the following: contingent processes and the states of affairs in which they issue do indeed mark out temporal intervals and instants (*qua* limits of such intervals) in the present/past linear and continuous temporal order. However, such contingent processes are generated with the passage of time. Consequently, they are never part of the future temporal order: that is, they do not define any temporal interval or instants in the future since they do not 'exist in the future'. The only intervals that are a part of future time, relative to a given now, are those defined by processes/events that are relatively necessary with respect to that time (which, according to one common ancient interpretation of Aristotle, are those that are temporally cyclical and unrestrictedly necessary). Thus, the temporal intervals marked out by the periods of various celestial

---

[34] While this temporal asymmetry does not figure in the *Physics'* discussion of time, it is a doctrine found in many places in the Aristotelian corpus, and many scholars have commented on it. One illustration: at *De Caelo* 1. 12. 283ᵇ13–14 Aristotle claims that potentiality—particularly in the contingent sense: the potentiality both for (becoming) Φ and for not (becoming) Φ—pertains only to the future, not to what already has happened (*tou gegonenai*); and at *Analytica priora* 1. 13. 32ᵇ10–13 he identifies the indeterminate (*to aoriston*) with the contingent.

bodies, which constitute necessary, eternal, and cyclical motions, are a part of the presently future temporal order, which is both separated from and made continuous with the past by the token-reflexive now. However, should I make an automobile trip tomorrow, the temporal interval defined by that continuous motion is not now part of the future temporal order, although (in the event that I do make the trip) it will *become* part of the past temporal order. So, in the following remark from *Phys*. 4. 13, I am inclined to think that Aristotle is thinking of the 'flood' (as he evidently does in *Meteorologica* 1. 14) as a necessary, eternally recurrent natural phenomenon:

'Some time' is a time defined relative to the now in the former sense [instantaneous sense]; as 'Troy was captured at some time' and 'there will be a flood at some time'. It is necessary that [these events] be determined relative to the now. Therefore, there will be some quantity of time from now to the latter event; and there was a certain quantity of time to the former.   (222ª24–8)

The future, according to this picture, is rather like the blank part of a copy book: it has only a minimal temporal structure, the temporal intervals and limit points 'ruled in' by necessary and cyclical natural phenomena (the movements of heavenly bodies and those natural, terrestrial periodic occurrences causally dependent upon them). The past, however, is a *plenum*, with these ruled spaces having been filled in by various contingent processes (e.g. the Trojan War and subsequent fall of Troy) and the temporal intervals and limit points defined by them. It is this asymmetry of future and past, I suggest, that lies at the conceptual heart of the 'flowing now' and A-series constituents of Aristotle's conception of time. The asymmetry of past and future in this sense—the past is 'fuller' than the future—is what gives time its direction, i.e. what is responsible for 'time's *arrow*'. And, I believe, it is here that we can see the reason why Aristotle, to quote Sorabji again, 'does not consider the flowing terminology inessential'. There will be *plenum* in the past direction in contrast to a largely 'unfurnished' future only relative to the supposedly 'flowing' or shifting now-position. This asymmetrical character of the Aristotelian conception of time may be modelled, as a number of interpreters of Aristotle have done,[35] by forward-branching, backward-linear 'tree'

[35] See e.g. my 'Necessity and Unactualized Possibilities in Aristotle', *Philosophical Studies*, 38 (1980), 287–98; 'Fatalism and Causal Determinism: An Aristotelian Essay', *Philosophical Quarterly*, 31: 124 (1981), 231–41. These essays are concerned with Aristotle's treatment of future contingent propositions and the issues of fatalism and causal determinism. The idea of the relative temporal indeterminacy of the future, which

structures. But if such a model is to come at all close to capturing
Aristotle's idea of the 'developmental' character of time, we must
envision the model as being viewed from a (dense and continuous) *succession* of nows along one linear (but not predetermined) branch of the
model. And here, of course, the notion of temporal flow is
reintroduced into the picture.[36]

According to the preceding interpretation of Aristotle's conception
of time, it is necessary and eternally recurrent processes that yield *Ur-
zeit*. On the one hand, they give time its underlying topological
structure as a linear continuum because there is an eternal sequence,
without beginning or end, of their tokens that are 'joined end to end'
without any intervening pause or gap: the posterior *terminus* of one
such token coincides with the prior *terminus* of its successor. *Ur-zeit*,
in this sense, also serves as the basis of Aristotle's metrical conception
of 'a time'—a quantitative unit of measure, or multiple of such units,
defined on this continuum. For periods of movement of celestial
bodies, considered as motion-types, define, respectively, units of
measure of which 'a time' is some *number* or multiple. On the other
hand, contingent, irregular, and idiosyncratic temporal processes give
rise to the asymmetry of past and future and, consequently, lie at the
root of Aristotle's version of time's arrow.

Of course, as we have seen, what is directly relevant to Aristotle's
kinematic analysis are the formal, structural features of stretches/
intervals of time—what one might call the *geometrical* features of
stretches of time conceived as infinitely divisible and continuous line-
segments. In the preceding chapter we discussed in some detail the
more formal aspects of Aristotle's kinematics. As we saw, that formal
analysis is embedded in his interval-based ontology of continua. We
now turn to the manner in which this formal analysis is embedded in
Aristotle's 'larger' metaphysical conception of *kinēseis*, in general, and
his conception of the identity conditions of local *kinēseis*.

the present account of Aristotle's version of time's arrow appeals to, is also relevant to
the analysis of Aristotle's conception of the contingency of the future, which is developed
in the essays cited.

[36] Although it is, I think, difficult to avoid terms such as 'flow', 'shift', or 'passage' in
discussing Aristotle's conception of time, such terminology is not to be understood as
implying that time in any literal sense moves or that the passage of time takes time. As
we saw, Aristotle maintains (*Phys.* 4. 12. 220ª32-ᵇ1) that time is not properly characterized as slow or fast.

THE METAPHYSICS OF *KINĒSEIS*

The Definition of Kinēseis

In Book 3 of the *Physics*, there occurs Aristotle's famous, formulaic, and obscure definition of *kinēsis* as 'the actuality (or fulfilment, realization, or actualization: *entelecheia*) of what exists potentially, *qua* a thing of that sort [viz., a thing that exists *potentially*]' (*Phys*. 3. 1. 201ᵃ10–11). It seems that, according to this account, process (*kinēsis*, in general) is the 'incomplete' actualization of a potentiality as opposed to a 'complete' actualization of a potentiality. The 'complete' actualization of the potentiality is a state of affairs supervenient upon the natural terminus of the *kinēsis*, i.e. the natural terminus of the former, incomplete actualization of the potentiality. Thus, to appeal to an Aristotelian example, the incomplete actualization of the potentiality of being a house (as possessed, for example, by the timber or stones) is the process of 'being built' or 'being fashioned into a house'; while the complete actualization is the state of affairs that supervenes upon the natural terminus of the process of being built or being fashioned into a house: the existence of a house.

The sense in which a process is an *incomplete* actualization of potentiality for, say, being *F* is that this actualization is effected in such a way that (*a*) its subject is not (yet) *F* and (*b*) the actualization of this potentiality for being *F* does not remove or destroy the potentiality. Waterlow comments that

Aristotle's definition of change does not state the obvious falsehood that the subject's not being F is a *sufficient* condition for its becoming F (cf. III. 2, 29–30). That would imply no difference between the actuality and the mere potentiality of change. But it says more than that becoming F is that for which not being F is *necessary*. It is not the case that every actuality that obtains only if the subject is in some negative condition is a change towards the corresponding positive one. That actuality of the statue-form belongs to the bronze only if e.g., helmet-form is lacking; yet the actuality of being formed as a statue is not that of becoming a helmet. If it were, by the same argument being a statue would be the same as becoming a set of coins, a set of nails, etc., and all the things that the bronze logically cannot be if it is a statue. The relation between the negative condition of the subject of change, and the actuality of change itself, is stronger than necessary but weaker than sufficient. The change is the active expression of the negative condition and is grounded in it.[37]

[37] S. Waterlow, *Nature, Change, and Agency in Aristotle's 'Physics'* (Oxford, 1982), 118.

The problem here, as Waterlow quite realizes, is providing an adequate characterization of this 'active expression of the negative condition [being not-F]' that is to be equated with the *kinēsis* of becoming F.

Waterlow suggests that an 'incomplete actuality [i.e. *kinēsis*] is one whose essential description requires a gerundive reference to a specific terminus *ad quem*':[38]

But a substantial point emerges when we consider that within the context of Aristotle's definition of process, 'potentially F' has the function of stating the *direction* of change. In other words, 'potentially F' harbours one purely intentional element, which it might be more apt to call 'gerundive', stating what *is to be* and would be *if* the change were to reach completion.[39]

However, as I think the preceding quotation suggests, this intentional or 'gerundive' character of Aristotelian potentialities seems just as applicable to the 'mere' (or 'entirely' unactualized) potentiality for being F as it does to the 'incomplete actualization' of this potentiality, i.e. the process of becoming F. The result is a conception of kinetic status that is, to quote Waterlow, 'relative to description':

A pile of stones on the ground is in a condition of natural stasis if we have regard to the earthy substance of the stone; but if a builder has dumped them there as the position most convenient from which to hoist them to an arch under construction, then from his point of view they are there only on account of not yet being somewhere else, and are therefore 'in process'. Again, kinetic status varies with the description: if we focus on 'being on the ground', and regarding 'being just here at the foot of the wall' as incidental, then we treat the stones as a case of earthy substance whose condition is static: for it is the nature of earthy masses to lie low, but not in one particular place rather than another; whereas if 'being just here' is not incidental (because central for the external agent's point of view), then under this description we are dealing with a *kinēsis*.[40]

Even if one accepts the notion that kinetic status is 'relative to description', a problem with Waterlow's analysis remains: it remains unclear how one is to distinguish between the 'mere' possession of a potentiality for being F *qua* potentiality and the 'incomplete actualization' of that potentiality in the form of the *kinēsis* of becoming F. For example, suppose that we are concerned with the pile of stones under

[38] Ibid. 131.
[39] Ibid. 123–4.
[40] Ibid. 128–9.

the description of 'material out of which the arch is to be constructed'. How are we to decide, according to Waterlow's account, whether the stones' 'being just here' on the ground below where the arch is to be erected is an expression of (a) the 'mere' potentiality of being fashioned into an arch (i.e. the potentiality solely *qua* potentiality, not *qua* any sort of actualization of that potentiality) or of (b) the actualization of that potentiality *qua* potentiality (thus, as Waterlow suggests, rendering the stones' presence just here an expression of their being 'in the process' of being fashioned into the arch)?

One might, I suppose, maintain that the distinction on which this question depends is a bogus one, at least in terms of Aristotle's discussion of *kinēsis* in *Physics* 3. According to such an interpretation, potentialities do not exist as 'mere' potentialities in my sense of 'mere': in so far as a subject possesses the potentiality for being F, it must possess that potentiality (at least) in the 'incompletely actualized' form of the *kinēsis* of becoming F. Although, perhaps, some work of Hintikka, Remes, and Knuuttila[41] can be construed as advancing such a view of Aristotelian potentialities and processes, I am not at all certain that it is a view to which Waterlow would subscribe.

This conception of the identity of potentiality and *kinēsis* does, however, manifest in more radical fashion a noteworthy tendency in Waterlow's analysis of Aristotle's account of *kinēsis* in *Physics* 3: the undermining of an intuitive, 'pre-analytical' conception of the distinction between a state (*stasis*) and a process or 'motion' (*kinēsis*). As Waterlow is quite aware, considerations of linguistic usage suggest, perhaps, that the 'intuitive' distinction we may initially (and rather uncritically) be inclined to make *should* be undermined. For it seems quite acceptable to describe myself as 'being in the process of driving across the country' or, simply, 'driving across the country' even though I am, at the moment, quite stationary in a motel room in Albuquerque. Similarly, I need feel no moral qualms about reporting to the administrators of my university that I am 'working on a book manuscript' even though I have been, for the last ten minutes or so, sitting immobile with a vacant mind, staring at the chalk board in my office.

A plausible reaction to this sort of consideration is to insist that

---

[41] The suggestion is made, with respect to real or full potentialities (i.e. resultant potentialities that are not in any way opposed), that 'as soon as there exists such a *dynamis*, a *kinēsis* toward its realization is initiated' (J. Hintikka, U. Remes, and S. Knuuttila, *Aristotle on Modality and Determinism*, Acta Philosophica Fennica, 29: 1 (Amsterdam, 1977), 73.

there is to be found in Aristotle's thought a 'formal, structural' distinction between *stasis* and *kinēsis* that represents an analysis of our
'intuitive' understanding of the distinction but which does *not*
precisely capture or map on to all 'process talk' and the grammatical
categories of verb aspect (e.g. imperfective versus perfect). It is true
that, prior to his 'metaphysical' definition of process in *Phys*. 3. 1,
Aristotle remarks on a principal feature of the mathematical/
structural concept, viz., the fact that *kinēsis* is to be included among
those things that are continuous (200^b17). However, the question
remains as to what the relation is between the metaphysical definition
and the 'narrower' sense of *kinēsis* according to which it is incompatible with *stasis*.

Waterlow's interpretation of Aristotle's metaphysical 'definition' of
'*kinēsis*' virtually guarantees that there will be tension between the
metaphysical definition and the narrower conception of *kinēsis*, which
opposes it to *stasis*. Commenting on the translation of '*entelecheia*' in
the metaphysical definition of *kinēsis* (the '*entelecheia* of what exists
potentially, *qua* a thing of that sort'), she notes

Some render this as 'actualization' and 'realization': misleading terms, in that
they can mean the *process* of becoming or making real or actual. Aristotle
cannot be read as defining process by 'actualization' in any such sense, since
that would be blatantly circular. Circularity apart, to offer such a definition
would be to give up the fight to show that process and change are themselves
real and actual.[42]

Waterlow maintains that 'if the word [*entelecheia*] did have a kinetic
meaning this would *ipso facto* render it unsuitable to stand on the right-
hand side of a *definition* of "process".'[43] In view of such a constraint on
the interpretation of the metaphysical definition, it seems unlikely that
the metaphysical definition could be understood as limited to the
narrower conception of *kinēsis*; indeed, it is far from obvious that the
definition could apply at all to the narrower conception. If *kinēsis* is
conceived as a *fundamental* metaphysical kind or category, any
definition of it will, in a sense, be circular. That is, we shall not succeed
in producing a *reductive* definition: one that 'reduces' *kinēseis* to
explicitly non-kinetic concepts or 'eliminates *kinēseis* in favour of the
non-kinetic'. Most often, I think, what seems to be definitional in
Aristotle is not reductive or eliminative but explicative. It would be

[42] Waterlow, *Nature, Change, and Agency*, 112.
[43] Ibid. 112, n. 16.

impossible to explicate that nature of Aristotelian *dunameis* (potentialities) without appeal to the notion of *energeiai* and vice versa. But I
think that no definition is possible that would reduce either category
to the other. Analogously, it seems likely that Aristotle does not intend
his metaphysical 'definition' of *kinēsis* to be reductive or eliminative;
rather, it is intended as an explication of process in terms of some
familiar Aristotelian metaphysical terminology.[44]

If this view of the metaphysical definition of *kinēsis* in *Phys.* 3. 1 is
correct, we need not be particularly concerned whether *entelecheia* — or
terms used to translate it — have kinetic connotations. It does seem that
Aristotle proceeds, in the sixth and eighth books of the *Physics*, to
explicate in the formal, structural way discussed in the preceding
chapter the nature of the sort of 'incomplete actuality' or 'actualization
of a potentiality *qua* potentiality', which he introduces in his metaphysical definition of *kinēsis*. However, a very real problem — which is
of considerable concern to Waterlow — is the fact that this formal,
structural 'refinement' of the metaphysical definition seems applicable
only to *kinēseis* in the 'narrower' sense in which they are contrasted
with *staseis*. Waterlow comments:

Thus although in III. 1, 200^{b}16–20, Aristotle names 'the infinite' as one of the
concepts to be examined in his philosophy of nature, on the ground that
process is continuous, and infinity rears its head in connection with continuity,
his actual analysis of process [i.e. the 'metaphysical analysis' in the third book of
the *Physics*] does not compel him to treat it as mathematically continuous or
infinitely divisible. This is an advantage, for had he restricted 'process' to
situations which it makes sense to describe in terms of mathematical continuity, he would have consigned to conceptual limbo a vast range of occurrences that we should naturally class as processes and becomings; including
many examples of his own. How could we begin to apply the model of the continuous series to getting healthy, or to house-building? It is not clear how any

---

[44] There is a large contemporary literature on Aristotle's definition of *kinēsis*. Particularly noteworthy is L. A. Kosman, 'Aristotle's Definition of Motion', *Phronesis*, 14 (1969),
40–62. Kosman discusses many of the same problems pertaining to the definition that
exercise Waterlow. The view that I express bears some affinity to that of D. W. Graham,
'Aristotle's Definition of Motion', *Ancient Philosophy*, 8 (1988), 209–15. Graham interprets the *definiens* in terms of a 1–place predicate 'the actuality of X *qua* X [or V-able *qua*
V-able]', rather than a 2–place predicate 'the actuality of X *qua* Y [or M *qua* V-able]': 'on
this interpretation, the *qua*-phrase does not serve to specify the X but only to call
attention to the formula of the expression itself; it invites us to consider the expression as
uniquely appropriate to the definition: the actuality of X itself, of X proper. If X stands for
a potentiality, then motion is the actuality of the relevant potential itself' (212).

type of change apart from locomotion (and increase and decrease so far as they imply locomotion of an object's boundaries) could be handled in this way.[45]

The motivation behind Waterlow's reading of the metaphysical definition of *kinēsis* is clearly discernible in the preceding quotation: if the definition is not read as being at least 'neutral' between the narrow sense of *kinēsis* in which it is contrasted with *stasis* and a broader sense, then it seems likely that forms of *kinēsis* other than locomotion get relegated, at least as far as the *Physics* goes, to a 'conceptual limbo'. This would be particularly true since the later discussion of process in *Physics* 6 and 8 seems to focus on *kinēsis* in the narrower sense.

Waterlow's anxiety concerning the non-locomotive forms of *kinēsis*—her concern whether much of Aristotle's analysis, in the *Physics*, of *kinēsis* is really applicable to its non-locomotive forms— seems to me to be quite legitimate. However, it is far from obvious that Aristotle intends his metaphysical definition to capture the broader sense in which processes can have stative constituents. Perhaps Waterlow's essential contention is that, irrespective of Aristotle's *own understanding* of his metaphysical definition, the definition can be given a consistent Aristotelian reading according to which it defines *kinēseis* in the broader sense. Chapter 3 of her *Nature, Change, and Agency in Aristotle's 'Physics'* does much, in my view, to substantiate such a contention. However, as I earlier suggested, her analysis leaves disturbingly vague the relation between the 'mere' potentiality, or potentiality 'pure and simple', for being F and the 'incomplete actualization' of that potentiality (i.e. its actualization *qua* potentiality) that the metaphysical definition identifies with the *kinēsis* of becoming or 'being on the way to' F.

Whatever the precise status of Aristotle's metaphysical definition, he seems to have believed that the metaphysical conception of process as an incomplete *entelecheia*, the *entelecheia* of what is potentially $[F]$ *qua* being potentially $[F]$, requires further analysis, which he attempted to give, at least for the special case of locomotion, in *Physics* 6 and 8. We discussed that analysis in Chapter 1. A question to which I shall return in Chapter 3 is whether there is to be found in the Aristotelian corpus any analogous further analysis of the non-locomotive forms of *kinēsis*. However, I turn next to a problem that develops for Aristotle with respect to the 'unity' or 'identity conditions' of local motions.

Are Kinetic Segments of Locomotions Locomotions?

If it is true that a body *A* can *have arrived* at position *P* (the spatial *terminus ad quem* of its continuous locomotion) at a temporal instant *t*, and if it is thus true that *A* can *be* at *P* at a temporal instant *t*, the following question arises: is it not the case that *A* also *has arrived* at and *is* at, in a continuous linear order, all the positions strictly between its initial position (*terminus a quo*), where it *remained* for a period of time before it moved, and its terminal (*ad quem*) position, where it comes to a stop and remains for a period of time? Such a view might suggest, first, that a single continuous (local) motion is, in some sense constituted of an infinite number of 'sub-motions': what I have termed kinetic segments are, in other words, promoted to the status of *kinēseis*, some of which overlap and each of which is demarcated by a pair of nows and a corresponding pair of spatial positions as starting time/place and ending time/place. A further 'simplification' leaves us only a dense and Dedekind-continuous linear array of pairs of instants and positions. The result is what I earlier termed the at–at ontology of motion, described by Russell with his customary lucidity (and tendentiousness):

> Motion consists merely in the fact that bodies are sometimes in one place and sometimes in another, and that they are at intermediate places at intermediate times. Only those who have waded through the quagmire of philosophic speculation on this subject can realize what a liberation from antique prejudices is involved in this simple and straightforward commonplace.[46]

Although, as I have already said, Aristotle ultimately resists both moves, he does flirt with at least the first move to a conception of a continuous *kinēsis* as, in a certain sense, constituted of other individually continuous *kinēseis*.

In *Phys.* 6. 6 he argues that 'what is moving will have moved' (237ª2–3) and, in fact, that 'everything that is changing will have changed an infinite number of times [*apeira*]' (237ª11). At the core of Aristotle's argument is the continuity (infinite divisibility) of time and the temporal continuity represented by the principle of the temporal non-supervenience of motion (TN-SK) discussed in the preceding section. Indeed, the immediate reason that Aristotle gives for the

---

[46] B. Russell, 'Mathematics and Metaphysicians', repr. of 1917 edn. in *Mysticism and Logic* (Totowa, NJ, 1981), 66.

second of the two preceding claims is that 'every time [interval] is divisible and a time [interval] is between nows' (237ᵃ10). So there certainly is the recognition by Aristotle that, in any continuous motion, it is possible to demarcate an 'indeterminate' number of distinct kinetic segments. This recognition, however, does not seem to be regarded by Aristotle as quite sufficient to establish that what is changing *has changed* (completed changes) previously, although it may be sufficient to establish that what is changing *was changing* (was undergoing the process of change) previously.

Aristotle connects the imperfective verb forms he employs in talking about change (e.g. *metaballein*, *to metaballon*, *kineisthai*, *to kinoumenon*) with the ongoing process of change and, hence, with what we have called kinetic segments. As he himself puts it, 'but it is also necessary that what has changed previously was changing [*metaballein*]; for everything that has changed from something to something has changed in [an interval of] time' (237ᵃ18–20).

To establish that everything that is moving must *have moved* (*kekinēsthai*) previously, however, Aristotle initially gives what must seem, from the contemporary perspective, an unnecessarily circuitous argument:

If in the primary time [of motion] *XP* a body has moved the distance *KΛ*, a body moving at the same speed and having started at the same time will, in half the time, have moved half the distance. But if the body moving at the same speed has moved a certain distance in a given time, it is necessary that the first body has moved the same distance in the same time, so that what is moving will have moved. (236ᵇ34– 237ᵃ3)

It might seem that the *second* moving body is entirely superfluous to this argument. Why does Aristotle not simply argue directly that, because a body moving at a constant speed traverses half the distance in half the time, the body *has* moved half the distance in half the time and that, therefore, owing to the infinite divisibility of time, it is always the case that 'what is moving will have moved'? The answer, I suspect, is that, with respect to locomotion, Aristotle connects the perfective-stative *kekinēsthai* ('has moved') with the state of having reached a position (the *terminus ad quem*) of a continuous motion in the sense *of having come to a rest* there. Aristotle would hold that the following two premisses are obvious: (1) that a body *B* moving at exactly the same speed as *A* and starting simultaneously with *A* but moving only half as long as *S* comes to rest at a position *C* that is half the distance from

A's *terminus a quo* to *A*'s *terminus ad quem*; (2) at the time *t* that *B* arrives at its resting-place *C* (which, as we have seen, Aristotle later, in *Phys*. 8. 8, argues is a unique now or temporal instant), *A* must be 'level with' (*kata*, i.e. neither in front of nor behind) B. Therefore, Aristotle evidently concludes, we are entitled to infer that A, while continuing to move thereafter, none the less arrives at the same position *C* at the same time *t* as does *B*, which rests (remains) at *C*.

What is wrong with this consequence? It is not clear that in Book 6 of the *Physics* Aristotle sees anything wrong with it. But there is a problem—or rather a congeries of closely related problems—pertaining to the unity of a continuous *kinēsis* to which it gives rise. Waterlow raises one such problem in characterizing what she regards as 'the fundamental error of' Book 6:

> What Aristotle fails to see there is this. If X is passing from A to B through the intermediate point I, then there is no single change occurring throughout the time of passage from A to B. For if one change (distinguished by reference to one pair of termini) is over at I, then at I *another* begins, even if X does not halt. It gets from A to B by a succession of changes A–I and I–B. Yet the account was intended to display each and every *single* change as 'containing' infinite others. . . . Thus infinite divisibility ensures that although in the end the object will *be* at B, it will not have arrived there by any single identifiable change; nor by a succession of these, since no change is single. One might ask why it should matter, seeing that the infinite proliferation does not entail that the object will never be at B. But it does entail that B is not reached by *change*. For only the specific is real, and there is no specific change or set of specific changes in which the passage consists. This amounts to a proof that the very concept of 'change' is incoherent: for change is nothing if not that by which something passes from one condition to another.[47]

There are, I believe, two issues raised in this subtle and acute passage. The more superficial, technical issue concerns the identity conditions for Aristotelian *kinēseis*. Perhaps not surprisingly, it proves the more tractable issue. I shall postpone until the next section discussion of the deeper issue, which pertains to whether *any* account of motion that conceives motion as containing an infinite collection of kinetic segments does not thereby render 'the very concept of "change" . . . incoherent'.

But what of the problem concerning the identity conditions for *kinēseis*? In *Phys*. 5. 4 Aristotle discusses the identity of motions at some length. For a motion to be one motion, in a numerical and

---

[47] Waterlow, *Nature, Change, and Agency*, 145–6.

'unqualified' (*haplōs*) sense of 'one', (i) there must be an (essentially) single subject or thing moved, (ii) the motion must be single in 'species' or type, and (iii) the 'when' during which the motion takes place must be a temporal interval that is 'one and not interrupted or intermittent [*mē dialeipein*]' (227^{b}20–32). These conditions are evidently intended to be individually necessary and jointly sufficient for the 'strong' or numerical identity of a motion (227^{b}27–9). While the first two are often more or less tacitly presupposed in Aristotle's discussions of motion elsewhere in the *Physics*, the third receives considerable attention. It is really a version of our temporal non-supervenience of motion principle TN-SK, intended to rule out pauses in a continuous motion. It is clear that, in this chapter, Aristotle understands the conjunction of the three conditions to be equivalent to the continuity of a motion: 'since every *kinēsis* is continuous, it is necessary that a *kinēsis* that is unqualifiedly one be continuous (since every [*kinēsis*] is divisible), and if [a *kinēsis* is] continuous, [it must be] one' (228^{b}20–2).

A problem with this account is that, understood in one way, it allows any proper kinetic segment of a continuous motion to be 'one motion', as well as the motion itself: for such a proper segment will (i) have one subject, (ii) be one with respect to the type of motion, and (iii) occur in a time containing no pauses, thus satisfying the temporal non-supervenience principle TN-SK if the motion of which it is a kinetic segment satisfies these three conditions. But then the three conditions cannot serve as 'identity conditions' *individuating kinēseis* in the sense of partitioning them into classes of non-overlapping temporal occurrences.

What is wanted in the statement of condition (iii) is a refinement of something like Aristotle's notion of a 'first or primary when' as used in *Phys*. 6. 5: the 'largest' temporal interval of motion satisfying conditions (i), (ii), and (iii).[48] This refinement captures, I believe, Aristotle's usual view concerning the identity of *kinēseis*. Each such *kinēsis*, at least if it is not eternal and if its 'subject' exists before and after the motion in question, is temporally 'bracketed' by periods of *stasis*. But there can be no such pauses falling temporally *within* a motion if it is to be accounted *a* (numerically and unqualifiedly unitary) motion. The doctrine of *Phys*. 6. 5 is that, in order for a body

---

[48] There is a largest such interval in the case of a finite stretch of motion: despite the fact that there is no first or last instant of mov*ing*, according to Aristotle, each such finite stretch is bounded in the prior and posterior directions by nows.

to complete any motion (to have moved), it already must have completed an indefinite number of other motions (must have moved an indefinite number of times). This doctrine seems to imply that the kinetic segments of motions are themselves motions. And it is inconsistent with what seems to be Aristotle's criterion of individuation of *kinēseis*, a criterion that implies that *a* (non-eternal) motion is 'punctuated at its temporal ends' by periods of *stasis*. It is this criterion of individuation, I believe—rather than the doctrine of *Phys*. 6. 5—which represents most closely Aristotle's considered opinion. In *Phys*. 8. 8 we find Aristotle 'refining' (i.e. correcting) the doctrine of *Phys*. 6. 5.

Local Motion as the Actualization of Potentiality qua *Potentiality*

In *Phys*. 8. 8 Aristotle suggests that a continuously moving body is at an intermediate (*meson*) position (between *actual* spatial *termini a quo et ad quem*) only at a temporal instant or cut (*en tomēi*) (262^b20–1) and that such a position can be considered a *telos* to which a continuously moving body comes only potentially (*dunamei*), not in actuality (*energeiai*) (262^b30–2). We might then be inclined to ascribe to Aristotle something like the following view perspicuously set forth by Waterlow:

The rolling object is not nowhere, but nor is it at any moment somewhere either, in the full-blooded sense in which it was and will be somewhere before and after the passage.... Rolling is an actuality whereby the subject is not actually anywhere, not yet nowhere, but (surely) potentially somewhere. But potentially *where*? There are many positions (perhaps we have to say infinitely many) which the continuously moving object neither was nor was not at: should we not then say that it was potentially at each? ... But potentiality is for the possibly actual; hence there is no such thing as *the* potentiality to be in P_m and P_n, etc. Should we then speak of the potentiality to be in them successively, or rather (as continuity demands) in a different one at a different moment? But the actuality that would correspond to this is the actuality of motion itself, since this simply *is* being in a different position at each moment; and the original problem survives, because the 'momentary being at' was just what seemed insufficiently real to be classed as 'really being somewhere'. Should we say then that the motion is an exercise of many potentialities, as many as there are positions? If so we lose the right to call it *the* exercise and *the* motion. In short, the logic of 'actual'/'potential' demands a *single* filling for 'is potentially at —'; and since potentiality is for things in the future, not the past, the reference will inevitably be to the latest position, or that where the motion ends.[49]

---

[49] Waterlow, *Nature, Change, and Agency*, 129–30.

This passages summarizes Waterlow's deeper metaphysical problem to which I alluded in the previous section. This problem might be characterized as follows: how to reconcile the Aristotelian conception of a (local) motion as the (incomplete) actualization of *a* (particular, individual) potentiality with a conception of the continuity of motion in terms of a body's having completed an indeterminate number of *other* motions.

One might, I think, initially be tempted to develop an 'Aristotelian' account of locomotion in conformity with the very general definition in *Phys*. 3. 1 of *kinēsis* as the actualization of a potentiality *qua* potentiality: the motion of a body from position A to position B is the actualization of the potentiality for that body to be in position B *by means of* instantaneously occupying (in the 'correct' temporal order) each of a dense and Dedekind-continuous linear array of loci; A, the 'first' locus in this ordered collection, is the *terminus a quo* of the body's motion, and B, the 'last' locus in the collection, is the body's *terminus ad quem*. The actualization of this potential for being at B—that is, the very process of the body's instantaneously occupying each of the positions strictly between A and B—is incomplete in a fairly obvious sense. When occupying the intermediate positions, the body is not yet at its *actual terminus ad quem B*. It is the actualization of a potentiality *qua* potentiality because the potentiality of the body to be at its *terminus ad quem B* remains 'intact' while the process is 'going on', i.e. during the time the body is instantaneously occupying each of the positions strictly between A and B. But this actualization is also incomplete in a second sense: it is the actualization of a potentiality *qua* potentiality that is *not* also a 'full-blooded' actualization. For, during the time the body is instantaneously occupying each of the positions strictly between A and B, it is—to use Waterlow's description—neither 'nowhere nor somewhere' 'in the full-blooded sense in which it was and will be somewhere before and after the passage'.

Waterlow's objection to such an explication, as I understand her, is that in the case of 'violent' locomotion (i.e. the locomotion of something that has not moved to its natural place), the talk of a potentiality and its actualization becomes vacuous—a mere verbal husk containing nothing of substance.

For where this [the last state or *terminus ad quem*] is not intrinsically directed, or not considered as such, the last state can only be identified (and the process fully specified) *ex post facto*. But this means that the process literally has no fully determinate description while taking place. But then it cannot count as an *actuality* while occurring—and if not then, when? Nor can it count as an incomplete actuality, for an incomplete actuality is one whose essential description requires a gerundive reference to a specific terminus *ad quem*. By contrast, a true account of the non-directed process *as* it is unfold*ing* ought to supply a description complete (or not incomplete) without any such reference, since in itself the process is not towards anything in particular.[50]

The objection that is raised in this passage strikes me as a serious one. But there are possible responses to it. One line of response that seems to be promising begins by pointing out the advantage of being able to apply the same analysis of motion in terms of the actualization of a potentiality *qua* potentiality to both natural and violent motion while, at the same time, maintaining sufficient flexibility in these concepts so as not to destroy the distinction. An important part of the distinction is that, in the case of violent motion, the spatial (and temporal) *terminus ad quem* can, according to Aristotle, be determined only *ex post facto* or *a fronte*. But the fact that the body that has undergone violent motion did have a *dunamis*, in *one* sense of this term, for being at its actual *terminus ad quem* is shown by the fact that it actually came to be at that position and not at some other. Of course, this *dunamis* will not be entirely similar to the *dunamis* of a body for moving to its natural place; but since we have a fundamental distinction between types of motion, it is perhaps not unreasonable to expect a correlative fundamental distinction between types of *dunamis*. According to this line of response, Waterlow's requirement that 'a true account of non-directed [violent] process *as* it is unfold*ing* ought to supply a description complete (or not incomplete) without any such reference [i.e. 'future-looking', *a tergo*, or 'gerundive' reference to the *telos / terminus ad quem*]' is too stringent: it rules out a priori the very possibility of applying the definitional schema of *Phys*. 3. 1 to violent ('non-directed') motion.

If we do allow such a *dunamis* in the case of violent motion, Waterlow raises a pointed question: is it 'indifferently' a *dunamis* of the body for being at its *actual* terminal position and a *dunamis* for being at the infinity of intermediate positions it 'traverses' but—according to Aristotle—neither arrives at nor departs from in moving to its actual *terminus ad quem*? I am not certain what the answer to this question, in terms of Aristotle's own physics, should be. Nor am I certain whether an affirmative answer would fatally compromise the attempt to com-

[50] Ibid. 131.

prehend violent motion under the definitional schema of *Phys*. 3. 1. It is ironical that classical (Newtonian) mechanics would have less difficulty with this objection. For, according to a classical Newtonian analysis, the totality of forces acting on a body that undergoes a certain local motion do specifically determine its actual *terminus ad quem* (if the subsequent interaction of the moving body with other bodies is ruled out or otherwise taken into account).

But there is a yet more fundamental problem with the preceding 'Aristotelian' account of locomotion, which I advanced as a possible interpretation of Aristotle's own conception of locomotion. The problem is that the account in effect assumes—as Waterlow does and as Russell does in the passage quoted earlier in this section—that continuous motion 'simply *is* being in a different position at each instant'.[51] This is what I earlier called the at–at ontology of motion. There is a strong tendency, from the contemporary perspective, to adopt the at–at ontology of motion as part and parcel of the standard contemporary mathematical and kinematic analysis of continuous motion. But, as I shall argue in Chapter 4, it is not *necessary* to do so; and, as I maintained in Chapter 1, it seems evident that Aristotle does *not*, in fact, do so.

Aristotle certainly seems to recognize that, if we consider any two actual or possible positions A and B (perhaps partly overlapping) of a body continuously moving from A to (or through) B, there will be a distinct intermediate (*meson*) position (perhaps partly overlapping one or both of the positions we are considering it to be between). He also recognizes that, *were* the continuously moving body traversing a spatial interval on which these positions can be demarcated to stop at C, it would take less time to complete its passage than were it to stop at B. It is to be emphasized that, owing to his conception of continuity (in sense (*b*): infinite divisibility) of spatial magnitude and motion, he holds that both these claims are true for *any* positions A and B that can be demarcated on the path of the continuously moving body. Hence, he *in some sense* holds the claims to be true for an infinite number of positions. But the relevant sense of 'infinite number', not surprisingly, is the Aristotelian sense of *potentially* infinite (i.e. 'no greatest') number. These *loci* are, for Aristotle, merely *possible* positions or stopping-places of the body: they do not form a collective totality that he *identifies* with the motion of the body.

[51] Ibid. 130.

This point emerges much more clearly, I believe, in Book 8 of the *Physics* than it does in Book 6. When Aristotle in *Phys*. 8. 8 discusses such intermediate positions of a continuously moving body—when he, for example, says that such a body is at such an intermediate position at a cut (262^{b}20-1) or that such a position is reached as a *telos* only potentially (262^{b}31-2)—he speaks of an 'indefinite', arbitrarily selected *meson*. In claiming that a continuously moving body is at such a position only potentially, he is simply saying that there is a legitimate sense of the modal 'could' for which it is true to say that the body *could* have stopped there but, in fact, did not. The consequence is that the doctrine of *Phys*. 6. 5—that, for a body to have moved, it already must have mov*ed* in the sense of having *completed* a distinct motion—no longer strictly holds. The body must have been *moving*; but according to the refinement of *Phys*. 8. 8, it did not *actually* arrive at (or depart from) any of these intermediate positions. So none of them marks the actual spatial *terminus ad quem* of the continuously moving body.

If (because of the infinite divisibility of time and spatial magnitude or distance) we were to speak of these intermediate positions of a continuously moving body as infinite in number, it would have to be 'infinite' in Aristotle's sense. The relevant sense in this context is the infinite with respect to division (*diairesis*): we have a finite distance that a continuously moving body has *actually* traversed; but it could have stopped there, or it could have stopped there, in between, etc., where the import of the 'etc.' is that the process of selecting another, distinct 'there' can always, in principle, be continued (beyond any finite number of steps). One might, in conformity with the terminology introduced earlier in Chapter 1, call this a sort of distributively dense conception of the positions (possible stopping-places) within a finite interval traversed by a continuously moving body. But I reiterate that Aristotle does not form a conception of such possible stopping-places as a collection of positions the instantaneous occupying of which might be identified with the continuous motion of the body.

Part of his objection derives from his strictures against a 'completed' infinity, i.e. treating an 'infinity' as a totality. But in this same chapter, *Phys*. 8. 8, Aristotle makes what Sorabji has characterized as a 'startling' and 'unexpected' concession in connection with his discussion of Zeno's Dichotomy paradox. In the case of the division of an interval (of spatial magnitude or time) into successive halves (i.e. [0,1/2], [1/2,3/4], etc. *ad infinitum*), Aristotle says that therefore it must be replied in answer to someone asking whether it is possible to traverse an infinity [of such halves] either in the case of time or in the case of length, that it is possible in one way but not in another. It is not possible [to traverse an infinity of such divisions] existing in actuality [*entelecheiai*], but it is possible [to traverse an infinity of such divisions existing] in potentiality. (263ᵇ3–6)

Sorabji comments that 'if [Aristotle] is to remain consistent, he needs to say in *Phys*. 8. 8 not merely that his divisions *exist* potentially (*dunamei onta*), but also that their *infinity* is potential as well (*dunamei apeira*), and that in the sense which I earlier defined of not being more than finite'.[52]

I suspect that if Aristotle is making a concession in this passage, it is a very small one. Immediately following the passage, Aristotle adds that 'the person who moves continuously has traversed an infinity [of distances] accidentally, but not unqualifiedly' (263ᵇ6–7). His point, I believe, is that, in a case of 'infinite division' such as the Dichotomy, one begins with a finite whole or totality (e.g. a finite distance or spatial magnitude) that is susceptible to a non-terminating process of division (e.g. halving). In traversing the given finite distance, one is traversing an infinity of distances (e.g. successive halves) 'accidentally' only in the sense that one is traversing a distance possessing the capacity or susceptibility to be subjected to a process of division that is infinite in Aristotle's 'constructive' sense: a process that can always, in principle, be carried a step beyond any finite number of steps.[53]

I do not think, therefore, that we find in *Phys*. 8. 8 any significant weakening of Aristotle's stricture against an actual or completed infinity.[54] This consequence, in itself, tells against any attempt to

---

[52] Sorabji, *Time, Creation and the Continuum*, 213.

[53] Of course, the claim that an infinity of runs is completed only in this potential sense apparently cannot be maintained for a staccato version of the Dichotomy, according to which the runner rests for a period of time equal to that which he takes to traverse 1/2 of the course, 1/4 of the course, 1/8 of the course, etc. The Dichotomy will receive further attention in Ch. 4.

[54] Where Aristotle *does* get into trouble, I think, is exactly where Philoponus says that he does. The fact that he holds that the cosmos has no beginnning in time suggests, as Philoponus claims, that there *has* been an infinite succession of days, generations of human beings, etc. up to the present time. See Philoponus *apud* Simplicius, *In phys.*, CAG 10, 1179. That is, it appears that such examples constitute totalities or actual/complete infinities of the order type (ω*) that is the inverse of that of the natural numbers. Simplicius interprets some remarks by Aristotle (as at *Phys*. 3. 6. 206ᵃ33–ᵇ3) as a sufficient answer to Philoponus: i.e. the elements of this supposed totality do not exist simultaneously and, hence, there is no such completed, infinite totality (*In phys.*, CAG 9, 506). Particularly in view of Aristotle's conception of the relative necessity and, it

identify motion with a body's being at different positions at different nows throughout some interval of time. However, a further consideration is the fact that such a collection of positions would have to be a *dense* linear array—unlike the positions of the Dichotomy (the 1/2 position, the 3/4 position, the 7/8 position, etc.), which are discretely ordered (i.e. each member that has a successor/predecessor has a unique successor/predecessor). As I argued in Chapter 1, there is reason to believe that Aristotle would have found the idea of a dense ordering of *actual* elements incoherent. Certainly, the definitions of *Phys*. 5. 3 entail that such a dense 'actual' ordering could never give rise to what is continuous. For continuity is defined as a species of contiguity, which, in turn, is a species of being 'in succession' (discretely ordered); but each element in a dense ordering has no predecessor or successor 'touching', contiguous to, or in succession to it. The one (distributive) sort of density that Aristotle *does* allow— which permits us always to fix a distinct position/point between two points/positions—is defined in terms of his conception of 'the infinite by division' as a non-terminating process. It is a process that necessarily cannot give rise to a 'totality' or 'completed' collection of elements.

Aristotle's *metaphysical* position, then, is in a certain sense even worse than Waterlow indicated in the passage quoted earlier. It seems clear that Aristotle would be unable to adopt an at-at ontology of locomotion according to which (continuous) motion *is* (essentially) an object's being in distinct positions at distinct instants throughout some interval of time (with, of course, some constraints on how the instants and positions pair up). The *very most* he could claim, I think, is that being in distinct positions at distinct instants (with the expected functional constraints on the pairing of instants and positions) is an accidental property of continuous locomotion. The relevant sense of 'accidental' is the *second* sense distinguished by Aristotle in *Meta*. 5. 30 (1025ª30–32), which parallels an account of a *proprium* (*idion*) specified in *Topics* 1. 5 (102ª18–19): a property which (i) is in some sense necessary to but (ii) is not a 'part' of, or does not manifest the essential nature of, the thing to which it belongs.[55]

appears, reality of the past, I do not find this response very compelling. I am inclined to think that these cases are not consistent with Aristotle's general strictures against infinite collections of elements. Cf. Sorabji, *Time, Creation and the Continuum*, 216–17.

[55] Of course, it is notoriously difficult to say just what the right sense of 'essential' is here. It does seem clear that it should be at least as strong as the notion of being

What is 'worse' about Aristotle's metaphysical position is that, according to this analysis, it is even more true that, for Aristotle, continuous locomotion is 'something of a mystery', to quote Waterlow.[56] The mystery, however, is entirely metaphysical or ontological. I hope that I was able to establish in Chapter 1 how closely Aristotle's formal, structural, or rational kinematic analysis of local motion agrees with the standard contemporary analysis. This agreement is impressive, I believe, despite the facts (i) that his analysis is expressed without the aid of the functional notation of calculus or real analysis and (ii) that he does not share the at–at ontology of motion or its nineteenth century set-theoretic underpinnings (both of which typically accompany the contemporary kinematic analysis of motion). In terms of the Aristotelian *metaphysical conception* of locomotion, one is left with the definitional formula of *Phys*. 3. 1 and, perhaps, the feeling that the concept of an actualization of a potential (of a body for resting at its *terminus ad quem*) *qua* that potential does capture within the Aristotelian metaphysical framework *something* of the nature of the continuous motion of a body to its *terminus ad quem*. However, whatever enlightenment the definition of *Phys*. 3. 1 offers, the appeal to 'actualization of a potential *qua* that potential' is not *kinematically* informative.

It is certainly possible to regard the abstract and kinematically uninformative character of Aristotle's attempts to characterize locomotion metaphysically as indicative of the shortcomings—perhaps remediable and perhaps not—of those attempts. Another viewpoint, however, is that Aristotle regarded *kinēsis*, pre-eminently exemplified by locomotion, as constituting a fundamental or close-to-fundamental ontological category. According to the latter view, it should be no surprise to find any possible metaphysical characterization of *kinēsis* abstract and kinematically uninformative.

This conception of *kinēsis* as ontologically fundamental or close-to-fundamental seems to me to be Aristotle's view, and to ground his anti-reductionism. By the thirteenth century the metaphysical analysis of motion had been more precisely developed. According to the *forma fluens* conception, motion is in the same ontological category as its *terminus*; in the case of local motion it is the continuous process of

predicable of every instance (*kata pantos*) discussed by Aristotle in *Analytica posteriora* 1. 4. 73ª28 ff. It is interesting to note that an example given by Aristotle is 'being contained in a line', which is predicated *kata pantos* of 'point'.

[56] Waterlow, *Nature, Change, and Agency*, 129.

attaining the spatial *terminus ad quem* of the moving body. Although the idea that the *terminus ad quem* of local motion is involved in the *definition* of that motion is an Aristotelian idea, and although Aristotle is sometimes cited as the proto-exponent of the *forma fluens* meta-physical model of motion, this model developed in a way that is quite un-Aristotelian. Nominalistic adherents of the *forma fluens* model, such as William of Ockham, decided that, since the *terminus* of motion is simply a positional state of the moving body and the motion itself belongs in the same ontological category as its perfection or *terminus*, the motion is to be identified with the positions of the moving body 'along the way' to its actual *terminus ad quem*.

The opposing, *fluxus formae* metaphysical model sharply distin-guishes the ontological status of the motion itself and that of the motion's *terminus*, regarding motion as a *qualitas* of the moving body—a quality subject to intension ('continuous increase') and remission ('continuous diminution'). The *fluxus formae* model, I believe, better captures the anti-reductionistic dimension of Aristotle's con-ception of motion. But it perhaps does not quite do justice to Aristotle's emphasis on the essential connection between motion and its actual *terminus ad quem*. I think that it must be admitted that Aristotle's own metaphysical conception of motion is in a more inchoate form than are these later scholastic models.

As we saw in Chapter 1, Aristotle proceeds, in the *Physics*, to a kinematic characterization of locomotion which—at least in its fundamentals—resembles a contemporary characterization. Without the aid of mathematical tools now regarded as essential for rigorously analysing the concept of continuous motion, Aristotle exhibits, it seems to me, a rather amazing 'intuitive grasp' of this concept. I am not suggesting that he never goes astray. For example, his readiness to equate a directional discontinuity with a pause in motion is an under-standable but unfortunate corollary of his analysis of the temporal limits or 'end-points' of stretches of motion. I also do not wish to give the impression that the mathematically grounded interpretation of Aristotle's kinematics in which I have engaged is, somehow, lying just beneath the surface of Aristotle's texts. What I do claim, however, is that such an interpretation can provide insight into Aristotelian kinematics and help to distinguish it from the underlying metaphysics.

It is clear that Aristotle's kinematic characterization of local motion is not regarded by him as a basis for a reductionistic ontological analysis of local motion: temporal stretches of continuous locomotion of a body are more ontologically real than the *instantaneous* position of a body. I shall suggest in Chapter 4 that it is only the development of the theory of transfinite sets in the latter half of the nineteenth century (along with the consequent point-set analysis of continuous magnitudes) that completes the transformation of the Aristotelian metaphysical undergirding of his kinematic analysis into the very un-Aristotelian at–at ontology of motion.

3

Aristotelian Kinematics and Non-Locomotive *Kinēseis*

I propose to consider in this rather brief chapter the extension of Aristotle's kinematic analysis of motion from the paradigm case of finite, bounded locomotion with definite, distinguishable *termini a quo* and *ad quem* to other sorts of *kinēsis*. From this examination I hope to be able to draw some conclusions concerning the basis of Aristotle's rational kinematics and metaphysics of motion—as well as the relation between his analysis of motion and his understanding of the way Greek verb aspect functions. The examination will focus, first, on circular or rotary motion as a cosmologically important special case of locomotion, next, on cases of change that apparently are *not kinēseis*, and, finally, on the kinematic characteristics of qualitative change or *alloiōsis*. I shall conclude the chapter with a summary of what I take to be particularly salient features of the discussion of Aristotle's physical theory that I have developed in this and in the preceding chapters.

ROTARY MOTION

In *Phys.* 8. 8 Aristotle adduces circular or rotary motion (*hē kuklōi kinēsis* or *phora*; *kuklophoria*) as a paradigm of continuous motion. In fact, he goes so far as to claim that 'with respect to no [motion] except the rotary is it possible to move continuously' (265ᵃ8–9). It is clear that this very restrictive and strong sense of 'continuously' implies not only continuity in Aristotle's kinematic sense, which was discussed in the two preceding chapters, but also eternity. It is *eternal* continuous motion, motion not punctuated by any discontinuities (in the form of pauses, according to Aristotle), that is continuous in the highest sense. Aristotle holds that motion that is continuous in this strong sense must be rotary motion. In fact, two of the kinematic 'mistakes' that we discussed in Chapter 1 occur in the course of Aristotle's attempt to rule out any non-rotary species of locomotion as possible candidates for continuous, eternal motion. Neither reversed rectilinear motion nor decelerating 'simple' rectilinear motion are continuous in the strong sense. In the first case, there must be a discontinuity (in the form of a pause, Aristotle believes), at the position(s) of reversal of motion. In the second case, it can take a continuously moving body only a finite amount of time to traverse a (*closed*) finite interval of distance; but the universe is of only finite rectilinear dimensions.

Our earlier discussion of these types of motion was cast largely in terms of the kinematics of the two cases. But, in the case of reversed rectilinear motion, Aristotle also considers an argument which he terms 'logical' (264ᵃ8) and which we might characterize as 'metaphysical'. The argument relies primarily on a metaphysical principle of continuous motion:

MPCM. Everything that is moving continuously . . . to where it comes as a result of that motion was formerly being borne to that very place; for example, if it comes to B it was being borne to B—and not just when it was close [to B], but straightaway as soon as it began to move. (264ᵃ9–13)

In the case of reversed rectilinear motion from A to Γ and back again to A, Aristotle maintains that MPCM entails (if the motion is continuous) that the body would have to undergo *simultaneously* the contrary motions of A to Γ and of Γ to A. Since this is impossible, he concludes by *reductio* that such reversed rectilinear motion cannot be continuous.

There seems, initially, to be a major problem lurking here. Circular motion appears as a perfect eternal exemplar of motion that is kinematically continuous: for each arc-interval of distance traversed there will be an interval of time such that, for any sub-interval of that time, the body will traverse a sub-distance of the given arc-interval in that sub-interval of time; and for any interval of time there will be an arc-interval such that, for any sub-distance of that arc-interval, that sub-distance will be traversed in a sub-interval of the given interval of time. However, in view of Aristotle's 'logical' or metaphysical principle MPCM, does it not follow that, for any two positions A and B in the circle traversed by a body undergoing continuous (and eternal) circular motion, the body is simultaneously moving from A to B and from B to A? And would this not constitute the very same sort of impossible simultaneous contrary motion that Aristotle believes he has located in the case of continuous reversed rectilinear motion?

Aristotle makes a valiant attempt to snatch victory from defeat. He begins by claiming that, in the case of circular motion, it is possible for a body to undergo simultaneously motion from position A and motion to position A 'with the same forward direction'.[1] He seems to go further at *De caelo* 1. 4. 271[a]19–22, suggesting that even circular motions in opposite directions (i.e. clockwise and counter-clockwise) are not contrary because (in 'completed' circular movements) they are both to and from the same place.[2] One wonders, however, why the same consideration would not undermine Aristotle's own argument that reversed rectilinear motion would involve the impossibility of simultaneous contrary motions. It seems that, in order both to maintain the MPCM and to prevent its application to circular or rotary motion in such a way as to show that such motion involves contrary motions, Aristotle must deny that any of the possible but not actual stopping-places of a body in continuous circular orbit are *actual termini* of the motion.

Such a move would accord with the general line on continuous motion taken by Aristotle in *Phys*. 8. 8, which we have previously discussed. And, indeed, we find Aristotle making this move in *Phys*. 8. 9:

Why should there be one limit rather than another on the [circular] line? For each [position or possible place] alike is beginning, middle, and end, so that [a body undergoing continuous circular/rotary motion] is always at the beginning and at the end and never there.   (265[a]32–[b]1)

The metaphysical problem that this move creates is fairly obvious. As Aristotle's paradigm of continuous locomotion, circular motion apparently cannot be given any teleological specification—even the *ex post facto* sort in terms of *actual termini a quo* and *ad quem*, which we invoked in the case of 'violent' or 'unnatural' rectilinear motion.

Aristotle has not entirely given up the game, however. I have thus far used both the adjectives 'circular' and 'rotary' in describing Aristotle's paradigm of continuous locomotion. The former term suggests, I think, a body moving in an orbit; there may be a centre of

---

[1] I follow Apostle's translation of *kata tēn autēn prothesin* here (*Aristotle's Physics*, 176). He understands the import of the phrase to be that 'the direction is always clockwise, or always counter-clockwise' (335, n. 59).

[2] Philoponus (*apud* Simplicius, *In Aristotelis de caelo commentaria*, ed. J. L. Heiberg, CAG 7 (Berlin, 1894), 189–90) takes vigorous exception to this argument. Fragments of Philoponus' influential treatise *De aeternitate mundi contra Aristotelem*, from which these objections come, have recently been collected in an English translation, with notes, by C. Wildberg, *Philoponus Against Aristotle, on the Eternity of the World* (London, 1987).

the circle described by the orbit, but the motion of the body may be conceived quite independently of anything else. The term 'rotary' suggests, on the other hand, a quite different picture: a sphere rotating about an axis is what immediately comes to mind. Although a fixed position on the surface of the sphere may describe a circular path, this motion is conceived in terms of, and taken to be dependent on the motion of the whole sphere. It is the picture of a rotating sphere to which Aristotle appeals in an attempt to retain the teleological component of his perfect form of locomotion. Since positions along the trajectory of a body in circular motion cannot serve this function, Aristotle turns to the centre of a (rotating) sphere (*Phys.* 8. 9. 265^{b}3–8):

For [the centre] is the beginning and the middle and the end of the interval of distance [*tou megethous*] [traversed in a situation of rotary motion]; consequently, since it is outside of the surface [of the sphere], it is not possible that there is a place that the moving body will rest as though it has arrived there (for it is always moving around the middle and not to an extreme position). On account, then, of [the centre's] remaining where it is, the whole is in one sense always at rest and [in another sense] always continuously moving.

Commentators, ancient and modern, have been uncertain concerning the import of Aristotle's claim concerning the centre's being the beginning (or *archē*), middle, and end of continuous circular or rotary motion; consequently, they have speculated freely on what this claim might amount to. For example, Ross (following Iamblichus) suggests that the centre may be the *archē* 'because the circle (or sphere) may be regarded as produced by the symmetrical fluxion from it in two (or three) dimensions'.[3] Aristotle *may* mean no more than that the centre of the sphere (or one entire diameter in cases where the axis of rotation remains constant) is the one part of the rotating sphere the distance to which remains constant *both* with respect to any fixed position not on the sphere *and* with respect to any fixed position on the rotating sphere. He may have taken the existence of such a *locus* as in some sense definitory of circular motion and, consequently, makes use of it to supply the 'missing' *termini* for 'strongly' (i.e. eternal) continuous motion.

It is perhaps worth noting that classical Newtonian kinematics makes essential reference to the centre of the circle in its description of circular locomotion. For example, in the case of circular motion, the 'position vector' describing the motion is typically (and naturally)

---

[3] Ross, *Aristotle's Physics*, 719.

thought of as rotating radius. And the limit concept of angular velocity ω of motion 'at an instant' is usually expressed in terms of radians per second or some related concept such as revolutions (circumferences) per minute. Aristotle's interest in the centre of rotation, however, does not seem to be kinematic. In fact, in one passage in *Phys.* 6. 10 he claims that, with respect to a rotating sphere, 'those [positions] near the centre and those at the surface and the whole [sphere] do not possess the same speed, so that there is not a single motion' (240^b15-17). The claim is not true for the classical modern concept of angular velocity, which is defined relative to the radius of rotation: there will be different radii for positions closer to and further away from the centre. But it is clear that what Aristotle has in mind is the *linear* distance of the arcs traversed at different positions in the same time; and, of course, this distance will be greater at positions further from the centre.

Aristotle's interest in circular motion seems largely metaphysical. He finds that, in order to preserve his metaphysical principle of continuous motion (MPCM above) and eternal circular motion as (paradigmatic) continuous motion, the *termini* of eternal continuous motion cannot be any (or all) of the instantaneous positions in the path of a body undergoing circular motion. A virtue of making the centre of rotation these *termini* is, as Aristotle says (265^b4), that they are outside (*eksō*) the path traversed by the body moving in a circle (or outside the path of a fixed position/body on the surface of a rotating sphere).

NON-KINETIC CHANGE

Aristotle's explicitly and repeatedly stated opinion is that there are forms of change (*metabolē*) that are not motions (*kinēseis*) in the broader sense of 'motion'—i.e. the sense which comprehends qualitative alteration, increase, and diminution, as well as locomotion. Consideration of several passages in which Aristotle discusses kinetic and non-kinetic changes suggests two fundamental features of his conception of *kinēsis*: (i) his conception of where one finds kinetic as opposed to non-kinetic change is heavily influenced by linguistic considerations, sc. the presence of verb forms characterized by semantically imperfective aspect; (ii) a picture, more or less literal, of what David Sherry has called the bounded 'path of change' also underlies Aristotle's conception of a *kinēsis*.

I am not particularly concerned with Aristotle's categorization of changes in *Meta*. 5. 1, in which generation and destruction are distinguished as non-kinetic forms of change. Rather, I am interested in two pictures of change. According to one, there is a continuous *kinēsis* temporally leading up to its *terminus* or completion, viz., a state or *energeia*. According to the second picture, there is no such process, but merely the event of the temporal inception of a *different* state or *energeia*.

In a difficult and much discussed chapter in the *Metaphysics — Meta*. 6. 9—Aristotle seems to attempt to explicate his notion of a *kinēsis* by means of what, from a contemporary perspective, might be called a linguistic criterion. Perhaps the linguistic basis of Aristotle's discussion in this chapter can be made most intelligible in terms of two semantic classes of Greek verbs distinguished by the linguist John Lyons.[4] There are 'action–event–state' verbs, in which the (imperfective) present tense is understood by Aristotle as connoting a kinetic process and the perfect-tense verb forms as connoting the state or denouement issuing from the event (often connoted by the aorist verb form) of the 'semantically successful' culmination of the kinetic process. On the other hand, there are 'event–state' verbs in which there is simply an event (typically connoted by the aorist) initiating a state connoted by either present or perfect verb forms.[5]

Aristotle, it seems, connects *kinēseis* particularly with the verb forms of Lyons' action–event–state verbs (or the action verbs of K. L. McKay) which contemporary linguists characterize by the phrase 'imperfective aspect' and which some ancients characterized by the term *paratatikos*. Imperfective aspect is characterized by McKay as 'present[ing] action as going on, in process, without reference to its completion'.[6] The *paratatikos*—which represents half of what seems to have been the fundamental Stoic system of aspectual contrariety, the *paratatikos/ suntelikos* or *suntelestikos* distinction[7]—was applied both to the imperfect and to the present tenses. *Paratatikos* connotes not only the

---

[4] *Structural Semantics: An Analysis of Part of the Vocabulary of Plato* (Oxford, 1972), 114–15.

[5] Lyons's distinction between action–event–state and event–state verbs is somewhat similar to McKay's distinction between action verbs and state verbs. Verbs of the latter category he characterizes as being 'essentially concerned with activities which are, or are very like, states of being' (K. L. McKay, *Greek Grammar for Students: A Concise Grammar of Classical Attic with Special Reference to Aspect in the Verb* (Canberra, 1977), 138).

[6] Ibid. 138.

[7] K. Schoepsdau, 'Zur Tempuslehre des Apollonius Dyskolos', *Glotta*, 56 (1978), 273–94; C H. M. Versteegh, 'The Stoic Verbal System', *Hermes*, 108 (1980), 338–57.

idea of processual duration but also, according to the *scholia* on Dionysius Thrax's *Ars grammatica*, the idea of incompleteness.[8] Aristotle's metaphysical/linguistic intuitions lead him, it seems, to find *kinēseis* beneath the imperfective or *paratatika* forms of action–event– state verbs, in which there is a clear semantic distinction between the process leading up to a resultant state of affairs and the resultant state itself. The sort of incompleteness that Aristotle in *Meta.* 9. 6 attributes to *kinēseis* is captured by the following considerations: from the fact that *x* is walking (*badizei*) [to somewhere specific] it follows that he has not walked (*bebadiken*) there; from the fact that *x* is building a house (*oikodomei*) it follows that he has not built [is not in the state of having completed the building of] that house (*ōikodomēken*); from the fact that something *x* is coming-to-be (*gignetai*), it follows that it has not come-to-be (*gegonen*); and from the fact that *x* is moving (*kineitai*) somewhere it follows that it has not yet moved (*kekinēken*) to that place (1048[b]31–3).

Event–state verbs, however, seem to supply Aristotle with at least one important source of non-kinetic change. Thus, when someone is in the 'act' of comprehending (*noei*: present, (pseudo)imperfective), he is at the same time in the state of comprehension (*nenoēken*: perfect) (1048[b]24). In such a case, there is no real distinction between the 'act' of comprehending and the state of comprehension. A person may have attained this state by the event of grasping or coming to comprehend (*enoēse*: aorist); but there is no imperfective *process* of comprehending that is incomplete in the sense that the state of comprehension is yet to be achieved while that process is going on. McKay comments that the syntactic 'perfect of such verbs has a meaning which to our eyes seems very similar to that of the [syntactic] imperfective'.[9] And so it also seems 'to the eyes of Aristotle'. The consequence at the meta- physical level is that, with respect to such event–state verbs, *kinēseis* tend to disappear.

One of the two examples of non-kinetic change adduced by Aristotle in *De caelo* 1. 11 seems nicely to exemplify the linguistic model of such change. Perhaps not coincidentally, it is an example that apparently was also used by Diodorus Cronus to illustrate his doctrine that *all* change is non-kinetic, a doctrine that we shall examine further

---

[8] See ibid. 342.

[9] McKay, *Greek Grammar*, 223–4. McKay believes, however, that for such verbs there typically are some subtle differences between present (grammatically imperfective) and perfect forms.

in Part II of this book. The example is that of touching or being in contact with (*haptesthai*), which is used by Aristotle to illustrate the following sense of the adjective 'ungenerated' (*agenēton*): something that now exists but formerly did not—but without there having been coming-into-being or generation (*geneseōs*) or change (*metabolēs*)—is said to be 'ungenerated' (280ᵇ7-8). At least in its middle or middle-passive sense of 'to touch' or 'to be in contact with', the verb *haptein* seems to exhibit the semantic form of event–state. Thus, the event of touching (aorist: *hapsasthai*) initiates both the activity of touching (present, (pseudo)perfective: *haptesthai*) and the (indistinguishable) state of touching or being in contact with (perfect: *hēpsthai*). There seems to be no imperfective, incomplete *kinēsis* of 'being partially but not fully in contact with'.

This linguistically based intuition is fortified, in Aristotle's case, by his formal analysis of touching in terms of 'extremities being together' (*Phys*. 5. 3. 226ᵇ23; *GC* 1. 6. 323ᵃ4). Since the extremities are limits of bodies, either these are together or they are not: there are no (continuous) degrees of being in contact which would permit one body gradually to *become* increasingly in contact with another until it is fully in contact with it. According to an Aristotelian doctrine enunciated in *Meta*. 3. 5 that we have previously discussed, the coming into contact of two bodies results in the destruction of a 'limit entity' (point, line, or surface) at the juncture of contact: where there were previously two such limit entities there is now but one, but neither limit entity has been the subject of any *process* of destruction (*to phtheiresthai*).[10]

Aristotle's other example in *De caelo* 1. 11 of 'ungenerated' change initially seems quite puzzling: it is moving (*to kineisthai*) itself. Clearly, *kineisthai* is a (paradigmatic) action–event–state verb. The semantics of the verb envisages an *atelēs*, imperfective process of changing (*to kineisthai*) to F issuing in the separate state of having changed to (*to kekinēsthai*), i.e. resting *at*, F. Of course, in the passage from *De caelo*, Aristotle says only that 'some' adduce the examples of touching and moving as illustrations of 'ungenerated' existence and non-existence. So we are not guaranteed that Aristotle himself accepts these as genuine examples. However, the example of touching fits so well his own conception, developed elsewhere, of what happens when two bodies come into contact that it seems reasonable to search for some Aristotelian sense in which motion might be said to be ungenerated.

---

[10] 1002ᵃ29–ᵇ11. Aristotle employs this account of non-kinetic 'generation' and 'destruction' of limit entities as an argument for their non-substantial ontological status.

First of all, it is clear that Aristotle does not wish to deny (as Diodorus does deny) that the *state* of having moved (*to kekinēsthai*) is imperfectively generated by a distinct process of moving (*to kineisthai*). Rather, it seems more likely that Aristotle's intent is to deny that the imperfective process or *kinēsis* of moving (*to kineisthai*) is itself the result of an imperfective process of generation. Perhaps most relevant to this point are Aristotle's arguments in *Phys*. 5. 2 that there cannot be 'change of change' (*kinēseōs kinēsis*) or a 'coming-to-be of coming-to-be' (*geneseōs genesis*). The doctrine that Aristotle there develops might be characterized as follows: while there certainly can be a coming-to-be or *genesis* of what has come-to-be or is (*to gegonēmenon* or *to gegōs*), there cannot be a *genesis* of the coming-to-be (*to gignesthai*) itself. The arguments he produces for this view are thoroughly metaphysical; that is, they go far beyond any straightforward linguistic considerations pertaining to verb aspect. And this is, in Aristotle's case at least, typical. Although he may begin with considerations of linguistic usage—and such considerations may serve as a controlling principle in his philosophical development of a topic—his philosophical analysis seldom fails to take him beyond such considerations.

One point where Aristotle seems to go beyond linguistic usage is in his development of a fundamental metaphysical component of his conception of *kinēsis*: a bounded 'path' of motion. This notion of a bounded path of motion supplies him with the raw material, so to speak, for his kinematic analysis of motion that we have previously discussed. It is this path or stretch of motion, for example, that is continuous, infinitely divisible, etc. It is also the concept of such a path of motion that helps to explain, I believe, some of the claims Aristotle makes concerning *kinēseis* as opposed to non-kinetic forms of change. Three of these claims are the following: (i) 'with respect to things of which there are no contraries (*enantia*), there is opposite change (*metabolē*) from the thing and to the thing—e.g. from being and to being—but not a *kinēsis*; and of such things there is no 'remaining' (*monē*), but only absence of change (*ametablēsia*)' (*Phys*. 5. 6. 230ª7–10); (ii) but a change (*metabolē*) that is only to some contrary [and not also explicitly from a contrary]—e.g. becoming white, but not from some [specified] state—is not a *kinēsis* (*Phys*. 5. 5. 229ᵇ10–11); (iii) in cases of *kinēsis* to (or from) an intermediate between contraries, 'the *kinēsis* makes use of the intermediate as a contrary in whichever direction the change occurs; e.g. [change] from grey to white [occurs] as if from black', etc. (*Phys*. 5. 5. 229ᵇ14–22).

The first of these claims emphasizes the importance of a pair of boundaries or limits, supplied by the contraries, to Aristotle's conception of a path of change. The contraries delimit the path of *kinēsis*. And, I think, Aristotle has in mind the sense of *enantion* (from e.g. *Categoriae* 10) that implies a middle (*meson*) between the contraries and that, consequently, allows for something to be neither (fully) in one contrary state or condition nor in the other. In other words, this is the space between the two limits of the path. The second claim emphasizes the necessity of a path that is bounded in *both* directions. Thus, while there may be a *change* of becoming white, in order for this change to be conceptualized as a *kinēsis*, a process or motion, it must be conceived as a path *from* some determinate state *to* the state of being white. This consideration supplies obvious additional support for Waterlow's suggestion that 'kinetic status varies with description'.[11] And, clearly, the conception of *kinēsis* underlying the claim goes far beyond the simple pairing of *kinēseis* with imperfective (present or imperfect) forms of action–event–state verbs. Finally, the last claim represents a principle of divisibility of *kinēseis*: by choosing a 'position' (e.g. grey) within a kinetic path (e.g. from black to white) and letting that position serve as a boundary or limit, it is possible to define another possible *kinēsis* (from grey to white) that corresponds to a kinetic proper segment of the original *kinēsis*. It is particularly this feature of Aristotle's 'path of motion' picture that underlies the bulk of his kinematic analysis of motion, which we discussed earlier, and that leads to his non-supervenience of motion (N-SK) principle.

As David Sherry points out, the picture of a path of motion seems particularly applicable to locomotion, the variety of *kinēsis* that is the principal object of Aristotle's kinematic refinement of the picture:

Locomotion fits admirably the paradigm of the geometric line [i.e. the geometric line-segment as a paradigm of a bounded, continuous path] since the path along which locomotion occurs is just a spatial magnitude; growth and diminution, too, fit the paradigm since a growing body, or point of a growing body, traces out a spatial path. The path of qualitative change, say from white to black, is a rather different case, though. The 'distance' from white to black seems to be nothing more than a metaphor, since there is no natural metric available for such qualities.[12]

---

[11] Waterlow, *Nature, Change, and Agency*, 128.
[12] 'On Instantaneous Velocity', *History of Philosophy Quarterly*, 3: 4 (1986), 395.

It is certainly true that, as we saw in connection with Aristotle's discussion in *Phys*. 4. 11 of the relations among spatial magnitude, time, and motion, he tends to regard the continuity of the spatial path of a moving body as essential to (a necessary condition of?) the continuity of the body's motion and of the time-interval within which it moves. It is to be noted, however, that there is even a difficulty in what seems to be the literal sense in which continuous locomotion exemplifies the picture of a kinetic path. The difficulty is that, at least in the case of bounded 'violent' or 'unnatural' motion, the *termini a quo* and *ad quem* are not, in any obvious Aristotelian sense, contraries of each other. Despite this difficulty, I think that Sherry is correct in his suggestions that what grounds the schematic picture of a path of motion is the geometrical picture of a line-segment and that this geometrical picture is largely responsible for setting the terms of Aristotle's kinematic analysis of motion. The question that Sherry is primarily interested in, and to which we next turn, is how this picture gets extended by Aristotle to qualitative *kinēsis* or *alloiōsis*.

QUALITATIVE *KINĒSIS*

In what sense is qualitative change continuous? Sherry provides a cogent answer to this question:

The model Aristotle had in mind is that qualitative change consists in a quality's spreading gradually [i.e. continuously] over a surface. The appropriateness of this model is buttressed by the recognition that there are only finitely many discriminable changes in qualitative change (*De sensu* 445^{b}21-29 and 446^{a}16-20). Thus the suggestion that the path of qualitative change is a continuum of qualitative states is quite foreign to Aristotle, and the path of qualitative change, as far as Aristotle was concerned, is indeed spatial . . . . On the other hand, we operate with two senses of 'the path of qualitative change.' One path is continuous and corresponds to the *extension* of a quality within a subject. The other path, though not recognized as such by Aristotle, corresponds to the *intension* of a quality . . . . The 'path' of intension is not continuous by Aristotle's own criterion and is therefore not really a path at all. It is the modern mind that sees such a path.[13]

Sherry's contention is that, for Aristotle, the only sense in which qualitative change can be said to be continuous is the sense in which a

---

[13] Ibid. 395-6.

quality comes to be possessed by a 'continuously greater spatial area' (e.g. surface area, in the case of colour) of its subject. Aristotle clearly suggests such a view in *Phys.* 6. 9 (240ª23-6). Elsewhere in his discussions of qualitative change it is perhaps not always so clear what his view is.[14] The *De sensu* passage seems to me to be particularly problematic.

Aristotle claims at *De sensu* 6. 445ᵇ22-3 that the 'species [or kinds: *eidē*] of colour, flavour, sound, and other sensibles are limited [or finite: *peperantai*]'. He then proceeds:

What is continuous is divisible into an infinite number of unequal parts, but only into a finite number of equal parts; and what is not essentially [*kath' hauto*] continuous [is divisible into] a finite number of kinds [*eidē*]. Since, then, the qualities [*pathē*] may be spoken of as 'kinds' and continuity always pertains to them, it is necessary to understand that the potential and the actual are different. On account of this, when a millet grain is observed, the ten-thousandth part escapes notice even though vision has covered it, and pitch in the interval between notes escapes notice even though one hears the entire musical phrase, which is continuous. The interval, that which is between the extremes, escapes notice. Similarly for very small parts of other sensible things. They are visible potentially, but not actually when they are not separated out. The one-foot length exists potentially in the two-foot length, but in actuality only when it has already been divided. When separated out, small increments might reasonably be [regarded as] dispersed into their surroundings, just as the bit of flavour is destroyed in the sea. But since the increment of sensation is not perceptible in itself nor separable (for the increment exists potentially in what is, more precisely speaking, [perceptible?]), so neither will it be possible actually to sense such a small sensible object when it is separated. But it will nevertheless be sensible since it already potentially is [sensible] and will be [sensible] in actuality when it is aggregated [with other such small quantities]. It has been stated, then, that some magnitudes and qualities escape notice, and what the cause of this is, and in what sense they are sensible and in what sense not. Whenever some of these are present in such a way as to be actually sensible— not just in the whole but in separation—it is necessary that their colours, flavours, and sounds be finite in number. (445ᵇ27-446ª20)

I have quoted at length from *De sensu* 6 because of the difficulty of the passage. What is Aristotle's point here? He has sometimes been understood to be contrasting spatial magnitude (*megethos*) and qualities

---

[14] For a general discussion of problems concerning the relation between the Aristotelian conception of *alloiōsis* and other aspects of Aristotle's physical theory, see G. R. Morrow, 'Qualitative Change in Aristotle's *Physics*', in I. Düring (ed.), *Naturphilosophie bei Aristoteles und Theophrast* (Heidelberg, 1969), 154-67.

(*pathē*) in something like the following way: while the transition that is locomotion is essentially a continuous path of motion connecting the *termini a quo* and *ad quem*, there are only a finite number of qualities between two contrary qualities (e.g. between black and white). Consequently, there cannot be an essentially or '*kath' hauto*' continuous transition from one such quality to another; rather, such a transition must come *epheksēs*—in discrete stages. While such an interpretation probably cannot definitely be ruled out, there seems to me to be little in the passage to support it.

To begin with, there is no apparent opposition between spatial magnitude and qualities in the passage; Aristotle evidently means his claims to apply to both alike.[15] These claims are, I believe, the following. When we attempt to divide up a kinetic path and separate out discrete, discriminable stages of the *kinēsis* in question, we shall be able to discriminate only a finite number of such stages. When, for example, we attempt to separate out and distinguish the distinct shades or *eidē* of grey that something passes through in changing from black to white, or the distinct notes produced 'as a stopper is moved along a vibrating string'[16] from one position to another, we shall be able to discern only a finite number of distinguishable shades and notes.

[15] In several places (e.g. *Historia animalium* 8. 1. 588^{b}4–16) Aristotle does speak of continuity (*sunecheia*) with respect to biological kinds. Herbert Granger ('The *Scala Naturae* and the Continuity of Kinds', *Phronesis*, 30: 2 (1985), 181–200) has distinguished 3 senses of continuity that might be invoked in this context. What he terms 'dense continuity' requires that kinds form a dense series: 'given any two kinds, A and B, a third kind C can always be distinguished between them in the series' (183). It seems that the series Granger has in mind would actually be, mathematically, a pre-ordering in terms of some such notion as similarity. (A *pre*-ordering because of the fact that it seems possible for there to be distinct kinds A and B that are equally similar to a 'reference' kind C; i.e. the similarity relation is not anti-symmetrical.) And Granger envisions a situation in which it is true, for any A and B, that there is a distinct C such that C is more similar to A than is B. In order to get continuity in the mathematical sense, another condition capturing Dedekind continuity would be required: if for a set Γ of kinds, there is a kind B such that for each $A \in \Gamma$, A is more similar to C than is B, then there is a 'least upper bound' for the set Γ—i.e. a kind D such that every A in Γ is at least as similar to C as is D and for which it is true that if any E also satisfies this condition (every A in Γ is at least as similar to C as is E), E is identical to D.

Granger prudently decides that it is unlikely that Aristotle has any such set-theoretic account of continuity (which requires an infinite number of actual kinds) in mind. What remains are 2 other senses of continuity. 'Strong continuity' would be modelled on Aristotle's formal account of continuity in the *Physics*—but without a set-theoretic ontology of kinds. When we sort individual organisms into kinds, any 2 adjacent kinds that we might distinguish will have a common boundary. The force of the common-boundary metaphor seems to be that individual organisms at the very fringes of a kind A will also be members ('at the very fringes') of an adjacent kind B. Granger rejects this interpretation in favour of a 3rd possibility, which he terms 'weak continuity'. In

It is the process of separating out that produces the shades from colour and the notes from sound as *actual* kinds or *eidē* of colour and sound, respectively. This process of separating out is also responsible for the finitude of kinds of colour and of sound. But an entirely analogous phenomenon apparently obtains in the case of continuous *magnitudes*. When we attempt to separate out and distinguish, say, sensible parts of a continuous, homeomerous thing or 'stuff', we shall be able to distinguish by sensible means only a finite number of such parts; and if we attempt to distinguish (possible) positions of a body continuously traversing a finite spatial distance, we shall be able to distinguish by sensible means only a finite number of these.

Does such a consideration mean that there cannot, strictly speaking, be a continuous transition from black through grey to white or from one note of the scale to a higher one? Not at all. What it *does* mean is that, for Aristotle, a continuous *path*, whether of magnitude or quality, is not to be identified with an ordered array or *series*—even a dense and Dedekind-continuous ordered series—of distinct stages. It is possible that the continuity of qualitative change is, as both Sherry and Sorabji have suggested, dependent on some continuous change involving magnitude. Sorabji, for example, understands Aristotle as classifying, at *De sensu* 6. 445^{b}28–30, qualitative change as being 'what is not in itself (i.e. essentially) continuous' (*to de mē kath' hauto sunechēs*), and evidently understands this phrase as connoting a sort of derivative or incidental (*kata sumbebēkos*) continuity. He proceeds to suggest that a '*continuous* movement of a stopper along a vibrating string' is responsible for 'a change to the next discriminable pitch, in the *discontinuous* series of discriminable pitches', and that 'in the case of colour, a change to the next discriminable shade, in the *discontinuous* series of discriminable shades .. may be produced by a *continuous* change in the proportions of earth, air, fire and water in a body'.[17] Although Aristotle does not actually make these claims in the passage, Sorabji's ingenious hypo-

this case there apparently would be a mathematically *discrete* pre-ordering of a finite number of kinds in terms of a notion of relative similarity; but there would be only small differences between 'successive' kinds so (pre-)ordered. This is such a loose sense of 'continuous' that it has nothing to do with continuity either in the contemporary mathematical sense nor, so far as I can tell, in Aristotle's technical sense. Although I find Granger's argumentation persuasive, I myself am not quite certain that Aristotle is not appealing to 'strong continuity' here. But it is *certainly* the case, as Granger notes, that Aristotle cannot be appealing to a set-theoretic notion of continuity involving a 'dense(pre-)ordering' of an infinity of actual kinds.

[16] The example is borrowed from Sorabji, 'Aristotle on the Instant of Change', 80.
[17] Ibid.

thesis as to what Aristotle *would* say about the underlying 'causal' processes of these changes may well be correct.

My suggestion, however, is that a discontinuous series arises only as a result of the process of attempting to separate out stages of a continuous process as distinct *eidē*—e.g. to separate out musical notes from the continuous 'matter' of sound or shades from the 'matter' of colour. Indeed, the very act of discriminating is a separating out, in this sense. Aristotle's text, I believe, at least leaves open the possibility of the following picture of qualitative change. There can be, say, a continuous gradation of colour from black to white. I have in mind a perfect version of the sort of graduated wash that one practises in a beginning class in water-colour painting. When we attempt to separate out discrete shades of grey in this continuous gradation, we shall be able to distinguish only a finite number of shades. Furthermore, precisely where we draw the boundaries between shades will be to a degree arbitrary; and there will be some insensible gradation of colour within each of the shades that we have distinguished. The principal moral to be gleaned from Aristotle's discussion in *De sensu* 6 of qualitative change is, I believe, that he does not conceive of continuity in terms of what might be called a set-theoretic ontology, e.g. as a dense and Dedekind-continuous linear ordering of discrete actual elements. Aristotle's ontology of the continuous is just the converse. What is fundamental is the continuous thing: the motion or the magnitude or the interval of sound of varying pitch. We can then distinguish or separate out parts, or positions, or qualitative *eidē*. But there are limitations to this process. There will be at most a finite number of such stages of *kinēsis* that can be actually discriminated by means of sensation; and, consequently, these stages must be discretely (successively) ordered. Even the theoretical infinite divisibility of spatial magnitude, time, or locomotion means simply, for Aristotle, that the *process* of division could always, in theory, be taken a step further than any finite number of divisions: this process does not yield a completed infinite totality of stages that can be identified with the magnitude, the time, or the locomotion in question.

AFTERWORD

Since the topic of the next chapter is the relation between Aristotle's physical and mathematical ideas, on the one hand, and ancient and modern mathematical developments, on the other, there is a bit of false advertising in the heading of this section: I have not yet finished with Aristotle or his physical theory. Nevertheless, it seems an appropriate place to underline what I take to be particularly significant features of the discussion, in this and the preceding chapters, of Aristotle's conception of *kinēsis*. Starting with a concept of process implicit in the system of Greek verb aspect, viz., in imperfective forms of action–event–state verbs, Aristotle proceeds to refine his analysis of *kinēsis*, an analysis which, for the most part, takes locomotion to be paradigmatic. Elements of this analysis that are, from the contemporary perspective, metaphysical or ontological and elements that are kinematic are closely interwoven. The picture of a path of motion, bounded at both ends, gives rise to the concept of a continuous locomotion, bounded by pauses or periods of rest at beginning and end. As we saw, the resulting kinematic conception of locomotion as continuous and infinitely divisible is strikingly similar to the standard contemporary kinematic conception. For example, the continuity of the function from time elapsed to distance traversed is implicit in Aristotle's principles of relative speed.

Despite this similarity to the standard contemporary kinematic analysis, Aristotle does not share the at–at ontology of motion. This metaphysical conception virtually requires—if motion is to be regarded as continuous—the set-theoretic analysis of motion in terms of sets of temporal instants and of spatial positions, both characterized by (non-denumerably) infinite cardinality and by linear orderings that are dense and Dedekind-continuous. Neither Aristotle nor (as I shall argue in the next chapter) the ancient mathematical tradition has the requisite mathematical concepts. For Aristotle, infinite divisibility is to be understood in terms of his own notion of infinity—here, division that can always, in principle, be taken a step further—rather than in terms of the density of actual, instantaneous positions of a moving body. And, as I shall further argue in the next chapter, something *superficially* very close to Dedekind continuity is implicit in Aristotle's formal conception of continuity in terms of a 'shared boundary'. The metaphysical upshot is that, for Aristotle, *kinēsis*—and, in the particular case, *phora* or locomotion—is ontologically prior to the instantaneous positions or possible but not actual stopping-places of the body undergoing the locomotion. There is no question of the ontological construction of continuous motion out of a collection of instantaneous positions of the continuously moving body.

In view of the fact that Aristotle would claim that only a finite number of such positions can be distinguished by sensation in any finite path of locomotion, a question arises pertaining to the basis of his commitment to the 'infinite divisibility' of locomotion (and of spatial magnitude and time). I shall suggest, again in the next chapter, that ancient mathematical practice is a plausible place to look for an answer to this question. More generally, I believe that the relation between Aristotle's analysis of time, spatial magnitude, and motion and mathematical considerations, both ancient and modern, is a topic worthy of further consideration.

4

Aristotle and the Mathematicians, Ancient and Modern

According to one popular tradition, a tradition that emphasizes the rational, system-building character of Plato's thought and the empirical, nature-investigating character of Aristotle's thought, Aristotle was markedly lacking in mathematical sophistication as well as in interest in mathematical issues. One might reasonably infer, from the more extreme versions of this view, that Aristotle (who spent twenty years in Plato's Academy) was granted a special exemption from the requirement that Plato, according to legend, set up in front of his school: *ageōmetrētos mēdeis eisitō* ('Let no one who is not geometrically minded enter').[1] However, another tradition pictures Aristotle, largely through his doctrine of the infinite but also through his philosophy of mathematics and general theory of scientific methodology, as a sort of *arbiter mathematicae*.

Not surprisingly, the truth probably lies somewhere between these two extremes. With respect to the former tradition, Aristotle's conception of mathematics certainly does differ from that of Plato: it is perhaps not unfair to say that he envisions a rather less exalted and comprehensive role for mathematical science than does Plato. And his doctrine of seeking only that degree of precision of which the subject-matter admits[2] naturally leads to caution with respect to the use of mathematical models in the explanation of phenomena. We would not, for example, expect to find Aristotle suggesting—even in jest—that the life of the person with a kingly, just soul is 729 times more pleasurable than the life of the person with a tyrannical, unjust soul.[3] On the other hand, while there is no evidence that Aristotle was a creative

---

[1] The legends pertaining to such an inscription are thoroughly discussed in D. H. Fowler, *The Mathematics of Plato's Academy: A New Reconstruction* (Oxford, 1987), 197 ff.

[2] *Ethica Nicomachea* 1. 3. 1094ᵇ11 ff.

[3] See Plato, *Republic* 9. 587b–e. Of course, it is generally true that few thigh-slappers are to be found in the Aristotelian corpus.

practising mathematician, there also is no evidence of mathematical illiteracy on his part. Indeed, particularly when he is dealing with physical topics, his use of mathematical considerations generally seems to be well-informed and to the point and his mathematical observations astute. In fact, in this chapter I shall hypothesize that some fundamental theoretical features of his physics derive from geometrical considerations.

The latter tradition, which pictures Aristotle as a mathematical arbiter, is more difficult to assess. For example, it is undeniable that Aristotle's conception of the infinite, set forth in the third book of the *Physics* and, for the most part, rigorously adhered to by Aristotle elsewhere, has had and continues to have great influence.[4] What is far less certain is the relation between this conception and ancient mathematical theory and practice. It may be virtually impossible to come to any very firm *historical* conclusions concerning this issue. But in the next section, I examine some *conceptual* issues pertaining to the relation between Aristotle's physical/mathematical thought and ancient mathematics.

ARISTOTLE AND ANCIENT MATHEMATICS

On what basis does Aristotle attribute various formal, structural properties—in particular, his version of infinite divisibility—first to spatial magnitude and then to time and locomotion? This question is particularly pointed because of the claim in *De sensu* 6 (which is entirely consonant with Aristotle's general theory of the 'infinite by division') that when we attempt *actually* to distinguish by sensation

---

[4] In contemporary mathematics, the Aristotelian influence (in some cases obviously mediated through Immanuel Kant) is often detectable in the so-called 'intuitionistic' tradition. Witness the following passage from M. A. E. Dummett, *Intuitionistic Mathematics and Logic*, pt. i (Oxford Mathematical Institute mimeo, 1974), 3: 'In intuitionistic mathematics, all infinity is potential infinity; there is no completed infinity. This means, simply, that to grasp an infinite structure is to grasp the process which generates it; to recognise it as infinite is to recognise that the process is such that it will not terminate. In the case of a process that terminates, we may legitimately distinguish between the process itself and its completed output: we may be presented with the structure that is generated, without knowing anything about the process of generation. But, in the case of an infinite structure, no such distinction is possible: all that we can, at any given time, know of the output is some finite initial segment of it. There is no sense in which we can have any conception of the structure as a whole save that we know the process by which it is generated.'

parts of something, there will be only a finite number so distinguishable. A large part of the answer, I suspect, lies in the influence of geometry on Aristotle. In *De caelo* he claims that the postulation of a smallest magnitude (*elachiston megethos*) would disturb (*kinēseie*) mathematics (1. 5. 271ᵇ10–12) and that the postulation of indivisible bodies (*atoma sōmata*) would be at odds with (*machesthai*) the mathematical sciences (3. 4. 303ᵃ20–21). I believe that Fred Miller is correct in his suggestion that atomist commitment to *elachista megethē* is Aristotle's 'main objection to the atomic theory'.[5] While Aristotle also complains in the passage from *De Caelo* 3. 4 that the postulate of indivisible bodies offends against what the senses seem to tell us as well as against accepted opinions (*endoxa*) and adds a physical argument against indivisibles, the argument 'from mathematics' seems to be Aristotle's strongest suit, as I suspect he himself was well aware.

What alternative to the postulation of least magnitudes is there if not some version of *to apeiron kata diairesin*, 'the infinite with respect to division'? An examination of the ancient geometrical treatment of this notion indicates, I shall argue, how closely Aristotle's general, philosophical account of *to apeiron* in this sense parallels geometrical practice. I use the verb 'parallels' here in order to avoid the issue of 'direction' of historical influence: was Aristotle's general account largely shaped by contemporary geometrical practice or did ancient geometers devise methods of proof (in particular, the so-called 'method of exhaustion') in adherence to the general strictures of Aristotle concerning *to aperion kata diairesin*?

In a very interesting essay, Wilbur Knorr suggests that the former is more likely to have been the direction of the influence than the latter.[6] Knorr argues (*a*) that the geometrical development of the method of exhaustion (about which more later) was largely autonomous, the result of a process of refinement of 'techniques employed by predecessors such as Hippocrates of Chios';[7] (*b*) that it is 'more plausible to view Aristotle's discussions in the *Physics* as an effort to *save* the infinite, in the face of a movement among geometers of his day to give up that concept'[8] than to suppose that the geometrical tradition was greatly influenced by Aristotle's discussion; (*c*) that, although it is clear that Aristotle was influenced, to a degree, by geometrical considerations in his physical

---

[5] 'Aristotle against the Atomists', 100.
[6] 'Infinity and Continuity', 112–45.
[7] Ibid. 143; cf. 135.
[8] Ibid. 121.

discussions, such influence was superficial and largely ineffective on account of Aristotle's lack of mathematical sophistication.[9] Consequently, according to Knorr, 'Aristotle's theory of the infinite shows remarkable insensitivity to the issues which must have occupied the geometers of his generation'.[10]

Of these theses, (*a*) and (*b*), at least if qualified a bit, have much to be said for them. The internal dialectic of ancient mathematics (i.e. the consequences of the developmental forces internal to the practice of ancient mathematics) has not always been sufficiently appreciated, and Knorr's work contributes significantly to correcting this situation. However, as the 'Platonic' metaphysics of Georg Cantor's *Grundlagen einer allgemeinen Mannigfaltigkeitslehre* illustrates, technical developments in mathematics can certainly be influenced by external, even philosophical concerns. There is no reason to think that the development of ancient mathematics was *exclusively* an autonomous affair, a matter of the card-carrying members of the club sorting things out among themselves over cigars and brandy, so to speak. (*b*) also seems to be a plausible suggestion. It is likely that there has been a degree of philosophers' *hubris* involved in the development of the picture of Aristotle (or Plato or Zeno of Elea) as an *arbiter geometricae*; on the other hand, the role of geometrical theory and practice on Aristotle's thought has not been adequately appreciated. None of this entails, however, the impossibility of influence in *both* directions. For example, it is possible to see Aristotle as canonizing for geometry views that he originally developed on the basis of geometrical influence.

It seems to me that (*c*), however, is at best an overstatement, although its place in the dialectic of Knorr's arguments is clear. If (*c*) were true, such mathematical incompetence on Aristotle's part would tend to support (*a*) and at least the latter part of (*b*) by making it unlikely that Aristotle would have been taken seriously enough to compromise the autonomy of development of ancient mathematics. As I previously mentioned, we have no reason to believe that Aristotle (or Plato, for that matter) was a creative practising mathematician. Not

[9] Knorr comments more than once on the imprecision (119) and 'awkwardness' (120, 122) of Aristotle's 'technical discussions' which employ mathematical principles. For a very different impression of Aristotle's mathematical competence see P. Feyerabend, 'Some Observations on Aristotle's Theory of Mathematics and of the Continuum', *Midwest Studies in Philosophy*, 8 (1983), 78: 'Aristotle was the foremost mathematical philosopher of his time, and he was well acquainted both with the technical problems and with the most precise ways of formulating them.'

[10] Ibid. 122.

unnaturally, then, we seldom find in Aristotle's corpus mathematical proofs reflecting (developing) standards of rigour characteristic of proofs of practising geometers. These facts, however, are quite compatible with a high degree of mathematical sophistication on his part. In such a context—i.e. when we are concerned with works that are not specifically works of mathematics—mathematical competence and sophistication may lie largely in the eye of the beholder. So, having made it clear that I disagree with Knorr on this matter, I leave the general issue and turn to several more specific (and, I hope, more manageable) issues. The first pertains to the relation between Aristotle's concept of the infinite by division (*diairesis*) and the geometers' so-called method of exhaustion.

Aristotle's 'Infinite by Division' and the Method of Exhaustion

The method of exhaustion, which according to virtually all commentators bears a singularly unfortunate misnomer,[11] occurs in a number of forms lucidly characterized by E. J. Dijksterhuis.[12] One form, which is termed 'the approximation method' by Dijksterhuis and of which Archimedes makes use, is the following. We construct a bounded monotonic increasing sequence[13] (e.g. areas of polygons inscribed in a conic section) $\{I_n\}$ of which the limit is area Σ (e.g. the area of the conic section in which the polygons are inscribed). We then find, by hook or by crook, a quantity K satisfying the following identity:

$$K = a_1 + \ldots + a_i + R_i, \text{ for each } i \geqslant 1 \tag{A}$$

such that

$$\text{for each } i, R_i > 0 \text{ and } R_i < a_i; \text{ and} \tag{i}$$

$$a_1 = I_1, \text{ and, for } i > 1, a_i = I_i - I_{i-1}. \tag{ii}$$

---

[11] E. J. Dijksterhuis, *Archimedes*, trans. C. Dikshoorn (Princeton, NJ, 1987), 130: 'for a mode of reasoning which has arisen from the conception of the inexhaustibility of the infinite, this is about the worst name that could be devised.'

[12] Ibid. 130–3.

[13] A monotonic increasing sequence is a denumerably infinite sequence within a set of elements that are at least partially ordered such that, for each element x_n in the sequence, there is an element x_{n+1} such that $x_n < x_{n+1}$. Such a sequence is bounded if there is in the set an element y such that, for each x_i in the sequence, $x_i \leqslant y$. A denumerably infinite sequence $\{x_n\}$ is monotonic decreasing if each $x_n > x_{n+1}$, monotonic non-decreasing if each $x_n \leqslant x_{n+1}$, monotonic non-increasing if each $x_n \geqslant x_n + 1$. Similar definitions of boundedness apply in these 3 cases. These concepts will be used several times in the present chapter.

It is then shown by *reductio ad absurdum*, on the assumptions that (L) $K < \Sigma$ and (G) $\Sigma < K$, that $\Sigma = K$.

In the case of (L), there is needed some proposition (such as Euclid's 10. 1) that is the 'converse' of Archimedes' axiom, i.e. a proposition which guarantees that if, starting with any two given magnitudes of which one is smaller than the other, we subtract a part $\geq 1/2$ of the greater magnitude, and then subtract a part $\geq 1/2$ of the remainder, etc., in some finite number n steps we will be left with a remainder less than the smaller of the two magnitudes with which we began. This proposition is used to show that there is some finite n such that $\Sigma - I_n < \Sigma - K$. But this conclusion, together with (A), yields a contradiction. Noting that $I_n = a_1 + \ldots + a_n$, we add K to both sides of the inequality. It then follows that $\Sigma + R_n < \Sigma$, which contradicts condition (i) on identity (A) above.

In the case of (G), the same 'converse' of Archimedes' axiom is used to establish that there is an n such that $a_n < K - \Sigma$. From (A) we know that $K - I_n = R_n$. From (i) above, we know that $R_n < a_n$. It follows that $K - R_n < a_n$, and (by transitivity of the $<$ relation) that $K - I_n < K - \Sigma$. This entails that $\Sigma < I_n$. But this result contradicts the assumption that $\{I_n\}$ is a bounded monotonic increasing sequence of which the limit is area Σ.

The only Archimedean example of this particular form of the method of exhaustion is Archimedes' 'strictly geometrical' proof (*Quadratura parabolae*, propositions 18–24) that the area of a conic segment bounded by an 'orthotome' (parabola) and a chord parallel to the tangent of the vertex of the orthotome is four-thirds the area of an inscribed triangle the base of which is the chord and the height of which is the distance from the chord to the vertex of the orthotome. Archimedes 'exhausts' the area of the figure bounded by parabola and chord by (a) constructing two triangles, one on each of the remaining two sides of the *original* inscribed triangle, (b) constructing four triangles, one on each of the remaining two sides of the two triangles constructed in step (a), (c) constructing eight triangles, one on each of the remaining two sides of the four triangles constructed in step (b), etc. *ad infinitum*. It is not necessary to go into the details of Archimedes' proof of the following claim. For our purposes, the following sketch of one step in the proof suffices. Let S be the area of the original inscribed triangle, S_1 be the sum of the areas of the two triangles constructed in step (a), S_2 be the sum of the areas of the four triangles constructed in step (b), S_3 be the sum of the areas of the eight triangles constructed in step (c), etc. Archimedes proves that S_1 is one-fourth of S, S_2 is one-fourth of S_1, S_3 is one-fourth of S_2, etc. (See Fig. 4)

From the contemporary perspective, it is quite natural to read Archimedes' proof as 'equivalent' to the determination of the area A of the parabolic segment as the 'sum of the infinite series' of areas of inscribed triangles:

$$A = S + S_1 + S_2 + \ldots + S_n + \ldots = S + \lim_{n \to \infty} \left(\sum_{i=1}^{n} S/4^i \right)$$
$$= S + \lim_{n \to \infty} \{(1 - 1/4^n)/S\} = 4S/3$$

In the discussion of the method of exhaustion in a 'contemporary' (now some twenty-five years old) mathematics textbook, Leo Zippin mentions that Archimedes 'encountered the series

$$1/4 + 1/16 + 1/64 + \ldots = 1/3' \tag{2}$$

and proceeds to characterize informally Archimedes' proof of this identity as follows:

'We divide a segment into four equal parts, we hold one for ourselves, give away two, and one remains. At this point three pieces have been handed out and we

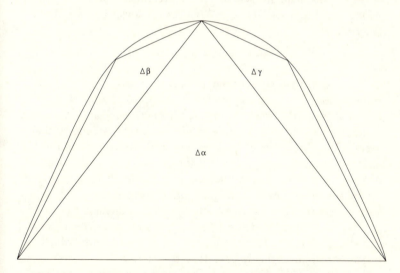

FIG. 4. The Quadrature of the Parabola: Archimedes' 'Rigorous' Proof Using the Method of Exhaustion

S = area $\Delta\alpha$, S_1 = area $\Delta\beta$ + area $\Delta\gamma$, etc. In contemporary terms, the area of the parabola is the 'sum' (limit of partial sums) of the infinite series $S + S_1 + S_2 + \ldots$.

hold 1/3 of the amount distributed. Next we take the remaining piece, divide it into four segments, keep one and give two away, so that again, one remains. After this step, it is again clear that we hold 1/3 of all that has been distributed, Next we divide the remaining piece into four equal segments, hold one, give two away, and one remains, As we continue this process, we hold exactly 1/3 of what has been handed out and a smaller and smaller segment remains to be distributed.' This is the meaning of the equation above. . . .

This method, which has in it all of the modern theory of limits, will be discussed more fully in Chapter 3. For the present, everyone will grant that it shows how the answer 1/3 can be guessed; and also that, if any answer is right, 1/3 is the one. Secondly, the argument shows that as one takes more and more terms of the series, the sum which one gets differs from 1/3 less and less. Thirdly, this fact corresponds precisely to the modern way of defining the *sum* of an infinite series *as a limit*, and so Archimedes' proof will seem to us entirely valid when we meet that definition.[14]

This is a beautifully lucid, compelling account of the identity (2). But Archimedes does not, in fact, prove (or assert) (2). Although it is natural, from the contemporary perspective, to read Archimedes' proof (*Quadr.*, prop. 23) as 'easily generalized to the infinite case', to do so is, I maintain, misleading. What Archimedes proves is that for *finite n* ≥ 1 (his proof is for $n = 4$ but *can* obviously be generalized to any *finite n*)

$$S/4^1 + S/4^2 + \ldots + S/4^{n-1} + S/4^n + (1/3)(S/4^n) = S/3. \quad (2a)$$

The reason that Zippin (and we) are so ready to generalize this result to the infinite case is intimately connected, I suspect, with the fact that we are prone to conflate the now familiar *mathematical* concept of a limit with a more intuitive concept, a concept that it seems clear that we and the ancients share. As we saw in the first chapter, Aristotle in *Phys.* 3. 6 recognizes cases such as the Zenonian dichotomy in which, as we successively divide all of a magnitude by means of a descending geometrical progression, and as we 'simultaneously' sum the parts obtained by this division, this inverse to the process of division produces sums that 'tend toward something definite' (206^b6)—namely, the whole with which we began. Aristotle explicitly says that the sum will not exceed this definite limit (ibid.). And since he has in mind a *diairesis* that results in a situation in which what remains of the magnitude so limited increasingly approaches (but never arrives at) nil, it is clear that he regards the correlative and inverse summing process as coming increasingly close to the limit (i.e. the whole with which we began). So Aristotle does have an 'intuitive concept' of a limit of an infinite process of summation—a process that can be *indefinitely* extended in the Aristotelian sense of being extendable beyond *any* finite number of stages. We here mean by 'limit' a least finite magnitude (i) which the process of summation never (i.e. at any finite stage) exceeds and (ii) to which the process of summation approaches closer at each successive stage but never (i.e. at any finite stage) reaches. There is no evidence, however, that Aristotle moves from this conception of limit (which obviously grounds the mathematical notion of a limit) to what I shall call the *mathematical sum/union* notion of a limit, which *by definition* serves as the sum or union of an infinite series.

I very much suspect that a similar situation is characteristic of ancient geometrical thought in general and, in fact, underlies the method of exhaustion. In the case of Archimedes, there can be little doubt that he recognized in his proof of *Quadr*. 23 that the identity (2a) entails that $S/3$ is the limit, *in the intuitive sense*, of the successive summation of a quarter of S, a quarter of a quarter of S, etc. For, from the identity (2a) it is clear that the sum of any n terms in the progression $S/4$, $S/16$, $S/64$, $S/256 \ldots$, $S/4^n$ (i.e. all the addenda on the left side of (2a) except the ultimate one) will not *exceed* $S/3$. Recall that the ultimate term, which must be added at any finite stage to obtain $S/3$, is one-third of the nth term in the progression. So, the larger n is the smaller the nth term will be. It is thus also clear that $S/3$ is the least magnitude to which the partial sums—as *we* would call them—in the infinite series approach ever more closely but to which none is equal. But here, too, there is no indication that Archimedes 'passed to the limit' in the sense of mathematical sum/union—that he inferred from (2a) something like (2).[15]

[15] It is perhaps worth noting that the *existence* of such a limit as 'sum' of an infinite series (limit of the infinite sequence of partial sums) depends upon Dedekind continuity. In order to infer from the existence of a bounded monotonic increasing (or non-decreasing) sequence (e.g. the infinite sequence of areas of polygons inscribed in a curved figure) to the existence of a limit of that sequence, it must be assumed that magnitudes of areas are Dedekind-continuous: i.e. if a set of areas is bounded above (if there is an area that is an upper bound of the set of areas), then it has a *least upper bound*. The Greeks of Aristotle's time were certainly acutely aware that not all such sets of areas have a *rational* least upper bound.

Rather than Zippin's characterization, the following seems better to capture Archimedes' argument:

We divide a segment into four equal parts, we hold one for ourselves, give two away and one remains. At this point, were we to receive 1/3 of the part that remains to be divided, we would have 1/3 of the whole. But, instead, we take the remaining piece, divide it into *four* equal segments, keep *one* [i.e. we get 1/4 rather than 1/3 of the remaining piece] and give two way, so that again, one remains. After this step, it is again clear that, were we to receive 1/3 of the part that remains to be divided, we would have 1/3 of the whole. But, instead, we take the remaining piece, divide it into four equal segments, hold one, give two away, and one remains. As we continue this process, we would hold exactly 1/3 of the whole were we to receive, in addition to what we have actually allocated ourselves, exactly 1/3 of what remains to be divided. But, at each stage, we shall receive only 1/4 of what remains to be divided. So in the process of dividing, allocating, and summing, we shall never *actually* 'make up the difference'—although, of course, the difference between 1/3 and 1/4 of what remains to be divided becomes 'increasingly less significant' because the quantity of what remains to be divided increasingly approaches (without ever 'arriving at') nil.

The point here is a fairly simple one. Evidently, for both Aristotle and Archimedes, adding or summing is a finite process that involves a finite number of addenda, although of course it is a process that is always *extendable* beyond any given stage in the sense that another addendum can always be added on to the sum thus far obtained. The *reductio* form of the method of exhaustion and, to borrow Knorr's apt phrase, its 'careful manipulation of finite magnitudes',[16] is a logically rigorous way of making use of the *intuitive* conception of a limit in geometrical proofs without making what Aristotle and geometers of Eudoxus' time and after would agree to be unscientific assumptions: that one can regard the limit of an infinite series as the result of performing *all* of an infinite number of additions; that one can regard an area bounded by a curve as the area obtained by taking the union of *all* of the members of an infinite collection of polygons inscribed in the area.

Knorr develops a hypothetical account of what an earlier proof of Euclid 12. 2 (the areas of circles stand in the same ratio as the squares on the diameters of those circles) by Hippocrates of Chios might have looked like. In the course of his exposition, he claims that the following

---

[16] Knorr, 'Infinity and Continuity', 135.

propositions would have been regarded as intuitively obvious by Hippocrates or a similarly competent geometer of his time:

Each circle is built up as the sum of square plus four triangles (yielding the octagon) plus eight more triangles (yielding the 16–gon) and so on. Just as any finite magnitude might be conceived as the sum of its half, quarter, eighth, sixteenth, and so on, so also the circle could be viewed as this sort of sum.[17]

In effect, Knorr is suggesting that not only what I have been referring to as the 'intuitive' but also the conception of a limit as a mathematical sum/union would have been obvious to an ancient mathematician with a modicum of sophistication. It is true enough that, from the contemporary perspective, the 'and so ons' in the preceding quotation present no difficulties. But this lack of difficulty is largely due to two facts: (i) In the arithmetic case, we have as a part of our mathematical tradition an extended notion of addition to rely on, one that goes beyond the finite procedure of arithmetic summation or elementary addition that we learn in school. (ii) In the geometrical case, our conception of the sum (union or join) of all the polygons inscribed in the circle is much less tied than it was for ancient geometers to the *process of constructing* the inscribed polygons, which of course can never be completed—i.e. ordered in terms of a discrete series of steps in which there is an *ultimate* step, a penultimate step, etc.

Knorr sees earlier geometers as possessing (perhaps in a rough, quasi-intuitive form) what I have called the contemporary notion of a limit as a mathematical sum/union—a notion that *identifies* a limit with the sum of an infinite series. And he sees later geometers, beginning about the time of Eudoxus, as using the method of exhaustion to place, as it were, this rough but, in some ways, very sophisticated mathematical notion on a rigorous and firm foundation. This view anticipates, as it were, the way in which fundamental concepts of the calculus, such as limit and continuity, were finally explicated in the eighteenth and nineteenth centuries: the standard modern *foundational* analysis of calculus bears some obvious analogies to the classical Greek techniques of careful manipulation of finite magnitudes. But, in order for there to be such a foundational analysis of calculus, harking back to Greek mathematical antiquity, the calculus had to be in place. There was not, of course, any such method of calculating with infinite quantities in place in Greek antiquity. It is perhaps more plausible to

---

[17] Ibid. 134.

regard earlier ancient geometers as possessing only the intuitive notion of a limit (which need not identify that limit with any sort of infinite sum, union, or join) and the later ancient geometers as devising the method of exhaustion as a technique for making rigorous geometrical use of *this* intuitive concept by means of a combination of *reductio* argument and careful manipulation of finite magnitudes.

Without attempting to decide any issue of priority with respect to Philosopher versus geometers, I suggest that the outcome of this geometrical development is the conception of the infinite (should one care to use that term) in terms of the correlative processes of indefinitely *extendable* processes of division and addition abstractly characterized by Aristotle in *Phys*. 3. 6. In other words, we see in Aristotle's texts a general conceptual account—a *Scientific American* account for the educated and interested layperson, if you like—of the 'scientific' notion of infinity that was applied technically, with increasing sophistication, by ancient mathematicians.

In the example from Archimedes' *Quadratura parabolae* previously discussed, we have a series of polygons inscribed in some curved figure the area of which we desire to ascertain. This series is infinite in the sense that it can always, in principle, be extended by the construction of a polygon in the area of the figure not yet circumscribed by any previously constructed polygon, while no such additionally constructed polygon will exhaust the remaining area. With respect to this remaining area, there is an important distinction to be drawn—one that goes to the very heart of the application of a converse principle of Archimedes' axiom, such as proposition 1 of Euclid 10, within the method of exhaustion. The *whole* of the remaining area will not be *fully* exhausted by the area of any finite number of polygons inscribed in that curved figure; but, for any *proper* sub-area of the remaining area, that area will be fully exhausted by the area of some finite number of inscribed polygons.

The method of exhaustion is a sophisticated application of indirect proof which uses these two propositions to specify the area of the curved figure, without making the 'unscientific' move of *identifying* the area of the curved figure with the *infinite* sum of areas of inscribed polygons. In the case of the proof of Archimedes, he obtains 'by hook or by crook' a quantity A which he wishes to prove to be the area of the curved figure. It is additionally ascertained that A is the sum of *any* finite sub-series of areas of n polygons so inscribed *plus* a remainder that is always equal to or less than the area of the last and smallest (*n*th) polygon in the finite sub-series. Archimedes thus obtains a series of areas that is infinite in the Aristotelian sense, connoting inverse processes of division and addition that can always be carried one step further. Another addendum can always be added to the sum thus far obtained by the process of addition; but each stage of this process is conceived as simply adding back a fractional part of *A* that has been divided off. So, the sum of parts of *A* 'added back together' never exceeds *A*; but just as the division of *A* into successively smaller parts never actually (at any finite stage) exhausts *A*, so the correlative addition obtains sums that are progressively closer to *A* but never actually reach it.[18]

Further, if the area of the curved figure differs from *A* it must differ from *A* by some finite amount: there are no infinitesimal or infinitely small differences in areas. But on the assumption that it does differ by such a finite amount, a contradiction is derived from the combination of (i) propositions concerning the inscribed polygons and their areas and (ii) some appropriate form of the converse of Archimedes' axiom.

K. M. Pedersen comments that

Among the mathematicians of the early 17th century there was a desire to find such a method of obtaining results which, in contrast to the method of exhaustion, would be direct. It would be well if the new method, apart from giving results, could be used to prove the relations achieved. Such a direct method might have been obtained had it been realised that

$$\lim_{n \to \infty} C_n = \lim_{n \to \infty} I_n \qquad (1.\,9.\,5)$$

and had *X* been put equal to that limit; however, this was not within the style of expression and power of abstraction of 17th-century mathematicians.[19]

This claim seems *a fortiori* applicable to mathematicians of the fourth and third centuries BC. Pedersen also makes the obvious point that, since the method of exhaustion essentially involves a *reductio*, the

---

[18] Again, the general assumption that the area of the figure must have some *definite* value *A*, whether *A* is commensurable or incommensurable with areas of the polygons inscribed in it, reflects the implicit assumption of Dedekind continuity of areas of figures.

[19] 'Techniques of the Calculus, 1630–1660', in I. Grattan-Guinness (ed.), *From Calculus to Set Theory, 1630–1910: An Introductory History* (London, 1980), 32. In his example of the method of exhaustion, alluded to by the identity (1. 9. 5) in this quotation, Pedersen considers what Dijksterhuis calls the 'difference form of compression method': a bounded monotonic decreasing sequence of circumscribed polygons (the C_i's) as well as a bounded monotonic increasing sequence of inscribed polygons (the I_i's) are employed. A claim analogous to Pedersen's for the 'approximation method' of exhaustion that we have been considering would read 'Such a direct method might have been obtained had *X* been put equal to $\lim_{n \to \infty} I_n$.'

'method can be used only if K [our A above—the value to be assigned to the unknown area or quantity X] is known in advance. This means that it needs to be supplemented by another method, if results are to be produced.'[20]

Aristotle abstractly characterizes this fact in his brief description of the inverse processes of division and addition. If we take a unit S as our K and successively divide this in terms of an appropriate decreasing geometrical progression (e.g. as in the 'Zenonian' bisection), the inverse process of addition tends toward S considered as a limit (but not a limit identified as the 'sum of infinite series'). In the example from the *Quadratura parabolae* that we have been considering, Archimedes uses a more sophisticated version of the same technique in conjunction with a *reductio* argument. Taking $S/3$ as his K, he finds that dividing this given in terms of a geometrical progression of fourths of fourths of . . . of S and performing the inverse summations obtains sums which approach ever more closely to his given K—namely, $S/3$. But none of these sums, irrespective of how many addenda it comprehends, ever equals $S/3$: there is always the remaining term $(1/3)(S/4^n)$ to be added in order to obtain $S/3$. There is no indication that Archimedes (or any other ancient geometer) thought that the remaining term could be eliminated by generalization from a series with a finite number of addenda to a series with an actually (denumerably) infinite number of addenda.

It is certainly the case that Aristotle's account of the sort of infinite-by-addition process that is the inverse of an infinite-by-division process captures a fundamental feature of the geometrical method of exhaustion: the geometrical process of division, and hence the inverse process of addition, does not terminate in any *finite* number of steps of division/addition. However, I have also made the stronger claim that Aristotle's refusal to consider the inverse processes as completed (or completable) at all—even in a so-called 'infinite' number of steps—accurately reflects a similar refusal on the part of ancient mathematicians. The failure to move from the intuitive sense of limit to the full notion of limit, identifying it with the infinite mathematical sum of an infinite series or the infinite union/join of a bounded monotonic

---

[20] Ibid. 31–2. Of course, there are analogously fundamental but 'useless' features of calculus. For example, the general definition of a definite integral,

$$\int_h^a f(x)\, dx = \lim_{n\to\infty} \sum_{j=1}^n (x_j - x_{j-1}) f(\xi_j)$$

(where the largest ot the $(x_j - x_{j-1})$s tends toward 0 as n increases without limit), is typically of little value in calculating the value of an actual integral.

sequence yields one of the most brilliant and sophisticated methodological developments of ancient mathematics. It is the failure to make this move that motivates the fascinating intricacies of the method of exhaustion: the skilful combination of *reductio* argument, appeal to a principle (such as Euclid's 10. 1) that is the converse of Archimedes' axiom, and 'careful manipulation of finite magnitudes'.

There is a final consideration that would have made it difficult, I believe, for Aristotle (and, perhaps, for ancient mathematicians as well) to accept the mathematical limit-as-sum or limit-as-union concepts. The difficulty in question is easily illustrated by the Zenonian dichotomy or bisection. Suppose that we agree to identify the unit interval [0,1] with the join of the infinite series [0,1/2], [1/2,3/4], [3/4,7/8], . . . , and say that the runner who has traversed the union of all these intervals has traversed the unit interval [0,1]. But has he? It would seem to have been within the capacity of both Aristotle and ancient geometers to recognize that the 'limit-point' 1 of the unit interval is not included in any of the Zenonian sub-intervals, and thus to have concluded that it could not be included in their 'infinite sum' or union, were such a concept to be admitted. The infinite union in question, if it is to be admitted, must be the half-open interval [0,1); it cannot be [0,1]. We have seen in previous chapters that Aristotle's conception of the nature of limit-points leaves no room for open or semi-open intervals considered as linearly ordered point-sets. And I believe that it is quite uncertain whether ancient geometry would have been able to accommodate these essentially topological notions any more successfully.

The contemporary tack, of course, is to invoke the concept of the metrical indistinguishability of the topologically distinct intervals [0,1] and [0,1). In the case of the Zenonian dichotomy, it then seems prudent to maintain, as does Gregory Vlastos, that traversing a topological interval metrically indistinguishable from [0,1] is 'a perfectly good way of "reaching"' the terminal point 1'.[21] However, from the ancient perspective, the fact that a supposed completed infinite summation might be understood as entailing the peculiar and, in a certain sense, untenable idea of traversing all the points before the terminal point without traversing the terminal point itself could have been interpreted as a *reductio* on the very idea of such a summation. It is a pity that there is (as far as I know) no textual evidence from antiquity bearing directly on this issue. But if one is to employ one's

[21] 'Zeno of Elea', in P. Edwards (ed.), *The Encyclopedia of Philosophy* (London and New York, 1967), 8, 374.

mathematical 'power of abstraction', to use Pedersen's phrase, in order
to set a limit equal to an infinite sum or union/join—if, in other words,
one is to transcend the ancient indirect and finitistic use of the limit
concept—it is an issue that must eventually be confronted.

Archimedes' Axiom and its 'Converses'

The actual axiom of Archimedes is stated as the fifth postulate in *De
sphaera et cylindro* and also, rather more informally, in the preface to
Quadratura parabolae:

With respect to the excess of unequal areas, i.e. the excess by which the greater
exceeds the less, we should be able, using this excess added to itself [some finite
number of times], to exceed any given finite area.[22]

More formally,

(AA1) for any x, y such that $y > x > 0$, and any z 'standing in
a ratio' to x and y, there is some natural number n such that
$n(y - x) > z$.

In the same preface, Archimedes says that a similar (*homoion*) lemma
was used in the proof that the volume of a cone is one-third of the
volume of the cylinder with the same base and height, a theorem that
Archimedes elsewhere (preface to *De sphaera et cylindro*) attributes to
Eudoxus. Hence the term 'axiom (or postulate) of Eudoxus' in the
mathematical literature. Some scholars would distinguish the postulate explicitly stated by Archimedes from the earlier 'postulate of
Eudoxus', and associate the latter with a principle implicit in Euclid's
definition 5.4 of magnitudes 'having a ratio to one another' (*logon
echein pros allēla*):

(AA2) for any x, y such that $y > x > 0$, there is a natural number
$n > 1$ such that $n \cdot x > y$.

Dijksterhuis makes the plausible suggestion that Archimedes states
the axiom in the form (AA1) in order to make it clear that he is ruling
out infinitesimal *differences* in magnitudes: 'he excludes the existence
of actual infinitesimals; the magnitudes he is going to discuss are to
form Eudoxian systems'.[23] However, I shall generally hereafter follow
contemporary usage, connoting the latter, 'Eudoxian' principle (AA2)
by the phrase 'Archimedes' axiom'.

[22] Preface to *Quadratura parabolae*, in *Archimede*, ed. C. Mugler, ii (Paris, 1971), 165.
[23] Dijksterhuis, *Archimedes*, 148–9.

Several principles might be counted as the 'converse' principles—I use this term in an intuitive, informal sense—of Archimedes' axiom. The most obvious candidate is, in fact, equivalent to it:

(CAA1) for any x, y such that $y > x > 0$, there is a natural number $n > 1$ such that $y/n < x$.

Since y/n must be greater than 0, it might thus seem that Archimedes' axiom implies the infinite divisibility of any magnitude x. This will be true only if we assume that, for each magnitude y and for each natural number $n > 1$, y/n is defined. But in the case of a 'quantum' or atomistic conception of magnitude, a magnitude constituted of, say, two such minimal quanta cannot be divided into three (non-null) parts, and *a fortiori* cannot be divided into three *equal* parts.

It seems reasonable to view (AA2) as a principle of 'comparability by finite addition' of any two *possible* magnitudes x and y. That is, for any two possible magnitudes, the smaller can be made to exceed the latter by being added to itself some finite number of times. Understood in this way, the principle is satisfied by a quantum conception of magnitude, according to which any possible magnitude is some finite multiple of the minimal quantum. This understanding of Archimedes' axiom suggests another 'converse' principle:

(CAA2) for any x, y such that $y > x > 0$, there is some natural number $n \geqslant 1$ such that $y - (n \cdot x) < x$.

The force of this principle is that any two possible magnitudes are comparable by finite subtraction: that is, for any two such magnitudes, some finite number of successive subtractions of the smaller from the larger yields a remainder (possibly null) less than the smaller. It will be noted that this principle also holds for a quantum conception of magnitude according to which every possible magnitude is a finite multiple of the minimal quantum.

As we previously remarked, Aristotle states versions of Archimedes' axiom in a number of places. One noteworthy example is *Phys*. 8. 10, where he states both (AA1) and the converse principle (CAA2): 'by continually adding to a finite quantity [itself], I shall exceed any definite quantity; and subtracting I shall similarly fall short [of any definite quantity]' (266^b2–4). In *De sensu* 6, Aristotle makes it clear that he understands the finitude of this process: 'that which is continuous [and finite] is divisible to an infinite number of unequal parts, but to a finite number of equal parts' (445^b27–8).

The latter quotation points toward an important distinction among

Archimedean-axiom 'converse' principles. 'True' converse principles, such as (CAA2), exhaust the difference between two magnitudes by means of a descending *arithmetic* progression. That is, the subtraction of a *constant* magnitude from the greater magnitude y yields, in a finite number of steps, a remainder less than the smaller magnitude x; of course, such a descending arithmetic progression also yields, in a finite number of steps, a null remainder. Such 'true' converse principles do not possess a high degree of geometrical usefulness—beyond, of course, the fundamental usefulness of the equivalent Archimedes' axiom itself.

What is of central usefulness in the method of exhaustion is a converse principle involving a descending *geometrical* progression or, more generally, a monotonic decreasing (or non-increasing) sequence converging to 0. The terms of such a sequence represent 'what is left' of the greater magnitude y, after successive subtractions of a *proportional* amount of the preceding term (minuend) in the series. Such a sequence has the property that, for any x, y such that $y > x > 0$, a magnitude smaller than x is reached in a finite number of 'proportional subtractions' beginning with y; but y is not exhausted—a null remainder is not reached—in a finite number of subtractions. Such considerations lead to another Archimedean-axiom converse principle:

(CAA3) for any x, y such that $y > x > 0$, if there is a monotonic decreasing sequence $\{y_n\}$ converging to 0 (where $y_1 = y$ and y_i ($i > 1$) is the remainder left after $i - 1$ successive 'proportional subtractions', beginning with y as first minuend), then there is some natural number $n > 1$ such that $y_n < x$.

Something like principle (CAA3) is what is usually needed in the application of the method of exhaustion. For example, if we are trying to establish that the area of a curved figure F in which we inscribe a polygon P having area K is $r \cdot K$, where r is some real number greater than 1, we do not want to exhaust the difference in area between inscribed polygon P and F 'too quickly'—i.e. in a *finite* number of steps—by the construction of other polygons on the sides of P. To do so would either, paradoxically, identify a complex inscribed polygon with the curved figure F or produce a complex figure *larger* in area than F (not *inscribed* in F) and, hence, be of no use in ascertaining the area of F. What we need is an infinite sequence of polygons $\{P_n\}$ 'between' P and F such that the difference in area between the P_is and $r \cdot K$ asymptotically approaches 0. We then use a principle such as (CAA3) to show that, if we suppose the area of F to be less than $r \cdot K$ by any amount d, there is an inscribed polygon I_n such that the difference in area between it and $r \cdot K$ is less than d. A contradiction is derived. Deriving a contradiction from the assumption that the area of F is greater than $r \cdot K$ by some amount d requires, in this case, a bit more work, but also invokes a principle such as (CAA3). In this sort of proof, no help will be obtained from a principle such as (CAA2), which tells us only that a quantity less than the difference d can be 'arithmetically' reached by repeated subtractions of some *constant* quantity from a larger magnitude.

I have already referred several times in the preceding section to an important ancient instance of (CAA3). It is proposition 1 of Book 10 of Euclid, sometimes referred to simply as the 'lemma of Euclid':

Two unequal magnitudes being set out, if from the greater there be subtracted a magnitude greater than its half, and from that which is left a magnitude greater than its half, and if this process is repeated continually, there will be left some magnitude less than the lesser magnitude set out.[24]

It seems clear that (CAA3) and Euclid's lemma require the infinite divisibility of magnitude in the Aristotelian sense of a process of division that can always be taken a step further—the sense in which he claims, as in *Phys*. 3. 7, 'the bisections of a magnitude are infinite' ($207^b 10$–11). Thus, such a principle involves more than Archimedes' axiom or the Eudoxian postulate (AA2) and its 'true' (equivalent) converse (CAA2), which are verified, as we saw, by an appropriate quantum conception of magnitude. Undoubtedly, ancient geometers recognized the importance of this assumption of the 'incompletable'

---

[24] *The Thirteen Books of Euclid's Elements*, trans. Sir T. L. Heath, iii (New York, 1956), 14. A contemporary formulation of Euclid 10. 1 appeals to a special case of an elementary but fundamental theorem concerning limits of sequences:

if $\{y_n\}$ is a monotonic decreasing sequence converging to 0 and $\{z_n\}$ is a monotonic decreasing sequence of real numbers such that, for each i, $z_i \leqslant y_i$, then $\{z_n\}$ also converges to 0.

For the 'lemma of Euclid' $\{y_n\}$ is set equal to $\{1/2^n\}$, yielding the Zenonian bisection or dichotomy. We are then guaranteed by the theorem that every sequence $\{z_n\}$ of remainders in which each remainder z_i is half or less of its minuend but non-null (i.e. in which each subtrahend is half or more of the minuend but not equal to it) is a monotonic decreasing sequence converging to 0. Suppose, then, that y is a given initial magnitude such that the 'first subtraction' from it yields as a remainder y_1, the 'second subtraction' yields y_2, etc. It then follows from the standard definition of the concept of a limit of a sequence that for any x such that $y > x > 0$, there is a natural number $n \geqslant 1$ such that $z_n < x$.

divisibility of magnitude as fundamental to their science as it developed (e.g. as essential to the theory of proportion). But the assumption is not made explicit in Euclid's proof of his proposition 10. 1.

The following is a sketch of Euclid's proof of 10. 1. Suppose that we begin with two magnitudes AB and Γ such that $AB > \Gamma > 0$. By Euclid's version of the Archimedean axiom (def. 5. 4) it follows that there is some positive integer n such that $n \cdot \Gamma$ (call this magnitude ΔE) $> AB$. Let ΔE be divided into n equal parts (each equal to Γ). Then let AB also be divided into n non-null proper parts such that the first of the n parts is greater than half of AB, the second part is greater than half the remainder (if the second part is the nth part, it *is* the remainder, of course; otherwise it is not equal to the remainder but more than half of it), etc. It is then follows inductively (Euclid actually considers the case $n = 3$) that, subtracting the 'first part' ($= \Gamma \leqslant \Delta E /$ 2) from ΔE and the 'first part' ($> AB/2$) from AB (yielding two 'remainders' of which the remainder of ΔE is greater than the remainder of AB), and then subtracting from these remainders the 'second part' ($= \Gamma \leqslant 1/2$ of the remainder) of ΔE and the 'second part' ($> 1/2$ of the remainder) of AB, etc., we arrive, in $n - 1$ steps, at an 'ultimate' (nth) part of ΔE ($= \Gamma$), which must be greater than the corresponding nth part of AB.[25]

[25] Appended to the proof is a 'porism' (corollary) to the effect that the proof also holds for the case of bisection or dichotomy—i.e. where the sequence of remainders of the larger magnitude AB is some initial segment of the sequence $\{AB/2^n\}$. Knorr ('Infinity and Continuity', 123–5) makes much of the *historical* difference between Euclid 10. 1 and this special case, which he calls the 'bisection principle' and which he connects with Eudoxus. In particular, he appeals to the fact that it is the bisection principle—rather than the more powerful lemma 10. 1—which is utilized in the 12th book of Euclid as (part of) the evidence for the hypothesis that 'Euclid presented Book XII largely in its early Eudoxean form but incorporated the later revised versions of proportion theory into Book V' (124). This hypothesis may well be correct: it does not seem that, in general, the proportion theory of Book 5 is as effectively employed in Book 12 as it might be. However, I do not believe that much support for the hypothesis can be derived from the distinction between Euclid's lemma and the bisection principle, since the bisection principle *is* explicitly covered by the proof of Euclid's lemma. Euclid's lemma does, however, represent a considerable *conceptual* advance over any possible earlier bisection principle. It does not require that the sequence of remainders, a sequence converging to 0, be a descending geometrical progression; *different* proportional parts of a given remainder (equal to or greater than a half of it) can be subtracted from different remainders in the sequence to produce the next term (remainder) in the sequence. This fact is particularly useful in geometrical cases, e.g. where polygons are being inscribed in a figure. In such cases, it can be proved geometrically that each new inscription-addition exhausts more than half of the remaining 'uninscribed' area, but the exact geometrical progression involved in the exhaustion of the area may not, at that stage of the proof, be

This proof, which appeals only to the Archimedean axiom and to elementary properties of inequalities, is straightforward except for the assumption that the larger of the two magnitudes (AB) can be divided into n parts, where $n \cdot \Gamma = \Delta E$ is some magnitude (by Archimedes' axiom) greater than AB. The assumption is, as one would expect, abrogated when we assume minimal, indivisible quanta of magnitude. For example, if Γ is equal to one such quantum and AB is equal to two quanta, then ΔE, in order to be greater than AB, must be equal to at least three quanta. But AB is not divisible into n (non-null) parts for any $n \geqslant 3$. What is needed (but left unstated by Euclid) is precisely the sort of 'infinity' of parts explicitly described by Aristotle in *Phys.* 3. 7:

It is always possible to think of a larger [number]. For bisections of a magnitude are infinite. So, this is possible potentially, not actually—a number can be comprehended that exceeds any finite multitude. But this number is not separable from the process of bisection; nor does the infinity 'remain' but, rather, it is coming-to-be. (207^{b}10–14)

A necessary requirement for obtaining, by induction, a *general* proof of Euclid's 10. 1 is the divisibility of the magnitude AB into an infinite number of parts in the ∞-sense of 'infinite'. As we have previously noted, ∞ does not designate any totality; it does not signify a cardinal or ordinal number. Rather, it signifies the *absence* of an upper bound. This is Aristotle's sense of the infinite by addition, to which he is alluding in the preceding quotation, although, of course, he invokes some typically Aristotelian metaphysical terminology in describing his conception. Characterized anachronistically—but not, I think, inaccurately—Aristotle's distinction between the potential and the actual is something like the distinction between ∞ and the Cantorian transfinite ordinal ω (or the Cantorian transfinite cardinal $\aleph_0$). The lack of a limit or least upper bound (indeed, the lack of an upper bound *simpliciter*) connoted by ∞ suggests a process that can be (i.e. *potentially* is) carried a step further than any finite number n of steps. But it is possible to interpret the notion of a limit ordinal ω, the set of *all* finite ordinals, as suggesting that a process (such as counting)—or the product of that process—can be conceived as completed or limited (and, hence, *actual*) despite the fact that the

'officially' known (see Archimedes, *Quadratura parabolae*). Or ascertaining whether there is a geometrical progression involved in the exhaustion of an area (or what particular progression it is if there is one) may not be important to the structure of the proof (see Euclid 12. 2).

process is unbounded in the sense of having no last step or stage. Aristotle, of course, firmly resists any such conception. Whether or not he was misguided in this resistance, he surely is correct in asserting that the mathematics of his day requires the ∞-conception of infinity. Without at least the ∞-conception, as Aristotle says, there will be 'magnitudes that are not divisible into magnitudes, and number will not be infinite' (*Phys*. 3. 6. 206ª11–12). Moreover, Aristotle is also correct in asserting that the mathematics of his day does not require anything like an ω-conception of infinity.

Aristotle's 'Infinite by Addition' and Euclid's Parallel Postulate

There is at least one area where it is arguable that Aristotle does dissent from what was (to become) ancient geometrical orthodoxy. According to a reasonable interpretation (initially advanced by Jaakko Hintikka) of Aristotle's account of the infinite by addition (*prosthesis*) in *Phys*. 3. 7, Aristotle makes a claim inconsistent with the famous parallel postulate (postulate 5 of Book 1) of Euclid. In *Phys*. 3. 7 Aristotle argues that 'it is not possible that there is an infinite with respect to the greater. . . . Since there is no infinite sensible magnitude, it is not possible that a magnitude exceed any definite magnitude. For then something might be larger than the heavens' (207ᵇ17–21). The problem develops when, later in the chapter, Aristotle argues as follows:

[The mathematicians] do not now need an infinite [in the direction of 'increase' or largeness] (nor do they use it); rather, [they require only the availability of a magnitude] that is as great as they wish. It is possible to divide in the same ratio as the largest magnitude a different magnitude of whatever size one pleases. So that, with respect to proof, whether a magnitude exists among those that are actual will make no difference to them. (207ᵇ29–34)

Had Aristotle stopped with the claim that all his contemporary mathematicians require is the availability of a finite magnitude (e.g. a line) as large as they wish—i.e. that there be no upper bound on *finite* magnitude—his claim would be quite unproblematic. He would simply be claiming that all the geometers require is the ∞-conception of infinity with respect to magnitude—for any finite magnitude s, there is available a magnitude $s' > s$. Talk of the existence of specific points infinitely distant from one another or the concept of a magnitude s' such that, for *every* finite s, $s' > s$, is not required and, in fact, has no use in the geometry of Aristotle's age. However, Hintikka has argued with considerable force that the latter part of the quotation takes Aristotle considerably beyond such a claim and places him on shaky mathematical ground.

According to Hintikka's interpretation, Aristotle

is also arguing that a geometer does not even need arbitrarily large potential extensions. . . . What Aristotle's statement therefore amounts to is to say that for each proof of a theorem, dealing with a given figure, there is a sufficiently small similar figure for which the proof can be carried out. In short, each geometrical theorem holds in a sufficiently small neighborhood. From this it does not follow, however, that the theorem really [i.e. universally] holds. There are in fact geometrical assumptions requiring arbitrarily large extensions. The best-known case in point is of course Euclid's fifth postulate, the famous 'axioms of parallels': 'If a straight line falling on two straight lines makes the interior angles on the same side less than two right angles, the two straight lines, *if produced indefinitely*, meet on that side on which are the angles less than the two right angles' (trans. by Heath). If there is a maximum to the extent to which lines can be produced, this postulate fails.[26]

There are a number of other Euclidean first principles, as well, that imply the indefinitely great extension of magnitude in one or more dimensions. The Euclidean definition (Book 1, def. 23) of parallel lines ('straight lines, which lying in the same plane and being produced indefinitely (*ekballomenai eis apeiron*) towards both regions [directions], that do not meet one another in either direction') is an example. Postulate 2 of Book 1, which licenses the production of a 'straight line-segment continuously in a straight line', is usually understood as allowing the ('unique') extension of a straight line-segment 'as far as one wishes' in either direction. And postulate 3 of Book 1, which licenses the production of a 'circle with any centre and any "distance" (radius)', is also usually understood, in Heath's words, as 'removing any restriction on the size of the circle'.[27]

The problem, then, is the following: Aristotle seems to realize that geometers appeal to the ∞-infinity of extension, the availability of magnitudes, lines, etc. 'as large as they wish' or without upper limit. But, Aristotle holds, the extent of the cosmos is limited. For Aristotle, geometers *qua* geometers deal with geometrical objects as *abstracted* from the physical world. 'In other words', to quote Hintikka,

---

[26] Hintikka, 'Aristotelian Infinity', repr. in *Time and Necessity* (Oxford, 1973), 119. Knorr ('Infinity and Continuity', 122) endorses Hintikka's interpretation of the passage.

[27] Heath, *Euclid's Elements*, i. 199.

a geometer deals with physical lines by abstracting from certain of their attributes... Now the real problem here is that some of the lines that a geometer needs do not seem to be forthcoming at all, and of course *this* existential problem is not alleviated by the possibility of abstracting from certain attributes of lines. If the requisite [physical] lines do not exist, there is nothing to abstract from.[28]

But Aristotle seems to be responding in *Phys*. 6. 7 above that there is no need for the geometer to be concerned *qua* geometer about whether his magnitudes, lines, etc. fall within the class of actually existent magnitudes, lines, etc. *because* any construction(s) in question can always be reproduced as similar construction(s) on a scale small enough to fall within the bounds of actually existent magnitudes, lines, etc. and, consequently, his theorems can always be proved. As Hintikka points out, however, 'for a sufficiently small neighbourhood' must be added as an essential qualification to this last claim. But this qualification, as both Hintikka and Knorr note, technically renders Aristotle's position inconsistent with 'Euclidean geometry' as that concept came to be understood.

The problem is exacerbated by the fact that Aristotle often seems to accept—ingenuously and without qualms—various geometrical principles entailing the lack of an upper bound with respect to magnitude. There are, for example, several arguments in *De caelo* 1. 5 which rely on assumptions closely related to the parallel postulate. One such argument purports to show that it is necessary that a body undergoing rotation must be finite:

If a body rotating in a circle is infinite, then the lines issuing out from the centre [i.e. the radii of the rotating sphere] are infinite. But then the interval between such infinite radii is infinite. By 'interval between' (*diastēma*) I mean [straight line] of maximal magnitude that touches the radii. It is necessary that this is infinite. In the case of finite radii, it will always be finite. But it is always possible to take yet more of the given [infinite radii]; so that, as we say that number is infinite, because there is no largest number, so the same account obtains concerning the distance [between infinitely long radii]. Therefore, if it is not possible to traverse the infinite, and if it is necessary that the interval between the radii of an infinite body is infinite, then it would not be possible for the body to move in a rotary fashion. But we see that the heaven turns in a circle, and we have determined by argument that the motion of such a body is rotary $(271^{b}29-272^{a}7)$

[28] Hintikka, 'Aristotelian Infinity', 122.

This argument is a bit puzzling. As we have seen, Aristotle recognizes a variety of the infinite by addition which is the inverse correlate of the infinite by division: there is no upper bound with respect to the *number* of parts that one can, in principle, separate off (and add back together) in the process of the infinite bisection of a finite, given magnitude. However, as Aristotle well recognizes, in such a case there is a limit (although this limit is not conceived by him as an infinite sum) of the *total quantity* of parts being correlatively separated off and added back together.

In *De caelo* 1. 5, however, Aristotle is using his notion of infinite by addition in connection with what *seems* to be a bounded line (e.g. a radius of a sphere) that, by supposition, *has* no upper bound! It appears that we already have a contradiction between the ∞- conception of infinity, to which Aristotle usually punctiliously adheres, and the idea of a sphere with an infinitely long radius. But let us pursue what seems to be his line of reasoning a bit further. Suppose that the radius from the centre of the earth to the outermost sphere of the heavens is infinite. That could only mean, according to Aristotle's conception of the infinite by addition, that there is no finite upper bound to the length of the radius—that however 'finitely far' we proceed from the centre outward, we can go yet further. It follows, however, that there must be an infinite maximal interval between *any* two radii. (One can think of a maximal interval as the greatest straight line or chord between two points equidistant from the centre of the sphere, one on each of the two radii.) '*Infinite* maximal interval' is, in fact, an oxymoron: according to Aristotle's ∞-conception of the infinite, what this phrase means is that there is no *maximal* distance between any two radii.

There apparently is a *reductio* implicitly present here. If there were such a maximal distance, that fact would entail that the radii could not be extended beyond the end-points of the interval. But then the radii would not be infinite. It follows, Aristotle seems to claim, that the outermost heavenly sphere, with infinite diameter, could not move at all. Any such movement can be conceived as some definite, angular movement, i.e. a superimposition of one radius of the sphere on to another distinct radius. Could such a superimposition occur? It depends upon how we conceive such a superimposition. It is true enough that, for any two points equidistant from the centre, one on each of the two radii, only a finite displacement is needed in order for them to coincide—i.e. for one to be superimposed on the other. But, by supposition, there is no upper bound on the distance of each of a pair of such points from the centre of the sphere. Consequently, if we conceive the superimposition of one radius on the other in terms of the superimposition of one member of *all* such pairs of points on the other, there is no upper bound of the linear distance that must be traversed in order to effect the superimposition. Aristotle seems to assume that to say that there is no upper bound of a linear distance to be traversed is just to say that the traversal of the distance cannot be completed, for the idea of completion implies the arrival at some position, which will be an upper limit of the (linear) distance traversed. A feature of this argument that remains puzzling is the fact that, while the argument depends upon equating 'upper bound' with 'finite upper bound' (and, more generally, assuming that 'bounded' implies 'finite'), it seems possible to make sense of the original supposition of a sphere with infinite radii only by thinking of the surface of the sphere as, in some sense, bounding a radius but not as being a *finite* least upper bound of a radius.

One might plausibly read Aristotle as affirming in this argument from *De caelo* 1. 5 that, for a given triangle, with the sides being finite segments of two of our infinite radii and the base being a given *diastēma* connecting the two end-points of these radius-segments, a similar triangle with arbitrarily greater base *diastēma* can be constructed. If one does so interpret Aristotle, he has accepted a proposition that the seventeenth-century mathematician John Wallis used in order to derive the parallel postulate.[29] Of course, Aristotle is employing the principle within the context of a *reductio* argument: his purpose seems to be to use the formal correctness of the principle to argue that, because of physical facts connected with the impossibility of infinite linear displacement entailed by any angular displacement of a cosmos of infinite radius, arbitrarily large triangles do not *actually* exist.

Furthermore, Proclus appeals to this passage from 1. 5 in order to obtain the following axiom:

if from one point two straight lines forming an angle [< 180°] are produced indefinitely, the distance between [the straight lines] produced indefinitely will exceed any finite magnitude.[30]

He then uses the axiom to derive the Euclidean parallel postulate. However, the Aristotelian principle is weaker than the parallel

---

[29] See the discussion in Heath, *Euclid's Elements*, i. 210–11.

[30] Proclus, *In primum Euclidis elementorum librum commentarii*, ed. G. Friedlein (Leipzig, 1873), 371. 14–17.

postulate. It rules out the elliptic counter-example to Euclidean geometry (in which there is an upper bound to the distance between straight lines) but not the hyperbolic counter-example (in which there is no upper bound to the perpendicular distance between two given parallel straight lines). In his proof of a lemma needed to derive the parallel postulate from Aristotle's principle ('If any straight line cuts one of [a pair of] straight parallel lines, it also cuts the other one'[31]), Proclus implicitly invokes the principle needed to rule out the hyperbolic counter-example, viz., the principle that there is an upper bound to the distance of the perpendicular from any point on one line to the other line. Although Aristotle's principle is weaker than the Euclidean axiom, it none the less would seem to imply the lack of an upper bound for any two divergent lines and, hence, the unlimited availability of spatial extension. But here, too, Aristotle uses his principle within the context of *reductio* argument.

Stronger but still indirect evidence that Aristotle accepted the Euclidean parallel postulate as a formally correct geometrical principle can be derived from a casual remark he makes at the end of *Prior Analytics* 2. 17 concerning the possibility of a false conclusion's being entailed by any number of different false premisses:

it assuredly is not absurd that the same false [proposition] should follow from a number of assumptions, e.g. that parallel lines should meet if an interior angle [on one side of a line intersecting two parallel lines] were to be greater than the exterior angle [i.e. the exterior angle formed by the other parallel line on the same side of the intersecting line] or if a triangle were to possess [angles] greater than two right [angles]. (66ª13–15)

We do not know, of course, the precise nature of the arguments Aristotle had in mind whereby the intersection of parallel lines might have been derived from these two assumptions, respectively. Heath produces plausible reconstructions of arguments whereby, 'in Aristotle's time', the two derivations could have been effected. Both of them rely on a proposition expressing Euclid's parallel postulate: if the two interior angles formed when one straight line intersects two other straight lines sum to less than two right angles, the latter two lines meet on that same side.[32] And I am unable to think of any way in which such arguments could avoid appealing to such a proposition. It seems likely, then, that Aristotle was familiar with (and accepted) something

[31] Ibid. 371. 24–5.
[32] T. Heath, *Mathematics in Aristotle* (Oxford, 1959), 29–30.

equivalent to the Euclidean parallel postulate—although, of course, he may not have recognized it as a 'first principle,' which cannot be derived as a theorem from the *remaining* first principles of geometry (i.e. that it is not a theorem of what we now call 'absolute' geometry).

Aristotle seems to accept the following propositions: (i) The subject-matter of geometry, i.e. what geometrical science is about is *megethos* (magnitude). (ii) *Megethos* has a dependent ontological status; more particularly, it depends for its existence on sensible or physical body (despite the fact that sensible/physical body is characterized by *megethos* not *qua* sensible or physical but *qua* intelligible). (iii) Sensible/physical body is bounded and finite in extent and, consequently, so is *megethos*. Yet Aristotle also gives evidence of accepting geometrical propositions implying an unbounded extent of *megethos*, a fact that appears to be logically at odds with the preceding propositions. How, then, can Aristotle blithely claim, as we have seen that he does in *Phys*. 3. 7, that 'whether a magnitude exists among those that exist will make no difference to [geometers]' (207^b33–4)? It might be thought that there is a rather easy answer to this question. Aristotle accepts various geometrical theorems (e.g. the sum of the interior angles of a triangle is always equal to the sum of two right angles) that entail that space is Euclidean in the sense of being flat rather than curved (elliptical or hyperbolical). But his conception of space is non-Euclidean in the sense that he thinks of space as bounded. I shall not here undertake consideration of the complicated question of whether the notion of a space that is Euclidean in the sense of being flat but non-Euclidean in the sense of being bounded is a coherent notion. A problem concerning *Aristotle's* apparent acceptance of such a conception of space is that, in the ancient tradition of 'Euclidean' geometry, the two features of the flatness and boundedness of space were logically united: theorems (such as those pertaining to the sum of the angles of triangles) expressing the flatness of space were proved using principles that entailed the unboundedness of space. And, as we have seen, Aristotle seems to accept principles that implicitly imply the lack of bounds of spatial *megethos*. How, then, did he justify a conception of space that was bounded but, in other respects, essentially Euclidean?

A plausible answer to this question may lie in Aristotelian meta-geometry or philosophy of mathematics. Jonathan Lear has argued that the Aristotelian texts we have pertaining to meta-geometrical considerations can be best understood in terms of the hypothesis that Aristotle held a sort of instrumentalist view of geometry:

Aristotle treated geometry as though it were a conservative extension of physical theory. If, as we have seen, one wants to prove of a particular bronze isosceles triangle *b* that it has interior angles equal to two right angles, one may 'cross' to the realm of pure geometrical objects and prove the theorem of a triangle *c*. . . . Aristotle tries to show how geometry and arithmetic can be thought of as true, *even though* the existence of separated mathematical objects, triangles and numbers, is a harmless fiction. That is, he tries to show how mathematical statements can be true in a way which does not depend on the singular terms having any reference or the quantifiers ranging over any separated mathematical objects. The key to explaining the truth of a mathematical statement lies in explaining how it can be useful.[33]

Such an instrumentalism could be employed to remove the sting from geometrical first principles which seem to imply an unlimited extent of *megethos*. Such principles can be admitted as useful or formally correct because they allow us to derive true geometrical conclusions and do not lead to false conclusions about *however much physical reality there, in fact, is*. But we need not take literally the existential implications about the extent of *megethos* that seem to be implicit in such geometrical principles. One plausible hypothesis is that it was on such grounds that Aristotle decided that 'with respect to proof, whether a magnitude exists among those that are actual will make no difference to [geometers]'.

From the contemporary perspective, physical reservations concerning ∞-infinite extension *in geometry* are likely to seem fundamentally misplaced. It is such reservations which yielded the preceding solution to the problem posed by the combination of Aristotelian doctrines of the ∞-infinitude of *arithmos* and of the finitude of *megethos*—in effect, a solution in the form of a sort of instrumentalist attitude toward geometrical principles that imply the ∞-infinity of *megethos*. But from the contemporary perspective, it appears that both these reservations and the Aristotelian 'solution' to them derive from an unfortunate confusion of theoretical mathematics with one area of its application, physics. In general, however, the ancient version of the distinction between the theoretical and the applied in geometry was much closer to the contemporary distinction between mathematics and engineering than to the contemporary distinction between mathematics and

---

[33] 'Aristotle's Philosophy of Mathematics', *Philosophical Review*, 91: 2 (1982), 187–8.

physics. In this regard, there are perhaps two other examples of ancient mathematicians who found the connection between a bounded, finite physical world and Euclidean geometry problematic. The chronologically later, less controversial example is Hero of Alexandria (first century AD?). An earlier, more interesting example is, I shall suggest, Aristarchus of Samos (first half of third century BC).

Hero's commentary on Euclid's *Elements*, according to Arabic sources, attempted to resolve difficulties or obscurities in some of the Euclidean proofs.[34] In the estimation of Heath, 'speaking generally, the comments of Hero do not seem to have contained much that can be called important'.[35] One variety of difficulty that Hero addresses, however, is of some interest from our current perspective. These are proofs that involve arbitrarily extended straight lines or auxiliary constructions larger than the figure that is the object of the theorem to be proved. Either Hero, or others whose objections he is willing to take seriously, are concerned lest there not be enough space (*topos*) to produce the required construction. Hero's response to this problem may be termed piecemeal: his strategy seems to be to look at the theorems one by one and, for those that require such larger constructions, to try to find alternative proofs that do not. He attempts to find a proof of a theorem applicable to any figure in 'real space' (on the assumption that real space, while otherwise essentially Euclidean, is none the less limited in extent) that relies only on constructions that can be realized in that limited real space.

One might think, with some reason, that with respect to *philosophy* of mathematics or meta-geometry, the approach of Hero is less sophisticated than that of Aristotle and, with respect to the actual mathematics, more problematic. And it is unfortunate that there do not seem to be extant any alternative proofs by Hero of such Euclidean theorems as proposition 29 of Book 1, in which the parallel postulate is employed for the first time in the proof of the following theorem: a straight line falling on parallel straight lines makes the alternate angles equal to each other, the exterior angle equal to the interior opposite angle, and the interior angles on the same side equal to two right angles. This theorem is used in Euclid's proof that the sum of the interior angles of a triangle is equal to two right angles (1. 32); and, in Euclid's proof of it, the fact that straight lines can be indefinitely extended figures quite essentially.

---

[34] See the discussion in Heath, *Euclid's Elements*, i. 20–4.
[35] Ibid. 22.

None the less, there is perhaps some point to Hero's concern. For part of Lear's account of the Aristotelian notion of geometry's being a 'conservative extension' of physical theory is the requirement that any geometrical theorem proved about a figure (figure-type) 'in the abstract' should be capable of being reproduced directly for any particular physical token of that figure-type. This requirement may be too stringent and, so far as I can tell, it is not certain that Aristotle would have subscribed to it. But if he did, problems can indeed arise concerning the direct translation of Euclidean proofs for very large physical tokens of figure-types or constructions when those Euclidean proofs appeal to larger 'auxiliary constructions'.

A nice example of Hero's method is proposition 20 of the first book of Euclid, the proposition that the sum of two sides of a triangle is greater than the remaining side. Euclid's proof, for arbitrary triangle $AB\Gamma$, requires the construction of larger triangles (e.g. $\Delta\Gamma B$ for the proof that $AB + A\Gamma$ is greater than $B\Gamma$) constructed by extending side AB to Δ, where $A\Delta$ is equal to $A\Gamma$. Suppose, however, we consider a physical token of a triangle for which it is the case that vertices A, B, and Γ are on (or very close to) the outermost sphere of the (finite, Aristotelian) cosmos. Then the triangle $\Delta\Gamma B$ cannot be constructed, and we cannot directly reproduce the Euclidean proof. According to Proclus, Hero (and Porphyry) produced alternative proofs in which 'the straight line is not projected out'. For example, in one proof angle A of triangle $AB\Gamma$ is bisected and line AE produced. It is then shown that $A\Gamma$ is greater than $E\Gamma$ and AB is greater than BE; hence, $AB + A\Gamma$ is greater than $BE + E\Gamma = B\Gamma$.[36]

What perhaps was a more radical attempt to preserve the Euclidean character of geometry may have been developed by Aristarchus of Samos. The story that I have to tell is merely a historically *possible* story. Although I cannot claim to be able to produce anything approaching a proof of its *actual* veracity, it does seem to me to be a plausible story. In the preface to the *Arenarius* (*Sand-Reckoner*), Archimedes makes two comments concerning Aristarchus. The first and more famous is that Aristarchus developed a heliocentric cosmology: 'he hypothesizes that the fixed stars and the sun remain immobile, that the earth is borne around the sun on the circumference of a circle, the sun lying at the centre of the orbit, and that the sphere of the fixed stars [lies] about the same centre as that of the sun'.[37] To this

[36] Proclus, *In Eucl.* 323.
[37] Archimedes, *Arenarius*, in *Archimede*, ed. Mugler, ii. 135. 11–15.

information, Plutarch adds that Aristarchus hypothesized that the earth rotates on its axis.[38] The second comment is that Aristarchus held that the magnitude of the outermost sphere is of such a degree that 'the circle on which he supposes the earth to orbit stands in the proportion to the distance of the fixed stars that the centre of a sphere stands in to its surface'.[39] With respect to the latter claim, Archimedes comments: 'But this is clearly impossible. For, since the centre of a sphere has no magnitude, neither can it be conceived as having any ratio to the surface of the sphere.'[40] Archimedes proceeds, in effect, to dismiss the second claim by conjecturing that what Aristarchus really meant (but awkwardly stated) was the following: if we accept the proposition that the earth is the centre of the cosmos, then the ratio of the earth to 'what is called by us the cosmos' is the same as the ratio of the (radius of the) circle in which Aristarchus postulates that the earth orbits the sun to the (radius of the) sphere of the fixed stars.

According to the second of the two accounts I shall give, however, Aristarchus is claiming that the distance from the centre of the cosmos, i.e. the centre of the sun around which the earth orbits, to the sphere of the fixed stars is literally infinite. To begin with, it seems clear that there is an intimate relation between the two doctrines ascribed to him by Archimedes, that of a heliocentric cosmology with immobile sphere of fixed stars and that of a cosmos with 'radii of (virtually?) infinite extent'. There seem to me to be two plausible accounts of this relation. The first is that, *beginning* with a heliocentric cosmology, Aristarchus adopted the postulate of a ('virtually'?) infinite distance between the orbit of the earth and the sphere of the fixed stars in order to account for the lack of observed stellar parallax. That is, if the earth orbits around the sun, its motion should, during a period of revolution, place it in different relative positions to the fixed stars, creating an apparent relative displacement of the stars among themselves during the period. However, if the relation of the diameter of the earth's orbit to the diameter of the outermost sphere is that of a point at the centre of the sphere to its diameter, it is obvious that the position of the earth in its orbital trajectory would not produce any apparent relative shift in position to the fixed stars (points) on the surface of the outermost sphere. This account has the merits of nicely fitting the way that Aristarchus expresses the 'infinite ratio' between

[38] Plutarch, *De facie quae in orbe lunae apparet*, 6. 923ª.
[39] *Arenarius*, 135. 15–19.
[40] Ibid. 19–22.

the diameter of the earth's orbit and the diameter of the outermost sphere. It also seems to accord with Aristarchus' interest in celestial mensuration, with which we are familiar from his extant work *De magnitudinibus et distantiis solis et lunae*.[41]

Heath has pointed out the possible relevance of lack of observed stellar parallax to Aristarchus' theory and, at the same time, has suggested that the proportion 'point: (surface of sphere of fixed stars) = (diameter of earth's orbit): (diameter of sphere of fixed stars)' is not intended by Aristarchus to be a mathematical fact:

He clearly meant to assert no more than that the sphere of the fixed stars is *incomparably* greater than that containing the earth's orbit as a great circle [read: so great as to make the diameter of the earth's orbit relatively insignificant in comparison with the distance to the sphere of fixed stars]; and he was shrewd enough to see that this is necessary to reconcile the apparent mobility of the fixed stars with the motion of the earth.[42]

It is to be noted that, as Heath says, variant locutions expressing the relation between point or centre and sphere seem to have been 'a common form of words among astronomers to express the negligibility of the size of the earth in comparison with larger spheres'.[43] Although such a locution does not seem to have been used elsewhere to suggest that the diameter of one sphere is negligibly small relative to another, it may have been so used here. The first hypothesis, then, is that Aristarchus appealed to a very great difference in diameter between that of the earth's orbit and that of the sphere of fixed stars— irrespective of whether this difference is literally infinite—in order to explain the lack of observed stellar parallax. This suggestion may well be correct. However, it has the disadvantage of not explaining why Aristarchus might have entertained the heliocentric hypothesis in the first place. As Ptolemy's *Almagest* (second century AD) makes clear, the geocentric hypothesis clearly seems the easier way of explaining absence of stellar parallax.[44]

An alternative account of Aristarchus' heliocentric hypothesis takes literally the attribution of an infinite diameter to the outermost sphere

[41] For the text, translation, and commentary, see Sir T. Heath, *Aristarchus of Samos: The Ancient Copernicus* (Oxford, 1913).

[42] Ibid. 309.   [43] Ibid.

[44] We do not seem to have here a possible 'Copernican' account of the preferability of a heliocentric cosmology as a theory that 'saves the phenomena' more simply than competing geocentric theories, e.g. by eliminating epicycles. For the postulation of a *circular* orbit of earth around sun as centre seems to encounter greater difficulties in accommodating the phenomena. See Heath, *Aristarchus of Samos*, 308.

of fixed stars. According to this account, the key to the motivation behind the heliocentric hypothesis lies in arguments such as those from Aristotle's *De caelo* 1. 5, one of which we examined earlier. To begin this alternative story, it should be pointed out that, as a pupil of Strato, successor of Theophrastus as Peripatetic scholarch, Aristarchus had an impeccably Aristotelian pedigree. According to the story that I wish to consider, Aristarchus particularly wanted to maintain that the cosmos is of infinite extent. A *literally* incommensurable relation—one for which Archimedes' axiom does not hold—between the diameter of the outermost sphere and any finite distance (such as the diameter of the earth's orbit around the sun) is not, according to this alternative story, something to be avoided, but a starting-point of his cosmological theorizing. But how is one to reconcile such a postulate with the Aristotelian arguments that the outermost sphere cannot move if one postulates infinite radii? Aristarchus' answer: make the outermost sphere immobile, place an immobile sun at its centre, and make the earth rotate on its axis and orbit around the sun. But what was the source of Aristarchus' desire to postulate an infinitely extended cosmos? Proposed answer: it was the desire of a mathematician with an essentially Aristotelian philosophy of geometry, in a generation following that of Euclid, to make the cosmos large enough to allow for arbitrarily long lines and arbitrarily great magnitudes.[45]

Making the outermost sphere of the cosmos immobile neutralizes one variety of Aristotelian argument against the hypothesis of a cosmos in which there is an infinite distance between centre and outermost sphere. However, it ignores a more fundamental Aristotelian objection to this hypothesis also set forth in *De caelo* 1. 5. In brief, this objection, which derives from Aristotle's strict adherence to the ∞-conception of infinity, is that the notion of an infinitely great magnitude and the notion of some limit to that magnitude (i.e. a limit to the dimension in which the magnitude in question is held to be infinitely great) are inconsistent. As Aristotle puts it, it is impossible that there should be 'a square that is infinite, or a circle or a sphere, just as [it is impossible that there should be] a line a foot long that is infinite' (*De caelo* 272^{b}20–1). According to the alternative story, Aristarchus maintains that, although the outermost sphere does not move,

---

[45] Strato perhaps helped pave the way for Aristarchus' doctrine of an immobile outermost sphere by several of his doctrines: his apparent denial of a cosmological role for unmoved movers; his elimination of the particular 'heavenly' 5th element, *aither*, with its natural circular motion.

it is still *there* as a supposed limit of the infinitely great radii of his heliocentric cosmos.

Perhaps recognition of this problem led Aristarchus to use a version of the astronomers' formula, describing the ratio of the radius of earth's circular orbit to the radius of the outermost sphere as being the same as the (supposed) ratio between centre and radius of a sphere, thus avoiding the use of the term *apeiron*. It is possible that, by the time of Aristarchus, this term had been largely limited to the Aristotelian (and general mathematical) ω -conception of infinity, and that Aristarchus, accustomed to this usage both as an Aristotelian and as a practising mathematician, would not wish to use the term to make his point. What Aristarchus needs is something like the ω -conception of infinity *as applied to spatial magnitude*, not just 'number'. Just as the first transfinite, limit ordinal ω serves as an upper bound of *all* finite ordinals, although it has no immediate predecessor, so Aristarchus needs his outermost sphere to stand at a transfinite limit distance (from any point in the cosmos) that is the supremum (least upper bound) of *all* finite distances. But his limit distance must not be reachable by any finite multiple of any finite distance. In other words, the outermost sphere would be a sort of singularity for Euclidean geometry (and for any Euclidean metric): the Archimedean axiom fails with respect to the concept of 'distance to the outermost sphere'. It is perhaps easiest to see Euclidean geometry as applying to the area contained by the sphere but not to the surface of the sphere itself.[46]

---

[46] Although the treatment of *measure* in modern mathematics has generally used real-valued measure functions and only the strict ∞-conception of infinity (connoting merely the absence of a real upper bound as a value of the function in question for a particular argument), there has been a tendency in geometry, originating in projective geometry, to make a move very roughly like the one Aristarchus needs to make. Thus we find the recommendation to understand ∞ and $-\infty$ as denoting 'points at infinity' (but not infinitely large numbers) in real analysis and, in geometry, the extension of the Euclidean plane by the addition of points at infinity (each such point being identified with an equivalence class of parallel lines in the plane) and a line at infinity (the totality of the points at infinity), together with a specification of the topological neighbourhoods of the points at infinity. See Behnke and Grauert, 'Points at Infinity'. Of course, the idea of the sun as *centre* of a sphere of infinite radius—or, indeed, the very idea of a *sphere* of infinite radius—seems to be quite problematic. In fact, Galileo illustrates a distinction between the potentially and the actually infinite in terms of a circle: although the length of its radius can be increased indefinitely with the plane figure retaining the form of a circle, if one attempts to think of a circle with an *actually* infinite radius, one no longer has a circle but a straight line (*Dialogue Concerning Two New Sciences*, trans. H. Crew and A. De Salvio (New York, 1914), 38–9). Cf. the idea, from differential geometry, of the horosphere: the 'limit surface' of a sphere of increasing radius, which is taken to be flat or plane-like in the sense of having zero Gaussian curvature.

In the case of Aristotle, we see him at least acknowledging the existence of a problem concerning the relation between physics and geometry—and perhaps providing a meta-geometrical, instrumentalist solution to that problem—a problem that hardly seems worthy of his attention, from the perspective of *our* understanding of Euclidean geometry. In the case of Hero, we see considerations that would nowadays be regarded as quite peripheral to pure mathematics directly influencing a mathematical research programme. And, according to the alternative account of Aristarchus' innovation, we see an attempt to 'save pure mathematics' by means of a heliocentric cosmology. The alternative story is presented merely as a possible hypothesis to explain the motivation behind Aristarchus' heliocentrism.

I do not believe that the peculiarity (from our perspective) of the idea that the first heliocentric theory in Western thought should have been devised in order to protect the Euclidean parallel postulate should count against this hypothesis. The fact is that many—perhaps most—ancients regarded the connection between physics and pure mathematics as being much closer than we would. A partial explanation of this fact is that the subject-matter of geometry was usually understood to be spatial *magnitude* and that spatial magnitude was usually—particularly in Aristotelian and Hellenistic thought—considered to be ontologically dependent on body, in some sense of 'body'.

The fact that the ancients did not always divide the pure from the applied in quite the same way that we do complicates the issue of the relative autonomy of ancient mathematics. For example, it has not been uncommon to view the paradoxes of Zeno of Elea as constituting an early important influence on the development of Greek mathematics. However, Knorr (and others before him) have argued— cogently, in my view—that there is virtually no evidence for specific, technical influence of the paradoxes on Greek mathematics. In the following section, I shall conclude my discussion of Aristotle and ancient mathematics with the argument that the lack of an ancient *mathematical* resolution of Zeno's Dichotomy paradox made the requirement of a philosophical analysis of the paradox, such as Aristotle's, all the more important.

Zeno's Dichotomy, Mathematics, and Aristotle

In contemporary accounts of Zeno's Dichotomy it is not unusual to find a quick mathematical solution given. The paradox is presented as follows: We suppose that a finite interval S is traversed by a runner moving at a constant speed in a finite time. But in order for the runner to traverse the interval S, he must traverse the sub-intervals $S/2$, $S/4$, $S/8$. . . . But, since the runner must take *some* finite amount of time (although a progressively smaller time because he is travelling at a constant speed) to traverse each of these intervals, and since there is an infinite number of them, it is concluded, paradoxically, that the runner cannot traverse the distance in any finite time. According to this interpretation of the paradox, the crucial assumption is that the 'sum' of an infinite number of terms, each of which is of some finite size or magnitude, must be infinite.

The quick mathematical solution, of course, denies this key assumption. If the runner is moving at a constant speed, just as he is traversing progressively smaller intervals of spatial magnitude as he approaches the goal, so also he is traversing these intervals in progressively shorter intervals of time. Just as there is a finite sum, namely, S, of the infinite series $S/2 + S/4 + \ldots + S/2^n + \ldots$ (identified as the limit of the sequence of partial sums, i.e. of the sequence $\{S(2^n-1)/2^n\}$), so also there is a *finite* time T which is the 'sum' of the infinite series, $T/2 + T/4 + \ldots + T/2^n + \ldots$, of time-intervals required to traverse each of the infinite number of spatial sub-intervals. Of course, this 'sum' is similarly defined as the limit of the sequence of partial sums.

We have seen that Aristotle, in *Phys*. 3. 6, recognizes that each of these processes of infinite addition has the appropriate limit (S or T), in the sense of a magnitude that is, in contemporary terminology, the least upper bound of the partial sums—but a least upper bound to which none of the partial sums, however great, actually attains. In his several discussions of the paradox, Aristotle's first and fundamental point is that a finite period of time can be infinitely, successively bisected in precisely the same way that Zeno conceives a finite spatial distance as being successively bisected.

Both length and time and, generally, everything that is continuous are said to be infinite in two senses: either with respect to division or with respect to their extremities. So while it is not possible to pass through what is infinite in extent in a finite time, it is possible [to pass through what is infinite] with respect to division; for the time itself is similarly infinite. (*Phys*. 6. 2. 233ª24–8)

In our first discussions concerning motion, we produced a resolution [of Zeno's Dichotomy] based on the fact of time's having in itself an infinite number [of potential divisions]. So there is no absurdity in supposing that someone traverses what is 'infinite' [i.e. infinitely divisible] in an 'infinite' [i.e. infinitely divisible] time.[47] For the infinite obtains in both length and in time in the same way. (*Phys*. 8. 8. 263ª11– 15)

Immediately after the latter passage, however, Aristotle proceeds to claim that, although this resolution of the paradox—in effect, pointing out that a finite interval of time T can be successively bisected just as a finite length S can, with T and S serving as the respective limits (least upper bounds) of the successive summing (computation of partial sums) of the divisions thus made—is 'adequate with respect to the questioner', it is not 'adequate with respect to the matter at hand and the truth' (263ª15–18). Aristotle here initiates the tradition, particularly instantiated in contemporary discussions of the paradox, of finding a deeper question underlying the paradox: whether it is possible to complete an infinite number of acts. His answer to this question is summarized as follows:

Therefore, one should reply to someone asking if it is possible to go through completely [*diekselthein*] what is infinite, whether in time or in length, that it is possible and that it is not. It is not possible [to go through completely what is infinite] in actuality, but it is possible in potentiality. What is continuously moving goes through an infinity accidentally, but not unqualifiedly. For it is accidental to the line to be an infinity of halves, while its essence and being is something else. (263ᵇ3–9)

As I stated in Chapter 2, I interpret this passage as being in conformity with Aristotle's general ∞-conception of infinity. The sense in which the runner goes through an infinity *in potentia* is simply that the finite distance S that a runner traverses (or the finite time T he takes to traverse it) can *qua* what is continuous be submitted in theory to a non-terminating process of bisection. Irrespective of how far this bisection is carried, (i) the process can always in theory be carried further and, hence, is not complete and (ii) the process can be correlated with an inverse process of addition of the parts thus far divided the sum of which approaches but never attains the initial distance S or time T.

The runner does not completely go through an infinity of halves (of S or T), however. Why not? Aristotle notes that *actually* going through

---

[47] For the phrase *en apeirōi chronōi*, see Ross's note (*Aristotle's Physics*, 714).

an infinite bisection would involve some actual marking-off procedure such as counting, stopping, or planting a flag-pole at $S/2, 3S/4, \ldots$ or at $T/2, 3T/4 \ldots$. Knorr comments that in a finite time 'This is clearly impossible—under the further assumption, which Aristotle would appear to admit, that any such single act of counting [or stopping, or planting a flag-pole] requires some minimal finite time'.[48] The idea is that, because of Archimedes' axiom, the 'sum' of an infinite number of such interruptions, if each interruption is *at least* some minimal length *t* in duration, would exceed any finite lapse of time. But, as Knorr also notes, what Aristotle actually says is that, since we are talking about an *actual* series of bisections, we are talking about what is *discontinuous* rather than what is continuous; so we are no longer dealing with the original Zenonian dichotomy. A number of contemporary philosophers have argued that even the completion of a discontinuous Zenonian 'staccato' dichotomy—in which the runner rests (for progressively shorter periods) between traversing each $S/2^n$ and $S/2^{n+1}$ pair of intervals—is 'kinematically possible'.[49]

Aristotle, however, surely holds that it is not possible. Although he may be making the assumption of a minimal temporal duration for each of the infinite interruptions, he does not explicitly state such an assumption. I suspect that his principal objection to the possibility of actually completing such a bisection is more fundamental. It is, simply, that the idea of actually completing an infinite bisection implies, for him, the reaching of an ultimate step or term; but his ∞-conception of

---

[48] 'Infinity and Continuity', 116–17, n. 11.

[49] See the discussion in Grünbaum, *Modern Science and Zeno's Paradoxes*, 82–6. Further developments are discussed in Grünbaum, *Philosophical Problems of Space and Time*, 630–45. In the latter, Grünbaum presents an instance of the staccato run, due to the physicist Richard Friedberg, in which 'the successive *peak* velocities and accelerations attained by Friedberg's *staccato* runner during the decreasing subintervals converge to zero as we approach the terminal instant' (640). A staccato run can thus be constructed such that the 'runner's velocity, acceleration (and *all* of the higher time-derivatives as well) vary continuously throughout the closed unit time-interval during which he traverses a unit distance' (ibid.). Grünbaum's conclusion that Friedberg's version of the staccato run 'obviates all of the kinematically and dynamically problematic features of the arithmetically simple example [of the staccato run]' suggests that he is equating the concept of kinematic possibility with the continuity of the function from time elapsed to distance traversed and the continuity of the (first and higher) derivatives of that function. Although Aristotle obviously does not have at his disposal the mathematical equipment employed by Friedberg, it does seem clear that some less precise but analogous conception of continuity of motion also figures largely in his conception of kinematic possibility. It is not clear, however, that for Aristotle such a continuity condition would be a sufficient as well as a necessary condition of kinematic possibility.

the infinite by addition is incompatible with there being such an ultimate step/term.

An ω-conception of the infinite supplies, in effect, completion of the series in the form of the limit (although, of course, there is no ultimate term, penultimate term, etc. in a well-ordered sequence of ordinal ω). The same point can be put more philosophically: possession of the concept of transfinite limit ordinal such as ω enables us to model the difference between *being in a position in which all tasks have been performed* (having reached the ω-state) and *being in a position in which the last task has been performed* (having reached the n-state, for some *finite*, natural n). I submit that, without at least an inchoate concept of such a transfinite limit ordinal, the distinction between having performed all the tasks and having performed the last task will not be a distinction made in the 'natural' way in which we are now capable of making it. Similarly, I think that the idea of the 'sum' of an infinite series *implicitly* appeals to something like an ω-conception of the totality of the addenda of the series (cf. being in the position of having added together *all* the addenda—i.e. not having left any out—but not having added a *last* addendum).

With the mathematical identification of the sum of an infinite series with the limit of the partial sums (and the attendant metrical identification of open, closed, and semi-open and semi-closed intervals of a continuous magnitude), the quick resolution of Zeno's Dichotomy becomes possible. There is a clear sense in which the continuously moving runner can be said to complete an infinite series of 'sub-runs' of distance $S/2$, distance $S/4$, ... in the form of traversing the *sum* of the infinite series of these distances, which is just S. At least in the case of the continuously moving runner, the metaphysical issue of whether the runner should be said to have completed this infinite series of sub-runs *actually* or only *potentially* would then seem to lose much of its importance.

For Aristotle, however, who lacks the requisite ω-conception of the totality of addenda of an infinite series, the metaphysical issue remains fundamental. The mathematics of his time does not supply him with the capacity for seeing the runner as completing an infinite series of runs *by means of* his traversing a distance that is the infinite sum of that distance's bisections because it does not supply him with the conception of the distance as the infinite sum of its bisections. How, then, is Aristotle to answer Zeno? His answer comes in two stages. First, when the distance S traversed (or the time T it takes the continuously moving runner to traverse it) is subjected to the process of bisection and the correlative, inverse process of addition of bisected parts, the sum approaches but does not attain or surpass the totality (S or T) as its limit or, in contemporary terminology, its least upper bound. There is no possibility that such a procedure can ever (i.e. in any finite number of steps) either surpass or reach the finite quantity with which we began. So, Zeno's argument *cannot* show **either** that the runner goes any further than the distance S he goes (takes any longer than the time T he takes to get there) *or* that he arrives at a distance of S after having traversed any *less* distance than S (arrives after a lapse of time T in any *less* time than T). These sorts of 'egregious' paradox cannot be derived from the Dichotomy, according to Aristotle.

Second, what the continuously moving runner *actually and really does* is to traverse continuously an interval of distance S in a time of duration T. He does *not* actually and really traverse an infinite number of sub-intervals or sub-distances. The sense in which the runner can be said to perform *in potentia* an infinite number of acts is simply the sense in which any continuous magnitude, e.g. the distance he traverses or the time he takes to traverse it, can in theory (i.e. in geometry) be subjected to the process of infinite division and the inverse process of infinite addition of bisected parts. But the sense of 'infinite' here is the strict ∞-sense, which does not supply a limit-concept that is identified with the completion of the correlative processes of bisection and of addition of the parts thus far separated off.

Such a strict (and, from the contemporary perspective, restrictive) ∞-conception of the infinite is the only one, I have suggested, that it is reasonable to suppose that Aristotle could have gleaned from the mathematics of his time. It is not wildly implausible to suppose that Aristotle's canonization of this strict, 'finitistic' ∞-conception of infinity influenced, in turn, later mathematical theory and practice. For example, the Aristotelian canonization of the strict ∞-conception may be at least partly responsible for the failure of ancient mathematics to make what in hindsight seems a small move from techniques such as the method of exhaustion to concepts central to the development of integration—in particular, to the concept of the sum of an infinite series as the limit of the sequence of its partial sums. But this, of course, is simply an educated guess the verification of which might or might not prove tractable to further historical investigation.

ARISTOTLE AND MODERN MATHEMATICS

There seem to me to be two principal *loci* of disagreement—which are particularly relevant to the analysis of space, time, and locomotion—between Aristotle and what might loosely be called modern mathematics. First, the adherence of Aristotle (and, it seems, ancient mathematics) to a strict ∞ -conception of infinity stands in opposition to later mathematical extensions of the conception. First, there developed the concept of the infinite sum of a well-ordered set of addenda of ordinal ω as the limit of the partial sums of addenda (under the same ordering). Later, continuous magnitudes were analysed in terms of ordered sets of transfinite (specifically, non-denumerably infinite) cardinality. A second and related *locus* of disagreement is found in the contrast between Aristotle's conception of the clear distinction between *number* or *multitude*, on the one hand, and *magnitude*, on the other, versus the later mathematical tendency to undermine this distinction—a tendency that eventually issued in the analysis of continuous magnitudes as multitudes or sets of intuitively discrete elements.

Before I turn to these two points of contrast between Aristotle's views and the subsequent development of mathematics, I wish to discuss briefly a charge levelled by G. E. L. Owen against Aristotelian rational kinematics: the principal item in this charge refers, in the words of David Sherry, 'to the unsalutary effect which Aristotle's dismissal of motion at an instant had upon the development of mathematical physics'.[50]

Aristotle's Dismissal of Motion at an Instant and the Development of Physics

Aristotle, as we know, was not a closet Newtonian. Although, as I hope I have established, there is much of interest in Aristotle's rational kinematics, the contemporary reader is less likely to become intrigued by what little rational dynamics there is in the Aristotelian corpus. In the *Physics*, one of the few noteworthy passages is *Phys*. 7. 5, where Aristotle claims that, at least in the case of 'unnatural' or forced

---

[50] 'On Instantaneous Velocity', 391. Owen makes the charge in two essays: 'Zeno and the Mathematicians', repr. in *Logic, Science, and Dialectic: Collected Papers in Greek Philosophy*, ed. M. Nussbaum (Ithaca, NY, 1986), 45–61; and the latter part of 'The Platonism of Aristotle', repr. in the same vol., 200–20.

motion, the force (*dunamis*, *ischus*) producing the motion varies *directly* with the 'mass' or weight of the body moved, *directly* with the distance it is moved, and *indirectly* with the time during which it is moved. To put the point rather anachronistically, Aristotle accepts something like the equation

$$F = ms / t.$$

That is, for Aristotle, a motive force is directly proportional to something like momentum, total quantity of motion, or, to use the apt phrase of Max Jammer, the 'cumulative determination' of motion.[51]

I. E. Drabkin, in a fine paper on Aristotelian dynamics, identified Aristotle's concept of *dunamis* in this passage with a special case of classical mechanics' concept of work (force multiplied by distance or that of power, work divided by time).[52] I believe that Owen is correct in his claim—one with which Drabkin in fact agrees—that any general identification of Aristotle's *dunamis* with the concepts of work or power of modern mechanics 'overlook[s] the difference between the conditions of uniform motion and of acceleration'.[53] Acceleration figures in both the concept of work and that of power, since they are both defined in terms of the *Newtonian* conception of force.

The idea that force is required for *sustaining* as well as *initiating* motion is deeply seated in Aristotle's thought and, indeed, in the physical theory of later Hellenistic philosophy (cf. the Stoic idea of an *aition sunektikon* or 'maintaining cause'). The dismissal of this idea, and correlative development of the idea that *alterations* in state of motion are directly correlated with force while the inertial maintenance of

---

[51] 'Energy', in Edwards (ed.), *Encyclopedia of Philosophy*, 2, 511–17.

[52] 'Notes on the Laws of Motion in Aristotle', *American Journal of Philology*, 59 (1938), 60–84. Drabkin is, in fact, in agreement with Owen's point, commenting that 'Aristotle, of course, has no generalized notion of "work" such as is found in modern mechanics, into which the modern notion of "force" enters' (73). Drabkin considers a special case of 'work' in which weights are lifted vertically through some distance at uniform speeds and an analogous special case of 'power' for such situations, and notes that, with the assumption of uniform speed, Aristotle's proportional identities follow (72–3). He adds, however, that 'no fruitful dynamics could result merely from this limited idea of "power" in the absence of a generalized notion of "force" and "work"' (73). Drabkin sees Aristotle's mechanics as being impeded 'by too close an adherence to the data of observation and by insufficient analysis and insufficient abstraction, a condition which was not overcome until two thousand years later' (82). In other words, Drabkin locates the inadequacy of Aristotle's dynamics in the Philosopher's failure to consider abstract, 'idealized' cases— the frictionless motion of a body in medium devoid of resistance, or the free fall of a body in vacuum.

[53] G. E. L. Owen, 'Aristotelian Mechanics', repr. in *Logic, Science, and Dialectic*, 331.

motion, in effect, requires no explanation, obviously lie at the very heart of Newtonian physics.

Owen's criticism pertaining to Aristotle's role in impeding the development of mathematical physics is not that he failed to recognize this key aspect of Newtonian mechanics—that Aristotle was not a proto-Newton. Rather, Owen complains that Aristotle's 'preoccup[ation] with the requirement that any movement must take a certain time to cover a certain distance',[54] that is, his insistence that for a body to move it must move *within* some interval of time, blinds him to the quite natural sense in which a body may be said to be moving *at* a temporal instant or durationless point. This neglect of what Owen regards as 'common idiom for us and for the Greeks' is tantamount, in his view, to 'a surrender to Zeno'.[55]

Unable to talk of speed at an instant, Aristotle has no room in his system for any such concept as that of initial velocity, or what is equally important, of the force required to start a body moving. Since he cannot recognize a moment in which the body first moves, his idea of force is restricted to the causing of motions that are completed in a given period of time. And, since he cannot consider any motion as caused by an initial application of force, he does not entertain the Newtonian corollary of this, that if some force F is sufficient to start a motion the continued application of F must produce not just continuance of the motion but a constant change in it, namely acceleration.[56]

One must, I believe, distinguish between a historical (or psychological) interpretation and a conceptual interpretation of Owen's charge. The historical—or, in the case of individual thinkers, psychological—influence of the Aristotelian stricture against instantaneous motion is doubtless a very complicated matter. David Sherry has argued, for example, that the method of geometrical representation of intension and remission of form developed by Nicholas Oresme in the fourteenth century was of great historical significance in providing a clear place for the concept of instantaneous velocity in the 'language game' of physics. The degree to which Aristotle's stricture actually impeded such moves is not clear; but Sherry does comment that 'as far as I can tell, the medievals did not recognize this tension between Aristotle's *Physics* and the direction of their own research. The explanation for this lies in what could be called "the purely grammatical character of their conceptual innovation."'[57]

[54] Owen, 'The Platonism of Aristotle', 218.
[55] Owen, 'Zeno and the Mathematicians', 60.
[56] Ibid., 61.   [57] 'On Instantaneous Velocity', 397.

At an ahistorical, conceptual level, however, it seems clear that whether something can correctly be said to be moving at an instant is, from the perspective of Newtonian mechanics, a purely metaphysical issue. In other words, Newtonian mechanics is metaphysically neutral with respect to the issue of motion at an instant; one can accept classical mechanics and adopt whatever position one will concerning this issue. The mathematical interpretation of such important instantaneous magnitudes in classical mechanics as velocity and acceleration involves, of course, derivatives (first derivative, in the case of velocity, second, in the case of acceleration) of position (*qua* vector) with respect to time. This is just to say that, when a vector function $\mathbf{f}$ maps times t on to position vectors $\mathbf{R}$, the instantaneous velocity $\mathbf{V}$ of the object at time t_0 is just the limit (if there is one) of the difference quotient $\Delta\mathbf{R}/\Delta t = \{\mathbf{f}(t) - \mathbf{f}(t_0)\}/(t - t_0)$ as t approaches t_0. But according to the now classical δ, ϵ-interpretation of the limit of a function, which was developed in its final form by Karl Weierstrass toward the middle of the nineteenth century, this claim is simply the following: the instantaneous velocity is set equal to that unique velocity vector $\mathbf{V}_0$ (if there is one) satisfying the condition

for each real number $\epsilon > 0$, there is some real number $\delta > 0$ such that, for any t in the domain of $\mathbf{f}$, $|\Delta\mathbf{R}/\Delta t - \mathbf{V}_0|^{58} < \epsilon$ if $|t - t_0| < \delta$.

So, when we speak of instantaneous velocity what we are referring to, mathematically, is the least (upper or lower) bound of a linearly ordered set of velocities in the full-blown sense: loosely, the limit of a set of (directional) distances traversed, each such distance being divided by the *period* of time taken to traverse it. As long as we have that limit available for purposes of calculation, it does not seem to be a matter of great *mathematical* or *physical* import whether we call it the instantaneous velocity of the object at t_0 or whether we say that the object is moving *at* the temporal instant t_0.

This analysis does suggest, I think, that there is *some* conceptual difference between instantaneous velocity and velocity in the full-blown sense. I have previously made the following suggestion:

it is open to the defender of Aristotle's resolution of the Arrow [which centres, of course, on the denial that the arrow is either moving or at rest at

---

[58] This quantity designates a length of vector differences, which is a scalar quantity and, thus, is comparable with the real number ϵ.

an instant] to claim that [instantaneous velocity] involves a *pros hen* homonymous use of 'velocity': instantaneous velocity is not velocity in the primary or focal sense, i.e. [directed] distance traversed divided by time *during* which it is being traversed, but the limit of an infinite sequence of velocities in this primary sense. Hence, the concept of instantaneous velocity need not imply that a body is moving or at rest at an instant in the way that the concept of velocity in a primary sense implies that a body is either moving or at rest during a (non-zero) interval or 'stretch' of time.[59]

Owen, however, believes that Aristotle should have used his doctrine of *pros hen* homonymy or 'focal meaning'[60] to assign appropriate derivative senses both to '[instantaneous] velocity/speed' and to 'motion/moving [at an instant]'.[61] One certainly *could*, from an Aristotelian perspective, do this. But, so far as I can see, one is under no logical, mathematical, or physical compulsion to do so. And I believe that it is quite unclear, from the historical or psychological viewpoint, to what extent Aristotle's 'failure to do this spoilt his reply to Zeno and bedeviled the course of dynamics'.[62]

Owen's attitude is largely determined, I believe, by his commitment to a premiss that he finds in Zeno's Arrow paradox:

(*b*) what is true of [the arrow] at each *moment* is true of it throughout the whole *period* [of its supposed continuous flight].

Now, Owen surely does not intend this premiss to hold unrestrictedly, i.e. for any property: for, according to the standard contemporary analysis, the arrow is at a unique spatial position at each moment in its flight; but, on the assumption that it moves, it is not at a *unique* position throughout the whole *period*. I assume that what Owen has in mind is simply the two states of being in motion and being at rest. In other words, (*b*) amounts simply to the claim that if the arrow is moving *at* each moment in an interval, then it is moving *throughout* that interval; and similarly for the state of rest. But I have argued that classical mechanics, according to the standard interpretation of the mathematics of that theory, does not force one to adopt this strongly metaphysical principle.

One could follow Aristotle and maintain that the arrow is neither

---

[59] 'What Worried the Crows?', *Classical Quarterly*, 36:2 (1986), 536, n. 10.

[60] This is the doctrine, used to particular effect in Aristotle's analysis of 'being' in terms of the *Metaphysics'* schema of categories, that (to put the point more linguistically or semantically than does Aristotle himself) a term can have distinct, non-synonymous meanings that are none the less all related to a core or focal meaning.

[61] 'The Platonism of Aristotle', 218.   [62] Ibid.

in motion nor at rest with respect to an instant. One could adopt Owen's suggestion, maintaining that the arrow is in motion (in a derivative, *pros hen* homonymous sense of 'motion') *at* each moment contained within a period of continuous motion (in the primary, focal sense of 'motion'). Or one could follow Russell's suggestion that the arrow is at rest at each such moment:

Weierstrass, by strictly banishing from mathematics the use of infinitesimals, has at last shown that we live in an unchanging world, and that the arrow in its flight is truly at rest. Zeno's only error lay in inferring (if he did infer) that, because there is no such thing as a state of change, therefore the world is in the same state at any one time as at any other.[63]

Whether Russell is being entirely serious here is unimportant. The metaphysical point holds irrespective of his intention. That is, Weierstrass's δ, ϵ-method for analysing the concept of the limit of a function, and hence of derivatives of a function, eliminates any real *mathematical* or *physical* impetus to 'resolve the issue of motion at an instant'. If one wishes, one can agree with Zeno in eliminating the notion of a state of change by claiming that a body is always in a state of rest at a moment but deny the premiss (*b*) attributed to Zeno by Owen and accepted by Owen himself. Or, if one wishes, one can follow Owen in retaining both (*b*) and the notion of a state of change, identified with motion at a moment. But, so far as I can see, either option (or Aristotle's *via media*, the elimination of talk of either motion or rest at a moment) is compatible with classical mechanics.

Where Aristotle and Modern Mathematics Part Ways

In this concluding section of the present chapter I recapitulate and expand upon some of the claims I have made earlier in Part I. In other words, this section can be regarded as a summary, from the contemporary perspective, of what I take to be the salient features of Aristotle's analysis of spatial magnitude, time, and motion as *continuous* phenomena.

The divergence between Aristotelian mathematical (or more generally, classical Greek mathematical) conceptions and those contemporary conceptions now considered standard is related, I shall suggest, to an analogous distinction between two models of physical reality, viz., a geometrical versus an arithmetic/algebraic point-set

---

[63] 'Mathematics and Metaphysicians', 63.

model of the structure of spatial magnitude, temporal extent, and locomotion. The most significant mathematical divergence, however, dates only from the point-set analysis of continuous magnitudes in the last half of the nineteenth century. Work on the conceptual foundations of calculus dating from the earlier nineteenth century can (but need not) be given an Aristotelian interpretation. The remarks of the founder of contemporary non-standard analysis, Abraham Robinson, are particularly apposite in this regard:

> When Weierstrass (who had been anticipated to some extent by Bolzano) introduced the δ, ϵ-method about the middle of the nineteenth century he maintained the limit concept in its central place. At the same time, Weierstrass' approach is perhaps closer than Cauchy's to the Greek method of exhaustion or at least to the feature of that method which was described by Leibniz ('*pour que l'erreur soit moindre que l'erreur donneé* . . .'). On the issue of the actual infinite versus the potential infinite, the δ, ϵ-method did not, as such, force its proponents into a definite position. To us, who are trained in the set-theoretic tradition, a phrase such as 'for every positive ϵ, there exists a positive δ . . .' does in fact seem to contain a clear reference to a well-defined infinite totality, i.e. the totality of positive real numbers. On the other hand, already Kronecker made it clear, in his lectures, that to him the phrase meant that one could *compute*, for every *specified* positive ϵ, a positive δ with the required property.[64]

The principal point of divergence between Aristotle and modern mathematics originates, later in the nineteenth century, in the analysis of continuous magnitudes as point-sets, a development that may be viewed as the completion of the process of arithmetizing continuous magnitude.

Aristotle's conception of number is a narrow (and, from the contemporary perspective, restrictive) one, according to which the concept is typically limited to the natural or counting numbers. In *Meta.* 5. 13 he draws a distinction between two sorts of quantity (*poson*): there is *plurality* or *multitude* (*plēthos*), which is to be understood as *numerable* (*arithmēton*) quantity; and there is *magnitude* (*megethos*), which is to be understood as *measurable* (*metrēton*) quantity. While a plurality is divisible into discrete parts, parts that are not continuous one with the other, a magnitude always is divisible (without limit) into parts that are continuous with one another (1020^a7–12). Aristotle elsewhere maintains that 'every number is

---

[64] 'The Metaphysics of the Calculus', in J. Hintikka (ed.), *The Philosophy of Mathematics*, (Oxford, 1969), 162.

known by the one' and that 'the one is the first principle of number *qua* number' (*Meta*. 10. 1. 1052ᵇ22–4). In the case of a plurality of discrete items, there is, so to speak, a natural unit of enumeration: the individual thing which, for the purposes of enumerating the items of the collection, is taken to be indivisible.

However, in the case of continuous magnitudes, enumeration requires the stipulation of a measure (*to metron*) as unit: 'in all these [continuous quantities], the measure and basic principle (*archē*) is something unitary and indivisible, since even in the case of lines, they treat the foot-length as atomic' (1052ᵇ32–3). A bounded interval of a continuous magnitude is not, of course, unitary and indivisible in an absolute sense (*haplōs*), since every continuous magnitude is, in the Aristotelian sense, infinitely divisible. However, it is unitary and indivisible *qua* principle of metrical enumeration, since 'number is a plurality of units' (1053ᵃ31).

Plurality (*plēthos*) has, for Aristotle, a strictly finitistic sense: a *plēthos* is a collection of some natural number $n > 1$ units. As a consequence of Aristotle's distinction between pluralities and magnitudes and his account of number as a plurality of units, it is clear that the contemporary notion of rational and irrational *numbers* would be quite foreign to his way of thinking. The division of the unit interval [0,1] that we associate with the rational *numbers* in that interval would be conceived by Aristotle as pertaining to the unit interval *qua* interval of continuous *magnitude*, not *qua* numerical unit. The result of division of the unit is not, in Aristotle's view, additional numbers that are constructed from the unit and combined with the counting numbers to form a new *numerical* ordered field. *Qua numerical* entity (as opposed to *qua* magnitude), the unit is indivisible.[65] Similarly, the

---

[65] Cf. J. Klein, *Greek Mathematical Thought and the Origin of Algebra*, trans. E. Brann (Cambridge, Mass., and London, 1968), 42, where Klein is speaking about later *Platonist* philosophy of mathematics as well as that of Aristotle: '"Fractions" are never anything but fractional parts of the thing as such which underlies the counting and which can, by reason of its *bodily nature*, be infinitely divided. In the realm of "pure" numbers, on the other hand, the *unit itself* provides the last limit of all possible partitions: all partitioning "will stop at one" (*katalēlksei eis hen*—Theon 18, 11 and 13 f.). Thus Proclus (*in Timaeum*, Diehl, ii, p. 138, 23) says: "Since each number is with respect to its own *kind* one and without parts but with respect to its own *material*, as it were, [cf. Domninus 415, 7; see also P. 32] divisible into parts, though not with respect to all of the material either; but rather what is ultimate [in it, i.e. the unit] is without parts even in the material, and in this ultimate thing [counting or calculation and, above all, partitioning] comes to a stop."' Klein's *opus*, which first appeared in German in 1934, is a classic work which still stands as a perceptive and immensely learned introduction to ancient philosophy of mathematics.

notion of 'irrational' belongs on the side of magnitude, as opposed to number. The ancient account of irrationals is, of course, part and parcel of ancient proportion theory. It is instructive to note that, in the primer of the theory of proportions that constitutes Book 5 of Euclid, the definitions and theorems are all stated in terms of *megethē*; neither *arithmos* nor *plēthos* occurs in these propositions.

The idea that *magnitudes* are infinitely divisible and hence foundationless—not multiples of some natural unit—is entirely Aristotelian. But the Aristotelian conception of number is quite different. Connected, as it is, with the idea of enumeration rather than mensuration, his notion of number does not extend to ordered fields (such as that of the rationals or of the reals) that are similarly foundationless.

In the last half of the nineteenth century, however, the development of set theory and, in particular, its early and intimate connection with the analysis of *point-sets*,[66] completed the eradication of the Aristotelian distinction between magnitude and plurality. In his *Grundlagen einer allgemeinen Mannigfaltigkeitslehre*, Georg Cantor made clear his conviction that concepts of physical magnitudes (such as spatial extension or time) as continuous implicitly appeal to a more fundamental mathematical (i.e. arithmetic) conception of a continuum. In the words of J. W. Dauben,

Drawing upon his theory of real numbers, Cantor wanted to develop a purely arithmetic analysis of the continuum. Given an n-dimensional space G_n, he defined an arithmetic point of the space as any system of n-tuples defined from real numbers ranging from $-\infty$ to $+\infty$. In his notation, $(x_1/x_2/ \ldots /x_n)$ was such an arithmetic point of G_n.[67]

Similarly, Richard Dedekind, at the beginning of his *Stetigkeit und die Irrationalzahlen*, notes that, when he had earlier given lectures on the calculus, he 'had recourse to geometric evidences', 'especially in proving the theorem that every magnitude which grows continually, but not beyond all limits, must certainly approach a limiting value'. He

[66] After his early work on trigonometric series and several significant results in analysis (e.g. the non-denumerability of the real numbers), Cantor published, between 1879 and 1884, a series of papers on *Punktmannigfaltigkeiten*, work that would be important to his later development of abstract set theory. See J. W. Dauben, *Georg Cantor: His Mathematics and Philosophy of the Infinite* (Cambridge, Mass., and London, 1979), ch. 4, 'Early Theory of Point Sets', 77–94.

[67] Ibid. 109.

immediately adds, however, that such evidences 'can make no claim to being scientific, no one will deny'.[68]

A problem entertained by mathematicians in the generations after that of Kronecker and Weierstrass was the task of reconstructing the continuous from what amounted to a set (*Menge*), according to Cantor's characterization of a set: 'any collection into a whole (*Zusammenfassung zu einem Ganzen*) M of definite and separate objects m of our intuition or thought. These objects are called the "elements" of M.'[69] Since the elements of a set are therefore discrete, in the intuitive, dictionary sense of being *intrinsically* separate and distinct, continuity must be reconstructed solely in terms of the *relational* ordering of the elements. Dedekind lucidly states an essential component (Dedekind continuity) of such a reconstruction:

In the preceding section attention was called to the fact that every point of the straight line produces a separation of the same into two portions such that every point of one portion lies to the left of every point of the other. I find that the essence of continuity lies in the converse, i.e. in the following principle:

'If all points of the straight line fall into two classes such that every point of the first class lies to the left of every point of the second class, then there exists one and only one point which produces this division of all points into two classes, this severing of the straight line into two portions.'[70]

Cantor developed a similar notion, which was later to constitute half of his concept of a *perfect set*, which in the *Beiträge* is presented as the conjunction of two conditions: (*a*) every element of the non-denumerable set is the limit of some denumerable, bounded monotonic ascending (descending) sequence (Cantor's 'fundamental sequences') of the set; (*b*) every denumerable, bounded monotonic ascending (descending) sequence of elements of the set possesses a limit that is a member of the set.[71] Condition (*a*)—which Cantor terms

---

[68] *Essays on the Theory of Numbers*, trans. W. W. Beman (Chicago and London, 1924), 'I. Continuity and Irrational Numbers', 1.

[69] G. Cantor, *Contributions of the Founding of the Theory of Transfinite Numbers* (*Beiträge sur Begruendung der transfiniten Mengenlehre*, pts i and ii), trans. P. E. B. Jourdain (New York, n.d.), 85.

[70] Dedekind, *Essays on the Theory of Numbers*, 11.

[71] Cantor, *Contributions*, trans. Jourdain, 128–36. Elsewhere Cantor uses what has come to be the standard, general topological conception of a perfect set: a set that is identical to its derived set or (equivalently) a closed set containing no isolated points. Cantor also appeals to a further necessary condition of a non-denumerable point-set's being a continuum. In the *Grundlagen* this condition assumes a metrical form: what Cantor calls 'connectedness' (*Grundlagen einer allgemeinen Mannigfaltigkeitslehre*, in *Gesammelte Abhandlungen mathematischen und philosophischen Inhalts* (Berlin, 1932), 194) and

the condition of the set's being 'dense in itself'—corresponds (roughly) to Dedekind's condition that every element/point of his linear set defines a particular *Schnitt* or cut; condition (*b*)—which Cantor calls the 'closedness' condition on the set—corresponds to Dedekind's principle stating the essence of continuity, namely, the requirement that every cut be correlated with a unique point/element of the linear set.

With respect to *Aristotle*'s analysis of continuous magnitudes, his 'problem' is not that he lacks the conception of Dedekind continuity. Rather, from the contemporary, point-set perspective, his strictly geometrical conception of magnitude gives him the concept too easily, making it trivial. Beginning with the idea of magnitude, a point is *constructed* by a cut or bisection; indeed, where there *was* potentially a *locus* (point) of bisection, there *are*, after bisection, two points: the two resulting *termini* of line-segments where they were cut.[72] It is only when the idea of a magnitude, *potentially* divisible without end (dense in the distributive sense, to use my earlier phrase), is replaced by the idea of an *actually* dense linear ordering of discrete elements that it becomes problematic whether a cut must yield two segments one and only one of which has a terminal element at the *locus* of the cut. Moreover, the point-set analysis of continuity makes possible the concept of a '(half)-open' interval, an actually dense linear ordering without a terminal point, whereas Aristotle's geometrical picture of magnitude and his constructive conception of points makes such a concept much more difficult to form. As we established in our earlier discussion of his physics, Aristotle's lack of this concept is one source of conflict between his analysis of locomotion and the contemporary standard kinematic analysis.

Another discrepancy between Aristotle's view and the standard contemporary view of continuous magnitudes is also a direct consequence of the point-set analysis. This discrepancy pertains to the various non-supervenience principles discussed earlier, which Aristotle accepts and contemporary analysis rejects. Let us consider once again two of these principles:

---

what is now sometimes referred to as 'well-chainedness'. In the *Beiträge*, it assumes the requirement that the linear continuum X contain a denumerable subset, of the order type of the rational numbers, dense in it (*Contributions*, 134–36).

[72] For more on the Aristotelian conception of continuity and its relation to contemporary topological conceptions, see my 'On Continuity', 1–12.

N-SM: Each partition of a continuous magnitude having positive measure or size into proper parts yields parts the sums of whose measure is non-nil.

N-SC: Each partition of a continuous magnitude into proper parts yields parts each of which is pairwise continuous with at least one other such part.

Holding that a continuous magnitude is constituted of nothing but continuous sub-magnitudes, which are potentially divisible *ad infinitum* and, hence, foundationless, Aristotle grounds both the positive size/measure and the continuity of the whole magnitude under consideration in the positive measure and continuity of these parts. That is, he holds that continuity and positive measure *cannot* supervene on elements that are not pairwise continuous and the pairwise sums of whose measure is always nil. According to the point-set analysis, however, such properties supervene on the point-set. A point-set can have positive measure although all the singleton subsets containing, individually, its elements (and, indeed, all its subsets of sufficiently smaller cardinality) have zero measure. And a point-set can be continuous although there is no sense in which its elements are pairwise continuous.

Although these 'supervenience phenomena' have been rendered perfectly consistent from a mathematical/logical point of view, their intuitive peculiarity still, occasionally, elicits comment. This intuitive peculiarity seems ultimately to be grounded in the following fact concerning the point-set (as opposed to Aristotelian) construal of continuous magnitudes: the *intrinsic* nature of the *ultimate* parts (i.e. points or elements of the set) is totally irrelevant to the formal, structural properties of the collection of these parts, according to the point-set analysis. From the point-set perspective, the elements/points are mere ciphers, since it is only their *relational* properties—or more properly, the relational properties of subsets of them—that are relevant to the formal, structural features of the whole. From the Aristotelian perspective, however, the continuity and positive measure of a quantity of continuous magnitude must be grounded, with respect to the parts resulting from any possible partition of the magnitude, both in the intrinsic continuity and positive measure of the parts and in the relation among the parts in the whole.

How great, then, are the differences between the Aristotelian conception of the continuous magnitudes of spatial extension, time, and locomotion and the standard contemporary point-set conception? On the one hand, the point-set conception makes possible the at–at ontology of motion, succinctly set forth by Russell in a passage that I previously quoted:

Motion consists merely in the fact that bodies are sometimes in one place and sometimes in another, and that they are at intermediate places at intermediate times. Only those who have waded through the quagmire of philosophic speculation on this subject can realize what a liberation from antique prejudices is involved in this simple and straightforward commonplace.[73]

There is, of course, a degree of *over*simplification in Russell's statement of the 'straightforward commonplace'. The standard contemporary analysis assumes not merely that a moving body is 'at intermediate places at intermediate times' but that the function from times to places is continuous. Moreover, it is standardly assumed that the (temporal) domain and (spatial) range of this function are *point-sets* (of temporal instants and spatial points or positions, respectively) that satisfy appropriate continuity constraints—although, as Cantor showed, it is possible to define continuous motion in a spatial point-set that is not, 'as a whole', continuous.[74] Russell's basic contention, however, seems to be a valid one: the point-set analysis of continuity suggests—even if it does not entail—the at–at ontology of motion. That is, this mathematical analysis makes plausible the decomposition of continuous motion into what seem to be non-motions—a set of motion slices or freeze-frames. And such a decomposition is certainly foreign to Aristotle's way of thinking about continuous motion.

Yet it is important to note that, in view of the dense and continuous ordering of these frames or slices, the essential *kinematic* features of Aristotle's analysis are retained. The frames/slices do not represent pauses of the moving object because they do not, individually, last or

---

[73] 'Mathematics and Metaphysicians', 66.

[74] Cantor showed in a paper of 1882 ('Ueber unendliche, lineare Punktmannigfaltig-keiten', pt. iii, repr. in *Gesammelte Athandlungen*, 149–57) that if, from a continuous domain *A* of *n*-tuples, a denumerable subset dense in *A* is removed, a continuous line 'given by a unique analytical rule' exists that joins any 2 points in the remainder. See the discussion in Dauben, *Georg Cantor*, 85–6. Interestingly enough, Cantor regarded the assumption that physical space possesses the structure of a point-set that is a three-dimensional continuum as an arbitrary assumption: 'The hypothesis of the continuity of space is therefore nothing but the assumption, arbitrary in itself, of the complete one-to-one correspondence between the 3-dimensional purely arithmetic continuum (x, y, z) and the space underlying the world of phenomena [*Erscheinungswelt*]' (Cantor, 'Punktmannigfaltigkeiten', 156, as translated in Dauben, *Georg Cantor*, 86).

endure for any period of time. Nor should such frames/slices be seen as positional states which the body *successively* occupies, 'jumping' or 'jerking' from one to another. Since the positions are densely ordered, there is no *particular* other place to which a body that is continuously moving can be jerked from any given place. According to the at–at account of continuous motion, as well as Aristotle's account, continuous motion always involves motion *through* a spatial interval or distance *during* a period of time. Within this period of time, the continuously moving body is always traversing densely and continuously ordered intermediate places; there is no jump, instantaneous or otherwise, from one place to another place without the traversal of such a continuum of intermediate places.

In sum, the nature of the difference between the Aristotelian and contemporary point-set pictures of motion is not kinematic: both pictures yield essentially the same conception of motion as continuous. Indeed, elementary but fundamental mathematical analysis of this conception of continuity (in terms of the continuity of function from time elapsed to distance traversed) need not be interpreted in terms of *point* sets nor be tied to the at–at metaphysical picture of motion— although, of course, such mathematical analysis *can* be, and typically is, so conceived. The difference is metaphysical, in a 'hard-core' sense of the term. Although his kinematic conception of locomotion closely agrees with that of the at–at metaphysic, *kinēsis* remains a fundamental, ontological category for Aristotle, not to be reduced to non-motions in the form of instantaneous spatial positions of the moving body.

We now turn, in Part II, to an examination of several ancient alternatives both to Aristotle's metaphysical and to his kinematic conception of motion, spatial extension, and time. The common ancient assumption seems to have been that the Aristotelian metaphysical principle of kinetic non-supervenience, i.e. the conception of locomotion as irreducible to anything but kinetic sub-segments, is closely tied to the Aristotelian kinematic conception of locomotion as continuous. In the present chapter I have maintained that the at–at ontology of motion, which severs this tie, becomes fully viable only as a result of mathematical developments that occurred in the second half of the nineteenth century.

PART II
Spatial Magnitude, Time, and Motion: Alternatives to Aristotelianism

Introduction to Part II

I propose to investigate in Part II two Hellenistic models of spatial magnitude, time, and motion—models that can be seen as conceptual alternatives to the Aristotelian model considered in some detail in Part I. One such model is the atomistic or quantum model, associated not only with Epicurean atomists but also with the 'Dialectical' philosopher Didororus Cronus, who was a contemporary of Epicurus. The other alternative model is Stoic in provenance and involves, according to the interpretation that I shall explore, the elimination of geometrical boundaries and other limit entities from the physical world. As I indicated in the Preface and Apologia, both these alternative models may be thought of as 'ungeometrical'. Unlike the Aristotelian model, both involve the refusal to apply the standard ancient 'Euclidean' conception of geometrical continua to the physical world. Owing to the close relation between physical science and geometry—a relation that was, in some respects, closer in antiquity than it is now—this refusal to countenance the application of the developing standard geometry to physical reality involves a criticism, sometimes quite explicit, of Euclidean geometry itself.

My investigation of the quantum and Stoic models may, with some justice, be thought to be rather narrow. First, my concern with the models is *primarily* conceptual, rather than historical. As many readers are no doubt already aware, there has been a major renaissance of interest in Hellenistic philosophical thought—or, more broadly, post-Aristotelian ancient philosophy—during the last fifteen to twenty years. Important philological and historical work, as well as impressive philosophical study of this period, continues. Although I hope to make judicious use of this research, I do not wish to represent Part II of this book as a comprehensive study of Hellenistic physics. I shall not be *centrally* concerned with the history of atomistic or Stoic physics, nor even with the very complex issues surrounding the actual historical connection between Aristotle and the Peripatetic tradition, on the one hand, and Epicurean and Stoic physical thought on the other.

The following investigation is primarily intended as a conceptual or philosophical investigation of two alternatives—of which there are scant but tantalizing historical traces—to an Aristotelian model of spatial magnitude, time, and motion, a model that combines the geometrical conception of infinitely divisible and continuous extension with some distinctively Aristotelian metaphysical underpinnings. My strong suspicion, to which I have already alluded and which I shall attempt to justify further in the following chapters, is that the *geometrical* conception of continuous magnitude and the Aristotelian metaphysics supporting that conception (particularly the Aristotelian elucidation of infinite divisibility in terms of potentiality) were considered, in the Hellenistic period, to be conceptually inseparable. Although I am certainly not unconcerned with 'history of *actual* philosophy', the 'history of possible philosophy' that I mentioned in the Preface and Apologia figures largely in Part II—partly because the paucity of hard evidence makes it virtually impossible to develop a philosophically engaging account that does not, at some point, transcend the data. However, I attempt to make clear to the reader my own sense of what is conjectural (and to what degree it is so) in the following analysis.

5
The Quantum Model: Spatial Magnitude

We, in our age, are quite accustomed to the idea that matter or corporeal substance comes in discrete quanta—chunks of some sort. Indeed, we are apt to regard as a priori implausible a conception of matter according to which it is radically continuous and *homeomerous*: a mass stuff each spatially determinable part of which, no matter how small, possesses no spatial interstices or natural joints, and is qualitatively identical to every other spatially determinable part of the same kind of stuff. A natural response to the conception of corporeal substance as a radically continuous *plenum* is, I believe, that this conception does not allow corporeal substance sufficient structure for the conception to be of any explanatory value in a physical theory. Upon reflection, then, it is perhaps a bit surprising how deeply entrenched in contemporary physical thought is the conception of space, time, and space–time as continua. Although there have been some contemporary physicists who have entertained the conception of quantized space, time, or space–time, these represent a minority position, as Richard Sorabji has pointed out.[1] It seems likely that the development of modern mathematics is at least partly responsible for the persistence, within the context of a physics of quantized matter, of the conception of space and time or space–time as continuous. For the structure of both (Cartesian powers of) the field of real and the field of complex numbers is continuous; so continuity figures largely in the development of modern mathematics beginning at least with the calculus. Consequently, there are advantages of mathematical expedience and simplification to the operative assumption that space and time or space–time possess a dense and continuous structure.

A similar proclivity toward a conception of magnitude as infinitely divisible and continuous characterized ancient geometry. As we saw in

[1] For references pertaining to quantized time in contemporary physics, see Sorabji, *Time, Creation and the Continuum*, 381–3.

the preceding chapter, Aristotle regarded the quantum assumption—that there is a least magnitude—as detrimental to mathematics. Cicero echoes this view in the *De finibus*:

This is certainly not worthy of the physical scientist—to believe that there is some minimal unit. And [Epicurus] assuredly would never have believed it if he had preferred to learn geometry from his own colleague Polyaenus rather than to make Polyaenus unlearn geometry.[2]

It is none the less true that ancient physical thought was not so heavily dependent upon mathematics that the very idea of 'doing physics' in isolation from the standard mathematics of the day would have seemed entirely ludicrous. I shall discuss the relation between the quantum theory and ancient mathematics in greater detail later in this chapter. At the present juncture, however, it is appropriate to note that, despite mathematical objections, the move from an atomist conception of material substance to an atomist or quantum conception of spatial magnitude and time was apparently an easier conceptual move in antiquity than it was later to become. According to most (but not all) scholars, such a quantum conception of spatial magnitude and time was developed by Epicurus; and it was certainly a central element of the thought of Diodorus Cronus.

There are two forms of the doctrine that spatial magnitude (or temporal extension) is constituted of quanta. According to the weaker form, it is a *physical* fact that corporeal objects are constituted of indivisible quanta. Such quanta are minimal or indivisible only in so far as it is a physical fact that any physical property F either characterizes all of a quantum of spatial extension or none of it. That is, such physical properties are realized only in integral multiples of a quantum. Similarly, in the case of a temporal quantum, it would be a physical fact that the universe is in a certain physical state throughout all of a temporal quantum or throughout none of it. This version of quantum theory assumes a sharp distinction between physical theory and the mathematics in which it may be formulated. Quanta of spatial and temporal extension can be characterized in terms of physical geometry and topology of *continuous magnitudes*. Consequently, such

[2] Cicero, *De finibus bonorum et malorum*, 1. 6. 20. According to the report of Cicero (*Academica* 2. 23. 106), Polyaenus was a 'great mathematician' who, after he had come to accept the doctrines of Epicurus, believed that 'the whole of geometry is false'. For more on the relation between Epicurus and his school to the ancient mathematical tradition, see the excellent paper of David Sedley, 'Epicurus and the Mathematicians of Cyzicus', *Chronache Ercolanesi*, 6 (1976), 23–54.

quanta will be, *qua* magnitudes of spatial extension or time, infinitely divisible; they will possess a particular shape, be of a specific size, have boundaries and edges, etc. According to this weaker form of quantum theory, considerable restrictions must be placed on what counts as a physical property. For example, if a spatial quantum is a cube having edges all of length *l*, this property cannot characterize any proper part of the quantum. Hence, such a property cannot count as a physical property in terms of which we just formulated the doctrine.

A stronger version of the quantum conception of spatial extension or time less sharply distinguishes physical theory from the mathematics applicable to the physical world. Spatial quanta (and/or temporal quanta), according to this form of quantum theory, are units that are indivisible from a geometrical/topological perspective, and not just from a 'merely physical' one. The former, weaker version of quantum theory has, I think, a greater appeal from the contemporary perspective. I suspect that *part* of the explanation for this is historical. The physical scientist has a highly developed mathematics of the continuous at his or her disposal. And it is very natural for us to conceive mathematics as an analytical, a priori tool which is applied to a synthetic, a posteriori 'remainder' of physical theory. It seems that in antiquity, however, the typical conception of the relation between mathematics and physical theory was a much more holistic one. The epistemology that underlies the standard contemporary conception of empirical physical theory and mathematics as an external but (if we are lucky) useful analytical tool developed—with vicissitudes—through a long historical period.

In the present chapter, I shall be primarily concerned with the second, stronger version of quantum theory. It is by no means certain that it was the stronger rather than weaker version of quantum theory that became orthodox Epicurean doctrine. The stronger version is the more conceptually interesting version, however; and I think that it is fair to say that the balance of the rather meagre evidence we have points in its direction. Although the exact historical connections are obscure, the quantum model can be interpreted, conceptually, as an alternative to the Aristotelian model, which we examined in Part I. But what sort of an alternative? I propose to consider the hypothesis that the quantum theory is, in part, a *metaphysical* alternative in which the role of the Aristotelian concept of potentiality is drastically attenuated. Although I attempted in Part I to distinguish conceptually the formal, structural elements of Aristotle's analysis of spatial magnitude, time, and motion from the metaphysical and ontological elements of that analysis, a 'moral' of Part I—it seems to me—is that, from the perspective of Aristotle, such a distinction is not really possible.

For example, although Aristotle's conception of locomotion as smooth or continuous has much in common with the standard contemporary kinematic analysis of motion, Aristotle does not accept what is often found as a metaphysical corollary of the contemporary analysis: the reduction of continuous motion to a dense and Dedekind-continuous, linearly ordered set of instantaneous positions of the moving body. Rather, I think Aristotle is quite serious in his claim (at *Phys*. 3. 1) that *kinēsis*—even in the special case of locomotion—is an ontologically primitive condition of a physical object, a primitive condition that involves an irreducible potentiality (for attaining the actual *terminus ad quem*, or completed, stative actualization of the *kinēsis* in question).[3] Although the notion of positions where the continuously moving body A (or some other continuously moving body moving synchronously with A) *could* have stopped prior to its *actual terminus ad quem* proves useful in Aristotle's kinematic analysis of locomotion, Aristotle does not *identify* any such collection of positions, considered as actual positions of the moving body, with the motion. Even the Aristotelian analysis of the infinite divisibility of continuous magnitudes such as spatial extension and time appeals to a fundamental and irreducible potentiality: such magnitudes are infinitely divisible in the sense that a process of actual division of a finite quantity of a continuous magnitude into sub-magnitudes *could*, in principle, always be carried beyond any finite number of stages of division. But here too, as I maintained in Part I, Aristotle exhibits no propensity to conceive a finite quantity of continuous magnitude as *actually* constituted of an infinite collection of such sub-magnitudes. In fact, in his philosophical lexicon (*Meta.* 5. 7. 1017^{b}1–9) Aristotle uses the example of the 'half line being in [the whole line]' (along with, *inter alia*, the Hermes in the stone) to illustrate the potentiality sense of *to einai* ('being') and '*to on*' ('what is').

The conception of primitive or 'surd' potentialities—which can be explicated only with reference to the temporally subsequent state of their actualization and cannot be reductively eliminated in favour of

---

[3] I follow Hintikka *et al.*, *Aristotle on Modality and Determinism*, in seeing Aristotle's definition of *kinēseis* in *Phys.* 3. 1 as creating a 'haven for *unrealized* potentialities' (73–4) and as implying that a potentiality can 'enjoy full actuality (as a potentiality not yet realized) only in the form of a *kinēsis* toward its realization' (72).

some state or states of full actualization—has often been the occasion, in individuals generally sympathetic to Aristotelian naturalism, of a sense of uneasiness. It has also been the basis, in other cases, of anti-Aristotelian gibes such as Molière's ridicule of 'dormitive powers'. In addition to epistemological concern about such potentialities (e.g. concern as to whether their explanatory role in any physical theory must not be viciously circular) there would have been ample reason in antiquity, at least from the time of Parmenides, to regard them as metaphysically suspect. For they seem to be outstanding candidates for occupancy of a dubious, 'bastard' ontological category between 'what is' and 'what is not'. It therefore seems plausible that an ancient attempt to eliminate the Aristotelian metaphysical category of *dunamis* or potentiality—which would, I believe, entail the attempt to eliminate the Aristotelian category of *kinēsis* or motion—might also lead to a rejection of Aristotle's formal, structural account of spatial magnitude and time and of kinematic analysis of motion. I argued in the last chapter that it is only with the development of real analysis and the theory of sets of transfinite cardinality in the late nineteenth century (and later developments in measure theory and dimension theory deriving from set theory) that there emerged a mathematically plausible alternative *metaphysical account* of continuous magnitudes and of continuous motion. Continuous magnitudes of finite positive measure and finite positive dimension could then be reduced, should one care to do so, to non-denumerably infinite aggregates of punctal elements, i.e. elements individually characterized by null dimension and null measure. And the at–at ontology of motion could then be invoked—as Russell in fact invoked it—in order to conclude that, *even in the case of continuous motion*, 'motion consists merely in the fact that bodies are sometimes in one place and sometimes in another, and that they are in intermediate places at intermediate times'.[4]

I submit, however, that such an alternative metaphysical picture was not feasible in antiquity. We certainly do not regard the conception of spatial magnitude, time, and locomotion as infinitely divisible and continuous as a peculiarly *Aristotelian* conception. And, largely because of nineteenth century mathematical developments which I discussed in the preceding chapter, we do not see these conceptions as wedded to the Aristotelian notion of potentiality. The situation appears to have been otherwise in antiquity, however. It may well then have seemed

---

[4] 'Mathematics and Metaphysicians', 66.

that, in order to rid oneself of Aristotelian *dunameis*, one also had to give up the concepts of spatial magnitude, time, and locomotion as infinitely divisible and continuous.[5] I shall return to more concrete consideration of this suggestion in this and the next chapter. But I shall begin with an examination of several atomist arguments for the constitution of physical magnitudes from quanta or *partes minimae*.

ARGUMENTS FOR QUANTA

Several interrelated arguments for postulating minimal quanta of magnitude are to be found in the ancient sources.[6] Although these arguments are not likely to strike the contemporary philosopher or scientist as very impressive, they perhaps possess more conceptual interest than would initially seem to be the case. I shall be particularly interested in them as presenting an alternative to the Aristotelian analysis of magnitude. Along the way, I shall also make some suggestions as to why such an alternative might have seemed attractive.

---

[5] The suggestion that a fundamental objection of Epicurus to the Aristotelian conception of continuous magnitudes was that the Aristotelian notion 'involved the notion of potentiality and this was in conflict with his fundamental principles' is made by David Furley in *Two Studies in the Greek Atomists*, Study I: *Indivisible Magnitudes* (Princeton, NJ, 1967), 128. The nature of this 'conflict' is not so obvious, however. Furley suggests (155), that 'it would seem to [Epicurus] contradictory to say that a finite magnitude is *potentially* divisible to infinity, and yet to deny that it consists of an infinitely large number of parts'. I am not sure that there is compelling evidence that this is Epicurus' belief. And Aristotle, through his careful analysis of the concept of ('potential') infinite divisibility, has surely made a cogent case that it is *not* inconsistent both to admit infinite divisibility—in his own *potentia*-sense of a (theoretically) indefinitely extendable process—and to deny that a finite magnitude *actually* 'consists of an infinitely large number of parts'. So, if Epicurus sees a problem here, I suspect that it pertains to Aristotle's uses of the potentiality–actuality distinction at precisely this juncture. The *nature* of any objections that Epicurus might have had to this metaphysical conception of *kinēseis* and *energeiai* is, I fear, a largely conjectural matter. However, in the course of this chapter and the next, I shall not refrain from making several conjectures pertaining to this issue.

[6] Whether Epicureans applied the notion of magnitude, as I am conceiving it in this chapter and the next, to both body and void is a difficult issue. I am inclined to think that they did and that the fact that they did is connected with their conception of void, not as the Democritean *ouden* or *to mē on*, but as a mass entity having a certain *phusis*, viz., intangibility and lack of resistance. In this connection, the characterization of Epicurean void by P.-R. Schulz as 'eine Art ideale Flüssigkeit' is attractive ('Das Verständnis des Raumes bei Lucrez', *Tijdschrift voor Filosofie*, 20 (1958), 29). This idea is defended and further developed in a very interesting paper by Brad Inwood, 'The Origin of Epicurus' Concept of Void', *Classical Philology*, 76: 4 (1981), 273–85.

The Combination of the Paradox of Measure and Analogy to Perceptible Minima

In Epicurus' *Letter to Herodotus*, we find the following considerations:

> Additionally, one must not hold that in a finite body there are infinite bits [or particles: *ongkoi*] however small. So not only must we deny division to infinity in the direction of the smaller, in order that we may not render all things weak and, in our conception of masses, we may not be constrained to waste them away, chafing away the things that are to what is nothing. We also must not accept that, among finite bodies, there is any passage to the infinite, not even in the direction of the smaller. For when one says that infinitely many bits inhere in something, however small they may be, it is not possible to see how this thing could still be limited in magnitude. For it is clear that the infinite number of bits must individually be of some size; and, then, whatever size they might be, their [combined] magnitude would be infinite.   (D.L. 10. 56–7)[7]

This passage can be interpreted as setting forth a version of what has, in recent times, come to be termed 'Zeno's paradox of measure'. The paradox, for which a fairly tenuous connection to Zeno of Elea can be established on the basis of several passages in Simplicius' commentary on Aristotle's *Physics*,[8] is set forth by Brian Skyrms as follows:

> Suppose that the line-segment is composed of an infinite number of parts. Zeno claims that this leads to absurdity in the following way:
>
> (I) Either the parts all have zero magnitude or they all have [the same] positive magnitude.
>
> (II) If they have zero magnitude, the line-segment will have zero magnitude, since the magnitude of the whole is the sum of the magnitudes of its parts.
>
> (III) If they have [the same] positive magnitude, then the line-segment will have infinite magnitude, for the same reason.[9]

As Skyrms points out, derivation of the inconsistency depends on (*a*) the assumption that a finite line-segment can be partitioned into an infinite collection of parts, (*b*) a principle of the measurability of these parts (i.e. the assumption that the concept of magnitude, zero or positive, actually applies to such parts), (*c*) an invariance assumption

---

[7] In citing from Epicurus' letters I shall follow the practice of citing, in the text, the particular location of the passage in the 10th book of Diogenes Laertius' *Vitae* (henceforward D.L.). A very full and useful commentary on the text of the *Letter to Herodotus* (*Ep. Hdt.*), from 56. 5 to 59, is given in Furley, *Two Studies in the Greek Atomists*, 7–27.

[8] Simplicius, *In phys.*, CAG 9, 139. 3–19 and 140. 27–141. 8.

[9] 'Zeno's Paradox of Measure', 226.

(i.e. the assumption that the parts all have equal magnitude), (*d*) Archimedes' axiom (irrespective of how large the finite positive measure of the line-segment is and of how small the finite positive measure of each part is, there is some *finite natural number n* such that the latter added to itself *n* times surpasses the former), and (*e*) a principle of ultra- (or complete, or perfect) additivity (the principle that, irrespective of the cardinality of a collection of real numbers, the concept of the sum of such a collection is defined).[10]

The standard contemporary resolution of the paradox, of course, denies proposition (II) as a corollary of the denial of (*e*), the principle of complete additivity. Despite the problems discussed in Chapter 1 concerning the formulation of anything like a principle of additivity for infinite collections addenda and, consequently, despite problems with the intelligibility of the idea of either the acceptance or denial of a principle of complete additivity, Skyrms seems to me to be correct in asserting: 'Neither the school of Plato, nor that of Aristotle, nor the Atomists appear to have challenged (II).'[11] Neither, so far as I am aware, is there any indication of an ancient mathematical challenge of proposition (II).

The absence in antiquity of anything like the contemporary resolution of the paradox—a resolution that not a few people today regard, at least on initial exposure, as unintuitive or *ad hoc*—leaves the ancient field largely to the Aristotelian resolution. Briefly characterized, the Aristotelian resolution is to nip the incipient paradox in the bud by denying (*a*). Aristotle, as we have seen, certainly accepts the infinite divisibility of a finite magnitude. But his thoroughly constructive, finitistic, ∞-conception of infinite divisibility precludes an actual or completed infinite partition of a finite magnitude. In the present context, the import of the Aristotelian ∞-conception of infinite divisibility is that there can be no partition of a finite magnitude that would yield an infinite collection of addenda, a collection that could be regarded as a totality and for which it thus makes sense to use such

---

[10] It is unclear from Simplicius' discussion how many of these principles Zeno might have had in mind or accepted. In Ch. 1 we discussed the problem of even formulating a principle of ultra or perfect additivity within the context of ancient mathematical or philosophical thought. And, as Malcolm Schofield indicates (G. S. Kirk, J. E. Raven, and M. Schofield, *The Presocratic Philosophers: A Critical History with a Selection of Texts*, 2nd edn. (Cambridge, 1983), 268), it is possible that Zeno did not have in mind an invariance principle, i.e. the necessary restriction of prop. III (in Skyrms's formulation of the paradox) to cases where each of the infinite number of parts has the same measure.

[11] Skyrms, 'Zeno's Paradox of Measure', 227.

notions as union or sum. The standard contemporary resolution admits such infinite partitions and attributes measure to each of the parts; but, in some cases (non-denumerable partitions) it denies that the notion of sum or addition is applicable. Aristotle, on the other hand, denies the possibility of any such partitions: this denial is part and parcel of his reiterated claim that points are not, strictly, 'parts' of the line (segment) and that line (segments) are not constituted of points. For points do not measure (*katametrein*) a line-segment. That is, no line-segment is an integral multiple of points; nor is the size of any line-segment an integral multiple of the sizes of points.

A number of scholars, for example, Skyrms[12] and Sorabji,[13] have seen something like (a part of) Zeno's paradox of measure being rehearsed by Aristotle in *GC* 1. 2, where he presents physical considerations that—so he claims—led Democritus to postulate invisible (*aorata*) and atomic magnitudes (*megethē atoma*) (316^{b}33; 317^{a}1). Aristotle's argumentation, which was considered in some detail in Chapter 1, involves the claim that if (*per impossibile*, in Aristotle's view) a finite magnitude were divisible into nothing but points, then, paradoxically, 'if all of them were put together, they would not constitute any magnitude' (316^{a}34). Aristotle explicitly rejects the atomic-magnitude resolution of the problem. Although, as we saw, the details of Aristotle's own alternative resolution are complicated and none too clear, his resolution involves the denial of the possibility of one sense of divisibility 'through and through' (i.e. a sense that would involve the divisibility of a finite magnitude into nothing but points or contacts):

It is not at all absurd that every sensible body should both be divisible at each individual point and also indivisible; for it will turn out to be potentially divisible but actually indivisible. But its being divisible everywhere at the same time even potentially would seem to be impossible. Because if that is possible, [the division] could happen, with the consequence not that it would actually at the same time be both indivisible and divided, but that it would be divided at each and every point. Nothing, therefore, will be left; and body, having been destroyed into the incorporeal, might again come to be either from points or absolutely nothing. But how could that be possible?   (316^{b}20–8)

Part of Aristotle's point may be that from

(1) At each point it is possible that a finite magnitude is divided

we cannot validly infer

[12] Ibid. 225–6.
[13] Sorabji, *Time, Creation and the Continuum*, 336–41.

(2) It is possible that at each point a finite magnitude is divided.

Such an inference involves a shift in position of universal quantifier and possibility operator (the inference of something of the form $M\forall a\Phi$ from something of the form $\forall aM\Phi$), a shift that, in contemporary quantified modal logic, is typically not valid. (Compare the inference from 'For each candidate, it is possible that (s)he wins the election' to 'It is possible that all the candidates win the election'.) Aristotle believes, however, that (2) is actually false and, as we also saw in Chapter 1, seems to argue—unhappily, from the contemporary perspective—for its falsity from the premiss that points are not successively ordered (*ephekses*).

I return, at long last, to the passage from Epicurus' *Letter to Herodotus*. The reference at D.L. 56, to division to infinity as 'chafing away the things that are to what is nothing' may represent one horn of Zeno's paradox of measure, that in which an infinite division of a finite magnitude results in parts (e.g. points) each having no magnitude. It is more clear that, later in the passage (D.L. 57), we get the other horn: if each of an infinite number of bits of a finite magnitude has some positive (invariant?) magnitude, then, paradoxically, their sum will be infinite.

What is, I think, particularly noteworthy in Epicurus' version of this paradox is the apparent lack of any consideration of the Aristotelian resolution of the puzzle. The import of Aristotle's conception of infinite divisibility as non-terminating is that the first horn of the paradox is removed: we never obtain an *actual* infinity of parts; rather, we can *always*, in principle, carry the cutting or division further. Hence, there is no concern about *this* sort of infinite division 'chafing away the things that are to what is nothing'. While Epicurus uses the same phrase as Aristotle,[14] *epi' toulatton* ('in the direction of the smaller/less'), to qualify the sort of infinite process he is discussing, he seems to be ignoring or conveniently forgetting the sense that Aristotle had attached to this phrase, a sense—as I argued in Chapter 4—shared with the ancient mathematical tradition. If, then, we interpret Epicurus as giving an argument for the constitution of magnitudes from indivisible quanta of some sort, an argument that is a version of what has come to be called Zeno's paradox of measure, his argument seems to represent no advance on the argument for minimal quanta

---

[14] See e.g. *Phys*. 3. 7. 207ᵇ4.

attributed by Aristotle in *GC* 1. 2 to Democritus. But Aristotle believes that he has refuted *that* argument.

If we look to the immediately following passage in Epicurus' text, however, we can perhaps discover some evidence that he is neither forgetting nor avoiding the Aristotelian attempt to undermine the paradox of measure. Recollecting that Democritus apparently employed such an argument as an atomist argument for minimal quanta of magnitude, let us consider the following remarks by Epicurus:

Since what is finite has an extremity [*akron*] that is distinguishable, even if it is not conceivable as existing by itself [*kath' heauto*], it is not possible not to think of what is in succession to this as being of the same sort; and thus proceeding forward with respect to what is in succession, it must be possible in this way to reach infinity in thought.   (D.L. 10. 57)[15]

Richard Sorabji has noted that, in Aristotle's arguments (as in *Phys.* 6. 1) to the effect that atomic constituents of magnitudes could not be either continuous with (*suneche*) each other or touching/in contact with (*haptomena*) each other, he leaves a loophole that later atomists were quick to take advantage of.[16] The loophole, apparently not ruled out by Aristotle, is the logical possibility of the arrangement of minimal quanta *merely ephekses*, 'in succession', *without* their touching (being in contact) or being continuous one with another. For, according to the definition in *Phys.* 5. 3, the state of affairs consisting in two things being in succession requires only that one be 'after' another with nothing of the same kind located between them (*Phys.* 5. 3. 226^{b}34–227^{a}6).

I suggest that atomists not only made general use of this loophole with respect to the issue of the arrangement of minimal quanta in larger masses (i.e. atoms, for the Epicureans). It also seems that Epicurus is making specific use of the loophole in D.L. 57 in order to undermine the Aristotelian refutation of the paradox of measure. I shall shortly return to the former, general use of the loophole. At present, I am concerned with its latter, specific employment. The reader may recall that in Chapter 1 the argument was advanced that in

---

[15] I here adopt Schneider's *kata⟨to⟩ toiouton* ('in such a way'), agreeing with Long and Sedley that it 'merely repeat[s] the sense of *houto*'. I cannot make out what, precisely, the force of their *kata tosouton* ('to that extent') would be as a qualification of the idea of reaching infinity in thought. See A. A. Long and D. N. Sedley, *The Hellenistic Philosophers*, ii (Cambridge, 1987), 33.

[16] Sorabji, *Time, Creation and the Continuum*, 367–75.

GC 1. 2 Aristotle does not rely simply on his own constructive or finitistic conception of infinite divisibility to establish the conclusion that a finite magnitude cannot be completely divided into an infinite of points, with no undivided magnitude remaining. The fact that points are not successively ordered seems to be a crucial premiss in Aristotle's *argument* that a completed division of a finite magnitude into nothing but points is not possible. In my earlier discussion I hypothesized an argument (unfortunately fallacious but perhaps from Aristotle's perspective not obviously so) from which he might have derived the impossibility of such a complete dissolution of magnitude into points, an argument that makes essential use of the fact that points are not discretely or successively ordered. I am not now concerned, however, with the nature of the connection of this premiss with the impossibility of such a dissolution, but with the fact that the non-successive ordering of points *does* figure, in Aristotle's discussion, as a premiss with respect to his conclusion concerning the impossibility of chafing away a magnitude into nothing but points (or other limit entities).

I suggest that Epicurus is here countering what he regards as the Aristotelian basis for avoiding the complete dissolution of magnitudes into limit entities. There is a great difference, according to the Aristotelian conception, between points or other limit entities *within* a continuous body or other stretch of magnitude (e.g. interval of time associated with a particular *kinēsis*) and the points or limit entities bounding or limiting such a body or actually demarcated stretch of magnitude. A continuous body or continuous stretch of magnitude has such limit entities within it only in a very special sense, according to the Aristotelian model: at most, they exist within such a body *dunamei* or potentially, as *loci* where the body/stretch of magnitude *could* actually be divided. On the other hand, the Aristotelian conception would seem to commit us to the *actual* (as opposed to merely potential) existence of some limit entities, e.g. the surface of a body, the *terminus* of a line inscribed in a wax tablet, or the punctal now (temporal *terminus ad quem*) at which a continuous *kinēsis* ends. There is no indication that Aristotle conceives of such entities as somehow spatially indeterminate or extended: they are true limits in the sense that they possess zero measure (are not extended) in at least one dimension; but there is an obvious sense in which they are 'objectively out there', a real feature of the physical world.

Aristotelian limit entities of this actual sort are assumable, I believe, to what Avrum Stroll, in a recent book on surfaces, terms the 'DS' conception of surfaces.[17] DS surfaces are geometrical or, in Stroll's terminology, 'abstractions' in the sense that they are 'true limits'—i.e. they have null measure or are unextended in at least one dimension. In other words, they are not corporeal in so far as 'corporeality' connotes possession of *three* dimensions. Yet DS surfaces are regarded as *belonging to* (and, indeed, as circumscribing and, hence, helping to define) the bodies or continuous stretches of magnitude that they demarcate. This second feature of DS surfaces is a particularly salient feature of Aristotle's discussion of such actual limit entities. It underlies, for example, his curious account of the division of a continuous line, which was noted in Chapter 1. When a continuous magnitude, e.g. a line, is *actually* divided, it is divided at a particular punctal position (*sēmeion*); but, once the division is effected, there are *two actual punctal* termini, each one defining the end of one of the two line-segments obtained from actually dividing the continuous line. Clearly, the motivation for finding two points where formerly there was but one (in the sense of punctal *locus* of division) is to ensure that each of the resulting segments has *its own proper terminus*. The idea that the limit of one of the segments might be thought of as located in the surrounding medium, once the division and separation has been effected, never seems to have occurred to Aristotle.

Although there is a sense in which, for Aristotle, mathematical objects (a concept under which he includes planes, lines, and points) cannot be 'in' physical objects, neither do they exist separated (*kechōrismena*) from sensible objects.[18] Aristotle's view is that geometry deals with things that happen to be physical or sensible but does not deal with them *qua* sensible things (*Meta*. 13. 3. 1078^{a}3–5). In exactly what way geometry *does* deal with sensible things is perhaps not clear, since Aristotle claims that 'sensible lines are not the sort of thing which the geometer talks about (for nothing sensible is thus straight or spherical; and the circle touches the straight edge not at a point but in the way that Protagoras used to say when he was producing *elenchi* against the geometers)' (*Meta*. 3. 2. 997^{b}35–998^{a}4). Although there may be some doubt as to the existence of actual (perfectly) straight

[17] *Surfaces* (Minneapolis, 1988), 46–50.

[18] See *Meta*. 3. 5–6, where Aristotle poses problems concerning the subject-matter of mathematics but does not answer them, and *Meta*. 11. 2. 1060^{a}36–^{b}19, *Meta*. 13. 1–3, 6–9, *Meta*. 14. 1–3, 5–6, where Aristotle reviews these problems, develops his own views, and criticizes alternative conceptions of mathematical objects.

lines or actual (perfectly) spherical objects in the physical world,[19] Aristotle does, in the preceding quotation, refer to sensible *lines*. And there is no reason, so far as I can determine, to deny that Aristotle believes that one does encounter actual surfaces (*qua* two-dimensional determinants of corporeal bodies, although perhaps not mathematical planes or spheres, etc.) and lines (*qua* one-dimensional determinants of 'faces' or surfaces of bodies, although perhaps not mathematical straight lines, circles, ellipses, etc.) in the sensible, physical world of things:

If one supposes as first principles lines or what comes from them (I refer to first surfaces[20]), these at least are not separate substances but cuts and divisions, lines of surfaces and surfaces of bodies, and points [are cuts/divisions] of lines;

[19] For a defence of the view that Aristotle *does* hold that, at least with respect to elementary geometrical entities (e.g. straight lines, circles), perfect instantiations are found in nature, see Lear, 'Aristotle's Philosophy of Mathematics', loc. cit., 161–92. There is an older tradition, represented by W. D. Ross and T. Heath, of interpreting Aristotle as invoking a notion of the 'intelligible matter' of the sensible, physical world, which Heath identifies with 'space or "extension"' (*Mathematics in Aristotle* (Oxford, 1949), 224). Mathematical objects, according to this interpretation of Aristotle, are then, in some *dunamis*-sense, instantiated in this intelligible matter. Heath (ibid. 226) succinctly presents the kernel of this interpretation as follows: 'Ross is obviously right in taking the sense of *hulikōs* ['materially'], as contrasted with *entelecheiāi* ['actually'–the passage referred to is *Meta*. 13. 3. 1078ᵃ31], to be that mathematical objects, straight lines, etc., though not actually and substantially present in sensible things, are potentially present, and their presence can be made actual by the geometer's power of *chōrismos*, "separation" (= abstraction).' For a contemporary development of this line of thought, see I. Mueller, 'Aristotle on Geometrical Objects', *Archiv für Geschiche der Philosophie*, 52 (1970), 156–71. For an interesting account of its Thomistic development, see P. O'Reilly, 'What is Intelligible Matter?', *The Thomist* 53: 1, 74–90.

Irrespective of the cogency of this interpretation of Aristotle's conception of mathematical objects in the sense of *straight* lines, perfect spheres, ellipses, planes, etc., there is yet another sense that one might attach to the phrase 'mathematical objects': surfaces *qua* actual 2-dimensional features of bodies, lines *qua* actual 1-dimensional features of bodies (e.g. their sharp edges), etc. I am not sure what view the tradition represented by Ross and Heath makes of mathematical objects in this latter sense. My own view, stated in the present text, is that while Aristotle does not hold that mathematical objects in this sense are substances or separable, he does hold that they are dependent but objective features of the sensible, physical world.

[20] It is far from clear what *epiphaneias tas prōtas* ('first surfaces') means here. The tradition which inteprets Aristotelian mathematicals as somehow intellectually instantiated in 'intelligible matter' (space or extension), interprets it as 'intelligible surfaces'. See e.g. Heath, *Mathematics in Aristotle*, 225. Another possibility is that the phrase refers to something like the elements constituting a composite surface in the sense of Hero (*Definitiones*, ed. J. L. Heiberg, in *Heronia Alexandrini opera qua supersunt omnia*, iv (Leipzig, 1903), def. 74, 50). E.g., first (primary or elemental) surfaces of a cone would be the circle constituting its base and the 'bent or curved triangle' constituting the remainder of its surface; the first surfaces of a cylinder would be the 2 circles constituting its bases and the 'bent rectangle' constituting the remainder of its surface, etc.

and, moreover, they are each limits of the same [i.e. appropriate kind of] things. And all these things inhere in other things, and none is separable. (*Meta*. 11. 2. 1060ᵇ12–17)

In the Aristotelian conception of limit entities—surfaces, edges, etc.—as objective but dependent features of the sensible, physical world, Epicurus perhaps finds a small rhetorical lever, which he hopes to put to good use. The Aristotelian must admit, as Epicurus puts it, that 'what is finite has an extremity that is distinguishable, even if it is not conceivable as existing by itself'. While insisting on the qualification of the impossibility of independent existence (an extremity must be an extremity *of* something), the Aristotelian will not reject the common-sensical claim that the extremity or surface of something is 'right there to be observed'.

Epicurus' next move, however, is where the trouble starts. Let us consider the 'spatial constitution' of a body with a distinguishable surface. Epicurus poses the following (rhetorical) question: do we not first think of the *actual* surface or extremity, and think of the internal spatial constitution of the body in terms of a unit 'of the same sort' (*toiouton*) *next in succession* to the actual surface, another such unit next to it, etc., until we fill up the internal spatial volume of the object? Our paradigmatic Aristotelian is committed to the conception of such units as true limit entities having null measure or being unextended in at least one dimension. Were he to be so unwise as to accept Epicurus' picture of the spatial constitution by the *successive* spatial filling up of a body with such units, he would apparently be committed to the unwelcome consequence of reaching the infinite, in *some* way, in his conception of the constitution of a finite magnitude. Such compliancy on the part of the Aristotelian would inevitably impale him on one horn (finite positive measure as the sum of an infinite collection of zero-measure addenda) of the paradox of measure.

To summarize, Epicurus has produced a 'slippery-slope'—or, better, 'slippery-surface'—argument against Aristotle's attempt to deprive the atomists of the paradox of measure as an argument for atomism. If the Aristotelian is going to admit the existence of limit entities in the form of surfaces and edges of bodies, is it not necessary to think of the spatial interior of a body as also filled up by similar entities discretely (successively) ordered? If the Aristotelian admits such an ordering *epheksēs*, what seems to be the basis of Aristotle's argument in *GC* 1. 2 for the impossibility of a complete dissolution of a finite magnitude into such limit entities—i.e. the fact that point is *not* next to point—is vitiated.

The standard *contemporary* response consists of three parts: (*a*) take the plunge down the slippery slope by admitting the possibility of a partition of a finite magnitude into an infinite collection of points or other limit entities; (*b*) insist that this infinite collection is densely, not discretely or successively ordered, and that the collection is of non-denumerable cardinality; (*c*) reject any principle of complete additivity, in particular, an additivity principle that would be defined for arbitrary non-denumerably infinite collections of addenda. Taking the plunge (*a*) is reasonable only if one has the conceptual and mathematical equipment to support (*b*) and (*c*).

But, as I have previously argued, neither Aristotle nor any other ancient philosopher or mathematician had such equipment. The case with respect to (*c*), formulation and denial of a complete-additivity principle, is, I think, fairly clear. But I have also suggested that, even with respect to (*b*), the idea of an *actually* infinite collection of densely ordered elements seems to have been generally problematic in antiquity, as it certainly was for Aristotle. The sort of density of points in a finite, continuous magnitude postulated by Aristotle is a sort of distributive density ultimately explicated in terms of his potentiality conception of infinite divisibility: another cut or division (point) can always, in principle be made between any two other cuts/divisions. But there is no sense in which the continuous magnitude is to be identified with anything like a densely ordered *actual* totality of such cuts, divisions, or points.

The geometrical usefulness of taking the plunge (*a*) is recognized a generation or two after Epicurus by Archimedes (although it is conceivable that the history of the geometrical use of (*a*) may go back much further, perhaps as far as Democritus' alleged discovery of the volume of the pyramid and cone).[21] In the *De mechanicis propositionibus*

---

[21] The attribution of this discovery to Democritus is made in the introduction to Archimedes' *De mechanicis propositionibus ad Eratosthenem methodus*. That Democritus may have analysed the cone (and pyramid?) into a collection of *laminae* is perhaps suggested by the paradox of the constitution of the cone attributed to him by Plutarch, *De communibus notitiis adversus Stoicos*, 1079e: if one cuts a cone by passing a plane through it, parallel to its base, what is the relation between the resulting 2 surfaces of the 2 segments (the conic frustum on the bottom and the smaller cone on the top)? Democritus apparently argued that if they are declared to be equal, the paradoxical result would be that the diameter of the cone cannot decrease with an increase in distance from the base and the 'cone' must in fact be a cylinder. But if the surfaces are declared to be unequal, the paradoxical result will be that the 'cone' becomes, in effect, a stack of cylinders of

ad Eratosthenem methodus (a work referred to by ancient writers but discovered only in 1899, hereafter referred to as the *Methodus*), Archimedes sets forth his method of discovery of a theorem his most formal proof of which in the *Quadratura parabolae* we discussed in Chapter 4: the segment of an 'orthotome' (parabola) possesses an area that is four-thirds the area of an inscribed triangle of the same base as the segment and equal height.

The procedure described in the *Methodus* involves 'balancing' (using a line-segment conceived as a lever) the parabolic segment against a triangle the area of which is four times that of the triangle inscribed in the parabolic segment (see Fig. 5). That is, consider the segment of a parabola $\alpha\beta\gamma$ bounded by straight line $\alpha\gamma$ as its base, inscribed triangle $\alpha\beta\gamma$, and right triangle $\alpha\zeta\gamma$, where $\zeta\gamma$ is tangent to the

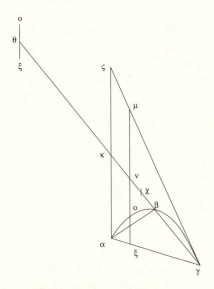

F IG . 5. The Quadrature of the Parabola: Archimedes' 'Discovery' Using Barocentric Analysis and the Assumption of Indivisibles

Each *in situ* line $\mu\xi$ of triangle $\alpha\zeta\gamma$ 'balances' the proper segment $o\xi$ of it that intersects parabola $\alpha\beta\gamma$, when that segment $o\xi$ is transposed in such a way that its mid-point is attached at θ.

decreasing diameter. The cone paradox and various solutions to it are further discussed in Ch. 7 below.

parabola and $\alpha\zeta$ is parallel to the axis of the parabola. Let κ be the mid-point of $\alpha\zeta$, and extend $\gamma\kappa$ to θ so that $\theta\kappa$ is equal to $\gamma\kappa$.

Archimedes proves that the area of $\Delta\alpha\zeta\gamma$ is four times the area of inscribed $\Delta\alpha\beta\gamma$. Although Archimedes never, so far as I have been able to determine, actually produces in the extant corpus the proof, it follows from proposition 14 of Book 1 of *De planorum aequilibriis sive de centris gravitatis planorum* that the centre of gravity of $\Delta\alpha\zeta\gamma$ lies on $\gamma\kappa$ at χ in such a way that $\chi\kappa$ is one-third of the distance of $\gamma\kappa$. If (i) we consider line-segment $\gamma\theta$ as a balance-lever with fulcrum at point κ, and if (ii) we could somehow attach parabolic segment $\alpha\beta\gamma$ at its centre of gravity to point θ, and if (iii) the parabolic segment so attached balanced $\Delta\alpha\zeta\gamma$ attached to the other side of the lever at point χ, we could apply the famous lever principle, prop. 6 of *De planorum aequilibriis* 1: commensurable magnitudes are in equilibrium at distances inversely proportional to their weights (or areas, in the case of plane figures). It would follow that the area of the parabolic segment $\alpha\beta\gamma$ is one-third of the area of $\Delta\alpha\zeta\gamma$. But, since the area of $\Delta\alpha\zeta\gamma$ is four times that of inscribed $\Delta\alpha\beta\gamma$, it follows that the area of the parabolic segment $\alpha\beta\gamma$ is four-thirds that of inscribed $\Delta\alpha\beta\gamma$.

The part of the proof that I am chiefly concerned with is (ii) and (iii) above—finding a way of attaching the parabolic segment $\alpha\beta\gamma$ to point θ and showing that it balances $\Delta\alpha\zeta\gamma$ attached at its centre of gravity at χ. In order to achieve this result, the following method is adopted. The parabolic segment is conceived as being constituted of parallel lines (such as $o\xi$ in Fig. 5); and $\Delta\alpha\zeta\gamma$ is conceived as being similarly constituted of parallel lines, each one of which is an extension of a parallel line of the parabolic segment (such as $\mu\xi$ in Fig. 5). It is then shown that each such line-segment $o\xi$ of parabolic segment $\alpha\beta\gamma$ balances the corresponding line-segment $\mu\xi$ of $\Delta\alpha\zeta\gamma$, when the segment $o\xi$ is conceived as being transferred to point θ and attached there at its centre of gravity (i.e. mid-point). That is, proportion theory is invoked to prove that for *each* such pair of segments $o\xi$ and $\mu\xi$, $o\xi\,/\,\mu\xi = \nu\kappa\,/\,\theta\kappa$, where ν is the centre of gravity (mid-point) of $\mu\xi$, which lies on the 'right side' of the balance lever $\gamma\theta$.

There are two key features of this procedure. First, there is a one-to-one correspondence, *of a particular sort*,[22] between line-segments of the

---

[22] Not every 1:1 correspondence between parallel straight line-segments of one plane figure and that of another (for which there is an invariant ratio between the lengths of these line-segments) can be used to establish the ratio of areas of the 2 plane figures. In other words, the technique of Archimedes' *Methodus*, which has affinities to the 'proto-

triangle $\alpha\zeta\gamma$ and 'balancing' lines of the parabolic segment $\alpha\beta\gamma$. This correspondence is established by the construction itself, since each line-segment of the triangle is balanced by a line-segment of the parabolic segment that is a proper part of it. Second, there is, in effect, the assumption that each figure can be partitioned into its respective parallel lines and, conversely, that each figure can be identified with the union of its respective lines. More specifically, it is assumed that, from the fact that each line of the triangle $\alpha\zeta\gamma$ *in situ* (i.e. at a variable distance from the fulcrum κ of the balance-lever) balances the corresponding line of the parabolic segment $\alpha\beta\gamma$ when it is transferred to the other end θ of the lever and affixed there at its mid-point/centre of gravity, it follows that the whole triangle *in situ* (i.e. when its centre of gravity is located at χ, the distance of which from the fulcrum κ is one-third of the distance of each 'arm' of the lever) balances the parabolic segment, when its centre of gravity is conceived as being attached at the other end θ of the lever. In other words, while the triangle is conceived as lying in the same plane as the lever and its centre of gravity is thus located on the lever at point χ, the parabolic segment is conceived as attached at its centre of gravity to the other end-point θ of the lever.

What is quite irrelevant to the procedure is any assumption concerning the *ordering* of the lines conceived as partitioning the plane figures or the *cardinality* of the collections that they constitute. It makes no difference whether these lines are conceived as densely or discretely (successively) ordered; it makes no difference what infinite cardinality is assigned to the collections they constitute. In fact, so long as they are thought of as *lines*—in the special sense that only their length determines the proportions interpreted as indicating balance—it makes no difference whether they are conceived as finite or infinite in number. Could the lines even be transformed into, say, very narrow segments having some width? No. For then a segment of the triangle

integration' techniques of the early 17th-c. mathematician Bonaventura Cavalieri, must be carefully applied in order to avoid fallacy. For example, if we consider all the straight line-segments (parallel to one radius-side) of a circle quadrant of a radius r and all the straight line-segments (parallel to a side) of a right triangle of side r, the members of these two sets can be put into a $1:1$ correspondence such that each line-segment of the triangle is equal to the corresponding line-segment of the circle quadrant. But it obviously does not follow that the area of the triangle is equal to the area of the circle quadrant. Cavalieri, aware of such problems, (in effect) required that the $1:1$ correspondence be established in terms of distance (of parallel line-segments) from a common *regula* (or reference line-segment). This restriction is satisfied by Archimedes' somewhat more complex procedure. See Pedersen, 'Techniques of the Calculus, 1630–1660', 32–7.

would not be a similar plane figure with respect to its proper part, a segment of the parabolic segment: the former would be a trapezoid, while the latter would have a curve (an arc of the parabola) as one of its sides. The result would be that the centres of gravity of the respective plane figures would depend upon more than their respective heights (lengths), and the reasoning that Archimedes employs to establish the proportions indicating the balance of the figures would no longer be valid.

Archimedes explicitly indicates that he does not consider his construction, with the preceding reasoning, to constitute a proof of the theorem. In this respect, I believe that Dijksterhuis is correct in claiming that the 'mathematical deficiency' that Archimedes sees in this heuristic method or method of discovery 'is a consequence of the use of indivisibles'[23] (i.e. the representation of the figures as unions of parallel lines). The problem is that Archimedes quite realizes that he is threatened by the one horn of the paradox of measure if he takes the plunge (*a*) by admitting a partition of a continuous magnitude into limit entities, here a partition of a two-dimensional plane figure into one-dimensional lines. Although he was one of the greatest mathematicians of all time, he did not have the combination of (*b*) and (*c*), the conception of a dense (and Dedekind-continuous) ordering of a non-denumerably infinite collection of limit entities and an appropriate, corresponding limitation of the additivity principle, to allow him to accept such a partition while avoiding the paradox of measure. So he finds himself in the following, psychologically awkward position. He makes good mathematical use of such partitions. That is, he in some sense thinks of the triangle and parabolic segment as being constituted of lines, and obtains fertile and demonstrably correct mathematical results from this way of thinking. But then he admits, along with Aristotle and Epicurus, 'but of course I don't literally mean it—because we all know that to conceive of what is continuous as constituted of an infinity of limit entities leads to paradox'.

My principal purpose in rehearsing in some detail Archimedes' plight is to illustrate, quite concretely, the sort of *mathematical* appeal— as well as, perhaps, the commonsensical appeal—of taking the plunge advocated by Epicurus: conceiving (supposedly continuous) magni-

---

[23] Dijksterhuis, *Archimedes*, 319. But see the discussion of Knorr (in his bibliographical essay appended to the most recent edition of this work, 435–8) concerning Archimedes' attitude to this application of the barycentric method, i.e. the method appealing to balance-lever and the idea of centres of gravity of plane figures.

tudes as internally constituted of the same sort of units as their boundaries or superficies. Epicurus, however, points up the problem. If we take this plunge *and* concomitantly retain the conception of such units as true limit entities (that is, as having zero-measure in at least one dimension), then we are in trouble. We are, at any rate, in trouble unless we happen to be twentieth-century mathematicians with the benefit of (*b*) and (*c*) to support us.

In antiquity, Epicurus invites us to join him in giving up the idea of such boundaries, surfaces, extremities, etc.—as well as the 'units of the same sort' that we find so natural and convenient to imagine as constituting the internal spatial structure of a magnitude so bounded—as *true limit* entities. Instead, he suggests, let us conceive of them as quanta, having some positive measure, but as minimal and indivisible in some conceptual or theoretical sense. Archimedes, as we have seen, gives no indication of willingness to accept the invitation. As we have seen, there is ancient evidence (for example, from Aristotle and, much later, from Cicero) that such a quantum conception was commonly (and correctly) regarded as being unscientific and as undermining the foundations of geometry.

From the evidence we possess, it seems unlikely that many Epicureans would have been impressed by arguments that their doctrine of *partes minimae* undermine geometrical science.[24] They are much more favourably disposed to considerations pertaining to sense (specifically, visual) discrimination, which they employ as part of their case for minimal and indivisible quanta. As we saw in Chapter 3, the

---

[24] For a nice summary of Epicurean attitude toward geometry, see the introductory section of Sedley, 'Epicurus and the Mathematicians of Cyzicus', 23–6. Proclus, in a passage cited by Sedley (*In Eucl.*, ed. Friedlein, 199–200), names 'the Epicureans' as 'setting out to overthrow geometrical first principles only' [sc., as opposed to undertaking a more encompassing sceptical programme] (199. 9–10). He then distinguishes those who, 'yielding with respect to the first principles, deny what is demonstrated from the first principles unless something else is conceded to them [the geometers], which is not settled beforehand by the first principles' (199. 11–14). As the one representative of such an approach, Proclus names the Epicurean Zeno of Sidon. Later (213. 15 ff.), Proclus says that Zeno denies the construction of the equilateral triangle (Euclid, 1. 1) 'unless it is conceded to them [the geometers, again] that it is not possible that there exist the same [i.e. common] segments (*tmēmata*) of two straight lines' (214. 21–2). I think it possible that the general sort of additional assumption that Zeno believes is necessary to the validity of geometrical proofs is, as Sedley implies ('Epicurus and the Mathematicians of Cyzicus', 24–5), the assumption of the actual existence of true limit entities: surfaces and planes lacking extension in 1 dimension, lines lacking extension in 2 dimensions, and points lacking extension in 3 dimensions. As an Epicurean committed to indivisible quanta, however, Zeno would not be prepared to concede this sort of assumption.

Aristotelian doctrine of *De sensu* 6 is a doctrine of perceptual minima: below a threshold size of the perceptible magnitude, 'the increment (*huperochē*) of sensation is not perceptible in itself nor separable (for the increment exists potentially in what is more distinctly [percept-ible])' (446ᵃ11–12). Since Aristotle also holds ('Archimedes' axiom') that a finite continuous magnitude can be divided into only a finite number of equal-sized parts (445ᵇ28), it follows that, because there is a minimal, threshold size for what is actually *per se* perceptible, there can be only a finite number, however large, of *disjoint* perceptible minima filling up any finite magnitude. And it seems that, on Aristotle's own terms, such minima, if actually separated out by perceptual discrimina-tion, would have to be arranged *epheksēs*, discretely or successively.

My point in returning to *De sensu* 6 here is to suggest that when Epicurus at D.L. 58–9 invokes the analogy he wishes to establish between perceptible minima and theoretical minima, this analogy has a certain dialectical force. For the Peripatetic tradition is apparently committed to accepting, in some form, the premiss of the analogy: some form of Epicurus' account of *perceptible* minima. In fact, the whole passage dealing with minima from D.L. 10. 56–9 has, according to the interpretation I am developing, a rather tight dialectical structure, which can be seen as especially directed against the Peri-patetics.

Epicurus begins by advancing a version of Zeno's paradox of measure as an argument for minimal, indivisible, extended minima as constituents of any finite and bounded magnitude. But, from *GC* 1. 2, it appears that Democritus had already done something similar; and Aristotle had incapacitated the paradox as an argument for such minima by arguing against the possibility of the dissolution of such a magnitude into nothing but points while retaining his own ∞-conception of infinite divisibility of a finite magnitude. He also apparently (and, from the contemporary perspective, unfortunately) had tied the impossibility of a complete dissolution of the magnitude into points to the fact that points in such a magnitude are not ordered discretely or successively. Epicurus counters that if one admits the objective but dependent existence of the extremities (surfaces, edges, etc.) of such a magnitude, it is entirely natural to (in fact, *impossible not to*) conceive the magnitude as internally constituted or spatially filled up by similar such units *successively ordered*. But, as we have seen, for the Peripatetic to make such an admission would be disastrous, in view of Aristotle's reliance, in *GC* 1. 2, on the lack of a discrete ordering of points as a guarantee of the impossibility of the complete dissolution of a finite magnitude into nothing but such limit units.

Now Epicurus turns to the analogy between theoretical or conceptual minima and perceptible minima. With respect to the latter, his conception does not differ much, at least at a superficial level, from that of Aristotle. He proceeds to argue on the basis of this analogy that magnitudes are constituted or spatially filled up by units successively ordered. Should this be granted, of course, Epicurus will have won: it cannot be denied, because of the threat posed by the paradox of measure, that these units are true quanta: although they are theoretically indivisible and without parts, they are extended, possessing positive 'measure'.

It must be understood of the minimum in sensation both that it is not the same sort of thing as that which allows of being traversed and that it is not completely unlike it. It shares a certain common property with what allows of being traversed: it is an interval but not constituted of parts. But when, on account of the resemblance due to the common property, we believe that some [part] of it is marked off, one on this side and one on that, it must be something equal [to the minimum] that strikes our attention. We, beginning with the first, see these [perceptible minima] in succession [*heksēs*], not in the same place, not touching part to part, but, rather, in their own proper manner serving as integral measures [*katametrounta*] of magnitudes—more of them for a greater magnitude, fewer for a smaller magnitude.

One must hold that the minimum in the atom is subject to this analogy. It is clear that it is only in smallness that that [i.e. the atom] differs from that discerned by sensation, but it is subject to the same analogy. So, in conformity with the present analogy we maintain that the atom has magnitude, merely setting forth something that is small on a larger scale. Moreover, it is necessary to think of these partless[25] minima as the limits of lengths supplying from themselves as primary units integral measurement for the greater and the smaller—by means of rational insight—with respect to what is invisible. For the common property obtaining between them and the changeable [i.e. sensible] things[26] is sufficient to take us this far; but it is not possible that a compounding

---

[25] I here follow von Arnim's emendation (accepted by Furley, *Two Studies in the Greek Atomists*, 25) of *amigē* ('unmixed', 'uncompounded') to *amerē* ('partless').

[26] Along with David Konstan ('Problems in Epicurean Physics', *Isis*, 70:253 (1979), 407), I adopt Furley's emendation of *ta ametabola* to *ta metabola*—i.e. 'unchangeable things' to 'changeable things' (*Two Studies in the Greek Atomists*, 26-7). However, von Arnim's emendation to *ta metabata*, i.e. to what is 'extended' in the sense of permitting passage from one part to another part, also seems possible. As Furley notes, the sense of the analogy requires a reference to what is sensible here. That desideratum seems to be satisfied both by his emendation and by that of von Arnim. Perhaps von Arnim's suggestion is marginally

should arise from the motion of these [minima within the atoms]. (D.L. 10. 59)

The preceding passage from the *Letter to Herodotus* clearly introduces what Sorabji has called 'a two-tier theory of atoms'.[27] At the 'top tier', the atoms, with their solidity and consequent impassivity, are the eternally stable ultimate elements [*stoicheia*] that are especially needed, according to an argument presented by Aristotle in *On Generation and Corruption* 1. 2, 'if generation and destruction are to occur by dissociation [*diakrisei*] and association (*sungkrisei*)' (*GC* 1. 2. 316^{b}35). The latter part of *GC* 1. 2 may suggest that Aristotle would admit the necessity of invisible corporeal elements *if* it were the case that all change—in a sense of 'change' that includes substantial generation and destruction—were simply a matter of dissociation and association. That all change is to be so analysed is, of course, a fundamental tenet of atomism. Earlier in the *Letter to Herodotus* Epicurus has taken Aristotle's point a step further:

Furthermore ... of bodies, some are associations [*sunkriseis*] and others are [the elements] from which the associations are formed. The latter are indivisible [*atoma*] and unchangeable—unless everything is going to be destroyed into what does not exist but, rather, be strong enough to perdure amidst the dissolution of the associations because they have the nature of *plena* and are incapable of being dissolved at any place or in any way. Therefore, it is necessary that the first principles be indivisible natures of bodies. (D.L. 10. 40–1).

At the bottom tier there are *minimae partes*, the indivisible quanta of magnitude, which are the principal topic of discussion of D.L. 10. 56–9, the passages which I have previously quoted and have been discussing. Irrespective of Epicurus' intentions, the argument in these passages for indivisible quanta can be viewed as distinct from the argument for *atoms*, which we find in Aristotle's *GC* 1. 2 and in the immediately preceding passage from the *Letter to Herodotus*.

The argument for such quanta of magnitude *begins*, as we saw, with a version of 'Zeno's paradox of measure'. A certain style of terminology and argument—e.g. the metaphors of everything being strong (10. 40) or being weak (10. 56) and talk, in both passages, of wasting away the things that exist to what does not exist—have led some commentators

favoured by the fact that *metabata* seems to have occurred—and the cognate noun *metabasis* certainly did occur—earlier in the passage.

[27] *Time, Creation and the Continuum*, 348.

to see the earlier argument for physical atoms as ultimate elements of change and the latter version of the paradox of measure at 10. 56. 5ff. as being essentially identical.[28]

It is uncertain, I think, whether Epicurus himself sees the two passages as presenting distinct arguments. The commentators who have claimed that, from Epicurus' view, the arguments are not really different may be correct. But Epicurus *should* (ideally) see them as distinct. The first (elliptical) argument is one which Aristotle gives some indication of accepting: *if* (counter-factually, according to Aristotle, but actually, according to Epicurus) all change, in the broadest sense, is a matter of association and dissociation, then invisible corporeal elements would have to exist. Whether Aristotle would additionally admit that these invisible corporeal elements must be indivisible and impassive is open to doubt. But that is Epicurus' view.[29] The second, more elaborate argument is a version of the paradox of measure, which Aristotle apparently has refuted: were it valid, it would entail, with respect both to any indivisible and unchangeable corporeal elements and to associations of these, that they must be constituted of minimal quanta of magnitude. Either the ultimate physical elements of association and dissociation (i.e. the atoms) would have to *be* such minimal quanta of magnitude or they would have to be constituted out of them. It is certainly logically possible that one could find persuasive arguments for indivisible and impassive 'building-blocks' of nature (perhaps arguments of an epistemological nature) without being persuaded (perhaps by some version of the paradox of measure) that there must be minimal quanta of magnitude.

Aristotle, as we have seen, was not persuaded by the paradox of measure and had produced an argument which, if interpreted

---

[28] Long and Sedley, *The Hellenistic Philosophers*, ii. 2, 33.

[29] The reason why there must be corporeal elements so small that they cannot be seen if *all* change is a matter of *sungkrisis* and *diakrisis* is fairly obvious: we do not, as a matter of fact, see such particles combining or separating in the case of *all* forms of change. But the inference to corporeal elements that are indivisible and unchangeable is more tenuous. It is not obvious that Aristotle makes it. For example, he says that *diakrisis* occurs into the (relatively) smaller, and *sungkrisis* out of the smaller (*GC* 1. 2. 317ª16). But must the smaller, at the level when it attains invisibility, be the *smallest*? One might argue, on behalf of Epicurus, that once one obtains invisible elements of association and a dissociation, there is no longer any explanatory purpose to entertaining the possibility that they might themselves be physically divisible or subject to change. Alternatively, one might argue that, unless one stops somewhere at the level of invisibility with physically indivisible and impassive elements, there would be an infinite regress with respect to the explanation of change in terms of the association/dissociation of smaller corporeal elements. It is not clear, however, whether such a regress would be vicious.

charitably, is a cogent refutation of the paradox *considered as an argument for minimal quanta of magnitude*. It is for that reason that, by the time of Epicurus, it will not stand by itself as an argument for *minimae partes*. Therefore, its supplementation by the analogy from perceptible minima to (supposed) real, theoretical/conceptual minimal quanta is crucial. And a reasonable hypothesis is that this supplementation was developed with an eye to Aristotle, who was responsible for the overthrow of the paradox of measure as an effective argument for minimal quanta. It seems to me unlikely that Epicurus regards the role of the analogy as being *simply*—in the words of Long and Sedley—to explain the 'nature [of the minima] and how they function mathematically within larger magnitudes' and that Epicurus believes that the 'existence of minima has already been proved' (by the paradox of measure).[30] If he *does* believe this, the belief is—even by ancient standards—a rash one.

Of course, as a piece of analogical reasoning, the analogy from the sensible to the conceptual is not a valid *deductive* argument and will, by contemporary lights, have relatively little suasive force. However, there is some evidence that, from the perspective of Epicurean 'canonic' (epistemology, logic, and theory of science), analogy occupied a central place in human knowledge. In his *Life of Epicurus* Diogenes Laertius states that, according to Epicurean doctrine, 'all our ideas have arisen from sensation, either by "impinging" [of effluences of atoms on our sense apparatus] or analogy or resemblance or composition, with ratiocination [*logismos*] contributing something' (D.L. 10. 32). And, with respect to existents, Epicurus claims in the *Letter to Herodotus* that, 'beyond [body and void] it is not possible to think of anything either by "preconceptions" [*perilēptikōs*] or by analogy from preconceptions' (D.L. 10. 40).[31] I think that a comment by Jürgen Mau made in another context (the discussion of geometrical theorems *discovered* by means of the use of minima, as in Archimedes' *Methodus*) is apposite:

It is an indispensable part of the Epicurean philosophical system that logically perfect proofs are neither necessary nor wanted. The only real criterion of truth is the *antimarturēsis* [falsifying sense evidence] and *epimarturēsis* [verifying

---

[30] *The Hellenistic Philosophers*, ii. 1, 42.
[31] See also the fragment from Philodemus, according to the text of Crönert, printed in C. Bailey, *Epicurus: The Extant Remains* (Oxford, 1926), Fr. 49, 132.

sense evidence], and it is not very likely that a theorem found in the above described way will ever be refuted by sense perception.[32]

Mau's comment seems to apply *a fortiori* to the conclusion of analogical reasoning from the larger, and thus sensible realm to the realm of insensibly small atoms. In effect, the Epicureans are pitting analogical reasoning about the insensible micro-level (which begins with what even the Peripatetics will agree is true of the sensible macro-level) against the dogmatic assertions of standard, ancient geometrical theory concerning the insensible micro-level. It is not surprising, then, to find ancient atomism, particularly Epicureanism, generally at odds with the standard mathematical science of the day. Indeed, problems concerning the nature of minimal quanta and the manner of their agglomeration in atoms—problems that constituted the basis of ancient criticisms of the quantum model and that have exercised contemporary scholars in their attempt better to understand ancient atomism—are largely geometrical. I shall return to these problems later.

One question concerning the relation between atoms and minimal quanta, however, is fairly easy to answer: why are there *two* tiers? That is, once the atomists have established, at least to their own satisfaction, the need to postulate indivisible quanta of magnitude, why not *identify* these quanta with the atoms, which are needed as elements of association and dissociation? At least part of the answer to this question must be, I think, the obvious one. To fulfil their role as elements of association and dissociation, as this role is conceived by ancient atomists in general, atoms must be characterized by differences of shape and size. And the most obvious way to conceptualize such differences involves attributing (proper) parts to atoms. Hence, the bottom tier, *within* the atom, of indivisible quanta.

As David Konstan has pointed out, however, considerations pertaining to diversity in size (and shape) of atoms does not explain why it is— as the Epicureans apparently held—that '*no* atoms may be exactly one minimum in magnitude'.[33] Konstan argues (to considerable effect, in my view) that the answer is that, for the Epicureans, indivisible quanta of magnitude are *essentially* (proper) parts: it is conceptually impossible

---

[32] 'Was There a Special Epicurean Mathematics?', in E. N. Lee, A. P. D. Mourelatos, and R. M. Rorty (eds.), *Exegesis and Argument: Studies in Greek Philosophy Presented to Gregory Vlastos* (Assen, 1973), 429.

[33] 'Problems in Epicurean Physics', 402.

that they should exist as discrete, atomic units. This issue, too, is intimately connected with geometrical considerations, to which I shall return. But the very idea that objective differences in the size of atoms are to be explained in terms of different integral multiples of indivisible quanta of magnitude instantiates another argument for the existence of such quanta, to which we next turn.

The Argument from the Objectivity of the Greater/Smaller Relation

There is a further variety of argument for the existence of indivisible quanta of magnitude that, initially at least, seems specious to the point of being silly. One example of it is found at the very beginning of the Peripatetic treatise *On Indivisible Lines* (*De lineis insecabilibus*), which presents a series of arguments for theoretical minima followed by (attempted) individual refutations of them.

If the properties 'many' and 'large' obtain and, in a similar fashion, their opposites 'few' and 'small', and if it is not the few ⟨and small⟩ but the many ⟨and large⟩ that admit virtually indefinite divisions [into parts], it is clear that the few and the small will admit only a limited (finite) number of divisions. But if divisions are limited, then it is necessary that something be a partless magnitude, with the result that in all things something partless will inhere, since the few and the small [obtain, in a relative sense (?), with respect to all things]. (968ᵃ2–9)

A version of the argument is also found in Lucretius' *De rerum natura*:

Moreover, unless there is a minimum even the smallest bodies will be constituted from infinite parts, since a part of a half-part will always have a half-part and nothing limits the division. Therefore, what difference is there between the greatest of things and the least? There will be no difference: for make the totality of things infinite to the greatest extent you please, and the smallest of things that exist will in a like manner consist of an infinity of parts. But because true reason protests and denies that the mind is capable of believing this, it is necessary to acknowledge oneself bested and that there exist things which are not possessed of any parts and are of the nature of minima. (1. 615–26).

The first quotation, in particular, indicates the attempt to undermine a rigid distinction—upheld, as we have seen, by Aristotle—between the notions of numerical plurality or multiplicity (*plēthos*) and magnitude (*megethos*). 'Many' and 'few', Aristotle insists, depend upon the existence of a counting-unit that, *qua* unit, is indivisible. And, typically, when we count, a 'natural' (intrinsic) unit is supplied by the things that we are counting: sheep or ions or sunsets. At the heart of the preceding argument is the supposition that magnitude must be treated on a par with plurality in this regard. As we saw in Chapter 4, the contemporary tendency has also been to undermine the distinction between plurality or number and magnitude; but this has been accomplished by an extension of the notion of number to ordered fields without a minimal unit, an extension that has weakened the connection between the notion of number and that of counting. However, ancient opposition to the distinction between number and magnitude—here represented by our argument—attempted to insist that magnitude, like number, is a concept that presupposes a fundamental unit.

The argument is that, without the assumption of such a unit, the objective distinction between large and small cannot be maintained, just as the objective distinction between many and few depends upon a counting-unit. The Peripatetic response, in *De lineis insecabilibus*, to the first argument, is not very informative (and the text of the response is quite corrupt). But it does point up the basic issue concerning the relation between number and magnitude. After disposing of the argument's peculiar identification of 'large' with 'admitting a practically infinite number of divisions' and 'small' with 'admitting only a finite number of divisions', the respondent comes to the basic point:

If, because the few in number admits only finite divisions, someone should judge that the small among lines [admits only finite divisions], he would be silly. For in the former case there is a generation [of numbers] from what is partless; and there is something which is the generative principle of numbers, and every number that is not infinite admits of only a limited number of divisions. But with respect to magnitudes, it is not the same.   (969ª12–17)

In other words, the distinction between large and small is not a matter of *number* of parts. So much seems clear from the Peripatetic response. But this response does not go very far. One might perhaps proceed a bit by claiming that there is still a sense in which the greater-than relation between two continuous magnitudes is objective. One might claim that it is an objective, invariant fact that the *ratio* of the length of continuous magnitude A to the length of continuous magnitude B is, say, 2:3, despite the fact it is no more true to say that A is constituted of 4 parts and B of 6 than it is to say that A is constituted of 34 parts and B of 51. Of course, to come to a judgement concerning relative magnitude, one must adopt a 'standard' or unit of measure, and there is a clear sense in which the procedure of fixing a standard is conventional. But that fact does not entail that the judgement pertaining to *relative* magnitude based on such a conventional standard is itself conventional. *Any* standard should give the same results concerning relative magnitude; and any standard should give the same result of incommensurability since, as recognized in the first scholium on Euclid 10, commensurability/incommensurability is a matter of nature (*phusis*), not stipulation or convention (*thesis*).[34]

One might, then, diagnose the fallacy of the argument from the objectivity of the greater/smaller relation as follows. It begins, correctly enough, with the idea that, since magnitudes (according to the non-quantum, infinitely divisible conception the argument seeks to refute) have no *intrinsic* metric, defined by number of minimal quanta, there is a sense in which the size or measure that we attribute to such a magnitude, considered *in itself* (i.e. without relation to other magnitudes) is conventional. But the argument then seems to infer, fallaciously, that *relative* size or measure—being greater than or smaller than—also is a matter of convention or *thesis* rather than a matter of *phusis*. The implication seems to be that, according to one convention, *A* might be larger than *B*, but, according to a different convention, *A* might be smaller than *B*.

Although there is reason to hold that this inference, in the bald way I have presented it, is not legitimate, there is also reason to think that this type of argument is not so egregiously absurd as it may first appear. Whether any more sophisticated elaboration of the argument was attempted in antiquity is not certain; we have, in so far as I am aware, no evidence of an attempt to take the argument further. However, there are reverberations of the argument in twentieth-century reflection on measure theory. Perhaps the way for such reflection has been prepared by relativistic physics. We are now becoming used to the idea, from the special theory of relativity, that there is no frame-independent notion of the ratio of two temporal intervals nor, consequently, of two spatial intervals.

Adolf Grünbaum has argued that, for dense and continuous manifolds, there can be only 'extrinsic' metrics, while discrete manifolds admit of 'intrinsic', 'cardinality-based' metrics, i.e. measures based on the number of quanta or chunks within an interval or

---

[34] The scholium, in fact, attributes this point, as well as the discovery of incommensurable magnitudes, to the Pythagoreans. See Heath, *Euclid's Elements*, iii. 1.

region.[35] There has been disagreement concerning the import of these claims, but several consequences seem relatively clear. For 'metrically amorphous' dense (and continuous) manifolds, the best we can hope for is agreement of results from the use of alternative metrical conventions—the hope that different possible standards of measurement will yield the same results. This, of course, does not always happen. Consider the simple case of two bars, A and B, and suppose both that B is much hotter than A and that the length of A and B cannot, for some reason, be directly compared (i.e. neither can be used as a ruler with respect to the other). Next consider two rods, r_1 and r_2, with which we shall measure A and B. Suppose that r_1 expands greatly in length when subjected to heat but that r_2 does not. Nor, let us assume, does B itself. It might turn out, then, that when rod r_2 is employed as rule, B is longer than A but, when r_1 is employed, A is longer. Note that we have a scientific theory, implicit in my description of the situation, that accounts for the discrepancy: what has happened is that, when placed in proximity to the hot B, r_1 has expanded, making B appear shorter than it actually is. So, this measurement can be dismissed as skewed or anomalous. Our scientific theory gives us reason to say that r_1 has not remained 'self-congruent' in length in transport from the region of the cooler A to that of the hotter B. The 'moral' of this simple story is that we customarily depend upon our scientific theory to provide some explanation when alternative standards of measure do not yield the same result and, thus, to write off one of the results as anomalous.[36]

Grünbaum, however, adduces an example of a scientific theory, the cosmology of E. A. Milne, that postulates a non-linear relation between the time v defined by periodic astronomical processes and the time t defined by periodic atomic processes.[37] I shall not go into the details of the relation, but merely note, as Grünbaum says, 'that two time-intervals which are congruent in one of these two time-scales

---

[35] This is a major topic of his *Philosophical Problems of Space and Time*, 2nd edn. See esp. ch. 16.

[36] In the situation I am imagining, what Hans Reichenbach terms a 'differential force' has been invoked to explain the fact that r_1 and r_2 yield different results. Consequently, r_1 either does not qualify as a 'rigid body', in Reichenbach's technical sense of this term, and thus cannot be the object of a coordinate definition in establishing (or using) a metric; *or* if it is to qualify as a rigid body and is to be employed metrically, we must correct for the effect (expansion and contraction) of such a differential force. See the discussion in Reichenbach, *The Philosophy of Space and Time*, esp. 10–37.

[37] E. A. Milne, *Kinematic Relativity* (Oxford, 1948), 22.

will be incongruent in the other'.[38] I believe that Grünbaum is correct in his claim that 'clearly, it would be utterly gratuitous to regard one of Milne's two congruences as bizarre, since each of them is presumed to have a physical realization'.[39] That is, in the absence of an intrinsic metric of time—such as that which would be supplied if time had a quantum or, to use Grünbaum's term, 'granular' structure that would be amenable to some sort of counting process—we have no reason to hold that one of the incompatible results given by these two metrics with respect to the size of a temporal interval is more correct than the other.

One might ask, as R. Swinburne did, if the supposition of an intrinsic metric really makes any difference in a situation in which different metrics yield incompatible results: 'But suppose that there turned out to be a thousand space atoms between A and B and a million between B and C when, by our ordinary criteria, the distances AB and BC were congruent with each other, what would we say?'[40] While Swinburne maintains that the 'fundamental' metric would remain the 'normal', extrinsic one (we would decide that 'some space atoms take up more room than others'), Grünbaum demurs:

It seems to me that if a manifold is worthy of metrical characterization, then the object of a metric on the intervals or point pairs of the manifold is to render *intrinsic* facts or tell the *intrinsic* story *in so far as is possible*.... We can presume that in a world whose physical *P[hysical]*- (and *T[emporal]*-) manifolds are indeed granular, the lawful behavior of physical entities would be describable more simply in terms of the intrinsic metric M_1, rather than being tied to the D_3 metric of the transported rods, if there are such at all. And, if the avowed function of a nontrivial metric is indeed to render an existing intrinsic equivalence relation but a particular metric is purported to do so while being extrinsic, then its ascriptions of metrical equality can be indicted as false.[41]

What we find here is a refinement of the argument from the objectivity of the greater/smaller relation. The ancient proponents of the quantum model argued that *without* an intrinsic, cardinality-based metric, the larger/smaller relation loses its objectivity and becomes merely a matter of convention. They proceeded to use this claim as a *reductio* on the model of spatial magnitude as continuous and divisible

[38] *Philosophical Problems of Space and Time*, 22.

[39] Ibid. 23.

[40] Review of A. Grünbaum, *Geometry and Chronometry in Philosophical Perspective*, *The British Journal for the Philosophy of Science*, 21 (1970), 311.

[41] *Philosophical Problems of Space and Time*, 556.

without limit and, consequently, as an argument *for* the quantum or granular model of spatial extension. Grünbaum, of course, does not indulge in any such *reductio* argument. But, to simplify a bit, he does hold that 'topological considerations pertaining to continuous P[*hysical*]-space' provide inductive support for a principle he finds in the inaugural dissertation of the nineteenth-century mathematician B. Riemann and which he calls 'Riemann's Metrical Hypothesis', a principle claiming that 'continuous *P*-space is intrinsically metrically amorphous'. And he adds that he has 'maintained that no corresponding conventional ingredient inheres in the *cardinality-based* metrical equalities of the intervals of a discrete *P*-space'.[42] One might maintain, with some reason, that considerations of sophistication, philosophical and scientific, entail a certain incommensurability between our original argument from the objectivity of the greater/smaller relation and Grünbaum's views concerning intrinsic versus extrinsic metrics. But I think that one can discern in Grünbaum's discussion conceptual reverberations of the issue lying at the heart of the original argument. The frequency with which we encounter such reverberations in the history of philosophical and scientific pursuits is, to my mind, striking.

The Argument from Commensurability

Since the ancient geometrical tradition seems to have been so clearly committed to a conception of magnitude as continuous and divisible without limit, the distaste with which many of the proponents of the quantum model regarded geometry is understandable. In fact, Epicurean aversion to and ignorance of geometry eventually became something of a rhetorical commonplace. More detailed consideration of the relation between ancient proponents of the quantum model and geometry will be postponed until the next section. However, there is one noteworthy attempt to use a geometrical concept to establish the existence of indivisible quanta of magnitude. Although, as one might expect, the attempt is a failure, it is, in my view, a rather interesting and instructive failure. The argument is the last of a series of arguments for quanta presented in the pseudo-Aristotelian *On Indivisible Lines*:

Moreover, from what the mathematicians themselves say [it follows that] there would be some indivisible line, as [the advocates of minima] say. For if

---

[42] Ibid. 498.

commensurable lines are those which are measured by the same measure, then however many lines may be commensurable are all measured [by the same measure].[43] For then there would be some length by which all these [commensurable lines] will be measured. And this is necessarily indivisible. For if it is indivisible, there will be parts of the measure; and these will be commensurable with the whole. The result would be that the measure of a certain part [e.g. a half] would be twice the half.[44] Since this is impossible, there must be an ⟨indivisible⟩ measure. And just as in the case of all lines that are [constituted] from the measure, similarly those that are measured once by it are constituted from partless units. (968^{b}5–15)

The subsequent attempted refutation of this argument is not very effective; and, in the comments accompanying his translation of *De lineis insecabilibus*, Harold Joachim misdiagnoses the problem—at least the principal problem—with the argument:

The fallacy is obvious, and is exposed at 969^b 10–12. Any line *AB* can become 'commensurate' with *some* line: but, because commensurate with *some* line, it is not necessarily commensurate with *all* lines, or 'commensurate' absolutely. One would indeed think the fallacy too obvious to have been committed.[45]

Two initial comments are in order. First, it is not at all obvious that the argument concludes (fallaciously, from the premiss that each line is commensurable with *some* line) that *all* lines are commensurable with each other. The argument is considering *all* lines that are commensurable with *each other* without making any assumption, one way or the other, as to whether this collection is coextensive with the collection of *all* lines (*simpliciter*). In the second place, neither Joachim nor the Peripatetic respondent addresses the heart of the argument: the claim that a collection of all lines commensurable with one another (whether

---

[43] I follow Bekker and all the MSS except N (as well as Joachim in his translation and notes) in reading *hosai d' eisi summetroi, pasai eisi metroumenai*. Apelt and (more recently) Cardini follow N in reading *metroumenai, pasai eisin summetroi*. See Pseudo-Aristotle, *De lineis insecabilibus*, with introd., trans., and commentary by M. Timpanaro Cardini, Testi e Documenti per lo Studio dell'Antichita, 32 (Milan, 1970), 50.

[44] Although the text here is most uncertain—I have basically followed Bekker in my translation—the argument seems clear enough. If there were proper parts of the unit of measure supposedly common to a class of all lines that are commensurable, that unit would have to measure such parts (i.e. the parts would have to be integral multiples of the whole), which is absurd. Cf. the proof of Euclid 10. 2, a *reductio* proof in which the contradiction is obtained by obtaining a length which a supposed measure must measure but which is of less length than the measure.

[45] H. H. Joachim (trans.), *De lineis insecabilibus* (Oxford, 1908), n. to 968^{b}10, 11, repr. in *The Works of Aristotle*, ed. W. D. Ross, vi, 6, *Opuscula* (Oxford, 1913).

or not that collection is coextensive with the collection of all lines) possesses a common measure.

In analysing the argument, the first question that arises is whether there is at least one such collection as that of *all* lines commensurable with each other. On the assumption (questionable, perhaps, in the case of *ancient* geometers) that the mathematicians are willing to allow infinitely large collections of lines, as well as the collection of *all* lines, the answer is 'yes'. The two-place relation 'X is commensurable with Y' is an *equivalence* relation. That is, it is reflexive (for all X, X is commensurable with X), symmetrical (if X is commensurable with Y, then Y is commensurable with X), and transitive (if X is commensurable with Y and Y is commensurable with Z, then X is commensurable with Z). Consequently, if we allow the collection of all lines, this relation will partition that collection into a group of mutually disjoint and collectively exhaustive sub-collections or 'equivalence classes' of lines that are commensurable with one another.

The argument then appeals to the same definition of commensurability as that given in Euclid 10, definition 1: 'commensurable magnitudes are defined as those that are measured by the same measure; incommensurable [magnitudes as those] of which it is not possible that there should be a common measure.' It is inferred from this definition that *for each equivalence class* of lines commensurable with one another there must be a common measure. Finally, in view of the notion of a common measure of a collection of lines—all of the lines in the collection are integral multiples of the measure—the argument concludes that the common measure *for each equivalence class* must be an indivisible quantum of magnitude relative to that class. If the distinction between commensurable and incommensurable is not vacuous (if *all* lines are not commensurable), the conclusion of such an argument would be not just that *one* indivisible quantum of magnitude exists, but that a *multiplicity* of such indivisible quanta exist, one for each collection of commensurable lines. Relative to each other, such minima apparently would be incommensurable.

From the contemporary perspective, at least, there is no problem with the idea of partitioning of *all* real-valued magnitudes or lines into equivalence classes of those that are commensurable with one another.[46] The problem arises from the use of the definition of commensurability.

---

[46] On the assumption that a real-valued measure can be assigned to magnitude, there is a non-denumerable infinity of such commensurability equivalence classes. Relative to such a measure, the class of all rational-valued magnitudes will represent 1 such class.

Suppose that $[X]$ is the equivalence class of all magnitudes commensurable with a given magnitude X. Then, from the definition of commensurability, it follows that

(1) For all magnitudes Y and $Z \in [X]$, there is a magnitude $W \in [X]$ such that Y and Z are each integral multiples of W.

However, for the argument we have been discussing to succeed, we must interpret the definition of commensurability as entailing

(2) There is a magnitude $W \in [X]$ such that, for all magnitudes Y and $Z \in [X]$, Y and Z are integral multiples of W.

Were principle (2) true, it would indeed follow that any equivalence class of commensurable magnitudes would contain a least member of which all the others are multiples. But (2) does not follow from (1). We find here yet another example of an illegitimate quantifier-shift. Although any two magnitudes in the class of all magnitudes that are commensurable with one another share a common measure, it does not follow that there is a common measure shared by any two magnitudes in the class.

None of this is clear from the Euclidean definition of commensurability, however. Since Euclid obviously means commensurability to be a property of collections of magnitudes and not merely a relation between *two* magnitudes (for in Book 10, proposition 4 he treats of 'three [and more] commensurable magnitudes'), his definition of commensurability should be: 'commensurable magnitudes are those that are *pairwise* measured by the same measure.'

Yet I do not think that the argument can *quite* be dismissed simply with the diagnosis of quantifier-shift fallacy. For if we again consider the equivalence class $[X]$ of magnitudes commensurable with an arbitrarily chosen magnitude X, it is true that for each and every natural number n, there will be a (single) common measure for any n members of the class. Euclid is well aware of this fact. Book 10, proposition 4 gives an algorithm for finding the greatest common measure of

For each irrational-valued magnitude i, any magnitude commensurable with it can be represented as the product of i and some rational r. Due to the denumerability of rationals, there is but a denumerable infinity of members of the commensurability equivalence class of i. Suppose that there is only a denumerable infinity of commensurability equivalence classes $[i]$ of irrational-valued magnitudes. Since every irrational falls into 1 (and only 1) such class, it would follow that there is only a denumerable infinity of irrational-valued magnitudes. But we know that there is a non-denumerable infinity of irrationals. Hence, there must be a non-denumerable infinity of commensurability equivalence classes of irrational-valued magnitudes.

any three commensurable magnitudes; and the porism to the proposition notes that the algorithm is extendable to (arbitrarily) more commensurable magnitudes. In brief, for any finite collection of commensurable magnitudes there will be a common measure. But, of course, this is a case where generalization to the infinite case does not hold: from 'for any n-member collection of commensurable magnitudes, no matter how large n is, there is a common measure for all of them' we cannot infer 'for any collection of commensurable magnitudes, there is a common measure for all of them'.

There are two ways that a rescue of the argument might be attempted. But both turn out to be unsatisfactory. First, it might be claimed that, for any magnitude, there are only a finite number of smaller magnitudes commensurable with it. But, so far as I can see, the only justification for such a claim would rest on some doctrine of indivisible quanta. So, as an argument *for* such quanta, the claim would render the argument circular. Second, it might be claimed that, although any finite magnitude is infinitely divisible, the greatest lower bound of the process of such division is not zero but some positive, infinitesimal magnitude. This is the way that Joachim apparently interprets the argument: 'There will be an actual length, or infinitesimal line, xy, which is the unit of measurement of them all. And xy must be indivisible.'[47]

There are many problems with such a view—both intrinsic, conceptual problems and problems with the view as an interpretation of the argument. The conceptual problems centre on the supposed indivisibility of such infinitesimals and the assumption of a unique such infinitesimal as the greatest lower bound of a collection of commensurable magnitudes. The recent mathematical theory of infinitesimals deriving from the non-standard analysis of Abraham Robinson offers no help here: his infinitesimals are divisible and none is the greatest lower bound of any collection of standard finite magnitudes. It is far from clear that any mathematically coherent conception of infinitesimals as indivisibles is possible. More to the point, however, a conception of magnitudes allowing for infinitesimals would necessarily not validate the Archimedean axiom. No *finite* compounding of the supposedly infinitesimal unit with itself would yield *any* standard finite magnitude. Consequently, such an infinitesimal magnitude could not serve as a *measure*, in the accepted sense of the term, of a collection of

[47] Joachim (trans.), loc. cit.

standard finite magnitudes. There seems, then, to be no reason to suppose that the indivisible measure envisioned by the proponents of our argument from incommensurability was conceived by them to be an infinitesimal. And such a conception apparently offers nothing of value in terms of improving the argument.

Although the attempt, on the part of advocates of indivisible quanta of magnitude, to use the geometrical conception of commensurability dialectically—i.e. to use geometrical theory to advance their quantum thesis—is unsuccessful, it probably is not the only instance of such a use of geometry to be found among ancient atomists. In the next section, I examine what I hypothesize to be another such case.

GEOMETRY AND THE QUANTUM MODEL

When Epicurus advised Pythocles to 'flee all *paideia*' (D.L. 10. 6), it seems extremely likely that education in the established geometrical science was part of what he had in mind. Indeed, Epicurean aversion to the geometers' *pulvis eruditus* ('learned dust/sand' in which diagrams used in proofs were sketched) eventually became something of a rhetorical commonplace. Cicero comments on this aversion and the consequent mathematical ignorance of Epicureans, attributing to it, among other deficiencies, the aesthetic blindness that renders them incapable of recognizing that a sphere is more beautiful than a cone, cylinder, or pyramid.[48] While there were some Epicureans who were— or previously had been—mathematicians,[49] it seems that the acceptance of the Epicurean world view generally involved, for these individuals, a conversion *from* the practice of geometry. Polyaenus, a 'first-generation' eminent Epicurean, who was perhaps the most distinguished of the mathematician converts, is described by Cicero as having come to believe that 'all of geometry is false' after he had accepted the views of Epicurus.[50] Zeno of Sidon is one of a few apparently exceptional Epicureans who, according to the account of Proclus in a passage cited earlier in this chapter,[51] continued to do mathematics after having become an Epicurean, arguing that (all?,

---

[48] Cicero, *De natura deorum* 2. 47-8.
[49] See the summary account in Sedley, 'Epicurus and the Mathematicians of Cyzicus', 23-6.
[50] Cicero, *Academica* 2. 106.
[51] Proclus, *In Eucl.* 199.

many?, some?) theorems of geometry did not follow without some additions to the (normally accepted?) set of postulates. I shall return to Zeno and the issue of an 'Epicurean geometry' later in this section. In general, there is reason for agreeing with Sedley that 'it seems that the wholesale rejection of geometry was still orthodox Epicureanism'.[52] Even wholesale rejection can come in several varieties, however. One sophisticated sort of wholesale rejection that seems particularly appropriate with respect to indivisible quanta—perhaps the *only* viable strategy here, in fact—is a geometrical stonewall: the entirely defensive posture of refusing to engage in geometrical argumentation with respect to indivisible quanta of magnitude because of the conviction that geometrical concepts are simply not applicable to such quanta.

Partes Minimae *and Geometry*

When one introduces indivisible quanta of magnitude, in the true sense of 'quanta' connoting 'positive measure' or bulk, protestations and pointed questions having an intuitive geometrical basis are almost certain to be voiced. What is the shape of such quanta? (Assumption: any spatial shape implies an organization of spatial proper parts, which contradicts the notion of a conceptually or theoretically indivisible spatial magnitude.) What are the dimensions of such a quantum? That is, how far is it from one side of it to another? (Assumption: any positive distance, specified in terms of some real-valued measure, means that we should, *theoretically* or *conceptually*, be able to talk about half of that distance, a quarter of that distance, etc.—even if, *as a matter of fact*, there are no separable bodies or particles that small.) Probably the most effective way of dealing with such questions is to deny their applicability to indivisible quanta. The questions only arise, it might plausibly be maintained, because the questioner mistakenly persists in (tacitly or explicitly) conceiving the quanta as embedded in a matrix or medium that is infinitely divisible and continuous. To what extent did ancient proponents of the quantum model of magnitude realize this strategy of rebuttal—which might be viewed as a form of stonewalling or refusal to play the geometers' game—to geometrical criticism of their doctrine?

An apparently early example of such a strategy is found in an argument for indivisible quanta found in *De lineis insecabilibus*. The

[52] Sedley, 'Epicurus and the Mathematicians of Cyzicus', 24.

argument is an argument for indivisibly minimal plane figures (in fact, squares), which immediately follows the argument from commensurability for indivisible lines that we discussed earlier and is, in fact, the same argument. The argument deals with all the squares constructed on 'rational' (*rhētōn*) lines, which are commensurable, and proceeds to argue as before from the definition of commensurability that such squares must have a partless measure (968^{b}15–17). The argument implicitly appeals to the Euclidean definition of rational lines (Book 10, def. 3) in terms of an (arbitrarily stipulated) line and all those lines that are commensurable with it 'in length and in square or in square only'. There are, in other words, lines in this class that are not commensurable in length. But, if the proponent of the argument is to consider *all* squares in a given commensurability equivalence class, this is the notion of rational line that he requires. That this is, in fact, the sense of 'rational' that he has in mind is shown by what follows:

> But if some such measure is cut along some prescribed[53] and definite line, [the resulting line] will not be rational or irrational or any of the other sorts of line of which the squares are rational, such as the *apotomē* and the *ek duoin onamatoin*.[54] [Such lines which might be constructed from a minimal square] do not have any natures in themselves, but relative to each other they will be rational or irrational.   (968^{b}17–22)

It is clear that, in order to avoid a *reductio* on the conclusion that there is a minimal square which is the common measure of an equivalence class of commensurable squares, the proponent of the argument does not wish to attribute to any lines at which a minimal square could be cut a nature of their own which would yield a square commensurable with the supposedly minimal square. What is perhaps surprising is that the possibility of such a minimal square's being cut should be entertained at all. A possible explanation is that the argument's author realizes that lines cutting the supposedly minimal square will yield commensurable squares. So such lines *should*, it seems, be rational in the Euclidean sense. For example, if we assign to the side of a minimal square unit measure, the diagonal of the unit square (of measure $\sqrt{2}$), will itself yield a square that is commensurable with (i.e. the double of)

---

[53] The term *tetagmenēn* used here does have a variety of technical, mathematical senses: e.g. 'regular' as applied to plane figures, 'ordinate' as applied to conic sections. Whether it might have a technical sense in the present context I have not been able to determine.

[54] See Euclid's Book 10, prop. 73 and 36, respectively, for accounts of these 2 sorts of line.

the unit square. But if we allow the possibility of dividing the unit square at the diagonal, then why can we not divide the diagonal by half (by considering the perpendicular from the base to the opposite angle of the two triangles resulting from cutting the unit square along its diagonal)? To do so, however, will yield a line (of measure $(\sqrt{2})/2$) which, like the diagonal, should be 'commensurable in square' with the unit square. But whereas the square on the diagonal is twice the unit square, the square on this line will be $1/2$ the unit square, which would be impossible if the unit square is to be the measure of all squares in its commensurability equivalence class.

In other words, although the first division of the unit square along its diagonal seems harmless (since its square is an integral multiple of the unit square), the division is a slippery slope that soon causes trouble for the thesis that there is a smallest square which is the measure of all squares in a commensurability equivalence class. The author of the argument forestalls problems by denying that such divisions of a smallest unit square have any nature of their own. There does seem to be some concession involved in the final clause—to the effect that such lines will be rational or irrational relative to one another. I do not know what to make of the concession; but the suggestion of Joachim is perhaps as good as any: 'Any such lines will, in fact, belong to a new order of lines, which may be expressed as rational or irrational in terms of one another, but not in terms of the ordinary geometry of lines.' Such a concession seems a dangerous compromise of the theoretical indivisibility of the unit square. A more thorough-going stonewall—i.e. the claim that there are no lines, points, or other sorts of part to be distinguished within the unit square—would probably have been a wiser move.

Some commentators have seen such a thoroughgoing stonewall in the Epicurean conception of the theoretically minimal parts of atoms. Sedley comments that 'I suspect that the Epicurean minimal unit, *to en têi atomôi elachiston*, was regarded as not having a geometrical shape, since to have a shape is to have parts';[55] Konstan 'I can only say that the Epicureans did not, I am sure, believe that the minimum quantity had edges';[56] Sorabji,

My suggestion is that [the minimal parts] have no shape at all. If they have no shape, Epicurus will be able to escape certain geometrical objections, for

---

[55] 'Epicurus and the Mathematicians of Cyzicus', 24
[56] 'Problems in Epicurean Physics', 405.

example, the objection that the diagonal of a square minimal part would have to exceed the side by less than a minimal length.[57]

The doctrine of radically shapeless, edgeless minima is appealing for precisely the reasons alluded to in these quotations. And I should like to believe that Sedley, Konstan, and Sorabji are correct in their inferences. But it must be pointed out that the ascription to the Epicureans of a doctrine of shapeless and edgeless theoretical minima is inferential; so far as I am aware, there is no *direct* statement of such a doctrine in the ancient sources.

More direct evidence of the stonewall response to geometrically grounded criticisms of indivisible quanta is the claim of Epicurus in the *Letter to Herodotus* 58, quoted earlier in the chapter:

We, beginning with the first, see these [minima] in succession [*heksēs*], not in the same place, not touching part to part, but, rather, in their own proper manner serving as integral measures [*katametrounta*] of magnitudes—more of them for a greater magnitude, fewer for a smaller magnitude.

Modern commentators, beginning with Jürgen Mau,[58] have seen in this passage an allusion to Aristotle's argument in *Phys*. 6. 1 (which was discussed in Chapter 1) that what is continuous cannot be constituted from indivisibles. Epicurus is agreeing with Aristotle that theoretically indivisible minima within aggregates (viz., within physically indivisible atoms) do not touch part to part, for they have no parts; nor are any two of them in the same place (which corresponds to touching 'whole to whole' in Aristotle's argument), because what is continuous has different parts that are 'separate with respect to place' (231^{b}6). Furley speaks of Epicurus as attempting 'to slip through a gap in Aristotle's net'[59] and Sorabji of Epicurus as using the 'loophole of postulating a merely successive relationship between conceptual minima'.[60] Although Sorabji is probably correct in admitting that this conjecture cannot 'be made certain', it seems likely not only that Epicurus did envisage a relationship of non-contiguous succession or discrete ordering but also that this is precisely the relationship among minima that Epicurus requires.

There has, however, been a variety of opinions advanced by modern scholars concerning the nature of the relation among indivisible

[57] *Time, Creation and the Continuum*, 372.
[58] *Zum Problem des Infinitesimalen bei den antiken Atomisten* (Berlin, 1954), 36–7.
[59] *Two Studies in the Greek Atomists*, 116.
[60] *Time, Creation and the Continuum*, 373.

quanta or *minimae partes* within the Epicurean atom. According to Sorabji's succinct summary,

Mau thinks that the relationship of minimal parts is unclear, Furley that it is edge-to-edge contact. Krämer sees Epicurus' answer in the phrase 'measuring in their distinct way', the distinctness (*idiotēs*) being opposed to coalescence. Konstan suggests that the smallest parts of the atom are inconceivable except as parts of a whole, and that it follows that no question can arise about how one part attaches to the whole.[61]

And Sorabji's own view, as we saw, is that indivisible quanta are 'successively' (discretely) but not contiguously ordered. There is a problem, it seems, with Furley's view. He suggests that, while the Epicureans identified the surface or extremity of an atom with the outermost layer of *minimae partes*, they should have maintained that surfaces, boundaries, edges, extremities, etc. are not parts. Presumably, then, surfaces, etc. would be true limit entities, lacking extension in at least one dimension. The response of Konstan, as far as it goes, seems to me to be apposite: 'I suspect that the notion of a boundary that was neither a part of matter nor physically separable from it would have smacked too much of idealism for Epicurus' comfort.'[62]

A further, related problem, however, is that the true limit conception of a surface, edge, etc. presupposes the idea of an infinitely divisible, continuous spatial extension. Let us consider a body A and the 'exterior' of A. If A has a surface in the true limit sense, it should be the case that when we consider a spatial interval (of just one dimension, in order to simplify matters) containing 'some of A' (on the right, say) and 'some of the exterior of A' (on the left), there is a sequence (actually, many sequences) of nested sub-intervals of a similar constitution that converge to a unique 'positional limit' that is the 'surface of A'. The existence of such a limit of convergence depends upon assumptions of the infinite divisibility and Dedekind continuity of magnitude.[63]

One might well attempt to *define* boundaries, extremities, edges, etc. in terms of such convergence. But even if one does not, it seems that the true limit conception of such entities necessarily involves convergence of this sort and, hence, at least the implicit notion of an

---

[61] Ibid. 374.

[62] 'Problems in Epicurean Physics', 405.

[63] It is Dedekind continuity that guarantees that there is a unique entity that is both the least upper bound of the A sub-interval and the greatest lower bound of the exterior-of-A sub-interval.

infinitely divisible, continuous 'environment' or matrix in which the entities possessing boundaries and edges are situated. So I believe that it is no mistake for the Epicureans to have avoided invoking a true limit conception of extremities and using such a conception to explain the relationship among their *minimae partes*.

There remain the other accounts of the relationship among indivisible quanta summarized by Sorabji. These do not seem to me to be incompatible. Central to the Epicurean conception of the relationship among indivisible quanta, I suspect, is Sorabji's conception of noncontiguous succession or discrete ordering. But it seems reasonable to assume that equally central is the entirely compatible claim of Krämer[64] that such quanta supply, 'in their own proper manner', a measure of all finite magnitudes (including, of course, atoms). And *katametrēma* (measure) can be read in the technical sense of 'defining all finite magnitudes as integral multiples of the atomic length', the sense insisted upon by Vlastos.[65] There will also be a certain lack of clarity about the relationship among *minimae partes* in the atoms, as Mau maintains, if one thinks of the quanta as embedded in an infinitely divisible and continuous matrix. For one cannot, on pain of inconsistency, answer the question that naturally arises when the quanta are pictured against such a background: how, in fine-grain detail, do adjacent quanta coalesce in an atom? Similarly, at least at the fine-grain level, all the preceding is compatible with Konstan's claim that 'there is no sense in inquiring how [a *minima pars*] might abut another object'.[66]

Konstan comes to this conclusion, however, not so much from geometrical considerations pertaining to indivisible quanta as from the claim—quite plausible in my view—that such quanta are regarded by the Epicureans as being *essentially* parts of larger wholes, viz., atoms. His argument, in a compressed form, is the following. Epicurus holds that what is capable of independent, substantial existence must have

[64] H.-J. Krämer, *Platonismus und hellenistische Philosophie* (Berlin, 1971), 243–4.

[65] G. Vlastos, 'Minimal Parts in Epicurean Atomism', *Isis*, 56: 2 [184] (1965), 136–7. Vlastos's view, which will be discussed in more detail in the text, is that the Epicurean minima (*ta elachista kai amerē*) happen (as a matter of *physical* fact) to represent the greatest common sub-multiple of the (finite) different atomic sizes. But this does not entail that such a minimum is theoretically indivisible, i.e. that it is a geometrically least magnitude. Of course, it will follow—and this is what I mean to emphasize in the text— that *if* Epicurean minima *are* indivisible quanta in this stronger, geometrical sense, then they are greatest common sub-multiples in Vlastos's sense.

[66] 'Problems in Epicurean Physics', 405.

parts—in particular, a surface, edges, 'interior', etc. But indivisible quanta are partless and, hence, do not have the capacity for independent existence: they must, essentially, be *minimae partes* of larger wholes (atoms, in the first place), wholes that are capable of independent existence precisely because indivisible quanta provide them with the surfaces, etc. requisite for such existence. Konstan then seems to conclude, on the basis of the lack of a capacity for independent existence of indivisible quanta, that 'Epicurus was not obliged to indicate how his minima, which were likewise inconceivable except as parts, were arranged in a larger mass'.[67] I do not see how this last conclusion follows.

Our sources agree that the indivisible quanta cannot be separated from atoms and regroup to form other atoms—probably for exactly the reasons adduced by Konstan. So Epicurus is clearly not obliged to explain any physical process of coalescence by which quanta might *come together* into a larger mass. But such a consideration does not render nonsensical, so far as I can see, the issue—one might term it a geometrical issue—of how indivisible quanta are arranged in an atomic mass. And Epicurus *does* address this issue in what is arguably the right way: indivisible quanta are successively but non-contiguously ordered and supply a measure (common sub-multiple) of the wholes which they constitute. What Epicurus is not obliged to answer, and what he apparently wisely resists answering, are questions (e.g. how does one quantum abut another?) that arise because of the tacit assumption of an infinitely divisible and continuous spatial matrix in which the quanta are embedded.

Konstan's paper raises another important issue concerning the spatial relation among atoms in composites. He sees Epicurus' doctrine of indivisible quanta as essentially *minimae partes* as a part of an attempt 'to solve the problem of contact among atoms, which is equivalent to the problem of boundary'.[68] The doctrine does supply atoms with surfaces (in the form, not of true limits but of an outermost layer of indivisible quanta). But does it 'solve the problem of contact among atoms'? Contact among atoms, in the sense defined by Aristotle, remains impossible. Surfaces (in the sense of layers of quanta) of two adjacent atoms cannot coincide because of the impossibility that two distinct corporeal quanta (i.e. pieces of the surfaces) should coincide or occupy the same place. And, of course, there are no

---

[67] Ibid.
[68] Ibid.

surfaces (in the true limit sense) of the surfaces (outermost layer of indivisible quanta) of atoms which could coincide.

Two main options present themselves. The first is that two successive atoms are always separated by *some* void. As Konstan notes, this view 'would explain [the Epicureans'] continued appeal to the principle that atoms are demarcated by void and that division is possible only where void subsists'. But Konstan also justly remarks: 'tempting as it is, I cannot find any evidence for this conception in the texts.'[69]

The other option is that, at certain *loci*, the surface of one atom is non-contiguously next to (non-contiguously succeeds) the surface of another *without any intervening gap of void*, just as Epicurus says that *minimae partes* within a single atom are arranged. The obvious problem here is why the non-contiguously, discretely ordered *minimae partes* of two such atoms do not coalesce to form a single, physically inseparable atom in the way that the non-contiguously, discretely ordered *minimae partes* of a single atom do. The only solution to this problem, so far as I can see, is to maintain that the explanation for the unity and physical indivisibility of the single atom is not geometrical or topological, since, according to this second possibility, the topological relation among the quanta in a single atoms would be the same as that among the 'union' of quanta in two atoms with surfaces that are, at least in some *loci*, successive (without intervening void). If the physical unity of the single atom—and the impossibility of multiple atoms coalescing to form a single, physically indivisible atom—is not to be merely a brute physical fact, the explanation of these phenomena would have to be, say, a 'chemical' explanation rather than a topological or mereological one.[70]

There is a strong tendency to represent the difference between the quanta within a single atom, on the one hand, and the quanta contained within two adjacent atoms, on the other, in a geometrical or topological manner. Thus, to quote Konstan, 'the former [minimal parts within an atom] constitute continuous matter, while the latter

---

[69] Ibid. n. 28.

[70] There is an analogous problem that arises, within the context of the geometrical conception of (physical) magnitude as infinitely divisible and continuous, concerning the relation of 2 physical bodies that are geometrically contiguous with respect to each other. The problem, which is rehearsed by Sextus Empiricus in *Adversus geometras* 61 ff. (*M* 3. 61 ff.), is the following. Since, according to the geometrical conception, 2 distinct but contiguous bodies have surfaces that are partly coincidental, why is it not the case that all such contiguous juxtaposition (*parathesis*) is union (*henōsis*)? Why is it not the case, e.g., that when we pull the 2 bodies apart, they come apart at a *different* place rather than the same one?

[atoms], precisely in that they have distinct surfaces which minima lack, can be brought into contact but cannot merge into a common corpuscle'. But, if we are take the doctrine of indivisible quanta seriously (as a geometrical or topological doctrine), there is a straight-forward sense in which the single atom is not continuous any more than multiples of adjacent atoms are. The single atom may be con-tinuous in the intuitive sense of constituting a natural, unitary whole without *separable* parts. But the topological/geometrical *analysis* of that continuity, which we may characterize as continuity in the topological sense, and which seems to have origins in Aristotle, cannot apply to such atoms. It should be noted, however, that although most contemporary scholars have tended to take seriously, in my sense, the Epicurean doctrine of minima, there has been at least one eminent dissenter: Gregory Vlastos. A consideration of his views seems essential in a consideration of the relation between the Epicurean ver-sion of the quantum model and ancient geometry.

An Epicurean Geometry?

At one level, the question of whether there was an Epicurean geometry can easily be given a negative answer. Vlastos is surely correct in claiming that there is no evidence for the existence of any ancient postulate set the intended model of which contains discretely ordered (and, at least for bounded constructions, a finite number of) 'Ur-elements'. It is not surprising that there should be no evidence of ancient axiomatic development of such a finitistic geometry. Vlastos comments, quite reasonably: 'I find it very hard to see what the finitist geometry ... would be like.'[71] In contemporary mathematics, such finite models typically arise in the algebraic study of absolute geometry, an approach in which fundamental concepts that are very abstract from the physical point of view replace the more intuitively comfortable concepts of elementary geometry.[72]

I believe that Vlastos is correct in pointing to the a priori implausibility of the ancient axiomatic development of a finitistic geometry; and I agree with Sedley that Vlastos 'spells out a strong

[71] 'Minimal Parts', 127.

[72] See e.g. H. Wolff and A. Bauer, 'Absolute Geometry', in Behake *et al.* (eds.), *Funda-mentals of Mathematics*, ii. 129–73. Absolute geometry is that part of geometry obtainable without any postulates (such as Euclid's 5th postulate of Book 1) that specify the curvature of the geometrical space—e.g. that specify whether space is 'flat' (Euclidean), parabolic, or hyperbolic.

argumentum e silentio against the existence of a special Epicurean geometry'.[73] Although Jürgen Mau has been cast in the role of a defender of the idea of a 'special Epicurean mathematics', the claims in his paper on this topic are actually quite modest: (i) the Epicurean rejection of *eis apeiron tomē* (divisibility 'to infinity') is the rejection of 'the mathematical axiom that any size can be bisected again and again *ad infinitum*',[74] and, consequently, the Epicurean *elachiston* or minimal quantum is, in some sense, *geometrically* minimal and indivisible; (ii) from the Epicurean standpoint, 'reasoning without the axiom of division *ad infinitum*' is reasonable because 'from the reliable testimony of Archimedes [Mau has in mind the *Methodus*] we know that it is possible to find new and true theorems without that axiom'.[75]

The point at which Vlastos's position seems to me to be weak is his premiss to the effect that, in the absence of a finitistic geometry in the rather narrow sense of a postulate set, analogous to that of Euclid but with an intended model of discrete elements, mathematically educated and interested Epicureans were faced with but two options: 'consign[ing] the whole of geometry to the devil'[76] or wholesale *mathematical* acceptance of the developing standard, Euclidean geometry. Perhaps some mathematically sophisticated converts to Epicureanism did choose the former alternative. Cicero's references to Polyaenus may be interpreted as implying, on Polyaenus' part, something of the aversion of the reformed smoker to cigarettes. But there were doubtless other reactions on the part of Epicurean mathematical *cognoscenti*. As Vlastos notes,[77] Demetrius of Laconia (second century BC) wrote a treatise on geometry; and Zeno of Sidon (second and first centuries BC), whom we mentioned earlier in a note in this chapter,[78] seems to have pursued mathematical matters as an Epicurean with a diligence sufficient to elicit a book-length response from the Stoic Posidonius.[79]

Proclus characterizes Zeno as maintaining that, even if the first principles of Euclidean geometry are granted, various theorems do not follow unless something else is added to the first principles. On this general basis, as well as some specific criticisms of Euclidean proofs by Zeno (as reported by Proclus), Vlastos proceeds to develop a picture of

---

[73] 'Epicurus and the Mathematicians of Cyzicus', 26, n. 24.
[74] 'Was There a Special Epicurean Mathematics?', 422.
[75] Ibid. 428, 429.
[76] Vlastos, 'Minimal Parts', 127.
[77] Ibid. 127, n. 35.
[78] See n. 24 above.
[79] Proclus, *In Eucl.*, 199–200.

Zeno as a 'constructive', but perhaps niggling and not very penetrating critic of Euclid:

> If Euclid's critic is to be judged by this recommendation [that an 'added assumption' to the effect that no two straight lines share a common segment of magnitude is needed to derive Euclid's proposition 1. 1 pertaining to the construction of an equilateral triangle] and its twin (that the same stipulation for circles should be added to the principles) the worst that we could say about him is that he is a severe and fussy, but certainly not an unfriendly, critic of the Euclidean systematization of geometry. He is, if anything, overanxious to perfect it.[80]

This picture of Zeno as a constructive critic of Euclid is intimately connected with Vlastos's general interpretation of Epicurean talk of partless, minimal quanta. His interpretation of minima is summarized by a proposition, characterized by him as a 'law of nature' and 'physical statement about the atoms', and designated 'L(I)':

> Atoms are so constituted that variations in atomic lengths occur only integral multiples of the smallest atomic length.[81]

With respect to L(I), Vlastos comments that 'if this were the law of nature it is meant to be, it should be compatible with *any* (self-consistent) mathematical system'.[82] But would it be? In order to avoid inconsistency, the notion of 'variations in atomic lengths' must be interpreted in such a restricted, artificial sense that L(I) becomes virtually vacuous. First, it is important to note that the 'smallest atomic length', designated q by Vlastos, does not represent any dimension of parts into which atoms may be *physically* divided because all atoms are *qua* atoms physically indivisible. Whether the dimensions or 'atomic lengths' of a particular atom are all integral multiples of a given q depends on what we count as dimensions or atomic lengths. For example, if the edges of a cubic atom count as dimensions and are each of atomic length $2q$, then the diagonal of the cube cannot count as a dimension/atomic length, for it will not be commensurable with the lengths of the edges of the cube. But we could just as well count the diagonal as a dimension/atomic length—by an appropriate *geometrical* construction of the cube—in which case its edges cannot be atomic lengths.

---

[80] 'Zeno of Sidon as a Critic of Euclid', in L. Wallach (ed.), *The Classical Tradition: Literary and Historical Studies in Honor of Harry Caplan* (Ithaca, NY, 1966), 154.

[81] 'Minimal Parts', 138.

[82] Ibid. 147.

Could we, rather arbitrarily, limit the concept of atomic lengths to the edges of solids? Not unless we want to rule out a variety of regular solids as possible atomic shapes. For a regular pyramid with square base of side $2q$ and height $2q$ will have edges with lengths incommensurable with q. Vlastos suggests that we might try to preserve q as minimal atomic length by supposing that 'all atoms, no matter how irregular might be their contours, could be (theoretically) broken down in the last analysis into parts of parallelepipedal shape, and the atomic lengths of the whole atom would be the set composed of all the atomic lengths of these component parts'.[83] Presumably, 'the atomic lengths of these component parts' refers to the lengths of the *sides* of the parallelepipeds, which will be multiples of q.

The problem with this suggestion is that, since we are referring to a *theoretical* breaking down rather than a physical one and since the theory in question is, according to Vlastos's assumption, Euclidean geometry, there are any number of ways of geometrically breaking down or carving up such atoms. Why, for example, think of a cube as geometrically constituted of smaller cubes with edges commensurable in length to the edges of the larger cube rather than as geometrically constituted of pyramids, which have edges not commensurable in length with the edges of the larger cube? And why think of atomic lengths as *sides* of parallelepipeds rather that, say, their *heights* (which may not be commensurable with their sides)? There do not seem to be any reasons, other than arbitrary geometrical stipulation, for ruling out geometrical decompositions of atoms that do not yield parts having edges the lengths of which are all multiples of some q. But when we invoke such geometrical stipulations we certainly appear to be placing *some* sort of limitation on Euclidean geometry.

It might be granted to Vlastos that the Epicurean doctrine that atoms are only found in a limited variety of sizes and shapes is a law of nature or physical statement without mathematical import. But I cannot see how restrictions on how we are to conceptualize, geometrically, the structure of atoms—which are *ex hypothesi* physically indivisible—can be anything but geometrical restrictions; and these restrictions must appear entirely arbitrary if we are assuming that Euclidean geometry characterizes the spatial matrix of atomic solids.

Other criticisms of Vlastos's interpretation of Epicurean minimal quanta have been given. Furley points out, for example, that since

---

[83] Ibid. n. 86.

Vlastos's interpretation does not attribute to the Epicureans the doctrine of minimal, discrete *spatial* distances, an infinite number of atomic shapes could easily be produced by slight spatial reorientation of the finite number of parallelepipedal solids into which each atom is properly (geometrically) analysed, according to Vlastos. In order to preclude an infinite variety of atomic shapes, then, Vlastos needs another principle (geometrical or physical?) restricting possible geometrical conjunctions of his canonical parallelepidedal solid atomic parts.[84] Furthermore, Sedley notes that the 'mathematical fragments of Demetrius of Laconia make it appear that the *elachiston* posed a threat to geometry; which on Vlastos's interpretation it would not do'.[85]

In sum, then, I think that there is reason to reject Vlastos's contentions that L(I), *qua* physical statement, captures all that the Epicureans intended by talk of 'least' and 'partless' magnitudes, and that mathematically sophisticated but physically orthodox Epicureans need not have had any *fundamental* objections to Euclidean geometry. At the very least, this contention would seem to need to be supported by a variety of stipulations and restrictions, which appear *ad hoc* and which are not obviously physical, rather than mathematical, in character.

To return to Zeno of Sidon, it is easy to see that, so long as Vlastos's interpretation of the Epicurean minimum stands, there is reason to maintain that Zeno's criticisms of Euclidean geometry must have been constructive. For example, according to Vlastos's interpretation of the doctrine of minima, Zeno would have no obvious *mathematical* objection to the additional assumption that he holds is necessary in order to derive the first proposition of the first book of Euclid—i.e. that two lines do not share a common segment of magnitude.[86] In general, Vlastos's L(I) could not constitute the basis of a denial of the existence

---

[84] Furley, *Two Studies in the Greek Atomists*, 42–3.

[85] 'Epicurus and the Mathematicians of Cyzicus', 26, n.26.

[86] The first proposition of Euclid's Book 1 is the construction of an equilateral triangle on any given straight line-segment $\alpha\beta$. The construction involves taking the given line segment as the radius of each of 2 overlapping circles, one having its centre at 1 end-point α of the line, the other having its centre at the other end-point β. Line segments $\alpha\gamma$ and $\beta\gamma$ are then drawn from each of the end-points of the line to an intersection γ (i.e. one of the 2 intersections) of the overlapping circles. Since $\alpha\gamma$ and $\beta\gamma$ are both radii of the circles, which are of equal radius, it follows that the triangle so constructed is equilateral. Zeno's point is that it must be assumed that the partially non-coincidental lines produced from the extension of $\alpha\gamma$ and $\beta\gamma$, respectively, do not have any common segments. Otherwise, the 2 lines might coincide for some interval *before* they reach γ, and the triangle produced would thus not be equilateral. See Proclus, *In Eucl.* 214. 18 ff.

of lines, points, surfaces, in the true limit sense, nor the denial of a *mathematical* conception of divisibility *ad infinitum*.

However, if L(I) is rejected as an interpretation of Epicurean minima—if, in other words, the doctrine of indivisible quanta *was* understood as having geometrical significance—a very different picture of Zeno's criticisms emerges. Then, it seems likely, as Sedley says, 'that Zeno regarded the additional premiss as false',[87] indeed, *mathematically* false. To show that a given theory requires, in order to derive its theorems, a postulate that one takes to be false—or that the theory entails a false proposition—can easily be presented as a quite destructive criticism of the theory, a *reductio* of the theory, in fact.

I very much suspect that such was the nature of Zeno's criticism of Euclidean geometry. But where does this leave Zeno and other Epicurean mathematicians? If we accept Vlastos's exhaustive dichotomy of adherence to Euclid or the complete assignment of geometry to the devil, the answer is obvious. But there are other options. Sedley mentions a sort of piecemeal, non-axiomatic 'applied geometry', the exchange of a mathematical science for 'an inexact but serviceable discipline'.[88] And I believe that Mau perhaps entertains the same hypothesis. Another possibility—in no way incompatible with a rough-and-ready *applied* geometry for use in mensuration and calculation—is the dialectical use of geometry. By 'dialectical use' I mean the criticism of Euclidean geometry not necessarily as an end in itself but as a tool in the development and clarification of atomist physical doctrines. Specific evidence for such an undertaking is, alas, scanty, to say the least. But in the following section I develop another speculative 'plausible story' of Epicurean criticism of Euclid's parallel postulate as a means towards clarifying the doctrine of the *parengklisis* or atomic 'swerve'.

Euclid's Parallel Postulate and the Atomic Swerve?

In his discussion of Euclid's parallel postulate (Book 1, Postulate 5), Proclus reports an argument that purports to establish the *contrary* of the parallel postulate, i.e. that 'it is impossible that lines produced at angles less than two right angles should meet'.[89] The argument is the following (see Fig. 6). Take two straight lines $\alpha\beta$ and $\gamma\delta$ and a straight line-segment $\alpha\gamma$, connecting them in such a way that the sum

---

[87] 'Epicurus and the Mathematicians of Cyzicus', 25.
[88] Ibid. 26.   [89] Proclus, *In Eucl.* 368. 27–369. 1.

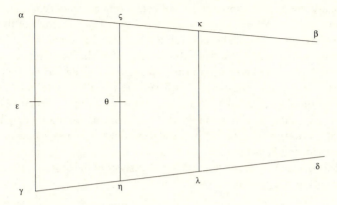

F IG. 6. The Argument that Non-Parallel Lines Do Not Intersect: The Case of Equal Angles

By contemporary lights, this case of the argument reported by Proclus is refuted by noting that the construction yields 2 infinite sequences of points, α, ζ, κ, . . . and γ, ε, λ . . ., both converging to a point of intersection finitely distant from α and from γ. Such a refutation depends upon the assumption of the infinite divisibility of extension.

of the interior angles ('on the right') is less than two right angles. Bisect αγ at ε and measure off a length αζ equal to αε on αβ and a length γη equal to γε on γδ. It is clear that αβ and γδ do not meet at ζ and η (that ζ and η are not, in fact, the same point). For if they did, the sum of two sides of a triangle (i.e. of αζ and γη) would be equal to the third side αγ, 'which is impossible'. So ζη must be a line-segment having some length. Bisect it at θ; and again measure out line-segment ζκ on αβ equal to ζθ and line-segment ηλ on γδ equal to θη. The same kind of argument can be used to show that lines αβ and γδ do not meet at points κ and λ. Since this process can be continued infinitely, which results in taking further and further segments on αβ and γδ, the argument's proponents, says Proclus, conclude that the straight lines do not meet anywhere.[90]

In his discussion of this argument, Proclus makes a promising beginning. He says that

although [the proponents of the argument] speak the truth, they do not say as much as they believe. That it is not possible to define the point of intersection in this straightforward way is true. However, it is not true that the lines do not meet at all.[91]

[90] Ibid. 369. 1–20.   [91] Ibid. 369. 21–370. 2.

The argument provides a method of generating a sequence of pairs of points on $\alpha\beta$ and $\gamma\delta$, respectively, and shows that, for each of these pairs, the members of the pair cannot coincide. However, as Proclus claims, it does not follow from this construction that the lines do not intersect. In some cases where the two angles ($\gamma\alpha\beta$ and $\alpha\gamma\delta$) are not equal, the point of intersection will fall *between* successive points on one of the lines yielded by the construction (see Fig. 7). Proclus *may* have had this case in mind in the first part of his more detailed response to the argument.[92] But this part of his response seems quite confused, and I shall not go into details. In general, after his promising initial comment quoted above, Proclus' analysis of the argument is disappointing.[93]

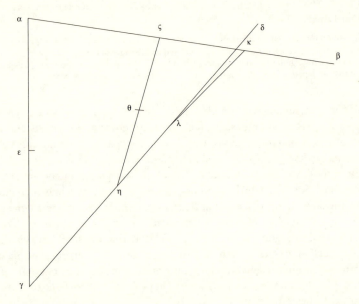

FIG. 7. The Argument that Non-Parallel Lines Do Not Intersect: The Case of Unequal Angles

The case of the argument for which the angles $\gamma\alpha\beta$ and $\alpha\gamma\delta$ summing to less than 2 right angles are unequal is refuted by noting that the lines $\alpha\beta$ and $\gamma\delta$ intersect *between* points generated by the argument's construction.

[92] Ibid. 370. 2–10.
[93] After the opaque argument at 370. 2–10, Proclus states the obvious, that the argument proves too much, noting that it will be refuted if a line can be drawn from α to

Another case that I wish to consider more closely is the case where angles $\gamma\alpha\beta$ and $\alpha\gamma\delta$ are equal. Here, according to the parallel postulate, line-segment $\alpha\gamma$ is the base of an isosceles or equilateral triangle having as (equal-length) sides segments of lines $\alpha\beta$ and $\gamma\delta$. In this case the sequence of points $\alpha,\zeta,\kappa,\ldots$ (on line $\alpha\beta$) and the sequence $\gamma,\eta,\lambda,\ldots$ (on line $\gamma\delta$) converge to the intersection of the lines (i.e. the vertex of the triangle) *as a limit of both sequences*. For each n, the pair of points which are the nth members of each sequence are some finite distance ϵ from the point of intersection; but for any distance ϵ, there is a natural number N such that for all $n > N$, the distance between the nth members and the point of intersection is less than ϵ. When Heath notes a certain similarity between this criticism of the parallel postulate and Zeno's paradox of Achilles and the tortoise,[94] he is evidently thinking of this particular case. Although the construction constituting the heart of the argument can be continued *ad infinitum*, the sequences of points resulting from the continued construction converge to a point finitely distant from α and from γ.

Proclus does not indicate the provenance of this argument, and, so far as I know, there is no evidence that would come close to deciding the issue. However, an interesting hypothesis, which I shall entertain, is that the argument is an Epicurean one. The one explicit principle employed in the argument that is mentioned by Proclus is Euclid 1, proposition 20: the sum of any two sides of a triangle is greater than the remaining side. Proclus reports that Epicureans used this theorem as an example of the lack of utility of geometry on the grounds that the theorem is 'clear even to an ass and requires no demonstration': the proposition belongs among *ta emphanē*, 'things that are manifest'.[95]

η. But if it cannot, the 1st as well as the 5th postulate of the 1st book of Euclid will be contradicted. Finally, Proclus comments that 'someone could say' (evidently, someone not assuming the parallel postulate) that straight lines whose interior angles total to less than 2 right angles but are greater than or equal to some angle α 'remain nonsecant'; but if the total is less than α, they intersect (370. 4–10). If one lets one of the interior angles remain a right angle and thinks of α as that angle of rotation of the other line, less than a right angle, at which the lines become nonsecant, α is the 'angle of parallelism' in Lobachevskian geometry. Heath notes the 'germ of such an idea as that worked out by Lobachewsky' (*Euclid's Elements*, i, 207.). But to press this point any further than does Heath (who simply mentions the point in passing) seems to me to constitute an example of the 'pernicious' variety of anachronism alluded to in the 'Preface and Apologia' of this study.

[94] Heath, *Euclid's Elements*, i. 206.

[95] Proclus, *In Eucl.* 322. 5–8. The ass enters in because of the Epicurean claim (322. 10–4) that a hungry ass will take a straight line to fodder rather than, so to speak, 'triangulating' to it. This is an argument for self-evident truth of the ancient variety that I

It will be noted that the rebuttal of the argument for the case we are considering, in which the two angles are *equal*, depends upon the infinite divisibility of magnitude. In effect, the construction of the argument yields a sequence of ever smaller similar isosceles or equilateral triangles, the limit of whose areas is zero. It is perhaps worthwhile to contemplate the argument within the context of the assumption of indivisible quanta of magnitude. Let us suppose, with Euclid, that two lines (whose interior angles in relation to an intersecting line are equal and less than 180^6) do intersect on the same side. Now, consider positions on the line when the two lines are two minimal units $(2q)$ apart. Bisecting this interval, we measure off a further minimal distance q on each line and ask if the lines intersect at the distance of q 'to the right' of the positions we are considering. The answer will have to be 'no' because, were it 'yes', we would apparently have a triangle with base $(2q)$ equal to the sum of its sides (each of minimal length q). Since the lines cannot intersect in anything less than a minimal distance q, two possibilities seem to remain. (a) The lines do not intersect at all. (b) Each line shifts or jumps (discontinuously) one minimal unit toward the other. So, on the assumption that lines have a breadth of minimal magnitude q, they will then be contiguous for a minimal distance q (or some integral multiple of q), and then they will coincide for a minimal distance q (or some multiple of q).[96] With respect to alternative (b), one 'straight line' will evidently have to shift to the position of the other: they cannot meet half-way, as it were, because that would involve a shift of $1/2q$ of each toward the other.

like to call 'birds b'lieve it; bees b'lieve it; even educated fleas b'lieve it'. Another noteworthy example is found in Sextus Empiricus, *Hypotyposeis* 1. 69, where the Stoic Chrysippus is presented as arguing that even a dog accepts a generalization of *modus tollendo ponens*: either *A* or *B* or *C*; but not *A* and not *B*; therefore, *C*. For, according to Chrysippus, a dog, coming to a triple fork in the road and not detecting the scent of its quarry in 2 of the 3 paths, will set off straightaway down the 1 remaining path without bothering to check for the scent.

[96] David Sedley has suggested to me a 3rd alternative. The straight lines are conceived as contiguous for (some multiple of) q and, then, as changing positions each with the other and remaining contiguous with each other for (some multiple of) q before diverging. Would this conception of each line 'quantum-shifting *over* or *past* the other', so to speak, constitute a counter-example to the conclusion that straight lines must either (i) share a common segment or (ii) not intersect? The answer depends, I suppose, on whether one takes this 'quantum-shift over/past each other' to be an instance of intersecting or meeting one another (*sumpiptousin allēlais*). If this identification is made, then this situation obviously does constitute a counter-example. But the identification need not, I think, necessarily be made. For in this situation, there is *no part*, whether segment or limit (e.g. point) at which the 2 lines intersect.

Which line is conceived as shifting and which is conceived as 'staying in position' seems an entirely arbitrary matter, from the geometrical perspective (see Fig. 8).

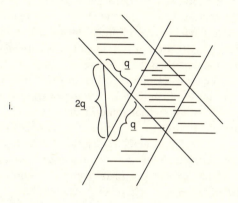

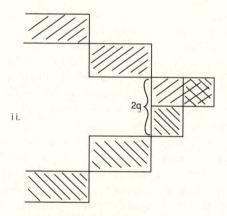

FIG. 8. The Argument that Non-Parallel Lines Do Not Intersect: 'Quantum Shifts' of Lines

(i) The sort of intersection of straight lines ruled out by prop. 20 of Book I of Euclid: the sum of any 2 sides of a triangle is *greater* than the remaining side. (ii) 'Quantum shifts' of non-parallel 'straight' lines. The primary 'moral' of this discussion is that a doctrine of geometrically minimal linear or scalar magnitude will affect the concept of angular magnitude.

What might one conclude from the 'Epicurean' argument that I have been imagining? First, it provides an argument (as qualified in the preceding note) that *if* some version of the parallel postulate is to be retained within the context of mathematical atomism, straight lines must either not intersect or must have a common segment. The import of this claim is more than the fairly obvious point that, if lines are conceived as having some (minimal) magnitude, their intersection or crossing must have some magnitude. The argument suggests that the common segment shared by intersecting parallel straight lines is achieved by a bending of one or other of the lines. But it is not a bending in the sense of continuous curving of the line; rather it is a discontinuous quantum shift or jump of the line. Such a proof would certainly give added force to the claim of Zeno of Sidon that Euclid's construction of an equilateral triangle in Book 1, proposition 1 assumes that straight lines do not have any common *tmēmata* (segments). If the parallel postulate *requires*, according to atomist lights, common segments intersecting straight lines while Euclid's proposition 1. 1 requires the contrary of this assumption, it is perhaps easier to see why Proclus should categorize Zeno among those who, in raising objections to this proposition, 'believed that they were refuting the whole of geometry'.[97]

Such an argument concerning the parallel postulate could also have been useful in developing the Epicurean doctrine of the atomic swerve or *parengklisis*. At *De rerum natura* 2. 244–5, Lucretius notes that the atomic *parengklisis* must not be held to be 'more than a minimum lest we seem to suppose oblique motions, and that the truth of the matter refutes'. Concerning the apparent distinction drawn in this passage between the swerve and oblique motion, Sedley suggests that an atom moving in a straight line 'can shift sideways by one *elachiston* without leaving that line'.[98] My suggestion is that Epicureans could have derived support for this very non-Euclidean doctrine from an atomistic criticism of the parallel postulate derived from the argument reported by Proclus. The idea is that the atomistic criticism of the parallel postulate shows that—at least in the case of non-parallel straight lines—a line can make such a 'quantum shift' *itself* and remain the same straight line.[99] Of course,

[97] Proclus, *In Eucl*. 214. 15–17.

[98] Sedley, 'Epicurus and the Mathematicians of Cyzicus', 25.

[99] Sedley points out that, in the case of 'natural' atomic motion and the *parengklisis*, we are evidently dealing with parallel straight lines with a privileged orientation (i.e. down/

that the argument's source was Epicurean and that some Epicureans made this sort of dialectical use of it is but a conjecture, supported by only a modicum of circumstantial evidence.[100]

It does, however, seem plausible that Lucretius' deprecation of oblique atomic motion is indicative of a notable insight on the part of mathematically sophisticated Epicureans: a doctrine of geometrically minimal *linear* magnitude will not leave unscathed the Euclidean doctrine of continuous and infinitely divisible *angular* magnitude. Consequently, the doctrine of minima will affect the angular as well as the linear components of atomic motion. Unfortunately, we do not seem to have much more evidence concerning the issue of angular magnitude and the angular component of atomic motion. As we shall see in the following chapter, this is only one of several aspects of atomic motion with respect to which the lack of extant information is exceedingly frustrating. We shall also see, however, that there is evidence of concerted attempts to develop quantum models of motion in opposition to the Aristotelian model discussed in Part I of this study.

up). And it is not clear that we would have reason to think of *these* lines as undergoing quantum shifts. Particularly if we do, it seems clear that the notion of parallelism will need to be reconsidered. As Michael Ferejohn expressed it to me, parallel lines will have to be far enough apart that they do not end up coinciding due to quantum shifts. Of course, it is possible simply to think of parallel lines in the privileged orientation as being *defined* by the motion of distinct atoms 'in free fall'—with or without a minimal swerve.

[100] I am indebted to Paul Vander Waerdt for bringing to my attention one additional piece of circumstantial evidence: a papyrus from Herculaneum (*P. Herc.* 1005. 7) attributes to Zeno of Sidon a title *Peri parengkliseōs kai tēs tou akroou prokatarchēs* ('On the swerve and the origin of the aggregate'). This at least shows that Zeno was interested in the *parengklisis*. Whether he connected that interest with his criticism of Euclidean geometry is, of course, another matter.

6

The Quantum Model: Time and Locomotion

It seems clear that, if spatial magnitude is constituted of discrete minimal quanta, Aristotle's analysis of motion, which was discussed in Part I, must be jettisoned. For the corner-stone of Aristotle's kinematic analysis of motion is its continuity; and, as we saw, the continuity of a locomotion requires its infinite divisibility (in Aristotle's 'constructive' sense) into kinetic segments, which in turn requires the infinite divisibility of the distance through which a mover moves and time in which it traverses that distance. Consequently, the atomic model of spatial magnitude will require a very different *kinematic* analysis of motion, at least at the micro-level. Some conception of motion as occurring in discrete quanta—hereafter referred to as 'quantum-motion'—seems to be necessary. Much of this chapter will be devoted to an analysis of such quantum conceptions of motion from a kinematic perspective. But various *metaphysical* issues concerning quantum models of motion are also central to the ancient discussions. In what sense are such models reductionistic? Do they result in the elimination of *kinēsis* as a fundamental ontological category or part of the furniture of the world? Is more than one metaphysical view of quantum-motion possible; and, if so, do we find representatives of these different metaphysical conceptions of quantum-motion? In order to begin our kinematic examination of quantum-motion, as well as our attempt to address these metaphysical issues concerning such motion, it seems necessary to return again to Aristotle.

ARISTOTLE ON THE RELATIONS AMONG KINDS OF QUANTUM

At several places in *Phys.* 6 Aristotle addresses the issue of the relationship among indivisible quanta of spatial magnitude, time, and motion. Irrespective of the cogency of the arguments he produces pertaining to this issue, his views—according to most contemporary commentators—were influential in the later development of conceptions of quantum-motion. In *Phys*. 6. 1 Aristotle makes a very strong claim: 'by the same argument, magnitude and time and *kinēsis* are all constituted from indivisibles and are divisible down to indivisibles, or none is' (231^b18–20). The claim is *too* strong. The doctrine of indivisible quanta of spatial magnitude does not *in itself* imply the doctrine of indivisible quanta of temporal duration (or vice versa). A doctrine of quantum motion (which allows for temporal jumps or instantaneous displacements over positive intervals of spatial magnitude) does not imply the existence of either spatial or temporal indivisible quanta. And, of course, a physical doctrine according to which corporeal substance comes in discrete, minimal quanta implies nothing with respect to the question of whether spatial magnitude, time, and motion are constituted of discrete quanta. The one legitimate entailment seems to be the following: a quantum structure of either spatial magnitude or time entails some form of quantum-motion.

We find Aristotle leading from his strongest suit. Most of the argumentation in *Phys*. 6. 1 is devoted to establishing the claim that 'if a magnitude is constituted of indivisibles, then also motion over this [magnitude] will be [constituted] of an equal number of indivisible motions' (231^b21–2). Although Aristotle's argumentation on behalf of this fairly obvious claim approaches overkill, his basic tenets concerning supposedly discontinuous local motion emerge in the course of his discussion.

Aristotle's aim is to show that if a magnitude $AB\Gamma$ is constituted of indivisibles A, B, and Γ, then the motion ΔEZ of a body Ω traversing that magnitude must be constituted of indivisibles Δ, E, and Z. In order to demonstrate this claim, he invokes the essentially linguistic principle that

it is necessary that something that is moving from one place to another should not, at the same time, *be in the process of moving* [*kineisthai*] and *have completed its motion* [*kekinēsthai*] to the place to which it was moving when it was moving (e.g. if someone is in the process of walking to Thebes, it is impossible that at the same time he be in the process of walking to Thebes and that he have completed his walk to Thebes). (231^b29–232^a1)

Aristotle then concludes by *reductio* that, since Ω is assumed to traverse the partless A in virtue of the motion (kinetic segment) Δ, Δ cannot instantiate both the *process* of Ω's going through A and the *achievement* (and ensuing state) of Ω's having gone through A. For, if

Δ did instantiate both process and achievement/ensuing state, it would be divisible. That is, *Δ* would be constituted of a part consisting of the process of moving and also a distinct part (or limit) consisting of the achievement or completion of that particular process of moving. Aristotle is apparently assuming that *Δ* is *not* divisible.

There is a fairly obvious problem with this argument: supposedly, Aristotle is trying to prove that *Δ* (as well as *E* and *Z*) are indivisible; and, since it seems he has not yet proved this, his implicit assumption of the indivisibility of *Δ* at this juncture would constitute a blatant *petitio*. Perhaps Aristotle believes that it is obvious that the divisibility of *Δ* would imply the divisibility of the (indivisible) spatial interval *A* with which it is *ex hypothesi* associated. He may think that, at the very least, the indivisibility of *A* implies that a supposed part of *Δ* that is the going-through-*A* and a supposedly distinct 'part' of *Δ* that is the having-gone-through-*A* cannot *both* be paired with *A*, as he has assumed in the hypothesis of the argument. (The only way both these supposed constituents of *Δ* could be paired with *A* would seem to require a pairing of the process of going-through-*A* with the interior, so to speak of *A*, and the achievement of having-gone-through-*A* with *A*'s 'right limit'; but the indivisibility of *A* would seem to preclude even this sort of distinction.)

According to the preceding considerations, Aristotle's argument may perhaps more usefully be interpreted as an attempt to spell out the nature of the parts of *ΔEZ* than as an argument for the indivisibility of *Δ*, *E*, and *Z*. What he has thus far obtained is the conclusion that, in the light of the unique pairing of *Δ* with *A* (*E* with *B* and *Z* with *Γ*), *Δ* cannot instantiate *both* the going-through-*A* and the having-gone-through-*A* (and similarly, of course, for *E* and *Z*). The remaining possibilities seems to be that the *kinēsis*-constituents *Δ*, *E*, and *Z* all instantiate either (i) the going-through of the corresponding indivisible spatial intervals or (ii) the having-gone-through of these minima. Aristotle fastens on the second option:

If, then, something is moving over the whole *ABΓ*, and the motion with which it is moving is *ΔEZ*, and if it never is moving but has moved over the partless *A*, the motion would not be constituted from motions but from jumps [*kinēmatōn*] and [would occur] by means of something that is not moving having completed a movement. . . . If, therefore, it is necessary that everything is either resting or moving, and something is resting with respect to each of the *ABΓ*'s, the result will be that something is continuously resting and, at the same time, moving.   (232ᵃ6–14)

It is important to note that the implicit *reductio* in the passage does not come until the end: Aristotle does not rely *simply* on the notion of something's having moved without being in the process of moving to obtain an absurdity. Rather, he seems to suggest that this notion implies that Ω, the body that is supposedly moving with respect to the whole spatial interval $AB\Gamma$, is resting with respect to each of its indivisible constituents. It is possible that he has in mind something like the following argument. Suppose that the length of the supposedly moving body Ω is equal to or larger than each of A, B, and Γ (a necessary supposition if these represent indivisible quanta of magnitude). Since Δ, E, and Z instantiate not *kinēseis* (mov*ings*) but *kinēmata* (having-moveds), then Δ, E, and Z must also instantiate *staseis* (restings) on the additional assumption that everything must be either moving or resting. Consequently, Ω must be resting with respect to each of the corresponding spatial magnitudes A, B, and Γ; and (since these partition the whole magnitude with respect to which it supposedly moves) Ω must paradoxically be resting with respect to the whole magnitude over which it, *ex hypothesi*, moves.

From Aristotle's own perspective, the *exhaustive* dichotomy of either-resting-or-moving may seem suspect. For, as we noted on a number of occasions in Part I, Aristotle maintains that a continuously moving body cannot be said either to be moving or to be resting with respect to the punctal now or temporal instant; so it also cannot be said to be moving with respect to any instantaneous position that we may imagine it to occupy during the course of its continuous motion. In the present case, however, we are dealing with spatial intervals that are indivisible but to which some positive measure is assigned. Aristotle seems to envision the following situation. Let us suppose that the length of Ω is one minimal unit (equal to A, B, or Γ) in the direction of motion. It is first the case, then, that it 'has moved into position A without having been in the process of moving into it'; then it rests for some period of time in that position; then we find that it 'has moved into position B without having been in the process of moving into it'. It then rests for some period of time in that position, etc.

Each of the 'having-moveds' is an instantaneous displacement from one position to the successive one. Consequently, it might be argued, if the *total* displacement of a body that is moving by instantaneous displacements or jumps (*kinēmata*) is not to be instantaneous, the body must rest or pause at each such *locus*. So the Ω really is resting with respect to each of A, B, and Δ. It might, however, be maintained that such a picture of instantaneous displacements interlarded with periods of *stasis* depends upon a conception of time as continuous and infinitely divisible: the resting of Ω at an (indivisible) spatial *locus* is associated temporally with a (divisible) interval of time, while the instantaneous displacement or jump is associated with the *limit* of such an interval. We will soon return to this issue. For the moment, however, we can characterize Aristotle's argument as follows. The supposition of indivisible quanta of spatial magnitude with respect to which a supposedly moving body moves implies that the 'divisions of its total motion' corresponding to each indivisible quantum of distance cannot individually both be (i) 'movings' (*kinēseis*) and (ii) 'having-moveds' (*kinēmata*). On the supposition that they are (ii) *kinēmata*, these are instantaneous displacements separated by temporal intervals of rest. So, the paradoxical result will be that 'something will be continuously resting and, at the same time, moving; for [*ex hypothesi*] it was moving with respect to the whole $AB\Gamma$, and it was resting with respect to each part and, consequently, with respect to the whole' (232ª13–15).

But what of alternative (i), the possibility that Δ, E, and Z instantiate not having-moveds or *kinēmata*, but movings or *kinēseis*? Nothing so far in the argument explicitly rules out the possibility of Δ's instantiating a moving; all that has been established, according to the most charitable interpretation, is that it cannot instantiate *both* a moving and a having-moved. Aristotle does not forget alternative (i): 'But if the indivisibles constituting ΔEZ are motions, it would be possible for something—although motion is present in it—not to be moving but to be resting' (232ª15–17). Unfortunately, he does not present any argument to support this claim. And I have not found much help in the commentators. Simplicius (who finds in the passage we have been discussing, 231ᵇ18–232ª17, four distinct *atopa* or absurdities entailed by the supposition that Ω *moves* with respect to the whole $AB\Gamma$ but only *has moved* with respect to its indivisible parts) hints at the argument that was probably foremost in Aristotle's mind: even if we assume that Δ, E, and Z are *kinēseis*, the very fact that the corresponding intervals A, B, and Γ are indivisible quanta entails that Ω must rest for some temporal interval at those positions.[1]

Aristotle's reasoning may have been that if Ω is associated with an

---

[1] See Simplicius, *In phys.*, CAG 10, 932–5.

indivisible interval for any non-null duration of time, Ω *cannot* be moving with respect to that duration of time; so it must be at rest with respect to it. Again suppose that the length of Ω in the direction of its movement is equal to A. According to the present line of reasoning, for Ω to be associated with A for some duration of time *and* for Ω to be correctly said to be moving for that duration, it would have to occupy, first, more and more of A until it fully occupies it and, then, less and less of A until it is entirely outside it. But this process implies the divisibility of A. Hence, for Ω to be associated with indivisible A for a non-null period of time, it must *remain* (i.e. be resting) at A for that temporal period. This argument has a certain cogency, I believe, if the non-null duration or *temporal* period with respect to which Ω is associated with A is assumed to be divisible. But if such a temporal period is *itself* an indivisible temporal quantum, it is not so obvious that Ω should be said to be resting (as opposed to moving) with respect to that quantum. We shall soon return to this issue. But first let us pause to take stock of Aristotle's argument that either spatial magnitude, time, and motion are all constituted of indivisibles or none is.

Thus far, we have not found much argumentation for this thesis. At its beginning, the passage beginning at *Phys*. 6. 1. 231^{b}21 looks as though it will be an argument that the constitution of a spatial interval from indivisibles implies the constitution of locomotion over such an interval from (the same number of) indivisibles. As it turns out, however, there is little if any explicit argument for this entailment. Most of what follows is an extended argument that the conception of spatial intervals as constituted of indivisibles gives rise to a paradox or absurdity: a body Ω that is traversing such an interval must be simul-taneously moving and at rest. This amounts to the claim that a cinematographic model of motion, i.e. a conception of periods of rest interlarded with instantaneous displacements (which do not *take* time), yields the following paradoxical consequence: a supposed interval of motion is partitioned in such a way that all of the sub-intervals of that partition are intervals of rest. Aristotle returns to the issue of the relation of indivisibles with respect to spatial magnitude, time, and motion only briefly at the end of the chapter. There he argues that infinite divisibility of length or spatial magnitude implies infinite divisibility of time (because a body moving at a constant speed equal to that of another body must, in traversing less distance, take less time) (232^{a}19–21). And, conversely, divisibility of time implies divisibility of length (because a body moving at a constant speed equal to that of another body must, in less time, traverse a shorter distance) (232ª21–2).

Although Aristotle continues his argument into *Phys*. 6. 2, where he introduces his principles of relative speed that we discussed in Chapter 1, *Phys*. 6. 2 simply works out what is already implicit at the end of *Phys*. 6. 1. Since the principles of speed to which he appeals entail (as we established in Chapter 1) the continuity of a function from times elapsed to distances traversed for a moving body, it is not surprising that these principles entail the infinite divisibility of spatial magnitude and time. So, as a number of commentators have noted, there is question-begging circularity involved in Aristotle's appeal to his conception of speed in order to prove that spatial magnitude is divisible without limit if and only if temporal extension is. The most charitable view of *Phys*. 6. 1–2 in this regard is that of Fred Miller:

Philosophers typically fall into circularity because they try to prove too much. Aristotle could have argued that given our commonsense beliefs about the faster and the slower, the continuity (or atomicity) of magnitude entails that of motion and time. That is, our prescientific or prephilosophical observations about bodies in motion commit us to the isomorphism thesis. This would be to argue from *ta phainomena*, as Aristotle often does.[2]

In summary, Aristotle's support of what Miller terms the 'isomorphism thesis'—i.e. Aristotle's claim that, as a logical/conceptual matter, either spatial magnitude, time, and locomotion are all constituted of indivisible quanta or none is—does not withstand close scrutiny. Consideration of instances where the isomorphism thesis does *not* obtain seems to be as important as consideration of instances where it does with respect to the later development of various conceptions of quantum-motion. The possibility of jumps or discontinuities of locomotion within the context of a conception of both spatial magnitude and time as infinitely divisible ('dense') and continuous is one violation of the isomorphism thesis which was briefly discussed in Chapter 1. Further discussion of this possibility will occur in a later chapter in connection with the idea of transition over a divisible spatial interval 'at one go' (*athroōs*), a Stoic idea that also reappeared among late Neoplatonists. Of more immediate interest is the conception of locomotion that results from the combination of a conception of time as infinitely divisible and a conception of spatial magnitude as constituted of indivisible

---

[2] 'Aristotle against the Atomists', in *Infinity and Continuity*, ed. Kretzmann, 106.

quanta: the 'cinematographic' model of motion, again to use Miller's terminology.[3]

CINEMATOGRAPHIC MOTION: DIODORUS CRONUS' VIEW?

The cinematographic conception of motion is, as I mentioned in the last section, particularly suited to a decomposition of motion into a series of alternating jumps or instantaneous displacements and pauses or intervals of *stasis*. According to this model of motion, an object occupies a fixed position for some lapse or duration of time; but at the posterior ('future-direction') *limit* of such an interval, it finds itself displaced by a minimal unit of distance in the direction of its motion. The temporal intervals of *stasis* need not be some indivisible quantum (or multiple of quanta) of time, but may be theoretically indivisible without limit.

An important feature of the cinematographic model is that motion cannot be a kinetic process of mov*ing*, which takes time. For, consider a body Ω of minimal length q in transit from one position A to an adjacent position B, both of minimal length q. Also consider any temporal instant t at which Ω is at A and any later time t' at which Ω is at B. Owing to the supposition of indivisible quanta of magnitude, at any time x such that $t < x < t'$, Ω must be either *fully* at A or *fully* at B: it cannot partially occupy either position. Consequently, there must be some t'' such that $t \leqslant t'' \leqslant t'$ with respect to which t'' exactly one of two situations obtains:

(a) for all $x \in [t, t'')$, Ω is at position A at time x and for all $y \in [t'', t']$ Ω is at position B at time y (which means that there is no last instant at which Ω is at A but there is a first instant at which it is at B);[4]

(b) for all $x \in [t, t'']$, Ω is at position A at time x and, for all $y \in (t'', t']$, Ω is at position B at time y (which means that there is a last instant at which Ω is at A but no first instant at which it is at B).

In either case, the transition from A to B is a displacement that is instantaneous, requiring no *lapse* of time whatsoever. And if *all* locomotion,

---

[3] Ibid. 103.

[4] I employ the standard mathematical convention for representing the interval of a continuous magnitude between 2 points (here, the temporal interval between 2 instants, t and t') by enclosing names of the 2 points in brackets. A square bracket indicates that the interval includes that endpoint (is closed at that end); a rounded bracket indicates that the interval does not include that endpoint (is open at that end).

over any multiples of q, is not to be instantaneous, a moving body must pause at at least some positions in the sense of resting or remaining at these positions for some non-null interval of time.

The sense of 'rest' or 'pause' here is a straightforward one: Ω rests (pauses) at a position A for a period i if and only if, for every now or temporal instant t that is a member of i, Ω is at position A at t. Suppose, however, that time (as well as spatial magnitude) is constituted of discrete, successive indivisible quanta; and consider the situation in which Ω is associated with successive spatial positions A, B, C, etc. at successive temporal quanta q, q', q'', etc. It is not now so obvious that we should describe Ω's movement in terms of alternating pauses and jumps or instantaneous transitions. We cannot, it seems, continue to conceive of jumps as instantaneous transitions in the sense of Ω's being in a certain position (e.g. A) for a certain *period* of time (e.g. i) but in a different position (e.g. B) at the *limit* of that time (and then for a successive period, e.g. i'). For if q and q' are truly discrete temporal quanta, there will be no such limit at which they are contiguous. And is it correct to say that Ω *rests* first at A for q, then at B for q', then at C for q'', etc.? According to the account of resting that I just gave, it is only vacuously true that Ω rests at A with respect to q: that is, it is only true that, for every now/temporal instant t that is a *member* of q, Ω is at A at t only because *there are no such t*s that are members of q.

Although our indivisible temporal quanta q have, *ex hypothesi*, dimension and positive measure or size and thus are not dimensionless, punctal nows, we seem to be faced with the same metaphysical options with respect to motion/rest 'at' these quanta as confront us with respect to motion/rest at temporal instants when we are dealing with continuous motion over continuous spatial intervals. We *could* say that Ω rests at a different position at each temporal quantum and jumps to a successive position in the sense, simply, of resting at a successive position at a successive temporal unit (without tying the transition to the inadmissible concept of a limit where one temporal quantum abuts the next).

We *could* follow Aristotle's doctrine concerning motion/rest at punctal temporal instants, maintaining that it is incorrect to speak of either motion or rest with respect to individual temporal quanta. According to this option, in order to speak correctly of motion or rest we must connect it with intervals of time in the sense of stretches constituted of *multiples* ($n > 1$) of temporal quanta. Then, Ω rests at position A for such an interval i just in case it is at the *same* position A at each quantum q contained in i; Ω is moving for such an interval i just in case it is at a *distinct* position at each quantum q contained in i. But, according to this option, the concepts of motion and rest apply *primarily* to temporal intervals i containing more than one temporal quantum q.

This option *could* be supplemented by adoption of the 'quantum-analogue' of the (un-Aristotelian) practice of speaking of motion at a temporal instant: we would then say that Ω is moving at a temporal quantum t just in case t is a member of an interval i with respect to which Ω is 'moving' in the primary sense. (A problem with this option is created by the fact that the account that I just gave of moving/resting with respect to an interval permits a quantum t to be the common *terminus* of intervals i and i' with respect to which Ω is, respectively, moving and resting—or vice versa. So a problem arises here that is entirely analogous to that pertaining to the status—with respect to motion/rest—of a temporal instant that is the common limit of contiguous stretches of motion and rest under the assumption of a continuous structure of time.)

In *Phys*. 6. 10 Aristotle considers the possibility of a sort of discontinuous motion which depends on time's being constituted of nows:

Motion of [what is partless] would only be possible thus: if a stretch of time were constituted out of nows. For then it would always at every now have moved and have changed so that it never would be moving but always would have moved. But that this is impossible was demonstrated before. For neither is a time constituted out of nows nor a line out of points nor a motion out of jumps [*kinēmatōn*].   (240ᵇ31–241ᵃ4)

Several scholars have made the plausible suggestion that the slight concession that Aristotle appears to make with respect to quantum-motion in this passage is fully and self-consciously utilized by the Epicureans. We shall return to this issue in the next section. For the moment, however, it is important to try to ascertain the nature of the concession that Aristotle seems to be making.

Although I do not think that it is by any means obvious what Aristotle is conceding, the most plausible hypothesis seems to me that he is making the following point. Suppose that a temporal interval (during which, we are supposing, a partless body traverses indivisible quanta of length) is constituted of nows. Whether we think of these nows as being punctal (having no dimension and no magnitude) or as indivisible temporal quanta (having dimension and minimal, positive magnitude) is not important; what is important for Aristotle's argument is simply the fact that they are ordered successively (*epheksēs*). At each of these discretely ordered temporal units, the moving body can be said to *have moved*, i.e. to have shifted its position (by an indivisible quantum q of magnitude). So the motion of the body would be constituted of these *kinēmata*, jumps or shifts. None the less, Aristotle says, this model allows us to say at any time only that the body *has moved*, never that it *is moving*. So where is the 'concession'?

Perhaps a clue that may help answer this question is found in the fact that earlier in this chapter (as well as in Aristotle's other account of the dissolution of motion into *kinēmata*, *Phys*. 6. 1, which we discussed in the last section) the notion of pauses or *periods* of rest figures largely. I suggested that in *Phys*. 6. 1, Aristotle derives his apparent absurdity not merely from the fact that motion with respect to intervals of length constituted of indivisible quanta would involve *kinēmata*, in the sense of instantaneous displacements of the moving body, but from the fact that the temporal interval i of supposed motion can be partitioned in such a way that *all* sub-intervals of i in that partition are intervals of rest of the moving body. Consequently, I suggest that the slight concession that Aristotle is making is the following. If time were constituted out of successively ordered indivisible units or nows, and if the moving body were located at a successive position at each successive temporal unit, an interval of motion of the body would be constituted of *nothing but kinēmata*: there would be no period of rest within this supposed interval of motion because the body is not located at any given position at more that one successive temporal unit or now.

Any concession in this passage is slight, because Aristotle proceeds to claim that even this dissolution of *kinēsis* into *kinēmata* has earlier been shown to be impossible. According to this account of Aristotle's concession, however, the reference to previous argumentation is not intended by him—or, at least, *should* not be intended by him—to be a specific reference to his earlier discussion in *Phys*. 6. 1 of the dissolution of motion into jumps. For the absurdity to which Aristotle argues in *Phys*. 6. 1 is not due to the *kinēmata per se* but to the fact that, when *kinēmata* are placed in continuous, infinitely divisible time, they must be separated by periods (i.e. divisible temporal intervals) of rest; consequently, a supposed interval of motion can be partitioned in such a way that all its sub-intervals are intervals of rest. Therefore, I suspect that the earlier demonstration to which Aristotle alludes is (as he himself implies at 241ᵃ2-6) his earlier argumentation that what is continuous (spatial magnitude, time, or *kinēsis*) cannot be constituted out of successively ordered indivisible minima. Of course, the very question at issue is whether spatial magnitude, time, and motion *are* continuous or not. And, irrespective of what Aristotle may believe, he is not in a position to produce an apodictic argument for his contention that they are. The best that he can do is to rely on *endoxa*, 'commonly held beliefs' and (as I have argued) on the assumptions of the best developed (geometrical) science of his day in order to support this contention.

We now return, at last, to Diodorus Cronus. It seems clear that he developed a theory of quantum-motion. The question is whether this theory was a cinematographic theory of quantum-motion. There can be little doubt, I think, either (*a*) that Diodorus, in explicit opposition to Aristotle, decomposed *kinēseis* into *kinēmata* or (*b*) that he connected this doctrine with his doctrine of minimal and partless quanta of spatial magnitude.⁵ At *M* 1. 311, Sextus Empiricus attributes a spatial version of Zeno of Elea's arrow paradox to Diodorus: 'that which is moving is moving either in the place at which it is or in the place in which it is not. But neither the first nor the second [alternative obtains]. Therefore, it is not the case that anything is moving.' At *M* 10. 85-6 Sextus explicitly connects Diodorus' version of the arrow with his doctrine of successively ordered indivisible quanta of magnitude:

Another weighty reminder of the non-existence of motion is provided by Diodorus Cronus, through which he shows that although nothing is moving [*kineitai*], it none the less has moved [*kekinētai*]. That it is not moving is a consequence of his hypothesis of indivisibles. For it behoves an indivisible body to be contained in an indivisible place and, on account of this, it is not moving in it [sc. the place where it is]. (For it fills it up; but it is necessary that a moving thing have a larger place [in which to move].) Nor is it moving in the place where it is not; for it is not yet in that place, so as to move in it. But, according to reason, it has moved. For what was formerly observed to be in this place is now observed to be in another place.

⁵ For the doctrine of 'minimal and partless bodies' (*elachista kai amerē sōmata*), see Sextus Empiricus, *M* 9. 363. For Diodorus as the originator of the 'minimal and partless' terminology, see Dionysius of Alexandria *apud* Eusebius, *Preparatio evangelica* 14. 23. 4 (= K. Döring, *Die Megariker: Kommentierte Sammlung der Testimonien*, Studien zur antiken Philosophie, 2 (Amsterdam, 1972), Fr. 116).

The connection between this spatial version of the arrow and Diodorus' doctrine of indivisible quanta of spatial magnitude is, as it happens, elucidated by Sextus himself:

Consequently, when Diodorus says, 'If something is moving, it is moving either in the place where it is or in the place where it is not', he says something fallacious and contrary to the conception of motion, inasmuch as that which is moving does not move either in the place where it is or in the place where it is not, but through both places: from the one and to the other. (*M* 10. 94)

I have argued elsewhere that this is precisely the sort of response that a proponent of *continuous* motion (such as Aristotle) ought to make to Diodorus' spatial version of the arrow paradox. Since there are an infinite number of possible stopping-positions strictly between the actual *terminus a quo* and actual *terminus ad quem* of a continuously moving body, and since, as Aristotle sees in *Phys.* 8, the body can be at such a position only at a temporal instant and not for any period of time, Aristotle's doctrine that a body neither rests nor moves at a temporal instant commits him to the proposition that the body *neither* moves nor rests at any of these positions—places where it (instantaneously) is, strictly between its actual *terminus a quo* and its actual *terminus ad quem*.[6]

When Sextus returns to this criticism of the spatial arrow at *M* 10. 105, he characterizes it in terms of the idea that 'that which is moving [has] two places, both that out of which it is moving and that into which it is going [*meterchetai*]'. What Sextus seems to have in mind is two (actual or possible) *loci* of a body, an arbitrary one *A* and one *B* that is exactly contiguous to the first in the direction of the body's motion. What the proponent of continuous motion says, then, is that when we say that the body *is moving* out of *A* and *is moving* into *B*, it 'has two places' in the sense that it is partly in *A* and partly in *B*, occupying increasingly more of *B* and less of *A* in the process of *moving* [*kineisthai*] from one place to the other. Of course, even if *A* and *B* are not contiguous but partially overlap, a similar account can be given.

To Sextus' (or Diodorus') question, 'when is that which is moving in the process of passing over out of the place in which it is and into the other place?' (*M* 10. 106), the advocate of continuous locomotion can reply, 'during the interval of time when it is partially (but not

    [6] M. J. White, 'The Spatial Arrow Paradox', *Pacific Philosophical Quarterly*, 68:1 (1987), 71–7.

completely) in "the other place"'. However, with a doctrine of indivisible spatial quanta, this answer does not work. If position A succeeds position B by a minimal quantum of magnitude, then we are faced with exactly the situation that Sextus proceeds to describe:

Then [is the moving body passing over out of A and into B] when it is in the first place, or when it is in the second? But when it is in the first place it is not *going into* the other place because it is still in the first place. But when it is not in that but in the second place, again it is not *going into* [the second place] but, rather, has already *gone into* it.

Although Sextus does not explicitly refer to Diodorus' doctrine of indivisible quanta of spatial magnitude in this passage (M 10. 105-7), it is here, I believe, that we can detect the substance of his earlier claim (M 10. 85-6) that Diodorus' doctrine that nothing is moving is a 'consequence of his hypothesis of indivisibles'.

Thus far, I have made no mention of *time* atoms, indivisible quanta of temporal extension, in connection with Diodorus. Whether Diodorus did think of time in terms of such a discrete structure is far from certain, although several recent commentators, notably Nicholas Denyer and Richard Sorabji, have argued for such an interpretation and I myself have accepted this view.[7] I think that it is fair to say that the basis of the interpretation of both Sorabji and Denyer rests upon a passage in which Sextus himself is recapitulating arguments (largely Diodorean) against motion:

Hence one ought to deprecate attacks of this sort [i.e. attacks on the possibility of motion which attacks Sextus takes to be fallacious]; instead one ought especially to use arguments such as these: If something is moving, it is moving now; if it is moving now, it is moving in the present time. If it is moving in the present time, it therefore is moving in an indivisible time. For if the present time is divided, it will certainly be divided into the past and the present, and thus will no longer be *present* time. If something is moving in an indivisible time, it is traversing indivisible places. If it is traversing indivisible places, it is not moving. . .   (M 10. 118-20)

---

[7] N. Denyer, 'The Atomism of Diodorus Cronus', *Prudentia*, 13 (1981), 33–45; R. Sorabji, 'Atoms and Time Atoms', in Kretzmann (ed.), *Infinity and Continuity*, 59–65; Sorabji, *Time, Creation and the Continuum*, 17–21, 369–71. Denyer and Sorabji both argue for Diodorus' acceptance of time atoms. Both in 'The Spatial Arrow Paradox' and in 'What Worried the Crows', I attributed such a view to Diodorus without much argument and in what I now regard as a much too casual way. The considerations that I adduced in the former article (76, n. 6) now seem to me very weak.

What follows is a repetition of the *spatial* version that Sextus has already (in several places) explicitly attributed to Diodorus. As Denyer notes,[8] Döring does not include this passage in his collection of fragments of 'Megarian' philosophers, apparently because of the lack of an explicit attribution of this version of the argument by Sextus to Diodorus. Of course the last part of the passage (which I have not quoted) *is* attributed by Sextus to him at other places; so it is only the passage I have quoted, the 'temporal prelude', that is in question. Sextus may here be giving a fuller version of the argument developed by Diodorus himself. But he also may be 'helping' Diodorus with his advice and, in effect, combining a spatial version of the arrow, due to Diodorus, with the well known temporal version of the arrow going back to Zeno of Elea: the supposedly moving arrow cannot be said to move at any now (temporal instant) falling in the period of time when it is supposedly moving; hence it cannot be said to move at all with respect to the period constituted of these nows.

I doubt whether it is possible to decide between these two possibilities with any degree of certainty. Denyer hypothesizes that Diodorus uses the time atomism (doctrine of indivisible quanta of time) of the 'temporal prelude' of this passage to establish the space atomism (doctrine of indivisible quanta of magnitude) that is essential to his spatial version of the arrow paradox.[9] This seems to me to be a possibility. But two relevant considerations are the following: (i) the argument for the indivisibility of the present is (as Denyer is fully aware) the same as that used by Aristotle in *Phys.* 6. 3 to argue that the present is an indivisible punctal *instant* or limit, and *that* sense of indivisibility of the present is (as Denyer also recognizes) of absolutely no help in establishing the existence of indivisible quanta of spatial magnitude; (ii) a discrete, quantum structure of spatial magnitude does not follow from a discrete, quantum structure of time, and there is, in fact, no hint of an *argument* for this entailment in the passage from Sextus, *M* 10. 118–20 quoted above.[10] In rebuttal to (ii), it might be

---

[8] 'The Atomism of Diodorus Cronus', 34.

[9] Ibid. 35.

[10] Denyer is aware of the fact that a discrete (or, in his terms, 'granular') structure of time does not, in itself, imply a discrete structure of spatial magnitude. He suggests that the granularity of spatial extension could be obtained, however, if one were to make the 'assumption that the thing in its journey from the one place to the other has passed through every intervening place. Of course, you may avoid Diodorus' spatial atomism by denying that assumption. But if you choose to maintain in this way that space is continuous you will still be giving a Diodoran account of what the thing's journey consisted

maintained that Diodorus was simply relying on the (fallacious) Aristotelian arguments for the isomorphism thesis to derive spatial quanta from temporal ones. Thus the historical situation stands.

I suggest, however, that as a *conceptual* matter Diodorus has some reason to eschew temporal atomism, adopting the cinematographic model of motion. This suggestion depends upon a certain view of Diodorus' motivation, which I have previously argued for, and which seems to be essentially accepted by Denyer. Diodorus is referred to as a 'Dialectician' (*Dialektikos*) in the ancient sources; and, traditionally, the *Dialektikoi* have been associated with the *Megarikoi* and *Eristikoi*. It had long been assumed that this 'triple succession' (*diadochē*) was characterized by a strongly dialectical or logical (even 'logic-chopping', in the case of the *Eristikoi*) methodology brought to the defence of an Eleatic metaphysics and (at least in some instances) of moral concerns deriving from the influence of Socrates. But in an influential paper David Sedley has argued that the notion of a unified Megarian (or Megarian-Eristical-Dialectical) school (*hairesis*) is mistaken and that the collection of the three groups into a 'succession' was the fabrication of Hellenistic doxographers committed to finding 'unifying threads' even where there was no historical basis for doing so.[11]

Although I have elsewhere expressed some reservations about the import of Sedley's conclusions,[12] the historical issues remain murky. What I still believe to be very likely, however, is the Eleatic motivation of Diodorus' denial of the process of locomotion: that he 'desired (*a*) to defend the denial of the reality of time and motion by his Eleatic "philosophical forefathers" against an ontological view according to which *processes* (*kinēseis*) are fundamental and (*b*) to reconcile what he would have considered to be the Eleatic metaphysical view with the view of common sense: things are different at different times'.[13] Denyer expresses what I take to be a similar view:

His argument against destruction and his argument against motion itself both have an Eleatic ring to their conclusions . . . furthermore, as we shall see, his denial of motion was not meant to be inconsistent with the thought that things

in: a discrete succession of places at which the thing paused *en route*, disappearing from one and reappearing at the next without ever passing through any places that intervened' (ibid. 39–40).

[11] 'Diodorus Cronus and Hellenistic Philosophy', *Proceedings of the Cambridge Philological Society*, 207 (1977), 74–120.

[12] *Agency and Integrality*, ch. 3, 'Diodorean Fatalism'.

[13] Ibid. 90.

are in different places at different times, as indeed his denial of destruction was meant to be consistent with the thought that a thing may exist at one time without existing at later ones.[14]

If the motivation lying behind Diodorus' paradox-mongering is Eleatic, there is a relatively straightforward rationale for his adoption of a quantum conception of spatial magnitude. By the time of Diodorus, there was a powerful response to Zeno's arrow paradox: that of Aristotle, according to whom the moving arrow neither is moving nor is at rest with respect to each now/temporal instant of the period during which it moves. Consequently, the arrow is neither moving nor at rest with respect to any of the possible (instantaneous) but not actual stopping-positions it traverses during its motion.

The passages from Sextus' *Adversus mathematicos* 10 discussed above suggest that this sort of response to the spatial version of the arrow may have been elaborated as follows. When we are dealing with contiguous places A and B, the *process* of moving *out of A into B*, connoted by the present-imperfective *to kineisthai*, is associated with the period of time in which the moving object is in *both* positions—i.e. the temporal interval in which it is occupying less and less of A and more and more of B. Diodorus is shrewd enough to see that the substitution of indivisible quanta of spatial magnitude for infinitely divisible spatial intervals vitiates this sort of rebuttal of the spatial version of the arrow. So his revitalization of the arrow paradox as an argument against the possibility of anything's being in the *process* of moving depends quite directly, as Sextus reports, on Diodorus' 'hypothesis of indivisibles' (*M* 10. 85–6). It is plausible that his Eleatic motivation thus sufficiently explains Diodorus' acceptance of a quantum conception of spatial magnitude. Whether he additionally appealed to an *argument* in support of this 'hypothesis' is quite uncertain; but if he did, it is unlikely that it was a valid argument.

If Diodorus saw himself in the tradition of Parmenides and Zeno, it is unlikely that he would have felt any impulse to undertake the project of 'solving the paradoxes of time', to use Sorabji's phrase[15]—or, indeed, any impulse to mitigate the paradoxicality of his own spatial version of the arrow paradox. For someone revelling in—rather than attempting to defuse—the paradoxicality of a view such as that

[14] 'The Atomism of Diodorus Cronus', 40.
[15] *Time, Creation and the Continuum*, 17. It must be noted, however, that Sorabji here makes only the weaker and very plausible claim that Diodorus' atomism 'gave him the *materials* for solving the paradoxes of time'.

developed by Aristotle in *Phys*. 6. 1, in which motion is resolved into *kinēmata* interlarded with pauses, the cinematographic model of motion would be quite attractive. A temporal stretch of supposed motion is partitioned into temporal sub-intervals *all* of which are intervals of rest of the supposedly moving body: *kinēsis* in the imperfective, processual sense of mov*ing* (*to kineisthai*) has been eliminated in favour of a series of successive states. These temporal intervals are clearly states of *rest* because of their divisibility: the body rests in a position for a certain *interval* or duration of time, for it is in the same position for every sub-interval of that interval.

If, however, one desires to minimize the paradoxicality of a conception of quantum-motion, the substitution of indivisible quanta of time for these temporal intervals of rest might appear attractive. If a moving body is at successive spatial positions associated with successive temporal quanta, it is not any more obvious that we should say that the moving body is at rest during, at, or with respect to such an indivisible quantum than it is that we should say that a moving body is at rest during, at, or with respect to a temporal instant when we assume a continuous, infinitely divisible structure of time. In the following section I shall consider the hypothesis that the Epicurean tradition used a doctrine of indivisible temporal quanta in this way—i.e. in order to develop a more respectable conception of quantum motion.

EPICUREAN QUANTUM-MOTION: THE MICRO-LEVEL

From Epicurus' own *Letter to Herodotus* two fundamental Epicurean doctrines pertaining to atomic motion are clear: (*a*) 'the atoms move continuously and eternally' (D.L. 10. 43); (*b*) 'furthermore, it is necessary that the atoms have an equal speed, when they are borne through the void and nothing strikes them' (D.L. 10. 61). According to the most common interpretation, which was adopted in the preceding chapter, the conception of indivisible quanta of spatial magnitude is also a fundamental Epicurean physical doctrine. So it follows that Epicureanism is committed to *some* conception of quantum-motion. There is more evidence than in the case of Diodorus Cronus that Epicurus (or later Epicureans) also developed a conception of temporal extension as constituted of successive, indivisible quanta. In his commentary on Aristotle's *Physics*, Simplicius characterizes the Epicureans as 'saying that magnitude, motion, and time are constituted out of what is partless'.[16] Similarly, Sextus describes the Epicureans as 'having assumed that all things [the context makes clear that by 'all things' he means 'bodies, places, and times'] leave off at what is partless'.[17] There is also a reference to the doctrine in one of the Epicurean papyri from Herculaneum.[18]

But what is the import of indivisible *temporal* quanta for the Epicurean conception of quantum-motion? It is possible, of course, that Epicurus and/or other Epicureans are simply (and uncritically) accepting Aristotle's fallacious arguments in *Phys.* 6. 1–2 for the iso-morphism thesis and concluding that, since they are committed to quanta of spatial extension, they are also committed to quanta of temporal extension. But, more significantly, it may also be the case that they are taking advantage of what I earlier called the 'slight concession' made by Aristotle at *Phys.* 6. 10. 240^{b}31–241^{a}1 with respect to quantum-motion in the context of a successive ordering of discrete nows or temporal units. At least one other recent com-mentator has seen the introduction of temporal quanta as a way to minimize the paradoxicality of the idea of quantum-motion, at least to the extent of satisfying Aristotle's characterization: 'just as motion is always other and other (*aiei allē kain allē*), so also is time' (*Phys.* 4. 11. 219^{b}9–10. Fred Miller comments,

The pure theory of atomism [i.e. a theory that postulates indivisible quanta of time as well as of spatial magnitude] can accommodate Aristotle's criterion of movement: the atomic body occupies a different atomic place at each atomic time. But the mixed theory with its 'cinematographic motion' does not satisfy this criterion of motion at all. Like modern cinematography, it substitutes an illusion for the real thing.[19]

Of course, I argued in Part I that 'occupying a different place at each time' is not regarded by Aristotle as an *analysans* of 'moving' (or of motion's being 'other and other'): Aristotle does not regard either the spatial trajectory of a continuously moving body or the temporal interval during which it moves as a dense and Dedekind-continuous *series* or linearly ordered set (of positions and instants, respectively).

---

[16] Simplicius, *In phys.*, CAG 10, 934. 25–6.

[17] Sextus, *M* 10. 143.

[18] P. Herc. 698, fr. 23 *N*. See W. Scott, *Fragmenta Herculanensia* (Oxford, 1885), 290. According to Long and Sedley, this and the passages from Simplicius and Sextus just cited are the only extant ancient references to an Epicurean doctrine of indivisible quanta of time (*The Hellenistic Philosophers*, ii. 46).

[19] 'Aristotle against the Atomists', 109.

But satisfaction of the different-place-at-different-time (hereafter DP/ DT) condition in the pure theory at least removes the temptation to think of the moving body as resting at successive spatial *loci*. This temptation, as we saw, is a very compelling one in the case of cinematographic conception of motion, and is perhaps the principal source of the paradoxicality of that conception. It is the feature that may lead us, in Miller's words, to regard the cinematographic conception as 'substitut[ing] an illusion for the real thing'.

While Diodorus may have been quite happy, according to the interpretation I have advanced, to substitute an illusion for the real thing, it seems unlikely that the Epicureans would have shared such a contentment with paradox. There is no apparent attempt on the part of Epicurus or other Epicureans to dismiss, in descriptions of atomic motion, present-imperfective verbal forms such as *kineisthai* (which connote the *process* of mov*ing*, according to both Aristotle and Diodorus) in the way that Diodorus does. Simplicius claims that

> they [the Epicureans] say that that which moves is moving [*kineisthai*] over the whole magnitude constituted out of partless units, but with respect to each of the partless units in it it is not moving, but has moved [*kekinēsthai*]. Because if one were to postulate that that which moves over the whole is moving over these [indivisibles], they would be divisible.[20]

This passage perhaps suggests that satisfaction of the DP/DT condition by a pure atomism that postulates temporal as well as spatial quanta, successively ordered, may have been regarded by Epicureans as sufficient to allow them to describe something (e.g. an atom) as mov*ing*, i.e. in the process of *kinēsis*, with respect to *intervals* of magnitude and of time, which will both be multiples of indivisible quanta. The passage may also suggest that the Epicureans were sufficiently intimidated by Aristotelian arguments (which assume the continuity of motion) to refuse to say that a body is moving with respect to an indivisible quantum of magnitude (and indivisible quantum of time): one can only say (at any *successive* temporal quantum?) that the body *has moved* over a quantum of spatial extension.

The reason that Simplicius gives for withholding the present-imperfective '*kineisthai*' from motion with respect to minima of magnitude (i.e. that talk of 'moving' with respect to such minima would, absurdly, imply their divisibility) implicitly appeals to an Aristotelian principle applying to what I earlier termed 'kinetic segments' or

[20] *In phys.*, CAG 10, 934. 26–30.

'stretches' of *continuous* motion. A moving body can be said to be moving with respect to a spatial interval ϵ only if both (i) the body moves over each proper sub-distance of ϵ (in less time than that in which the body moves over the whole of ϵ) and (ii) ϵ is divisible into proper sub-distances.

It is worth noting that, from a (contemporary) logical perspective, condition (ii) is not superfluous. Without it, it would be trivially true that a body moves over a spatial minimum: since there are no proper sub-distances of such a minimum, it is trivially true that a moving body moves over all of them. Whether the Epicureans whom Simplicius is castigating denied the possibility of saying that an atom is mov*ing* with respect to a quantum of magnitude or time is uncertain. They may have. But it is also possible that Simplicius (who is in the midst of explicating Aristotle's argument from *Phys*. 6. 1 pertaining to the absurdity of the decomposition of *kinēseis* into *kinēmata*) is simply giving an Aristotelian response to a later, un-Aristotelian theory, a theory which he regards as an impertinence in view of the passage he is discussing.

Need the Epicureans have denied that atoms are moving with respect to indivisible quanta of spatial magnitude or of time? I do not think so. As I suggested in the preceding section, the same variety of *metaphysical* options concerning motion/rest at an indivisible time seem to be available in the case of indivisible times that are quanta (i.e. have positive dimension and measure) as are available in the case of indivisible times that are punctal (i.e. lack positive dimension and measure). It is possible, by adopting the correct set of principles, consistently to sustain any one of the following claims. (*a*) The moving body is moving at a temporal quantum contained in an interval (multiple of quanta) during which it is held to move. (*b*) The moving body is at rest at any such temporal quantum. (*c*) The moving body is neither moving nor at rest at such a temporal quantum.

We have here analogues of three metaphysical views pertaining to motion at an instant, within the context of continuous motion, views that were discussed in the second section of Chapter 4: (*a*) is the 'quantized-time' version of the view advocated by G. E. L. Owen, (*b*) corresponds to a view offered (although perhaps not wholly seriously) by Russell, and (*c*) corresponds to the doctrine of Aristotle. Of course, an advocate of option (*a*) must not speak of motion *during* a temporal quantum if such a locution is understood as implying that a continuous stretch of motion or kinetic segment is being paired with that quantum: that a certain distance traversed by the moving body is to be paired with the temporal quantum in such a way that there are decreasing sub-distances of that distance which are paired with decreasing sub-intervals of the temporal quantum. It will be remembered that Aristotle uses an appeal to the concept of moving in the sense of effecting the continuous traversal of a positive distance to argue against the claim that a moving body is moving with respect to (during) a temporal instant. Just as it is incumbent upon the advocate of motion at a temporal instant to distinguish the sense of 'motion' figuring in the metaphysical concept of motion at an instant from the notion of a kinetic segment, it is incumbent upon the advocate of motion at an indivisible temporal quantum to make an analogous distinction.

In the task of fleshing out such a distinction, however, the advocate of motion at an instant has an advantage in the form of aid from classical mathematics. That is, since the range of the measure functions assigning values to interval of time and spatial magnitude are real numbers (and hence characterized by density and continuity), and since the values assigned to velocities are vectors in the real plane (and, hence, characterized by properties analogous to the density and continuity of the reals), there is the limit notion of instantaneous velocity which may (but, as I have previously maintained, *need* not) be used to lend kinematic substance to the metaphysical notion of motion at an instant. The mathematics used to define such a notion is that of continuous structures, not discrete ones. And, even though the proponent of quantum-motion has a *metaphysical* option analogous to that of motion at an instant, the existence of this option does not mean that quantum-motion so conceived can be thought of as continuous in the mathematical sense. The *kinematic* analysis of such quantum-motion would necessarily look quite different from the Aristotelian kinematic analysis of continuous motion and its modern mathematical counterpart.

THE EPICUREAN CONCEPTION OF SPEED: MICRO-LEVEL AND MACRO-LEVEL

I have thus far not said much about the second fundamental Epicurean doctrine concerning atomic motion, which I stated at the beginning of the last section: (*b*) 'furthermore, it is necessary that the atoms have an equal speed, when they are borne through the void and nothing strikes them' (D.L. 10. 61). Within the context of a pure atomic theory, i.e. a theory that postulates indivisible quanta of time as well as of motion, the doctrine of *isotacheia*, or equality of speed of all atoms, appears to follow from the other fundamental doctrine (*a*) of the continuous[21] and eternal motion of all atoms. For no atom can take any time less than one indivisible time quantum to be shifted one indivisible quantum of distance. Suppose, on the other hand, that it takes some temporal interval *i*, which is a multiple of time quanta, to be shifted one quantum of distance. Two possibilities then present themselves. (i) The atom is *not* shifted in position for some (all but one) of the quanta contained in the interval *i*. But then the DP/DT condition is violated, and the atom does not seem to be continuously and eternally moving. (ii) The atom traverses a quantum of distance in the temporal interval *i* in such a way that the DP/DT condition is satisfied. The only way that I can see in which such a situation could be interpreted involves the postulation of distinct positions *within* the minimal distance of magnitude, which, of course, is not possible.

A problem with this analysis is that it seems to imply *unqualified* atomic *isotacheia*. But (*b*) may be read as implying a qualified *isotacheia*: atoms move at the same speed only if they are not slowed down by collisions with other atoms. According to one fairly common tradition of interpretation (represented, for example, by Bailey[22]), Epicurus has phrased (*b*) in a rather misleading fashion: all he means is that an atom in moving from position *A* to position *B* will arrive there faster if it proceeds (more or less) directly than if it is deflected by collisions and, hence, takes a more circuitous and longer path from *A* to *B*. Another interpretation (represented by Bignone[23]) represents an atom as 'missing a beat'—i.e. remaining in the same position—at the time (temporal quantum) of collision with another atom. But this view obviously violates the DP/DT condition and, hence, the continuity of atomic motion (according to the most plausible view of what continuity of motion amounts to within the context of a theory of quantized spatial magnitude and time).

Drabkin argues for 'a change from maximum velocity to a lower (but

---

[21] Of course, the sense of 'continuous' here is neither the Aristotelian nor any contemporary technical sense. The term must simply connote motion that is 'unceasing' in the sense of motion that satisfies the DP/DT condition discussed in the last section.

[22] *Epicurus*, 219.

[23] E. Bignone, *Epicuro* (Bari, 1920), 229–31.

not zero) velocity during the finite moment of impact, followed, as before, by maximum atomic velocity as the new trajectory begins'.[24] He adds that the 'measure of velocity in these cases would be, as before, the distance between the position of the atom at successive units of time'.[25] In view of the argument of the preceding paragraphs, however, I am afraid that I cannot see how any atom could be displaced by anything other than one quantum of distance relative to one quantum of time (when it is assumed, of course, that both time and spatial magnitude are discretely constituted). For if an atom is displaced by more than one quantum, it will have been displaced by a (finitely) *divisible* interval of distance—of, say, nq, where $n > 1$ and q is the minimum magnitude of distance or spatial extension. Since the interval of displacement nq *has* subdivisions, it surely makes sense to inquire into the manner of its displacement by a subdivision of the interval, say, the *first* distance of one quantum away from its original position. It cannot have been displaced by this distance in anything less than or more than one quantum of time. The apparently paradoxical consequence is that the atom will at the same time (relative to a given temporal quantum) be moving at 'unit speed' c (one q per temporal quantum) and at nc.[26]

If this argument has force, there does not seem to be an obvious way of avoiding an unqualified *isotacheia*—a universal, constant 'unit speed' c for all atoms at all times—if a doctrine of indivisible temporal quanta is combined with that of indivisible quanta of spatial magnitude and if 'continuous' atomic motion is interpreted in terms of satisfaction of the DP/DT condition. In fact, Simplicius notes in passing that the Epicureans maintain that 'everything is moving at the same speed through partless [intervals of distance]'[27] in order to avoid paradoxes (e.g. proper parts of what is assumed to be indivisible) resulting from

[24] E. Drabkin, 'Notes on Epicurean Kinetics', *Transactions and Proceedings of the American Philological Association*, 69 (1938), 367.

[25] Ibid. 369.

[26] It might be thought that an analogue of this argument is applicable to supposed spatial discontinuities of motion within the context of a theory of both time and space as infinitely divisible and continuous. But such a discontinuity must be an *instantaneous* displacement over a finite and divisible spatial interval. It is true enough that the body would traverse all proper sub-intervals of this interval in the 'same time' (i.e. instantaneously). But since the 'time taken to effect the displacement' is no time at all, the body really is travelling at no speed (i.e. there is no ratio of distance traversed to the time taken to traverse it). Consequently, it is not possible to derive the (apparent) absurdity that the body is, at the same time, moving at different speeds.

[27] *In phys.* CAG, 10, 938. 21–2.

the assumption of different speeds. In making this remark, the commentator doubtless is assuming a concept of continuously varying degrees of speed: he is discussing *Phys*. 6. 2, which contains Aristotle's principles of relative speed from which we derived, in Chapter 1, the mathematical continuity of motion. But, as we have just seen, such a strong assumption is not needed in order to derive paradox from a supposition of differences in atomic speed.

The claim that *panta* (everything) is moving at the same speed certainly would not be understood by Epicurus as applying to things (complexes of atoms) at the macro-level of which we have sense experience. Although the Epicurean account of the relation between the invisible micro-level of atoms and their insensible motion and the visible macro-level of compounds (*sungkriseis*) and their sensible motion is not (in extant material) as clearly delineated as the contemporary philosopher would like, it seems fairly certain that the Epicurean tradition did not want to dismiss the macro-level as illusory, denying it *any* positive ontological status. As we saw in the last chapter, Epicurean epistemology makes essential use of analogical argument beginning from sense experience in the development of fundamental metaphysical doctrines. So it clearly is to the advantage of Epicureans to save, in some fashion, the phenomena of sensation.

In the particular case of locomotion, the problem of saving the phenomenon of variable (and apparently continuous) motion at the macro-level is particularly pointed in view of the existence of a constant speed for all atoms. Epicurus, in the *Letter to Herodotus*, indicates that he is at least aware of the problem:

Collision and lack of collision take on the appearance of slowness and quickness.| Furthermore, it will be said that with respect to compounds one [atom][28]

---

[28] The syntax of the beginning of this passage is ambiguous: the *hetera*—i.e. the one thing that will be said to be faster than another—can be understood as referring either to a *sungkrisis* (compound of atoms), as in Hicks's Loeb translation of Diogenes Laertius, or to an *atomon* (*within* such a compound), as in the translation of Bailey (*Epicurus*, 37) and that of Long and Sedley (*The Hellenistic Philosophers*, i. 48). Helpful discussion of this passage with Paul Vander Waerdt and David O'Conner have convinced me that the most plausible account of the argument of the passage (to be discussed below) requires the translation of Bailey and of Long and Sedley. I was originally bothered by a concern that has also been expressed by Mau: 'Der konzessive gen. abs. *tōn atomōn isotachōn ousōn* fordert ein anderes Satz-Subjekt als "Atome" ' (Mau, *Zum Problem des Infinitesimalen*, 41). But (*a*) Epicurus' Greek sometimes departs from textbook paradigms and (*b*) the rule *is* sometimes intentionally violated when the genitive absolute clause is being emphasized. The force of the genitive absolute must, it seems, be 'contrastive', expressing what *in fact* is the case in contrast to what some critics will *say* is the case, if the interpretation of

is faster than another, whereas [in fact] atoms are possessed of equal speed. [This will be said] because of the fact that atoms in agglomerations are borne to one place even in the least continuous time[29], although in times comprehensible [only] by reason[30], they are not borne to one place but, rather, constantly collide up to the point where the continuity of their motion should come within the purview of sensation. The *further* supposition concerning what is unseen, i.e. that, therefore, those times comprehensible through reason also possess continuity of motion, is not true with respect to the present issue, since it is everything that is observed by direct perception or that is grasped by the understanding that is true.   (D.L. 10. 46b|10. 62).

The sense of this passage can best be construed, I think, essentially along the lines set forth by Bailey in his commentary. Some might think that, since one sensible object (compound of atoms) moves twice as fast as another, the atoms in that compound are moving twice as fast (and in the same direction as the compound itself) as the atoms in the other compound. But this is not so: atoms, even atoms in compounds, all move at the same speed, but in compounds they 'vibrate', moving in short, rectilinear trajectories and in all directions owing to their 'constantly jostling one against another', to use Bailey's translation. We are then cautioned against inferring by an *uncritical* analogy from a truth apparent to the senses (that compounds move, in an apparently continuous fashion, at varying speeds) to the (false) conclusion that atoms move, individually, in the same manner.

What, of course, is left rather vague is the relation between the discontinuous *isotacheia* of individual atoms (even those in compounds) and the apparently continuous motion, at different speeds, of the compounds constituted from those atoms. The gap

Bailey et al. is adopted. Bailey (*Epicurus*, 220– 2) has extensive and, in my view, basically right-headed notes on this paragraph.

[29] For a general discussion of the 2 kinds of time see Mau, *Zum Problem des Infinitesimalen*, 41–5. I agree with Long and Sedley (*The Hellenistic Philosophers*, ii. 45–6) *contra* Mau that the phrase 'least continuous time' connotes a *perceptible* time: viz. one in which motion *looks* continuous. Long and Sedley make the plausible claim that such a time 'is, presumably, not the shortest perceptible time ... [because] The shortest perceptible time would be seen as partless, so that no change could be discerned during it' (ibid.). Implicit support for this last claim comes from the discussion of perceptible minima in the *Ep. Hdt.* (D.L. 10. 58).

[30] Long and Sedley agree that the times 'apprehended by reason' 'are periods of time too short to be detected by the senses' (*The Hellenistic Philosophers*, ii. 45); but they conjecture that, since there is no compelling evidence for the doctrine of indivisible temporal quanta in the *Letter to Herodotus*, 'a comparatively early work written around the time of [Epicurus'] arrival in Athens', an Epicurean doctrine of temporal minima, successively ordered, post-dates the *Ep. Hdt.* (ibid. and *The Hellenistic Philosophers*, i. 51).

between *apparent* continuity and micro-level discontinuity of motion is not difficult to bridge if the indivisible quanta of spatial magnitude (and, perhaps, of time) are small enough. In fact, we in the age of cinematography are in a better position than ancient Epicureans to appreciate that what looks to be continuous may not, when subjected to fine-grain analysis, be so. The issue of different speeds of compounds of atoms which are individually all moving at the same speed raises more problems, however. It seems highly probably that Epicurus regarded the velocity of the sensible complex as, in some way, the resultant of the velocities of the individual atoms constituting it. Bailey asks the crucial question, 'What then is the atomic difference between the bodies *A* and *B* which causes the difference in the speed of motion of the aggregate body?', and answers, 'It is simply that in *A* more atoms are moving in the direction of the whole body than in *B*; in *B* there is more *antikopē*, it is more retarded by adverse atomic motion and therefore as a whole body moves slower.'[31] So far, perhaps, so good. Unfortunately, however, Bailey is more specific elsewhere:

Imagine that each body consists of 24 atoms: if in *A* 16 are moving from east to west and 8 in other directions more or less impeding, whereas in *B* 8 only are moving from east to west and 16 in other directions, *A* travels from east to west twice as fast as *B*.[32]

Drabkin has pointed out that the principle of proportionality implicit in Bailey's example is much too crude to work. For example, if all 24 atoms in a third body *C* moved in east-to-west direction, we would not expect the whole to move only three times as fast as *B* but, rather, at atomic speed. Drabkin also considers another interpretation of Bailey's example: 'that the velocity of the compound bears to maximum atomic velocity the same ratio as the number of atoms moving in the direction in question bears to the total number of atoms'.[33] But he easily shows that such a principle also will not work:

For if only one atom, in the case cited by Bailey, were moving in the given direction, not only would the compound not be moving in that direction with 1/24 of atomic velocity, but there would, in fact, be no reason for supposing that it would move in that direction rather than in any one of 23 other directions.[34]

---

[31] *Epicurus*, 220–1.
[32] C. Bailey, *The Greek Atomists and Epicurus*, (New York, 1964), 335.
[33] 'Notes on Epicurean Kinematics', 371.
[34] Ibid.

The fact is that even the beginnings of what Drabkin terms 'the quantitative analysis involved in this problem' would involve much more complex mathematics (e.g. vectorial analysis) than anything suggested by Bailey. While 'avoiding a precise mathematical formulation', Drabkin ingeniously extrapolates from 'Epicurean assumptions' concerning the resultant motion of complexes of atoms. For example, a ball batted lightly moves more slowly than a ball batted hard because

in the second case, the surface of contact between bat and ball being greater, there is a larger number of collisions between bat-atoms and ball-atoms, and, because a plurality of bat-atoms has, at every instant, been moving in the given direction (or in directions more or less close to it), the proportion of ball-atoms set in motion in that direction (or in directions more or less close to it) is, to begin with, greater in the second case than in the first. As a consequence, since the ball-atoms which had actually been in collision with the bat-atoms in turn collide with other ball-atoms and these, in turn, collide with others, the tendency of the motion of the ball to persist in the given direction is stronger in the second case than in the first. But eventually the mutual impacts of the atoms within the ball and the impact of atoms from without reduce the plurality of atoms moving, at every instant, in the given direction (or in directions more or less close to it) until eventually this plurality is entirely cancelled and the ball comes to rest. This will be a longer process, of course, in the second case than in the first because there is a greater plurality to overcome.[35]

Unfortunately, we do not have evidence to support even this degree of *conceptual* sophistication (leaving aside the issue of 'precise mathematical formulation') in the Epicurean application of their 'fundamental assumptions' concerning motion. Consequently, I am inclined to think that Drabkin may be overstating his case a bit when he remarks, at the conclusion of his stimulating paper, on 'the remarkable advance that [Epicurean science] represents in dealing with the specific problem in this paper, the linking of the microscopic and the macroscopic worlds in a single kinetic theory'.[36]

Drabkin himself notes Epicurus' 'contempt for the mathematical treatment of physical problems'[37] and speculates that the 'distaste of the Epicureans for mathematics' contributed to the 'lack of a quantitative treatment' of physical problems, which, in turn, helps to explain the lack of Epicurean 'immediate influence in the history of physics'.[38] This may indeed be part of the story. But, from a more general and less

---

[35] Ibid 372.
[37] Ibid. 371.
[36] Ibid. 374.
[38] Ibid. 374.

technical perspective, part of the problem is the considerable degree of conceptual vagueness about the relation between micro-level and macro-level. This vagueness may, in turn, be related to the questionable ontological status, in Epicurean thought, of 'phenomenal' properties (of sensible compounds of atoms)—a questionable status that is particularly understandable if the plausible hypothesis of Long and Sedley concerning Epicurus' motivation is correct:

Epicurus, as part of his rearguard action against Democritean scepticism, defends their reality [i.e. that of secondary qualities or phenomenal properties at the macro-level], but keeps atoms free of them on the grounds of the enormous explanatory power that this confers on the system.[39]

It is, I hope, neither unfair nor condescending to suggest that the forte of the Epicureans was the sketching of a big picture rather than detailed conceptual or technical analysis. It is conceivable that some of the more mathematically minded Epicureans (e.g. Zeno of Sidon) may have attempted to explicate in greater detail the relation between micro-level and macro-level motion. But it is also possible that Epicurean analysis of this problem never progressed much beyond general principles as applied by Epicurus himself in the *Letter to Herodotus*.

OVERVIEW

According to the hypothesis I have been developing, there may have been a considerable difference in motivation between Diodorus' employment of the quantum model of spatial magnitude, time (?), and motion and that of the Epicureans. Diodorus' use of the model represents, according to this hypothesis, a 'new Eleaticism'—an *elimination* of *kinēseis* and, hence, of any 'surd' or ontologically primitive conception of potentiality from the world. His version thus satisfies, with a vengeance, the general characterization of the quantum model that I gave at the beginning of Chapter 5: a *metaphysical* alternative (to the Aristotelian model) in which the role of the Aristotelian concept of potentiality is drastically attenuated.

The Epicurean use of the model, according to the picture I have been developing, may have been rather less radical. To begin with, the Epicureans were not interested in reviving Eleatic metaphysics but in

---

[39] Long and Sedley, *The Hellenistic Philosophers*, i. 57.

reviving and refining the atomist response to Eleaticism. *Kinēsis* is not to be *eliminated* but to be *explained*, reductively, in terms of the (unchanging) 'primary' properties of atoms and the (changing) relations among atoms—broadly speaking, the association and dissociation of atoms. It was argued in the first section of Chapter 5 that the Epicureans were faced with two options with respect to the constitution of their fundamental elements of association and dissociation, viz. the atoms: (*a*) each atom is constituted of a finite number of indivisible quanta of magnitude, discretely or successively ordered; (*b*) each atom is divisible without limit, in the Aristotelian sense, according to which the division can theoretically be carried beyond any finite stage but never terminates.

There is, of course, a third option: (*c*) each atom is constituted of an *actual* infinity of (equal-sized) parts. But this option was not viable in antiquity because of its susceptibility to the paradox of measure. It is only in fairly recent times that a mathematical tradition (viz. the rejection of a principle of complete additivity) has developed that permits (*c*) to be accepted without paradox. (*b*) seems to have been not only the Aristotelian choice but also the 'official' choice of ancient mathematics, enshrined in the ∞-conception of infinite division. But the sort of infinite divisibility required by (*b*) depends quite directly on a conception of 'surd potentiality': a given atom would not consist of any actual *archai* of magnitude, i.e. *actual partes minimae* the number of which determine its size. With respect to a conception of magnitude as determined by number of parts, its magnitude would be grounded only in the surd potentiality of non-terminating, foundationless division. According to the proponents of the quantum model, this is no grounding at all. For example, as we saw in Chapter 5, proponents of indivisible quanta worried that relinquishing such an *actual* grounding of foundational minima would compromise the objectivity of the greater/smaller relation; and in the Epicurean view, atomic size is surely one of the objective, primary properties of atoms. Aristotle had held that the notion of number or *multiplicity* (*plēthos*) depends upon an indivisible unit. Ancient quantum theorists maintain (in opposition to Aristotle and the geometers) that the same must be true in the case of magnitude (*megethos*).

Firmly committed to indivisible units of magnitude, the Epicurean advocates of such quanta soon decided (perhaps aided by the arguments of Aristotle and the precedent of Diodorus Cronus) that motion had to be quantized, in some way or other, as well. In this chapter I have maintained that we have no evidence that the Epicureans wished to emphasize or play upon the paradoxicality of quantized motion—in the way that Diodorus apparently *did* wish to play upon its paradoxicality. I have also argued that the introduction of indivisible temporal quanta is, in fact, a conceptual boon in the project of minimizing this paradoxicality—although (as I hope I have made clear) whether any Epicureans were actually so motivated with respect to the doctrine of temporal minima is a highly conjectural matter.

Whatever the exact motivation, the result of the Epicurean investigation of atomic motion seems to have been the use of a DP/DT principle to *analyse* (reductively) motion into a series of positions occupied by an (atomic) body at successive times. In other words, we seem to find an ancient version of the at-at ontology of motion, in which the positions of the moving body, as well as the times of its occupation of these positions, are ordered discretely (*epheksēs*). As I suggested at the end of Chapter 4, there seems to be reason to think that in antiquity the *metaphysical* idea of conceiving motion simply as the occupation of a sequence of positions at a sequence of times (i.e. the at-at ontology of motion) was intimately tied to the *kinematic* idea of quantized motion, or motions constituted of *kinēmata* rather than of foundationless sequences of kinetic segments. And in the Epicurean analysis of motion we surely find an example of this connection.

The connection in antiquity was, I believe, closer than that of historical accident. For to combine the at-at ontology with a kinematic conception of motion as continuous requires a conception of the continuous in terms of dense and Dedekind-continuous linear ordering of intuitively discrete limit entities (e.g. temporal instants, spatial points, or instantaneously occupied positions of the moving body). And there is good reason to think that such a conception was not included in the conceptual repertoire of either ancient philosophical or mathematical analysis. Consequently, it seems altogether plausible that, in antiquity, kinematic continuity (of spatial magnitude, time, and motion) would have been regarded, quite reasonably, as bringing along the metaphysical baggage associated with what was, without doubt, the pre-eminent ancient conceptual analysis of continuous spatial magnitude, time, and locomotion—that of Aristotle. So rejection of the conception of divisibility *in potentia*, rejection of the conception of *kinēsis* as a particular sort of potentiality (a *dunamis* that is actualized *qua dunamis*), etc., could naturally have been seen as enjoining the adoption of some version or other of the quantum model.

The disjunction 'either Aristotelianism or the quantum model' seems, to us, a strange one: the disjuncts cut across categories rather than carving up, in a neat and exhaustive logical fashion, one category. I hope that I have been able to make a case that the presentation of this disjunction as an apparently exhaustive dichotomy would not have seemed so strange in the third or second or first centuries BC. But, from the ancient perspective, are there no other possibilities with respect to the analysis, 'physical' and metaphysical, of spatial magnitude, time, and motion? One other possibility that seems worth exploring originates from our painfully scant information about the physical thought of the 'Old Stoa'. I conclude this study with a consideration of this possibility.

7

The Stoic Model

According to one plausible interpretation of the meagre extant evidence, the Stoic conception of spatial magnitude, time, and motion did not differ greatly from the Aristotelian conception—at least with respect to the formal, structural features of spatial magnitude and of time and rational kinematics. The Stoics certainly agreed with both the Aristotelian and geometrical traditions in holding that spatial magnitude is infinitely divisible. And, as we shall see, some *testimonia* suggest that this infinite divisibility was conceived in terms of the Aristotelian (and geometrical) ∞ -conception of infinity discussed in Part I. This tradition of interpretation of Stoic physics, which might be termed conservative, minimizes the significance of those *testimonia* that attribute 'strange' physical doctrines to the Stoics, maintaining that these reports represent misunderstandings (wilful or ignorant) of the Stoic theory which they report. And, indeed, much of the evidence does come from sources that are polemical and hostile to Stoicism, such as Sextus Empiricus and Plutarch. Representative of the conservative interpretation of Stoic physics are the notes of Harold Cherniss to his Loeb translations of Plutarch's *De Stoicorum repugnantiis* and *De communibus notitiis adversus Stoicos*. On the other hand, there is a radical tradition of interpretation of Stoic physics, perhaps particularly represented by S. Sambursky's monograph *Physics of the Stoics*, in which the *testimonia* are taken more at their face value. That is, the fragmentary, strange evidence is generally interpreted as indicative of Stoic physical theory, rather than as indicative of *misunderstanding* of the theory; and some attempt is made to develop a 'big picture' of Stoic physics in which the strange doctrines do not seem so strange.

Particularly in view of the paucity and nature of the evidence, there is much that can be said in favour of each of the approaches, the conservative and the radical, to the interpretation of Stoic physics. The conservative approach exemplifies the virtues of prudence and common sense. And in circumstances of uncertainty—where we are dealing with little actual evidence and the motivation underlying some of the most important *testimonia* is suspect—the virtues of prudence, caution, and common sense should not casually be dismissed as pedestrian. However, conservative interpretation is apt to result in a short and not very interesting story about Stoic physics.

In order to determine whether there is anything conceptually interesting about Stoic physics, it is, I think, necessary at least to explore some 'radical' hypotheses. These may ultimately be rejected; and it may turn out that the preponderance of historical evidence suggests that Stoic theorizing about the physical world was—at least with respect to the analysis of spatial magnitude, time, and motion— sufficiently dependent upon Aristotelian (and standard ancient geometrical) concepts that it does not deserve the status of a competing model. But in this chapter, I propose to pursue a more radical line of interpretation by way of the development of some hypothetical theses concerning the Stoic analysis of the physical world. This approach has the added virtue, I believe, of exploring some conceptual alternatives to the Aristotelian and quantum models of spatial magnitude, time, and motion; and this exercise may help us to deepen our understanding of these models.

THE REMOVAL OF LIMIT ENTITIES FROM THE PHYSICAL WORLD

Galen reports a Stoic definition of 'body' as 'extension in three dimensions along with resistance [*meta antitupias*]'.[1] With such a (natural and plausible) account of body, it follows that limit entities, which by definition lack extension in *at least* one of the three dimensions, do not qualify as body. But what ontological status do limit entities then have? According to Proclus, 'we should not believe, as the Stoics are wont to suppose, that limits of this sort—I mean [limits] of bodies—subsist [*huphestanai*] in mere thought'.[2] Diogenes Laertius, in noting that Posidonius held that surface exists both in thought (*kat' epinoian*) and in reality (*kath' hupostasin*),[3] seems to be contrasting him with other Stoics (perhaps particularly Apollodorus, whose definition

---

[1] *De qualitatibus incorporeis* 10, cited in H. von Arnim, *Stoicorum Veterum Fragmenta*, ii. (Leipzig, 1923), fr. 381. Reference to von Arnim will hereafter be in the form '*SVF* 2. 381'.

[2] *In Eucl.* 89. 15–18.

[3] D.L. 7. 135.

of body in terms of extension in three dimensions he has just reported), who held that surface exists only *in intellectu*.

While Plutarch evidently interprets the Stoic denial of corporeal status to limit entities as implying that they are to be included (along with *lekta* or propositions, the void, place, and time) in the Stoic ontological class of *asōmata* or incorporeals,[4] Long and Sedley suggest that the polemical context of Plutarch's remark renders his account suspect. They think that it is more likely that the Stoics placed such limit entities (along with fictional entities) in a category of mental constructs that 'fall[s] altogether outside the corporeal–incorporeal dichotomy'.[5] If we accept Long and Sedley's interpretation of the Stoic analysis of limit entities as mental constructs (irrespective of the issue of whether they also are to be accounted *asōmata*), the question remains whether the phrase 'mental constructs' is to be understood as connoting a degree of falsification or misrepresentation of the way the physical world really is.

It is logically possible, of course, to maintain that, although surfaces and other limit entities are mental constructs (i.e. not corporeal), they none the less are mental constructs (*a*) which are essential to our understanding of the physical reality and (*b*) which cannot correctly be said to misrepresent, falsify, or distort that physical reality.[6] One might term this the Kantian sense of 'mental constructs'. On the other hand, it is easy to understand the notion of limit entities as mental constructs (particularly when limit entities are placed in the same category as fictional entities[7]) as equivalent to the idea that such limit entities are geometers' fictions and, hence, involve a degree of *mis*representation. While admitting the possibility of a more conservative interpretation, I propose to explore the more radical inter-

---

[4] Plutarch, *De comm. not.* 1080e.

[5] *The Hellenistic Philosophers*, i. 301. See also their Stoic 'ontological stemma', ibid. 163.

[6] Some evidence, of which Cherniss makes much, for the more conservative view is Plutarch's comment at *De comm. not.* 1080e that the Stoics 'say that bodies touch one another at a limit, not at a part; and the limit is not a body. So, then, a body will touch a body with something incorporeal—and, then again, it will not touch it because there is something incorporeal in between.' The last comment, reminiscent of similar arguments in Sextus, shows how far Plutarch is willing to go in making his case for the inconsistency of Stoic thought. But the former comment, if it actually represents Stoic doctrine (which, of course, is not certain—particularly in view of the need for it in Plutarch's subsequent polemical argument), suggests a view according to which the incorporeality of limit entities does not at all preclude their actually existing, *qua* the limits of what *is* corporeal, in *hupostasis* or substantial (physical) reality.

[7] Ibid.

pretation of the Stoic doctrine that limit entities exist only *kat'*
epinoian. According to such an interpretation, a more accurate conception of spatial magnitude, time, and motion can be gained by dispens-
ing with the imposition of such fictions when we engage in the analysis
of physical reality. But what sort of model or picture might have
resulted when (according to the radical interpretation) the Stoics
separated limit entities from *hupostasis* or actual (physical) reality is
not at all obvious.

Infinite Divisibility and Fuzzy Boundaries

Suppose that we regard all surfaces, edges, points, etc. as elements of a
mental grid imposed on spatial extension and time. What do we have
when we remove the grid? According to the picture I am considering,
we have infinitely divisible spatial magnitudes. But an infinite sequence
of such nested intervals (a monotonic non-increasing sequence) does
not converge to some limit entity or boundary—a surface, line, or point.
Rather, convergence is to some interval of indeterminacy or fuzziness.
While such an interval is itself theoretically indivisible *ad infinitum*,
there is a sense in which it represents an ontologically foundational
level of physical reality. So, according to the picture I am attempting to
describe, the indeterminacy or fuzziness is not merely an *epistemic*
feature of our interaction with the world.

As an illustration of this view, consider a three-dimensional body
A surrounded by its spatial environment B. We consider a three-
dimensional region i of spatial extension that clearly contains some
of A and some of B and increasingly small regions i' nested in i.
According to a doctrine of geometrical realism (shared, I believe, by
Aristotle and, generally, the ancient mathematical tradition), there
can be constructed a monotonic non-increasing sequence of such
regions which converges to a two-dimensional limit entity, i.e. the
(geometrical) surface of A or interface between A and its surrounding spatial environment. According to the present interpretation of the Stoic view, however, convergence is to a
three-dimensional region of indeterminacy, which represents the
merging of the corporeal body A into its corporeal spatial environment. Since this region is itself divisible *ad infinitum*, one could
designate a two-dimensional limit within it as the surface of A. But
such a designated surface would be entirely a (physical) geometer's
artifice, having no more *ontological* claim to be the surface of A than

any of the infinite other two-dimensional limits that might be so designated within the region of indeterminacy/fuzziness.

This picture of the Stoic removal of limit entities from physical reality represents the topological aspect of the unity that the Stoics ascribed to the cosmos or 'whole' (*to holon*). It is the passive aspect (*corpus universum*) of this whole which is characterized by Calcidius as having 'parts [that] are inseparable and that mutually cohere with one another'.[8] This picture has also been invoked by Sambursky:

> Instead of the surfaces of two adjacent bodies touching each other, we now have a picture of the infinite sequences that envelope the surfaces, *merging into one another and thus forming a narrow zone where the extremities of these bodies enter into a mixture*. In this way the corporeality of the contact is maintained and any conceptual difficulty is removed which might arise from the notion of two-dimensional surfaces entering into the description of physical phenomena which are taking place in three dimensions.[9]

Giving some account of this Stoic view in terms of standard mathematics is a tricky business. The contemporary mathematical treatment of *continuous* magnitudes essentially involves the assumption that, for each cut or certain kind of bipartition of a region of such a magnitude, there is a unique limit entity—i.e. point, curve, or surface.[10] Perhaps the best place to look for contemporary elucidation of the Stoic idea is the non-standard mathematics based on L. A. Zadeh's fuzzy-set theory.[11] Zadeh's ideas can apparently be extended to create a fuzzy point-set topology. It should be emphasized that such a

---

[8] Calcidius, *Timaeus a Calcidio translatus commentarioque instructus*, ed. J. H. Waszink (London and Leiden, 1962), 293. According to Sextus Empiricus (*M* 9. 332 = *SVF* 2. 524), the Stoics distinguished between the cosmos/whole, which is finite, and the 'combination' of cosmos and surrounding void, which is infinitely extended. Long and Sedley point out that the *corpus universum* in the passage from Calcidius cannot refer to the cosmos/whole (because it is characterized as *determinatum* and, later in the passage, reason is said to pass through it); they suggest that it is an 'unusual expression for the passive *archē*' (*The Hellenistic Philosophers*, ii. 268).

[9] S. Sambursky, *Physics of the Stoics* (New York, 1959), 96 (emphasis added).

[10] For a discussion of the role of such a principle of continuity in elementary geometry, ancient and modern, see Heath, *Euclid's Elements*, i. 234–40.

[11] I am very grateful to David Bostock for pointing me in the direction of fuzzy-set theory as a possible contemporary tool for explicating the Stoic removal of limit entities from physical reality. He also did me the service of dissuading me from pursuing another, inadequate strategy for explicating this doctrine. For an introduction to fuzzy set theory and some of its applications, see L. A. Zadeh, *Fuzzy Sets and Applications: Selected Papers by L. A. Zadeh*, ed. R. R. Yager, S. Ovshinnikov, R. M. Tong, and H. T. Nguyen (New York, 1987); P. Wang and S. K. Chang (eds.), *Fuzzy Sets: Theory and Applications to Policy Analysis and Information Systems* (New York and London, 1980).

conceptual use of Zadeh's ideas is quite unhistorical. In particular, the Stoics held that three-dimensional regions of spatial (corporeal) magnitude are fundamentally real. The mathematical construction of fuzzy regions of this sort from sets of unreal limit entities (e.g. points) would doubtless have seemed Pickwickian to the Stoics. None the less, such a construction is capable of modelling some features of the Stoic removal of limit entities from physical, spatial reality.

The basic idea underlying fuzzy-set theory is quite simple. In standard set theory, an item either belongs to (is a member/element of) a set or does not belong to the set. In place of a set X itself, we can speak of X's characteristic function, which will assign to each member of some universal set a particular value (say, 1) if the item is a member of set X and another value (0) if it is not a member of X. In standard set theory, characteristic functions are binary-valued since it is assumed that there are only two states that an object can be in with respect to a certain set—either the state of being a member of it or the state of not being a member of it. The characteristic function of a fuzzy set, however, can take any value in the closed real interval [0,1]. Intuitively, such an innovation suggests the possibility of grade of membership in a set, with grade of membership becoming higher as the characteristic function's value approaches the limit 1 and lower as the value approaches the limit 0.

While the idea of grade or degree of membership may initially seem rather strange, it perhaps seems somewhat less strange when the sets in question are point-sets, used to represent intervals or regions of continuous magnitude. To return to our earlier example of a three-dimensional body A surrounded by its spatial environment B, let us consider a characteristic function f_A on the point-set consisting of the union of A and B that is intended to capture the idea of A's being a fuzzy object that 'blends' with its surrounding spatial environment. f_A will assign the value 1 to points 'clearly' in the interior of A. But let us suppose that there is a region of width ε in lieu of a two-dimensional surface of A. Points within this surrounding belt-like region will be assigned values by f_A less than 1 and greater than 0, continuously approaching 1 as we move to the interior of the belt and continuously approaching 0 as we move to its exterior. Points clearly outside the belt, in region B, will be assigned the value 0. According to this picture, object A is certainly bounded: it is surrounded by a spatial region of points all assigned the value 0 by f_A. But it seems that we would not want to say that there is anything like a *least* bound of A. Of course, we could *stipulate* an interpretation that would yield a surface or least bound of A: e.g. all points assigned 1 by f_A belong to A, all points assigned a lesser value do not; or all points assigned a value greater than 0 by f_A belong to A, all points assigned 0 do not; or all points assigned a value of greater than or equal to 0.996 by f_A belong to A, all points assigned a lesser value do not; etc. But according to the Stoic view I am attempting to model, such stipulations correspond to nothing in physical reality. What obtains in reality is *simply* the continuous blending of A with its surrounding environment through region ε.

With this contemporary picture as an explicatory tool, I turn now to some issues that arise in the ancient literature with respect to Stoic physical theory. In *De communibus notitiis* Plutarch seems to raise two problems with a Stoic doctrine combining infinite divisibility and the removal of limit entities from the physical world:

Furthermore, it is contrary to common sense [*para tēn ennoian*] that ⟨there should be⟩ in the nature of bodies neither an extremity [*akron*] nor anything that is first or last at which the magnitude of a body terminates but, rather, that it should always be the case that, however much is taken, the appearance of some part beyond it extends the substance indefinitely and indeterminately. For it will not be possible to conceive one magnitude as being either greater than or less than another if there turns out to be an infinite procession of the parts of both alike. The nature of inequality will be destroyed. For, when we think of things as unequal, one leaves off and the other exceeds and surpasses by their ultimate parts. But if inequality does not exist, it follows that neither will irregularity [or unevenness: *anōmalia*] or roughness of body. For irregularity is inequality of one surface with itself, and roughness is irregularity along with hardness. None of these is left intact by those [Stoics] who do not terminate body at some ultimate part but infinitely extend all things in terms of number of parts. (*De comm. not.* 1078e-1079a)

There is some considerable unclarity in the argumentation of this passage. If we understand by *eschaton* ('ultimate') a *minimal* quantum of corporeal extension, the argument can be read as a version of the 'argument from the objectivity of the greater/smaller relation' discussed in Chapter 5 (pp. 220-5): to deny the existences of a minimal unit of magnitude, which is the common measure of all magnitudes, is to sacrifice the objectivity of the greater/smaller relation among bodies. Luria has so construed the passage.[12] In a note to his Loeb translation of *De communibus notitiis*, Cherniss—with great certitude—

[12] S. Luria, 'Die Infinitesimallehre der antiken Atomisten', *Quellen und Studien zur Geschichte der Mathematik*, 2, pt. B (1933), 169.

dismisses this account.[13] I am not so certain as Cherniss. But I do follow him in holding that the sense of *eschaton* here is that of the *terminus* or boundary of a body or finite area of magnitude. This seems particularly likely in view of the discussion of irregularity (*anōmalia*) and roughness (*trachutēs*) in the latter part of the passage.

Another issue concerns Plutarch's use of the term *meros* ('part') in connection with *eschaton*, Cherniss claims that Plutarch 'disregards the distinction which [the Stoics] drew between *peras* [limit] and *eschaton meros* [ultimate part]' and that 'the Stoics did not deny "extremities" to bodies but insisted that these extremities are incorporeal limits and not parts of the bodies which they limit'.[14] In other words, Cherniss is adopting the conservative interpretation to which I earlier alluded. That is, the attribution of incorporeal (or mental) status to limits does not literally involve removing these limit entities from the world; it only involves the fairly obvious and uncontroversial claim that they are *limit* entities and not bodies (i.e. are not extended in *all* three dimensions).

According to a more radical strategy of interpretation, the passage has two arguments to make concerning the Stoic removal of 'ultimate parts'—*in the sense of limits*—from physical reality. The first argument is that, without surfaces limiting a body, the body would be infinitely (*eis apeiron*) extended. This argument is easily answered by noting that a body or magnitude can be *bounded* and thus finite without having a *least bound*. As we saw above, body *A* clearly is bounded in the sense of surrounded by a spatial environment that is unambiguously *B* (not-*A*). But the fact of boundedness does not, according to our picture, entail the existence of a surface or least bound.

The other argument in the passage is rather more interesting. Although the text is less than pellucid, I take the essence of Plutarch's other argument to be that, without limits of bodies (and, more generally, of magnitudes), there must be indeterminacy with respect to the issue of the equality of such magnitudes. What determines the equality, in the most strict theoretical sense of the term, of linear interval *A* and linear interval *B*? A natural, intuitive answer is that they are equal in this strict, theoretical sense just in case one can be superimposed on the other in such a way that the two *termini* or endpoints of *A* coincide, respectively, with the two end-points of *B*. But

[13] H. Cherniss, *Plutarch's Moralia, in Seventeen Volumes*, xiii, pt. 2 (Cambridge and London, 1976), 813, n. *b*.

[14] Ibid. 811, n. *c*.

without such end-points (or other limit entities such as linear edges and surfaces when we consider magnitudes of two and three dimensions), *this* particular theoretical sense of equality is untenable. According to Plutarch's subsequent argument, inequality is thus also abolished because, so he suggests, A is unequal to B when both (i) one end-point of A is superimposed on the 'analogous' end-point of B and (ii) the remaining end-point of A does *not* coincide with the remaining end-point of B but either falls short of or falls beyond it.

There are a number of ways to respond to this argument. But the course I shall explore (with the suggestion, to be elaborated later, that Chrysippus may have pursued it) begins with the claim that the Stoic removal of limit entities from the world allows for *discriminable differences* between magnitudes A and B—that A may, to use the terminology attributed to Chrysippus by Plutarch, 'project above or beyond' (*huperechei*) B.[15] To what do discriminable differences in magnitude, e.g. cases where A projects beyond B, 'retrench' or converge? That is, if one imagines the difference between A and B as becoming less and less, what is the limit of this process?

Where A and B are linear magnitudes, the standard theoretical answer is, of course, a point—a point at which their *termini* coincide and they become exactly equal. But, according to our radical interpretation of the Stoic removal of limit entities from the physical world, there are no such points (or other limit entities) to which a sequence of intervals (representing discriminable differences between A and B) converge.

A plausible hypothesis, which I shall adopt, is that discriminable differences in magnitude retrench to a lack of discriminable difference ε, which is regarded as itself an interval that is theoretically infinitely divisible. But differences of magnitude falling within ε are fuzzy. That is, the value of the greater-than relation for magnitudes A and B (in that order) is 1 when A is discriminably greater than B—greater than B by at least ε. But if the difference between A and B falls within ε, the value of the greater-than relation falls, in a continuous fashion, between 1 and 0. And, of course, when B is discriminably greater than A, the value of the greater-than relation for magnitudes A and B becomes 0.

According to the interpretative hypothesis that I am considering, the interval ε has both ontological and epistemological significance. It

---

[15] Plutarch, *De comm. not.* 1079d ff. This is the famous discussion of the pyramid and cone, to which I shall soon return.

is possible to 'precisify', by stipulation, the larger-than relation so that differences in the magnitudes *A* and *B* falling within the interval ε are significant—i.e. so that such a difference makes one magnitude larger (*meizon*) than the other. But, since such a difference is not discriminable, the larger magnitude cannot be said to 'project beyond' (*huperechei*) the other. Having introduced the interpretative hypothesis of fuzzy topological regions and fuzzy metrical relations, I wish to reconsider the (in)famous problem of the cone, as reported by Plutarch in *De communibus notitiis*.

The Cone Problem: Four Resolutions

The beginning of the so-called 'cone passage' does not deal with the example of a cone (which is attributed to Democritus by Plutarch) but with the example of a pyramid. Plutarch implies that the example of the pyramid is due to Chrysippus himself:

> In addition to these things [Chrysippus], puerile fellow that he is, says that, if a pyramid is constituted of triangles, the sides are certainly unequal along their juncture but do not project out where they are larger. (*De comm. not.* 1079d)

The example has been interpreted in many ways. It seems to me most likely (although by no means certain) that both 'triangles' and 'sides' (*pleurai*) refer to the faces of the pyramid and 'juncture' (*sunaphē*) refers to the edges where the faces meet. What Chrysippus is alluding to is what we would call the *continuous* inclination of these edges toward each other (viewing the cone from base to apex; inclination *away* from each other viewing it from apex to base). As we proceed (up or down) the pyramid, the distance across a triangular face (parallel to the base) from one such edge to another certainly becomes 'unequal' to what it was: it becomes sensibly less as we proceed up the pyramid and sensibly greater as we proceed down.

Chrysippus' view seems to be that, as we proceed down the pyramid from any given place along a face, the distance across the face from edge to edge becomes 'greater but does not exceed or protrude'. The apparent inconsistency of the last concept, of course, is what earns Chrysippus Plutarch's scorn. I follow Long and Sedley in believing that the puzzle that Chrysippus is concerned with here is 'essentially identical to the cone puzzle'.[16] At least it seems likely that Chrysippus' account of what we would call the *continuous* change in distance from

[16] *The Hellenistic Philosophers*, i. 302.

edge to edge across a (triangular) face of the pyramid is the same as his account of an analogous continuous change with respect to the (diameter or circumference) of a cone as we proceed from apex to base.

We are not given an explicit puzzle or paradox in the discussion of the pyramid. But we are given an explicit puzzle in the immediately following example of a (right circular) cone. The Democritean paradox is the following. Suppose that we divide a right circular cone into two segments by passing a plane through it parallel to its base (yielding a conic frustum 'on the bottom' and a smaller cone, similar to the original one, 'on the top'). What are we to say about the resulting *two* circular surfaces of these segments (the base of the smaller cone and the top of the conic frustum)—are they (i.e. their diameters) equal or unequal? Evidently the paradox, as propounded by Democritus, is that we can make neither response and still retain our cone 'as a cone'. (*a*) If we say 'unequal' we make the sides of the cone, as they incline toward its vertex, 'irregular' (*anōmala*), and the cone 'receives many step-like indentations and roughnesses'. But (*b*), if we say 'equal', 'the segments will be equal and the cone will undergo a transformation making it appear as a cylinder, since it is constituted of equal and not unequal circles, which is the utmost absurdity' (1079e).

Long and Sedley designate as one of two 'important assumptions' made by Democritus the proposition that 'a solid can be analysed somehow as *consisting of* a series of plane figures, the cylinder for example being describable as a stack of equal circles'.[17] In Plutarch's report of one horn of the paradox above, the participial clause modifying 'cone' ('constituted [*sungkeimenos*] from equal and not unequal circles') certainly seems to manifest such an assumption. But it is perhaps not so clear that *Democritus* would have made such an assumption. And the assumption surely would have been rejected by both Aristotle and the Epicureans—for different reasons. In the case of Aristotle it would have been rejected because of his doctrine that what is continuous cannot be constituted of such limit entities. In the case of the Epicureans, it would have been rejected because of their doctrine (as we have interpreted it) of the physical/geometrical non-existence of such limit entities.

However, the particular design of the paradox has the effect, I think, of forcing the potential paradox-solver to go beyond this (possible)

---

[17] Ibid.

initial objection. This feature of the design of the paradox is the fact that the plane cutting the cone parallel to its base is conceived as dividing the cone into two *separated* segments with two *separate* surfaces where once the segments were united (to form the 'whole' cone). Although this assumption may seem to introduce an awkward 'physical' element into the paradox, the assumption can be idealized in an appropriate geometrical fashion. We can assume that the cutting is 'geometrically clean': the slice can be conceived as perfectly parallel with the base and as yielding a perfect geometrical partition of the cone into *two* segments (i.e. no 'sliver' is cut out by the 'perfectly thin' knife/plane). This picture obviates the need for a stronger assumption, the other 'important assumption' attributed to Democritus by Long and Sedley: 'the two contiguous surfaces of two bodies in contact are not coincident but directly *adjacent*'.[18] Neither the Aristotelian nor the standard (ancient or contemporary) geometrical analysis would accept such an assumption. But both Aristotle and the contemporary paradox-solver are still faced with two distinct surfaces when the cutting is thought of as resulting in the spatial *separation* of the conic frustum and the smaller cone.

The idea that these segments of the original cone are spatially 'pulled apart' renders impossible the view of Cherniss that the 'cutting plane' that divides the cone into segments 'is [the *single*] incorporeal *peras* of their division and contact'.[19] Cherniss's assumption that we are dealing with, in effect, only *one* circular surface lies at the heart of his conservative interpretation of Chrysippus' resolution of the paradox. The fact that we can, it seems, consider the segments as spatially separated supports the contention of Long and Sedley that Cherniss's 'interpretation is not entirely satisfying'.[20] Before returning to what Chrysippus (*apud* Plutarch) says about the paradox, I shall examine several other possible responses to it.

A 'Standard' Contemporary Resolution. According to a standard contemporary account, if we consider any circular section *a* of the cone, any circular section *b* above it (i.e. closer to the vertex) will have a smaller diameter. But there will always be a distinct intermediate circular section *c* between *a* and *b* such that the diameter of *c* is less than the diameter of *a* but greater than the diameter of *b*. Suppose, then, that

---

[18] Ibid.
[19] *Plutarch's Moralia*, viii. 2, 820–1, n. *b*.
[20] *The Hellenistic Philosophers*, i. 302.

we slice the cone parallel to its base at a circular section *a* and think of the two resulting segments, the bottom conic frustum and the top conic segment, as being pulled apart from one another. We then must decide whether the circular section *a* is the surface of the bottom segment or the top segment; and this decision seems an entirely arbitrary one. Let us say that circle *a*, having diameter *s*, is the (top) surface of the bottom frustum. What of the top segment? If we think of the diameter of *a* as being measured between two lines, *l* and *k*, on the side of our original cone, then every two points on *k* and *l*, respectively, that are equidistant from the vertex of the cone determine the diameter of a circle 'in' the top segment. And for *every* real-valued distance $s' < s$ (the diameter of *a*), there will be a pair of points on *k* and *l*, such that *s'* is the distance between them. But since there is no *s'* that is 'immediately less' than *s*, there is no circle *b* 'in' the top segment that can serve as the limit or bottom surface of that segment. But, surely, there *is* a bottom surface of the top segment—particularly if, as we assumed, there is a top surface of the bottom frustum.

It is to be emphasized that the sense in which a circle is 'in' a segment is the sense in which its diameter is determined by two points *on* the lines *k* and *l*, which are lines along the side of the *original* cone. It is obvious what has happened. When we pass a plane parallel through the cone parallel, we conceive it as bisecting *k* and *l* at two points equidistant from the cone's vertex. Then, quite arbitrarily, we assigned those points to the bottom conic frustum when we thought of the two segments as being spatially separated. This leaves the remaining, top segments of *k* and *l* 'open on the bottom end' since we are identifying each of the lines *k* and *l* with a dense and Dedekind-continuous, linearly ordered set of points. It seems clear that, if we do not want to think of the top segment as lacking a bottom surface, we need to 'add' end-points from the 'surrounding (continuous) spatial matrix' to the open segments of *k* and *l*, respectively, and regard *those* two 'added points' as determining its surface. The distance between those two added points and, thus, the distance of the diameter of the bottom surface *b* of the top segment will be *s*, the same as that of the diameter of *a*, the top surface of the bottom frustum.

It seems utterly arbitrary to claim that the surface of the bottom conic frustum 'belongs to *it*' but that the surface of the top segment 'belongs to the surrounding spatial matrix'. The apparent 'moral' is that, when we apply the point-set analysis of continuous magnitudes within a *quasi*-physical context such as our example, where the segments are conceived as being spatially separated, our best choice for the concept of a surface is what Stroll calls an 'LS' or 'Leonardo surface'. Such a surface is 'abstract' in Stroll's sense: that is, it is a true limit entity lacking *at least* one dimension. However, as Stroll says, the key feature of such a surface 'is that for Leonardo a surface does not belong to either of the elements whose boundary it forms'.[21] Essentially the same point can be put in a more topological manner. If we are to conceive a region of magnitude (in the intuitive sense) as a point-set, then surfaces of that region pertain not to that point-set but to its *closure* or, more properly, to the *boundary* or *frontier* of the set, which is the intersection of its closure with that of its complement.

An Aristotelian Resolution. The natural Aristotelian resolution of the cone problem is the ancient resolution that comes closest, I believe, to the contemporary resolution that I have just discussed. The difference, of course, is the underlying ontology of what is continuous: Aristotle is unwilling to identify a continuous magnitude with a dense and Dedekind-continuous, linearly ordered collection of limit entities. Thus the cone is not a dense and continuous stack of circular sections, parallel to the base. Nor are the lines k and l along the side of the cone, to which reference was made in the preceding section, to be identified with a dense and Dedekind-continuous, linearly ordered set of points. How, then, would Aristotle conceive the result of the action of cutting the cone parallel to its base and pulling apart the resulting segments? The answer is found, I believe, in his doctrine of the 'generation' of limit entities discussed in Part I. Such an actual division results in two *actual* surfaces where, prior to the cutting, there was but a (single) *locus* of *potential* division. This Aristotelian doctrine is well attested. We do not, however, have direct evidence as to what Aristotle would have said about the relative size (of the diameters) of the two resulting circular surfaces. But it is, I think, overwhelmingly likely that he would have regarded them as equal.

It is only with respect to the underlying ontology of magnitude that such an Aristotelian resolution of the problem differs from the standard contemporary resolution. According to both resolutions, the diameters of circular sections above an arbitrarily selected cut a of the cone (at a distance h from the base) converge to the diameter d of that cut as least upper bound.

[21] Stroll, *Surfaces*, 46.

According to the second horn (*b*) of the paradox, if we say that the surfaces of the two segments are equal in diameter, we end up transforming the cone into a cylinder. Implicit in this claim is the inductive proposition that if, for a given cut, the (upper) surface *a* of the lower segment and the (lower) surface *b* of the upper segment have the same diameter *d*, then *all* cuts above this one will yield surfaces of diameter *d*. This proposition would hold only if both (A) the cone may be partitioned into segments the lower and upper surfaces of which have the same diameter and (B) the set of segments of such a partition is discretely ordered in terms of distance from the base. That is, according to assumption (B), when we consider any member of the partition, if there are other segments in the partition further from the base, there is an immediate successor to the segment in question, a segment that is 'next closest' in distance to the base in terms of its original position in the cone.

Aristotle, of course, rejects (A). Any possibly actual partition of the cone will contain a finite number of segments. While such segments are ordered discretely or *ephekses* and the top surface of one has the same diameter of the bottom surface of its successor (if it has a successor), none of the segments will itself be cylindrical: the diameter of its top surface is less than that of its bottom surface. Of course, a partition of the cone into a number of segments greater than any given natural number *n* can always, in theory, be effected. And the diameter of the top surface of a given segment in the partition can be made to approach the diameter of the bottom surface of *that same segment* 'as a limit' by increasing the number of segments in the partition. But the limit can, according to Aristotle's strict adherence to the ∞-conception of infinity, never be reached.

A contemporary analysis avoids the same horn (*b*) of the paradox by denying (B). Such an analysis may countenance the partition of the cone into the set of its circular sections. Since these 'segments' have no height, their bottom and top surface have the same diameter because it is the *same* circular section. Hence, condition (A) is satisfied. But the ordering of these segments (in terms of their distance from the base of the cone) must be a dense and Dedekind-continuous linear ordering. Such an ordering is not discretely ordered: that is, no circular segment/section has an immediate successor that is 'next closest' in distance to the base of the cone.

Consequently, the inductive proposition does not succeed. We cannot infer, from (i) the existence of a segment/section with both 'top' and 'bottom' surfaces (here, the same surface) of diameter d and (ii) the claim that any cut of the cone will yield a bottom segment the top surface of which is the same diameter as the bottom surface of the segment above it, the consequence (iii) that *all* the segments/sections in the partition of the cone above the segment/surface with diameter d also have diameter d. The reason that the inference is invalid is that the partition of the cone into segments/sections is such that the section of diameter d does not have an immediately succeeding 'neighbour' section immediately above it. However, *this* fact, obvious from the contemporary perspective, means that, when we consider an actual geometrical/physical slicing of the cone and the separation of the resulting segments, if we identify a given section a of diameter d as the top surface of the bottom conic frustum, then the bottom surface of the top conic segment (also of diameter d) cannot be a member of the partition of the cone into circular sections of null height. It must be supplied from outside, as it were, as the limit of the sections constituting the top segment. Of course, the same point holds *mutatis mutandis* if we identify a as the bottom surface of the top segment.

The Aristotelian and contemporary views of this problem may be contrasted as follows. Aristotle's unwillingness to countenance a partition of the cone into an infinite set of limit entities (circular sections) results in his acceptance of both the following propositions: (1) the facing surfaces of the two segments of the geometrically conceived cone (when we think of the cone as divided and the segments as spatially separated) are both equal in diameter; (2) both these circular surfaces are *geometrical* parts of the resulting segments. As we have seen, however, there is a sense in which the contemporary willingness to countenance the partition of the cone into a set of circular sections requires that, when we consider such a division and spatial separation of segments, the facing surfaces of the resulting segments cannot *both* be considered geometrical parts of the original, geometrically conceived cone. The sense in which the two surfaces cannot both be geometrical parts of the cone is, simply, that the surfaces cannot be two distinct members of the partition of the original cone into circular sections.

Both the Aristotelian and the contemporary analyses have basically the same *mathematical* view of the relation between any two distinct cuts of the cone. (For example, between any two cuts there will always be a third 'theoretically possible' cut of an intermediate diameter.) And both can successfully avoid horn (b) of the cone paradox. But the fact that, for Aristotle, the geometrical cone cannot be partitioned into a set of such cuts while, according to a standard contemporary analysis, it can be so partitioned leads to very different ways of avoiding this horn of the paradox.

An Epicurean Resolution. I shall assume that the Epicurean doctrine of indivisible quanta was a geometrical doctrine in the sense of our earlier discussion of the quantum conception of spatial magnitude, time, and motion. Given this assumption, we can see that Epicureans are vulnerable to the second horn (b) of the cone paradox. For condition (A) above is satisfied in such a context: whether or not the cone could *physically* be partitioned into segments or slices having a depth or thickness of only one quantum q of magnitude, such a partition is *conceptually* possible; and, of course, this will be the 'finest' partition. Although one of these segments does not literally have a top and bottom surface,[22] it does seem that it cannot have any smaller diameter on top than on bottom. We are, in fact, talking about just one diameter in the sense of the multiple of q (number of quanta) across the segment (without implying that this is the diameter of a circle in the traditional *geometrical* sense of 'circle'). Condition (B) is also satisfied: these minimal segments are discretely ordered in terms of their distance from the base of the cone. So, were an orthodox Epicurean to maintain that any cutting of the cone yields two segments for which it is true that the top surface (segment one quantum thick) of the bottom segment has the same 'diameter' as the bottom surface of the top segment, such an Epicurean does fall victim to horn (b)—the cone will be transformed into a cylinder.

It seems most plausible for such an Epicurean to embrace horn (a) of the paradox. Any 'theoretical cutting' of the cone (which will always be between adjacent minimal segments) yields a top segment with a bottom surface (minimal segment one quantum thick) the 'diameter' of which is smaller by some multiple of q than the 'diameter' of the top surface of the bottom segment. The conic surface then *does* become *anōmala* or irregular and 'receives many step-like indentations and

---

[22] According to the argument of Ch. 5, a conception of spatial magnitude as quantized does not admit the notion of surfaces as (2-dimensional) true limit entities because the limit notion implies the infinite divisibility and continuity of spatial magnitude. Surfaces, for the Epicureans, become an outermost layer of quanta; but here we are *ex hypothesi* dealing with a segment of the cone that is but one quantum q thick. So it would also seem strange to talk about its surface(s) in the Epicurean sense.

roughnesses'. In other words, the *geometrical* cone disappears and, in its place (and also in the place of the pyramid), we find something that has more the appearance of a ziggurat when it is subjected to fine-grain analysis.[23] For the geometrically orthodox Epicurean, as I am conceiving him or her, being impaled on horn (*a*) of the paradox will not be a painful experience. An orthodox Epicurean already holds geometry (that is, the standard ancient geometry of the infinitely divisible and the continuous magnitude) to be false.

A Stoic Resolution. What I signify by 'a Stoic resolution' is an attempted resolution attributed by Plutarch to Chrysippus in *De communibus notitiis*:

[Chrysippus] says that the surfaces are neither equal nor unequal but that the bodies [*sōmata*] are unequal because of the fact that surfaces are neither equal nor unequal. (1079 f).

The account is short and, as Long and Sedley have noted,[24] Plutarch can be a 'malicious reporter' in a polemical context (which this surely is). It is not surprising, then, that the nature of Chrysippus' attempted resolution of the puzzle remains controversial. In fact, there seems to me to be little likelihood that any consensus will ever be achieved with respect to this matter. None the less, I shall not refrain from adding to the speculation, taking as my starting-point the 'radical interpretation' of the Stoic removal of limit entities from the realm of *hupostasis* or actual (physical) existence.

Cherniss maintains, reasonably enough, that Chrysippus withholds *both* of the contrary predicates 'equal' and 'unequal' from the noun 'surfaces' because a presupposition of the attribution of both these adjectives fails to be satisfied:

Chrysippus meant simply that neither of the predicates, 'equal' and 'unequal,' is applicable to what Democritus called the 'surfaces,' because these are in fact just the single geometrical plane which cuts the cone into segments and is the incorporeal *peras* of their division and contact . . .[25]

---

[23] David Bostock suggests that the description of the resulting figure as 'irregular' or 'Ziggurat-like' is appropriate only if we think of Epicurean spatial quanta as having edges and surfaces. He indicates that the Epicurean might maintain that what we *mean* by a 'regular' slope of 45° for a right circular cone just is 1 quantum of 'indentation' of diameter *per* 1 quantum of rise in height. This point seems to me to be quite correct. However, it does involve a denial of the accuracy of developing Euclidean geometry with respect to the applicability of that geometry to physical magnitude.

[24] *The Hellenistic Philosophers*, i. 302.

[25] *Plutarch's Moralia*, xiii. 2, 820–1, n. *b*.

Long and Sedley also consider such an interpretation[26] but wisely reject it. As we have seen, this interpretation will not do if we adopt the quasi-physical perspective according to which the cone is geometrically (i.e. perfectly) bisected and the segments are then spatially separated. From such a perspective, there must be *two* surfaces if there are any surfaces at all.

Pursuing an alternative, radical interpretation of the Stoic abolition of limit entities, we might hypothesize that Chrysippus' intent was to deny that the surfaces of the resulting segments are neither equal nor unequal because there are no such surfaces at all. According to this interpretation, the denial of the existence of such limit entities enables Chrysippus to avoid the paradox rather than resolve it. Given such circular surfaces, we evidently must say either that each *epharmozei* (exactly fits or coincides with) the other or that they do not so coincide. *Epharmozein* (a term that is used in a later passage in Plutarch's criticism of Chrysippus, to which I shall shortly return) is a geometrical term, which in the active voice typically connotes the sort of coincidence between one geometrical entity and another when one is conceived 'as actually *moved* and *placed upon* the other'.[27] I suspect that Long and Sedley are correct in their suggestion that 'Chrysippus is genuinely puzzled by the relationship of the two surfaces produced by slicing a cone or pyramid latitudinally'.[28]

Faced with (1) two distinct surfaces that are 'geometrical' (i.e. limit) entities and (2) the geometrical conception of exact coincidence, Chrysippus does not see any way of resolving the paradox. Horn (*a*) is unacceptable because of the discontinuous *anōmalia* it yields; and horn (*b*) yields the even more paradoxical transformation of a cone into (a single) cylinder. Of course, in view of the common Stoic assumption of the infinite divisibility of magnitude, Chrysippus need not have been so afraid of horn (*b*). But, although the 'Aristotelian' resolution was conceptually available, there is no evidence that it was *historically* available to Chrysippus in this particular context, as an actual precedent on which he might have relied. Furthermore, the Aristotelian resolution depends upon the distinctive Aristotelian metaphysical doctrine of the having-coming-to-be—but without there being a

---

[26] *The Hellenistic Philosophers*, i. 302.

[27] Heath, *Euclid's Elements*, i. 224 ff. Heath notes that 'in the passive, *epharmozesthai*, the verb means "to be *applied* to" without any implication that the applied figure will exactly fit, or coincide with, the figure to which it is applied' (224).

[28] *The Hellenistic Philosophers*, i. 302.

process of coming-to-be—of *two* limit entities. Before the slicing and physical separation of segments there was a single (potential) circular *locus* of division, while after the slicing and spatial separation there are two circular surfaces. The Aristotelian metaphysical construal of this transformation might well have been unacceptable to a Stoic.

Whatever the case with respect to the options available to Chrysippus, it appears likely that his comment, 'the bodies are unequal because of the fact that the surfaces are neither equal nor unequal', is directed primarily against horn (*b*). That is, the two resulting segments of a latitudinal bisection of the cone (= 'the bodies')[29] can be unequal (*not* distinct sections both having the appearance of cylinders of the same diameter) because these segments do not have circular geometrical surfaces. Chrysippus may have believed that the geometrical coincidence of such circular surfaces would render the cone vulnerable to horn (*b*)—i.e. the paradoxical transformation of the cone, once sliced, into two cylinders.

Perhaps this response is acceptable as far as it goes. *One* way of avoiding horn (*b*), although certainly neither the Aristotelian nor the standard contemporary way, is to deny that the segments created by the division and spatial separation of the cone *have* surfaces which either coincide in size or fail to coincide. But this response does not go far. Horn (*a*) does not seem to be explicitly dealt with by Chrysippus in Plutarch's report.[30] And it seems to be reasonable to wish to know more about how the two segments *are* related. Although these segments may lack circular surfaces in the geometrical sense, they are two bodies that are limited latitudinally, and their latitudinal ends

[29] Since there are, according to the radical interpretation, no 'geometrical objects' there is all the more reason for Chrysippus to adopt a corporeal conception of the cone and its segments.

[30] There *may* be a reference to horn (*a*) a little later at 1080a: 'the inequality of the bodies, surely, and not of the surfaces produces the roughnesses round about the cone which he regards with suspicion'. But it is not clear what the point of the remark is. Cherniss (*Plutarch's Moralia*, xiii. 2, 823, n. *b*) follows Pohlenz in regarding the remark as a direct quotation of Chrysippus, although it does not appear as a fragment in the von Arnim collection. The referent of the 'he' would then be Democritus. I think that it is possible, however, that the remark is not a quotation of Chrysippus, but Plutarch's own and that the referent of the 'he' is Chrysippus. Its import would then be something like the following: he (Chrysippus) is worried about avoiding horn (*a*), which introduces 'step-like indentations' along the side of the cone; but such indentations are, strictly speaking, the result of the inequalities of *bodies* (three-dimensional sections of the cone); so simply denying the existence of surfaces (which must be either equal or unequal) does not in itself eliminate the possibility of indentations produced by difference in size of the *corporeal* segments produced by latitudinal slicings of the cone.

surely must be admitted to have a circular appearance even though there may not actually be circular limit-surfaces demarcating these ends.

What, then, can we say about the relation between these two ends? Sambursky makes the following comments pertinent to this issue:

> The Stoics therefore discarded the conception of the distinct surface of a body, or generally the distinct boundary of $(n-1)$ dimensions forming the surface of a figure of n dimensions ($n = 1, 2, 3$), and replaced it by an infinite sequence of boundaries defining the surfaces of inscribed and circumscribed figures which converge from both sides to the figure in question and thus define it as a dynamic entity.[31]

Long and Sedley also speak, more cautiously, of Stoic 'attempts to describe the difficult mathematical notion of convergence on a limit'.[32] Although I too am pursuing the radical interpretation according to which limit entities are removed from physical reality, I wish to demur a bit here. Although I think that there may well have been a rough and ready, intuitive notion of convergence involved in the Stoic conception of the 'ends' of bodies—e.g. the latitudinal ends of the conic segments— it seems to me doubtful that this conception had a very close connection with modern mathematical notions of convergence.

Aside from the issue of the mathematical acuity and interest of the Stoics, there is a *metaphysical* problem apparent in the quotation from Sambursky. Replacing 'the distinct surface of a body' by a convergent infinite sequence of Xs would perhaps have been a mathematically feasible move for Chrysippus. He was an almost exact contemporary of Archimedes; and Archimedes (as well as earlier geometers, it seems) made use of such constructions in applying the method of exhaustion in calculating areas of plane and solid figures. (In Chapter 4, however, I questioned whether we have any reason to believe that any ancient mathematician thought of such a convergent 'infinite' sequence of figures as a 'whole' or 'completed totality'.) But a convergent infinite sequence has to be a sequence of *somethings*—values for 'X' above have to be filled in. The most likely candidates for filling in the 'X' are boundaries or limit entities of some appropriate sort, as indicated in the quotation from Sambursky. But there seems to be something decidedly Pickwickian about doing away with a 'distinct boundary' of a body and replacing that idea with the idea of the 'outer aspect of the

---

[31] *Physics of the Stoics*, 96.
[32] *The Hellenistic Philosophers*, i. 302.

body' as 'an infinite sequence of *boundaries*' converging to the 'missing' boundary/surface. *If* the Stoics actually did away with boundaries, in the sense of the radical interpretation, I doubt that they were Pickwickian in this particular manner.

Where does this leave us? It seems reasonable that Chrysippus would have held that the ends of the segments resulting from the latitudinal slicing of the cone do not *discriminably* differ in diameter. But, I suggest, he may have held that the end of the bottom segment 'is larger [*meizon*] but without projecting or exceeding [*huperechein*]'. Plutarch attributes this concept to Chrysippus at *De comm. not.* 1080c, after his account of the cone paradox. Although the attribution does not occur in conjunction with his explicit discussion of the cone paradox, it does, additionally, occur earlier in *De comm. not.* in connection with Plutarch's account of Chrysippus' pyramid problem. My suggestion, then, is that Chrysippus held that the two ends of the conic segments do not differ in size to any discriminable extent: the top of the bottom conic frustum does not 'stick out' or 'protrude' (*huperechei*) beyond the bottom of the top conic section when the segments are juxtaposed. But the size of the top of the lower frustum is (indiscriminably) greater than the bottom of the top conic segment. And this fact *explains* why the union of the segments yields a *cone*, the size of which gets progressively smaller toward its vertex, rather than a cylinder.

I am, therefore, qualifiedly agreeing with Long and Sedley's comment that Chrysippus' view was that 'the two adjacent faces cannot be perfectly equal, yet there is no finite quantity by which the one exceeds the other'.[33] An initial qualification that I would make substitutes 'discriminable quantity' for 'finite quantity' in this sentence. Whether the 'indiscriminably small difference' might have been equated by Chrysippus with 'difference smaller than *any* finite difference' is a fascinating issue to which I shall shortly turn.

However, three concluding remarks concerning Chrysippus' resolution of the cone problem seem to be in order. (1) If we are speaking of a *geometrical* cone, the assumption that the adjacent but separated surfaces (in the geometrical sense) should *not* be perfectly equal is, by both Aristotelian and standard mathematical lights, misguided. (2) The radical interpretation of the Stoic doctrine of limit entities, together with the fact that Chrysippus evidently used the term 'bodies' in connection with the segments of the cone, indicate that there may

---

[33] Ibid.

be no *geometrical* cone problem, according to Chrysippus, because the limit entities to which geometrical analysis pertains do not exist *kath' hupostasin*. (Chrysippus may have been willing, however, to envisage a *physically* idealized cutting of the corporeal cone, in the sense of a clean cutting with no sliver taken out.) (3) Particularly if limit entities are not to figure in the analysis of the cone problem, neither the modern *mathematical* notion of convergence nor any of its ancient geometrical forerunners is likely to be of much use in elucidating Chrysippus' resolution of the cone problem.

Discriminable and Indiscriminable Differences. In the section 'Infinite Divisibility and Fuzzy Boundaries', I advanced the hypothesis that the Stoics might have developed a view in which discriminable differences of magnitude retrench, not to any limit entity such as a point, line, or surface, but to an indiscriminable difference in magnitude, which is itself theoretically infinitely divisible. For example, a metre stick is discriminably longer than a yard stick. And if we shorten by small increments the metre stick, it approaches the length of the yard stick. What is the limit of this process of shortening? According to the classical geometrical view, if we consider the lengths of yard and metre sticks geometrically, we 'theoretically' approach as limit a closed interval of magnitude (identified with the length of the metre stick, geometrically conceived) that 'exactly coincides' [*epharmozei*] with the closed interval that is identified with the length of the yard stick, geometrically conceived. That is, when we place the two 'left' (or two 'right') end-points of the intervals one on the other, the remaining end-points will also coincide. According to the present hypothesis, however, the Stoic process of shortening the metre stick would retrench to an interval which is indiscriminably different in length from the interval defined by the yard stick. Since the Stoics have removed (according to the radical interpretation) limit entities from the world, there is no such thing in nature as exact equality of magnitude. So discriminable differences in magnitude always converge or retrench to an indiscriminable difference, which itself is theoretically divisible and which I earlier identified as ε. According to this hypothesis, ε does not merely signify a limitation of the physical accuracy of our measurement techniques, although such considerations could have been at least partly responsible for the Stoic denial of the existence of limit entities *kath' hupostasin*. ε apparently has *some* sort of ontological status.

Unfortunately, there is no obvious and explicit evidence, so far as I am aware, for a Stoic doctrine according to which intervals of spatial magnitude retrench to such an interval ε rather than to a limit entity such as a point. However, two passages may be read as suggesting such a doctrine. The first passage pertains to time and suggests a conception of intervals of time retrenching to 'nows' conceived as short intervals rather than as either indivisible quanta or punctal limits. At *De comm. not*. 1081c Plutarch characterizes the Stoics as 'not admitting a least [*elachiston*] time and not wanting the now [*to nun*] to be partless'. The former prohibition seems to be directed against a doctrine of temporal quanta: *elachiston chronon* connotes, I take it, a minimal *quantum* of time rather than a punctal limit. The second prohibition seems to be more inclusive. The requirement that *to nun* should not be without parts would seem to preclude not only a conception of the now as an indivisible temporal quantum (*elachiston chronon*) but also a conception of the now, such as that of Aristotle, according to which the now is a partless temporal *limit*.

It is true that Plutarch attributes to the Stoic Archedemus of Tarsus a conception of *to nun* as 'a kind of juncture or meeting' (*harmēn tina kai sumbolēn*) of what is past and what is present (1081e). This *may* (but I think need not) be a doctrine of the now as an indivisible limit. Plutarch proceeds, however, to attribute the following conception of the present to Chrysippus:

but in the third, fourth, and fifth books of his 'On Parts', [Chrysippus] affirms that, of present [*enestēkotos*] time, some is going to be while some has already been. (*De comm. not*. 1081f)

It seems clear that the point of Chrysippus' claim is that the present is really a stretch of time in which it is at least theoretically possible to imagine a distinction between earlier and later. Of course, he may simply be pointing out that now locutions often designate, depending upon context, *discriminable* stretches of time—a 'present' second, minute, day, year, generation, *etc*. However, there remains the question of what, if anything, such discriminable intervals of time retrench to or converge on. If they retrench to a punctal temporal limit—but a limit that is not to be thought of as 'now' or present, then (as Plutarch is quick to note) there is a problem of consistency concerning this conception of the now as a context-dependent (discriminable) stretch of time and concerning another doctrine attributed by Plutarch to Chrysippus. Plutarch reports that 'Chrysippus ... says in his book "On the Void" and in certain others that the past and future parts of time do not obtain [*huparchein*] but subsist [*huphestēkenai*], while only the present [*to enestēkos*] obtains' (*De comm. not.* 1081f). On the one hand, Chrysippus seems to maintain that the present can always be 'shaved away' into past and future. But on the other, he maintains that it is only the present that enjoys the ontological status of obtaining or existing. The problem is that the shaving away of present into past and future would seem to leave nothing to enjoy this ontological favour.

I have elsewhere discussed possible interpretations of the relation between these Chrysippean doctrines, including the possibility (which I do not think can be dismissed with certitude) that they are inconsistent doctrines coming from different parts of Chrysippus' huge corpus.[34] Another possibility, of course, is polemical distortion on the part of Plutarch. But I remain attracted to the idea that, for Chrysippus, discriminably long intervals of time retrench to nows or presents that are theoretically divisible *intervals*. Such an interval ε is indiscriminably short in the sense that, although its divisibility entails that a distinction between earlier and later can theoretically be stipulated *within* it, such a past/future distinction cannot be *discriminated* within it. Moreover, the ontological character of ε as a region of indeterminacy or fuzziness means that such stipulated and indiscriminable past/future distinctions *within* ε do not have the same degree of reality as discriminable past/future distinctions, which involve temporal stretches longer than ε.

I conjecture that it is the token reflexive now in the sense of such an interval ε to which Chrysippus accords the ontological favour of existence. The past and future that merely subsist are not the merely theoretically stipulable past/future within ε but rather the *discriminable* past and future on either side of it. It must be admitted, however, that, with respect to this account, conjecture far outstrips the evidence.

A second passage that may suggest the retrenchment of discriminable intervals of magnitude to a very small indiscriminable interval ε is a passage in which Sextus Empiricus is criticizing the Stoic doctrine of motion 'all at once' (*athroōs*) over a divisible interval of magnitude. I shall discuss this doctrine in greater detail in the next section. At present, however, I am concerned with the three options that Sextus considers with respect to the spatial interval over which such motion

[34] 'Zeno's Arrow, Divisible Infinitesimals, and Chrysippus', *Phronesis*, 27: 3 (1982), 246–8.

athroōs might occur. The interval might be (1) infinite (*aoriston*), (2) a place defined precisely (*pros akribeian*), 'a distance greater than which by even a hair's breadth the thing moving all at once will not be able to pass through', or (3) a 'small but not precisely bounded place' (*mikron men, ou pros akribeian de periōrismenon topon*).[35] Of course, these three categories might simply be categories supplied by Sextus. But I suspect that he adds the 'peculiar' finite category (3) of a small but not precisely determined interval of spatial magnitude because such intervals actually were posited in (some) Stoic physical theory. Such an interval could well have been an indiscriminably short but theoretically divisible interval ε.

Might Chrysippus have attached any definite mathematical significance to the notion of 'being greater but not exceeding' (*meizon ou mēn huperchon*), interpreted as 'being greater by (some part of) an indiscriminably small but theoretically divisible interval ε'? The idea of something's *both* being greater than *and* exceeding nicely expresses the idea of something's being *discriminably* greater because of the literal meaning of *huperechein*: to protrude or stick out. But, as Cherniss notes, *huperechein* also has a mathematical use.[36] In the references to Plato and Aristotle cited by Cherniss (*Phaedo* 96e, *Parmenides* 150d–e, *Topics* 125a), *huperechon* (and its cognates) seems to be used in apposition to *meizon* ('larger'). Perhaps the use of *huperechein* in the sense of 'to be greater by a "definite" amount' can be read into later uses of the term, as in Definitions 4 and 5 of Book 5 of Euclid, definitions in which the term is used by itself, not in conjunction with *meizon*.

It is in the fifth postulate of Archimedes' *De sphaero et cylindro*, however, that we find the most interesting use of *huperechein*:

Moreover, of unequal lines and unequal surfaces and unequal solids, the greater [*to meizon*] exceeds [*huperechein*] the lesser by the following amount: when that amount is added to itself it is capable of exceeding any given [magnitude] of the sort that are compared with one another.[37]

This postulate, the so-called Archimedean axiom that we discussed in Chapter 4, can be interpreted (1) as claiming that when one magnitude *A* is *greater* than *B* then *A* *exceeds* *B* and (2) as defining 'exceeds' as 'being greater than a "definite" amount' where 'definite'

---

[35] Sextus Empiricus, *Hypotyposeis* (*PH*) 3. 79–80.
[36] *Plutarch's Moralia*, xiii. 2, 819, n. *d*.
[37] *De sphaera et cylindro*, post. 5, in *Archimede*, ed. Mugler, i. (Paris, 1970), 11.

has the following sense: *A* exceeds *B* by a *definite* amount $C = (A - B)$ just in case, by some finite number *n* of additions of *C* to itself, any give magnitude comparable to *A* and *B* can be surpassed. According to the interpretation of Dijksterhuis, which I am adopting, the content of the postulate

may be briefly summed up as follows: if two magnitudes satisfy the axiom of Eudoxus in respect of each other, their difference also satisfies this assumption in respect of any magnitude of the same kind homogenous with both.

To express it in modern terms, [Archimedes] excludes the existence of actual infinitesimals; the magnitudes he is going to discuss are to form Eudoxian systems.[38]

A possibility—although not much more than that—is that Chrysippus, in maintaining that a magnitude *A* can be 'greater than but not exceed' *B*, means to deny the axiom of Archimedes, who was his almost exact contemporary. If this is so, Chrysippus is claiming that *A* can be greater than *B* by an indiscriminable amount ε which is an infinitesimally small amount in the following sense: there is no natural number *n* such that ε added to itself *n* times exceeds *B* or *A* (or any magnitude that can stand in a definite ratio to them).[39]

According to this possibility, Stoic indiscriminably small differences would gain not only an ontological status but a mathematical one. Over the years a number of scholars have entertained the possibility of a Stoic conception of infinitesimal magnitudes. Perhaps most recently, this idea has been hinted at in connection with the cone paradox by Long and Sedley:

The two adjacent faces cannot be perfectly equal, yet there is no finite quantity by which the one exceeds the other. (Similar agonies can result from an attempt in arithmetic to find a difference between ten and nine-point-nine recurring.)[40]

The problem, of course, is that in real analysis there are no infinitesimals: there is no quantity that is non-null but less than every positive 'finite quantity'; and there is no difference between ten and 'nine-point-nine recurring' *without end*. Long and Sedley (following Sambursky) implicitly connect these Chrysippean 'agonies' with a sort of crude fumbling toward 'the difficult mathematical notion of con-

---

[38] *Archimedes*, 148–9.
[39] See 'Eudoxus' axiom', Euclid 5, def. 4.
[40] *The Hellenistic Philosophers*, i. 302.

vergence on a limit'.[41] But the standard contemporary δ, ϵ-method of explicating convergence on a limit is, in effect, a way of dismissing such 'agonies' as the result of mathematical mistakes and of showing that there is no need for the inconsistent notion of infinitesimals. That is, despite the Leibnizian notation dy/dx for the first derivative (for any x) of a function $f(x) = y$ that specifies y as a value of x, the standard contemporary mathematical analysis does not understand 'dx' (or 'dy') as specifying some supposedly infinitesimally small value of 'x'. Rather, 'dy/dx' signifies the limit of the difference quotient '$\Delta y/\Delta x$' ($|y - y_0|/|x - x_0|$), as the value of 'x' approaches ever more closely to x_0. And the δ, ϵ-method of defining a limit uses only the *finite* real-valued intervals δ and ϵ to define the limit of $f(x) = y$ as the value of 'x' approaches x_0: A is this limit if and only if, for every positive real-valued interval ϵ, there is some positive real-value interval δ such that $|y - A| < \epsilon$ if both $0 < |x - x_0| < \delta$ and x is a member of the domain of the function.

The δ, ϵ-method of interpreting convergence (as well as its finitistic ancient analogue, the method of exhaustion, employed by Archimedes and others) depends quite directly on the acceptance of Archimedes' axiom: if one magnitude is greater than another, then it exceeds that magnitude by a *definite, finite* amount, an amount that when added to itself n times, for some natural number n, exceeds any given finite quantity.

I believe that if Chrysippus was a victim of the 'agonies' noted by Long and Sedley (as he may well have been), it is much more likely that he was led to a denial of the Archimedean axiom for his 'indiscriminably small differences ϵ' than to an analysis of the δ, ϵ sort, the effect of which would be to deny any special mathematical status to such differences. In an earlier essay I examined Chrysippean indiscriminably small intervals not in terms of the mathematics of real analysis and its δ, ϵ-analysis of convergence to a limit but in terms of the non-standard analysis developed by the contemporary mathematician Abraham Robinson and its divisible infinitesimals.[42] My purpose in that paper was to explore the extent to which the infinitesimals of Robinson's non-standard analysis could (*a*) provide a resolution of Zeno's arrow paradox and (*b*) could accommodate some puzzling Stoic doctrines concerning spatial magnitude, time, and

[41] Ibid.
[42] White, 'Zeno's Arrow, Divisible Infinitesimals, and Chrysippus', 239–54.

locomotion. Although I probably did not make the point as clearly as I should have done, I did not mean to suggest that Chrysippus developed anything close to a coherent *mathematical* doctrine of infinitesimals.

Indeed, there are various layers of plausibility that may be distinguished with respect to the interpretation of Stoic physical doctrine I have been pursuing. First, it seems to me very likely that Chrysippus (and perhaps other Stoics) did possess some concept of indiscriminable differences in magnitude as very small, not precisely bounded, and theoretically divisible intervals. Second and more doubtful, but still, in my view, quite plausible, is the hypothesis that these fuzzy ε-intervals were accorded a special *ontological* as well as an epistemological status. In other words, they 'take the place of' points or other limit entities in the actual, physical world. More doubtful yet although, I think, just possible is the hypothesis that Chrysippus accorded these ε-intervals some *mathematical* status by denying that some such principle as the Archimedean axiom applies to them. Although the restriction of Archimedes' axiom is an important step in formulating a mathematically coherent conception of infinitesimal magnitudes, such a restriction does not, in itself, constitute anything like a mathematical theory of infinitesimals. And it seems *prima facie* quite unlikely that Chrysippus (or any other philosopher or mathematician of antiquity, for that matter) might have proceeded, mathematically, beyond the denial of the Archimedean axiom.

If, by some chance, Chrysippus did conceive his indiscriminable differences as infinitesimal intervals, in the sense of intervals that are so small that they do not satisfy the Archimedean axiom, it is perhaps worth noting that such Chrysippean intervals would share two additional properties of the contemporary infinitesimals of Robinson's non-standard analysis.

First, Chrysippean indiscriminably small intervals evidently would be infinitely divisible in the same way that any standard, finite magnitude is. According to Diogenes Laertius,

Chrysippus says that [division] is infinite ⟨not *to* an infinite⟩; for there is not something infinite at which the division arrives. Rather, it is inexhaustible. (D.L. 7. 150)

This statement looks, of course, very much like an expression of the classical, Aristotelian account of the meaning of 'division to infinity'. At the very least, it precludes reaching an infinitely small *terminus* of division beyond which division cannot proceed. In the case of Robinson's theory, there is an ambiguity with respect to '*terminus* of infinite division'. Standard *finite* division (e.g. bisection) of a finite quantity yields only increasingly small *finite* quantities. *Infinite* division may be said to 'reach a *terminus*' in the form of infinitesimal quantities, quantities that do not satisfy the Archimedean axiom. But such a quantity is not a *terminus* in the sense of an indivisible end of division, for it is itself divisible.

A more intriguing analogy occurs with respect to indiscriminably small differences conceived in terms of Sextus' category of 'small but not precisely bounded' intervals. If, as I suspect, this category represents an actual Stoic concept, it seems plausible that it originates from the fact that—particularly at the micro-level—it makes no sense to think of intervals as precisely bounded because there are no limit entities *kath' hupostasin* to serve as their bounds. There is an analogous lack of precise bounds for Robinson's infinitesimals. Not only are Robinson infinitesimals divisible (i.e. for each infinitesimal there is a smaller one); it is also the case that, for each infinitesimal interval, there is a greater one, still infinitesimal. Moreover, in Robinson's field of hyper-real numbers into which the infinitesimals are 'fitted', there is no smallest standard real number, greater than all infinitesimals. Consequently, there is a Dedekind discontinuity between the class of infinitesimals and the class of standard real numbers (linearly ordered in terms of the greater-than-or-equal-to relation). Consequently, the infinitesimal gap in Robinson's field of hyper-real numbers between zero and the beginning of the standard, positive reals cannot be assigned a precise size or measure either in terms of some *definite* infinitesimal or in terms of some standard, positive real number. The gap is, as it were, infinitesimally small, generally speaking, but no *specific* infinitesimal number can be assigned to it as its size.

Yet even the basic conceptual fit between Stoic indiscriminable differences and Robinson's mathematical infinitesimals is hardly perfect. If we think of an indiscriminable difference ε in purely epistemic terms, it seems to me implausible to suppose that such an interval would satisfy the principal characteristic of Robinson's infinitesimals, namely, their failure to satisfy the Archimedean axiom. For if we identify an indiscriminably short interval ε with an infinitesimal and identify an interval of discriminable length with one of some finite, standard length, it seems unintuitive to maintain that ε added to itself *any* finite number of times will fail to yield an interval of discriminable length. The fact of the matter is that, even were we to admit infinitesimals via Robinson's non-standard analysis or some theory similar to it, it makes sense to assume that there are epistemically indiscriminable differences in magnitude that are intervals of (standard) *finite* length and, hence, are intervals that *do* satisfy the Archimedean axiom. That is, for some finite n, the result of adding such an indiscriminable interval to itself at least n times will be discriminable. Suppose that we accord an ontological status and not merely an epistemic one to indiscriminably small, fuzzy intervals ε. The question whether such intervals are also to be thought of as true mathematical infinitesimals arises again with respect to a Stoic conception of locomotion, to which I next turn.

LOCOMOTION: THE DOCTRINE OF MOTION *ATHROŌS*

The doctrine of locomotion *kata athroun* or *athroōs*, 'all at once' (or, to use Sorabji's phrase, 'at one go'[43]) seems to be associated with the Stoics by Sextus Empiricus. In *Adversus mathematicos* 10 Sextus attributes (at the beginning of the passage: *M* 10. 123) the view in question to those who maintain that 'all things are divided "to infinity"'. He also implies but does not actually state[44] (at the end of the passage: *M* 10. 142) that the conception of motion *athroōs* that he has been criticizing is due to the Stoics. There is a parallel passage, without any specific attribution, at *Hypotyposeis* (*PH*) 3. 76–81. Sorabji has discussed the later history of the conception of motion *athroōs*, which reappears in Damascius, the last of the Platonic Successors,[45] and makes its way into Islamic thought.[46] In this section, I shall be principally concerned with an investigation of what the conception of motion *athroōs* through a divisible interval might have meant to the Stoics. My assumption (an assumption of which we cannot, I fear, be

---

[43] *Time, Creation and the Continuum*, 53.

[44] What he actually states is that the Stoics' conception of motion involves the infinite divisibility of 'bodies, places, and times' (*M* 10. 142). His strategy in the preceding passage has been to argue that, whether motion over 'divisible intervals' of spatial magnitude is analysed in terms of motion *athroōs* or in terms of the moving body's always traversing a former sub-interval of distance in a former sub-interval of time, the concept of motion over such divisible intervals gives rise to paradox.

[45] Damascius *apud* Simplicius, *In phys. (corollarium de tempore)*, CAG 9, 796 ff.

[46] Sorabji, *Time, Creation and the Continuum*, 52–63, 384–402.

completely certain[47]) is that the conception was part of some Stoic doctrine of motion.

In the 'Corollary concerning Time', appended to his commentary on Book 4 of Aristotle's *Physics*, Simplicius discusses Damascius' version of the doctrine. There it is suggested that the doctrine of motion *athroōs* was employed by those who 'confute the argument of Zeno'.[48] The parallel passages (*PH* 3. 76; *M* 10. 139–41) from Sextus suggest that the doctrine was used as a means of circumventing a version of Zeno's Dichotomy paradox, the version according to which the convergence of bisections is to the place of departure, i.e. the *terminus a quo* rather than *terminus ad quem* of a given finite interval of distance. Before something that is (continuously) traversing a given interval of distance reaches the *terminus ad quem*, it must first reach the mid-point; but before it can reach the mid-point, it must reach the mid-point of the first half (the quarter-point of the entire distance); but before it can reach the quarter-point, it must reach the mid-point of the first quarter (the eighth-point of the entire distance); *etc. ad infinitum*. Sextus' argument is that, according to a conception of motion *kata to proteron proteron* (i.e. motion in which 'the former [part is traversed] before' the latter), 'it is impossible to discover among the infinity [of sub-intervals thus generated] any that is first from which the thing which is said to move will move' (*PH* 3. 76).

As we noted in Chapter 4, there was not a quick and easy mathematical resolution of the Dichotomy available in antiquity, a resolution whereby the distance traversed could be *mathematically identified* with the sum of an infinite series of addenda (i.e. with the limit of the infinite sequence of partial sums). In antiquity, the Aristotelian analysis came closest to the standard, contemporary resolution. Aristotle holds that there is no 'first' distance away from the *terminus a quo* that the continuously moving body traverses. But in order to prevent this fact about continuous motion from creating a problem with respect to the Dichotomy, Aristotle appeals to the metaphysics of his actuality–potentiality distinction. There need be no concern about there being no 'first sub-motion' completed by the moving body because the *continuously* moving body does not *actually*

---

[47] It is at least conceivable that it was *Sextus* who, in devising arguments against the possibility of motion through an infinitely divisible distance (a doctrine that undoubtedly was Stoic), adopted the conception as one of the 2 ways such motion could occur as part of his strategy of argument.

[48] Simplicius, *In phys.*, CAG 9, 796. 32–797. 2.

complete the infinite series of sub-motions postulated by the Dichotomy. And the only sense in which the body may be said *potentially* to do so is the 'harmless' sense in which the entire distance traversed may be bisected in the manner of the Dichotomy. The product of this process of bisection cannot be regarded as a totality because the process generating it is an ∞-infinite process and, hence, cannot, in principle, be regarded as completable.

For those ancients who did not wish to accept the metaphysics undergirding Aristotle's solution of the Dichotomy, it remains a problem. Advocates of a quantum conception of spatial magnitude, of course, have a ready-made solution to the problem, since the 'infinite bisection' giving rise to the puzzle is impossible and the spatial quanta constituting *any* finite distance are finite in number and discretely (successively) ordered. It is possible that Stoics, who may not have wished to embrace the Peripatetic metaphysics of potentiality and actuality and who certainly did not wish to adopt a quantum conception of spatial magnitude, turned to the idea of motion *athroōs* through a *divisible* interval of distance. This idea may initially seem to be only a 'minor variant' of the quantum conception. That is, it may seem that motion, when subjected to fine-grain analysis, is resolved into 'jumps' that are, individually, effected 'at one go' rather than part-by-part. The only difference from the quantum model will be that such indivisible jumps traverse small spatial distances that are *theoretically* divisible *ad infinitum*. There apparently is no sense in which an indivisible jump over such an interval so divides it, however. This idea of indivisible jumps 'over' theoretically divisible distances is susceptible to a variety of interpretations. In what follows I explore the most important of these interpretations.

Motion Athroōs *as Discontinuous Motion*

According to what is perhaps the most straightforward way of interpreting the notion of motion *athroōs*, motion becomes discontinuous and, indeed, is resolved into discrete jumps. According to such an interpretation, while Stoics held that time and spatial magnitude are infinitely divisible and continuous, they postulated a discrete, quantum structure for motion. So their solution to the Zenonian Dichotomy is very similar to that of a pure quantum theory of the sort discussed in Chapter 6. Although—unlike the account of a pure quantum theory— the distance traversed may be infinitely divisible, the motion involved in traversing it is not. There is a first indivisible movement away from the *terminus a quo*, in the form of a jump; and, indeed, all of the object's motion across a finite interval is resolved into such jumps or displacements. The difficulties that arise for such a conception of motion are similar to those discussed in Chapter 6. But in this case of a mixed quantum conception of motion, according to which motion comes in quanta but time and spatial magnitude do not, the problems are perhaps more severe.

The passages from Sextus do not make it clear whether motion *athroōs* over a divisible spatial distance is to be understood as a literally instantaneous displacement, a displacement that takes no time whatsoever to occur. But this seems one possible interpretation of the doctrine. If this interpretation is adopted, 'motion' becomes radically discontinuous: jumps or instantaneous displacements are interlarded with pauses, *periods* of time in which the 'moving' object remains stationary in a particular *locus*. Such pauses are necessary because, without them, *any* motion through *any* spatial distance would apparently occur instantaneously, a consequence that clearly does violence to the senses and to reason. Despite its retention of infinitely divisible time and spatial magnitude, such an analysis of motion would be virtually the same as that of Diodorus Cronus, who evidently believed that his account *eliminates kinēsis*, in a fundamental metaphysical sense. It is perhaps noteworthy that, with respect to an assessment of this interpretation of the Stoic conception of motion *athroōs*, we do not have evidence that the Stoics held that their theory of motion in any sense eliminates motion. Nor do their critics make *this* particular criticism of the Stoic theory.

Another possibility, suggested by the quotation of Damascius from Simplicius' 'Corollary concerning Time', is that a jump or movement occurring *athroōs* somehow 'takes time'. The quotation ends with a puzzling claim:

consequently, that in which the present motion occurs is a present time which, like the motion, is infinitely divisible; for each is continuous, and everything that is continuous is infinitely divisible.[49]

The first puzzle concerning this claim is how the 'present motion' (*kinēsis hē enestōsa*), which Damascius is evidently identifying with a jump (*halma*), could be conceived as infinitely divisible. Simplicius' verdict, somewhat simplified, is that Damascius' conception is

[49] Damascius *apud* Simplicius, *In phys.*, CAG 9, 797. 11–13.

incoherent. The idea of an *actually* (*energeiai*) present time, demarcated by a present jump (*bēma*) and bounded on either side by a punctal now, is inconsistent with a continuous nature of time, the nature or being of which is its 'becoming' (*to tou chronou eidos en tōi ginesthai to einai echon*).[50]

Moreover, if even a supposedly minimal motion is conceived as infinitely divisible at least with respect to the time it takes, can it not be divided—at least in theory—into linearly ordered proper parts in the manner of Zeno's Dichotomy? And will its status as a transition that is effected in one go (*athroōs*)—rather than gradually, part by part—not be vitiated? Sorabji suggests that the answer is that 'the leap can be thought of as infinitely divisible, because the distance traversed would be infinitely divisible, and another jump could be across a shorter distance'.[51] Note that Sorabji says '*another* jump': *this* jump cannot 'take time' in the sense that in a shorter time *this* body making *this* jump traverses a shorter distance on pain of fatally compromising the very notion of motion *kata athroun*, as contrasted with 'gradual' motion or motion *kata to proteron proteron*.

Consequently, if a jump is claimed to 'take time', that claim must mean, simply, that the body is at rest for a certain period of time in position *A* and there is an instantaneous displacement to a position *B* some divisible interval of distance away. The displacement of the body takes no time to occur; and the displaced body is located at none of the intervening possible places as a result of its displacement. In other words, this conception turns out to be identical to the conception we just examined: motion is resolved into a sequence of interlarded jumps and pauses. The only other way that I see in which a jump could both 'take time' and remain a *jump*—as opposed to gradual, divisible motion—is for the body 'moving' from *A* to *B* to disappear at a certain instant from *A* and at some later instant reappear at *B*, having been nowhere at all during the intervening interval of time. This would be a conception of a motion *athroōs* even more paradoxical than one that resolves motion into a sequence of pauses and instantaneous jumps.

Sorabji notes that

Damascius seems to think that all bodies, and hence the stars in particular, move by leaps, and stellar leaps are so arranged that they serve as a clock, marking off corresponding leaps in time. The combination of divisibility and

---

[50] Ibid. 798. 24–6.
[51] *Time, Creation and the Continuum*, 53.

indivisibility which we have seen to belong to the leaps of *motion* is supposed to be transferred to the *temporal* leaps. But it is hard to see with temporal leaps how they can be indivisible. Presumably, time is thought of as standing still during a stellar rest, and as suddenly moving on at its end, without ever advancing part way. That is the idea, but why should we not give sense to the idea of a period of celestial rest having progressed part way, by making use of *additional* clocks which are out of phase with the celestial clock by amounts as small as we please?[52]

This passage points up the difficulty of the 'combination of divisibility and indivisibility', to use Sorabji's phrase, that seems to be implicit in the conception of motion *athroōs*. Sorabji's plausible suggestion is that both spatial magnitude and time are infinitely divisible in the sense that there is, in principle, no lower bound to the spatial distance or temporal interval with respect to which a kinetic leap or instance of motion *athroōs* could occur. But, according to the present interpretation, any *given* instance of motion *athroōs* will be discontinuous: the body moving *athroōs* across a divisible distance will apparently not traverse any sub-distance in a shorter time. Since, according to the argument above, a body moving *athroōs* does not literally 'take time' to effect its jump, it is easier to see why, as Sorabji notes, that when he speaks of 'leaps' of *time*, Damascius refers 'to the intervening period between two instantaneous transitions, a period in which, as we shall see, time is supposed to stand still'.[53]

Therefore, according to this account, locomotion is radically discontinuous—constituted of instantaneous, indivisible jumps alternating with periods of rest, when the moving body remains stationary at a spatial *locus*. The theoretical divisibility of spatial magnitude and time means only that, in principle, there is no lower bound either on the distance instantaneously traversed or on the temporal intervals of rest separating such instantaneous transitions. It is possible, of course, that the Stoics did develop such a conception of motion. But the very fact that the conception really is a *quantum* conception of motion, very similar to conceptions discussed in Chapter 6 despite the fact that it does not assume a quantum conception of either spatial magnitude or time, may suggest that it is somewhat anomalous, considered as a part of that theory. For the general tenor of Stoic physical theory seems to involve considerable emphasis

---

[52] Ibid. 55.
[53] Ibid. 53–4.

on continuity, at least in an intuitive sense of this term. Therefore, it is worth considering several alternative accounts of motion *athroōs*.

Motion Athroōs *as Infinitesimally Brief Motion*

As we previously noted, if we consider the version of the Zenonian Dichotomy in which the distance to be traversed (say the unit interval [0,1]) is decomposed into an infinite sequence ([1/2,1], [1/4,1/2], [1/8,1/4], etc. *ad infinitum*) converging to the *terminus a quo* (0), we note that the *terminus a quo* is not an element of even the 'infinite union' of these closed sub-intervals. Even were one thus to consider the sub-intervals as a totality and to regard as unobjectionable the fact that this sequence of sub-intervals has no first member, it might still seem that an initial *motus* is required to connect up the *terminus a quo* with the sequence of Zenonian sub-intervals regarded as a totality. We here have another of the 'agonies' alluded to by Long and Sedley.[54] There is no finite distance by which the *terminus a quo* (the '0 point') precedes the totality of initial ('left-hand') points of the Zenonian sub-intervals, although the 0–point does indeed precede *all* such points. As we saw in Chapter 4, the standard analysis would address this problem by the *metrical* identification of the left-closed interval [0,1] and the left-open interval (0,1], the latter being identified as the 'infinite union' of the Zenonian sub-intervals [1/2,1], [1/4,1/2], [1/8,1/4], ...

The topology and real analysis underlying this resolution of the problem were not worked out in antiquity, however. Hence, the problem—if recognized—would have seemed more severe than it now does. The 'small but not precisely bounded' intervals mentioned by Sextus *could* have been invoked to solve the problem and bridge the apparent gap between the *terminus a quo* and the Zenonian sub-intervals. In order to avoid contradiction, such an interval would have to be infinitesimal, i.e. a quantity not satisfying Archimedes' axiom in the sense that no finite additions of such a quantity itself will ever equal or exceed any finite (real-valued) quantity. We noted earlier the implausibility of identifying such infinitesimals with the indiscriminably small differences between two (discriminable) magnitudes.

There are additional problems with invoking infinitesimals to resolve this version of the Zenonian Dichotomy. First of all, there is no

[54] *The Hellenistic Philosophers*, i. 302.

first (nor last) infinitesimal magnitude that the moving body traverses: a coherent theory of infinitesimals (and a theory that satisfies the Stoic requirement of divisibility *ad infinitum* of magnitude) will not postulate a smallest infinitesimal. Second, there is no first *finite* distance traversed. The infinite process of Zenonian bisection is in no way curtailed within the context of a coherent conception of infinitesimal magnitudes. In fact, a non-Archimedean theory of infinitesimals such as Robinson's results in 'more' divisibility rather than 'less'.

The fact that an interpretation of the 'small but not precisely bounded' intervals in terms of true infinitesimals in no way yields an initial sub-interval for the Zenonian Dichotomy seems to me significant. Of course, it is extremely unlikely that any ancient philosopher or mathematician could have worked out mathematical details of a conception of true infinitesimals much beyond the claim that the Archimedean principle does not apply to them. But, aside from this consideration, it seems that such a conception would not have been regarded by ancient philosophers or mathematicians as a useful tool for dealing with the Dichotomy. Ian Mueller remarks that 'the standard Greek notion of composition appears to be juxtaposition or concatenation'.[55] 'Concatenation' and 'juxtaposition' imply, I think, not only a *discrete* ordering of elements but also—if we are dealing with a concatenation/juxtaposition that is supposed to yield an *actual* composite—an ordering in which there is a first (and last) element.

Aristotle is able to avoid the Dichotomy by the invocation of metaphysics. The sub-intervals yielded by (either form of) the Dichotomy do not constitute an *actual* totality. Consequently, we need not worry about the mathematical or physical *identification* of the 'collection of all sub-intervals' with the original interval.

But for an ancient thinker who might have been tempted to identify the unit interval with the concatenation/juxtaposition of Zenonian sub-intervals, the absence of an initial sub-interval remains a problem. A theory of infinitesimals, if mathematically coherent, will not be of any help in the resolution of this problem. What is needed is the conception of a small, finite interval which is immune to the trouble-making infinitely continuable process of Zenonian bisection, but which also does not yield the paradoxical-seeming consequence of discontinuous, quantum motion. On the face of it, these seem to be incompatible

[55] 'Geometry and Scepticism', in J. Barnes, J. Brunschwig, M. Burnyeat, and M. Schofield (eds.), *Science and Speculation: Studies in Hellenistic Theory and Practice*, (Cambridge, 1982), 82.

desiderata. In the next section, however, I explore a final interpretation of motion *athroōs* that attempts to reconcile the continuity of motion with the avoidance of an infinite, Zenonian bisection.

Motion Athroōs *as Continuous but 'Fuzzy' Motion*

Just as we can discriminate between the length of a metre stick and that of a yard stick, we think that we can discriminate 'smooth' motion across an interval equivalent to that difference of magnitude.[56] It is plausible, however, that as we decrease this interval we arrive at a 'small but not precisely bounded' interval ε of magnitude which is so small that we cannot detect continuous motion—or, indeed, any motion—across it. Such a spatial interval, as well as motion across it, are indiscriminable. It seems reasonable to assume that we reach such a magnitude ε as a consequence of a *finite* number of bisections of any finite interval of magnitude. Since I am assuming the radical interpretation of the Stoic removal of limit entities from the physical world, Zenonian bisection of a discriminable interval of magnitude proceeds as follows. It is possible to bisect a unit interval 'within a margin' $1/2 \pm$ ε; and it is possible to bisect the remainder, yielding a remainder $1/4 \pm$ ε; *etc*. But eventually (i.e. in a finite number of steps) we will arrive at an indiscriminably small remainder $\leqslant$ ε.

According to the radical interpretation of the elimination of limit entities, this picture has an ontological as well as an epistemic significance. That is, it is not merely a practical or physical limitation on the accuracy of our perception or of our measuring devices[57] that yields, in a finite number of steps, an indiscriminably small and 'not precisely bounded' (*ou pros akribeian periōrismenon*) interval. The fuzziness represented by such an interval ε could not, in principle, be eliminated or lessened; rather, it represents an ontological indeterminacy that is built into the physical world, a world in which there are no limit entities.

What, then, of motion *athroōs*? One could, of course, conceive of

---

[56] Of course, at least since the advent of cinematography, we have realized that, when a discretely ordered sequence of images is passed very quickly through our visual field, we are easily fooled into thinking that we are perceiving continuous motion.

[57] There has not been much discussion, in so far as I am aware, of ancient *theoretical* accounts of the effect on scientific knowledge of physical reality by such limitations on the accuracy of measurements. A very interesting, seminal piece on this topic is G. E. R. Lloyd, 'Observational Error in Later Greek Science, in Barnes *et al.* (eds.), *Science and Speculation*, 128–64.

such motion as a quantum jump, an instantaneous displacement across an indiscriminably small but finite, theoretically divisible, and 'fuzzy' (not precisely bounded) interval ε. But to do so results in a discontinuous conception of motion with its paradoxical-seeming consequences, which were discussed in Chapter 6 and which Sextus makes the most of in his account of motion *athroōs*. To begin my 'preferred account' of motion *athroōs*, I turn to Long and Sedley:

A less risky, and much more Stoic, reading is that these are portions of motion which are completed *legato* and not in stages, It is, after all, their view that limits subsist only as constructs of thought. Thus there are only as many dividing points on a runner's journey as anyone may choose to mark off in thought. At some point our mental power to mark further divisions will fail us, and we will be left with an undivided, although divisible, portion of distance, which can consequently be traversed with a single undivided motion.[58]

Elaborating on and modifying this suggestion a bit, I should like to make the following suggestions. Motion *athroōs* across an indiscriminably small interval ε would be *legato*, in a certain sense. That is, ε is not an indivisible quantum but a theoretically divisible interval. But the division within it is the result of a 'precisifying' of a linear ordering relation that is, at the level of ε, ontologically fuzzy/indeterminate. That is, the before/after relation *fully* obtains for *loci* separated by intervals of magnitude greater than ε. But, as we get to *loci* separated by intervals of ε or less, it is neither determinately true nor determinately false that one is before the others: the value of the before/after relation for such points is somewhere within the open interval $(0,1)$. Of course, we can precisify the before/after relation in such a way that we can theoretically stipulate, with as fine a degree of accuracy as we like, that points within a distance ε are either before or after each other. But this stipulation will be 'theoretical' in the sense of 'arbitrary': that is, it will not have the same ontological reality that the separation of points by a distance greater than ε has.

Motion across an interval of magnitude ε is not exactly quantum displacement. We *can* always precisify within the interval, to whatever degree of precision we like, in such a way as to say that less of ε is traversed in less of the indiscriminably small time-interval in which the continuously moving body traverses ε. None the less, infinite Zenonian bisection of ε or of the motion across it does not correspond with the same sort of physical reality to which corresponds *finite* bisection of a

[58] *The Hellenistic Philosophers*, i. 303–4.

larger interval (or the motion across it). That 'ontologically real' bisection is finite because it must terminate in a fuzzy or indeterminate interval $\leqslant \varepsilon$. In other words, *real* bisection of spatial magnitude, time, or motion always occurs with respect to a fuzzy margin of indeterminacy $\pm \varepsilon$, a fact which means that *real* bisection is finite. I would reiterate the point that, according to the radical interpretation of the Stoic elimination of limit entities, this indeterminacy was conceived by the Stoics in ontological as well as in epistemic terms.

In response to the claim of Long and Sedley that, against the Stoic conception of motion *athroōs*, Sextus 'very pertinently argues the necessity *in physical fact* that any motion whatever possess constituent stages',[59] my imaginary Stoic could admit the 'theoretical divisibility' *in some theoretical sense* of motion *athroōs* and of the fuzzy, indiscriminably small spatial interval ε across which such motion occurs. But such a Stoic could claim that such divisibility cannot be conceived in terms of ontologically real Zenonian bisection. Ontologically real division is not really precise but always must be understood in terms of a fuzzy margin $\pm \varepsilon$. And such division will take only a finite number of steps to reach the indiscriminably small interval of indeterminacy $\leqslant \varepsilon$. As I have emphasized, this fact is an ontological fact about ineliminable indeterminacy characterizing the structure of continuous physical reality (spatial magnitude, time, and motion), a fact which derives from the radical interpretation of the Stoic elimination of limit entities from physical reality.

CONCLUSION

One fairly obvious conclusion to be drawn from this and preceding chapters pertains to the great variety of senses, ranging from 'pre-analytical' to technical, that can be assigned to 'continuity' and its cognates. The Stoic removal of limit entities from the physical world results in a sort of intuitive or 'pre-analytical continuity' of *to holon*, the entire physical cosmos. One physical object is so topologically interconnected with its environment that there are no joints, so to speak, between them; they insensibly blend into one another just as the metrical greater/less-length-than relation insensibly blends into the same-length-as relation and continuous motion insensibly blends into

[59] Ibid. 304.

rest. And, as I have now suggested more than once, continuity in this intuitive sense is to be thought of not just as an epistemic limitation but as an ontological fact deriving from the removal of limit entities from the physical world and the ontological indeterminacy introduced by the elimination of such limits *kath' hupostasin*. In effect, regions of indeterminacy/fuzziness are substituted for precise limits in the forms of surfaces, boundaries, lines, and points.

It is continuity in this intuitive sense that particularly interests Sambursky. He gives a physical account of it in terms of the Stoic notion of *tonikē kinēsis* or 'tensional motion':

the picture we get of the Stoic notion of hexis is a fairly clear one. Physical bodies have coherence and definite properties by virtue of the everlasting movement of a very tenuous and elastic medium pervading them. Since matter is conceived as strictly continuous, the medium performs its tensional fluctuating motions within matter itself, being united with it in total mixture. The dynamic concept of hexis by which the physical state of a body is defined is thus akin to what we would call today a field of force. The Stoic notion of continuity, applied to the phenomena of the physical world, has therefore led, by the intrinsic logic of scientific thought, to the concept of forces acting in accordance with the principle of continuity, these forces being the cause of the cohesion of matter as well as of its specific physical qualities. If we exclude Empedocles ... it was the Stoic School who first conceived forces of a well-defined nature as being active in matter and giving it definite shape. The ingenious picture of tensional motion by which the Stoics gave expression to the continuous as well as the dynamic character of this force, at the same time confining its field of action to a body which as a whole might well be at rest, is similar to that of a standing wave or stationary vibration in modern physics.[60]

To oversimplify, Sambursky attributes the lack of true limit entities ('geometrical' boundaries, surfaces, etc.) and the resulting fuzziness in the Stoic conception of the physical world to their conception of physical phenomena as the product of *tonikē kinēsis*, 'fields of force' the dynamic or oscillatory character of which produces this fuzziness in nature.

Sambursky fully recognizes, I believe, the speculative character of his view. He is also aware that this view both goes beyond the bounds of interpretative safety and must, when we attempt to conceptualize it in any detail, seem parasitic on later, much more sophisticated scientific theories. His picture is none the less an interesting one and may be more or less correct. It is, I believe, largely compatible with the

[60] *Physics of the Stoics*, 31–2.

interpretation of the Stoic conception of spatial magnitude, time, and motion that I have developed in this chapter. But—as in previous chapters—I have here concentrated on the formal, structural analysis of these physical quantities rather than on Stoic 'physics', in Sambursky's more inclusive sense of that concept.

Peroration

There is a tradition of concluding a book such as this with a peroration. In the case of a book containing as much technical and historical material as this one, there is something to be said for this tradition—for concluding with a peroration in the dictionary sense of 'emphatic recapitulation or summary'. I should like to introduce my brief peroration with a rather long quotation taken from the introductory essay (by A. D. Aleksandrov) to the mathematical *summa* edited by Aleksandrov, Kolmogorov, and Lavrent'ev. In a section entitled 'The conflict of opposites: discrete and continuous', Aleksandrov writes

Here we encounter two contrasting kinds of objects: on the one hand, the indivisible, separate, discrete objects; and on the other, the objects which are completely divisible and yet are not divided into parts but are continuous. Of course, these contrasting characteristics are always united, since there are no absolutely indivisible and no completely continuous objects. Yet these aspects of the objects have an actual existence, and it often happens that one aspect is decisive in one case and other in another.

In abstracting forms from their content, mathematics by this very act sharply divides these forms into two classes, the discrete and the continuous.

The mathematical model of a separate object is the unit, and the mathematical model of a collection of discrete objects is a sum of units, which is, so to speak, the image of pure discreteness, purified of all other qualities. On the other hand, the fundamental, original mathematical model of continuity is the geometric figure: in the simplest case, the straight line.[1]

The opposition between the continuous and the discrete described by Aleksandrov has been the principal theme of this book—and has given the book its title. Aristotle maintains this opposition in a sharp and, from the contemporary perspective, perhaps a rigid way. Although continuous spatial magnitude, time, and motion cannot be

---

[1] 'A General View of Mathematics', in A. D. Aleksandrov, A. N. Kolmogorov, and M. A. Lavrent'ev, (eds). *Mathematics: Its Content, Methods, and Meaning*, trans. S. H. Gould and T. Bartha, i (Cambridge, Mass., 1969), 32.

reduced to what is discrete, the discrete is not ontologically eliminated from the *plenum* that constitutes the cosmos. Discrete *limit entities* are very much a part of Aristotle's topologically continuous world. They are present as surfaces and edges of bodies, as the punctal temporal *termini ad quem* of processes, etc. And, of course, discrete first substances or *tade tina* ('this-suches'), and natural kinds that are 'multiplicities' (*plēthē*) of these first substances, are fundamental Aristotelian metaphysical principles.

Ancient quantum theorists, however, undermined the opposition in the most radical way—by, in effect, eliminating the continuous in favour of the discrete. For reasons we have discussed, the ancient conception of material substance as constituted of discrete quanta gave rise to the idea that (geometrical) mathematical science, because of the assumptions of infinite divisibility and continuity that it makes concerning its subject-matter, is 'false'. That is, geometry does not accurately characterize its subject-matter.

On the other hand, Stoic physical thought emphasizes continuity (in an intuitive sense of the term) in the physical world at the expense of discreteness. According to the interpretation of Stoic physics that I pursued in the last chapter, discrete limit entities are banished from the physical world. Again, for a contemporary version of such a view, I quote Aleksandrov:

But ideally precise geometric forms and absolutely precise values for magnitudes represent abstractions. No concrete object has absolutely precise form nor can any concrete magnitude be measured with absolute accuracy, since it does not even *have* an absolutely accurate value. The length of a line segment, for example, has no sense if one tries to make it precise beyond the limits of atomic dimensions. In every case when one passes beyond well-known limits of quantitative accuracy, there appears a qualitative change in the magnitude, and in general it loses its original meaning. For example, the pressure of a gas cannot be made precise beyond the limits of the impact of a single molecule; electric charge ceases to be continuous when one tries to make it precise beyond the charge on an electron and so forth. In view of the absence in nature of objects of ideally precise form, the assertion that the ratio of the diagonal of a square to the side is equal to the $\sqrt{2}$ not only cannot be deduced with absolute accuracy from immediate measurement but does not even have any absolutely accurate meaning for an actual concrete square.[2]

One characteristic of the view set forth in this quotation would, I believe, be quite appealing to both ancient quantum theorists and

---

[2] Ibid. 31–2.

advocates of our Stoic model. It is the tendency—perhaps somewhat ambivalently expressed in the quotation—to deny the meaningfulness of certain mathematical concepts (or, at least, to suggest the loss of original meaning of these concepts) at the level where these concepts lose their applicability to physical reality. The fact that Aleksandrov believes that there *is* such a level depends, of course, on his acceptance of contemporary physics, with its quantized conception of matter. In this particular respect, the ancient atomists were in a similar position. Although ancient Stoics did not hold a conception of material substance as quantized, it seems likely that they too believed that 'no concrete object has absolutely precise form nor can any concrete magnitude . . . even *have* an absolutely accurate value'.

That such views concerning the physical world should have been interpreted—by both friend and foe, apparently—as undermining standard ancient mathematical science (Euclidean geometry, in particular) is indicative of an ancient philosophy of geometry that ties mathematics quite closely to the physical world. The same connection is conversely illustrated by Aristotle's very geometrical conception of the physical phenomena of spatial magnitude, time, and motion. Such a normative connection between mathematics, even pure mathematics, and physical science outlived its ancient instantiations. Part of the basis of Kronecker's objection to Cantorian mathematics was his belief that Cantor's transfinite mathematics 'lacked (physical) content'. Far from dismissing such criticism, Cantor attempted to argue for such content to his work. And in a recent, influential, and very controversial book, *Mathematics: The Loss of Certainty*,[3] Morris Kline argues as a historical thesis that the divorce of a pure mathematics from physical science has resulted in paradox-mongering and sterility within modern mathematics.

So we see that another perennial theme has also arisen in the ancient material that we have been examining: the constraint, theoretical and operational, on mathematics by physical theory (and any underlying metaphysics that may be associated with that physical theory). And, of course, the other side of the coin is the constraint on physics by currently accepted mathematical theory (and any underlying metaphysics that may be associated with that mathematical theory).

In conclusion, I return to the theme with which I began this

[3] (Oxford, 1980).

peroration—the opposition between continuity and discreteness. At a *mathematical* level, means for overcoming this opposition were not available until the latter part of the nineteenth century. As Aleksandrov says,

In the seventies of the last century there arose a theory of real numbers which represents an interval as a set of points, and correspondingly the range of variation of a variable as a set of real numbers. The continuous again consisted of separate discrete points and the properties of continuity were again expressed in the structure of the set of points that formed it. This conception led to immense progress in mathematics and became dominant.[4]

Ancient mathematics supplied no such aid to Aristotle and his successors in overcoming the opposition between continuity and discreteness.

In the absence of such aid, Aristotle probably was wise to maintain the opposition. And he (perhaps with the aid of ancient geometers) was certainly very clever to maintain this opposition in terms of the related notions of a foundationless ontology of the continuous, the ∞-conception of infinite divisibility, and the metaphysics of potentiality. It seems to me unfair to fault Aristotle for jumbling together mathematics, physics, and metaphysics, although it is arguable that that is what he has done. Great mathematical ideas usually arise within a context of human interests that are not *exclusively* mathematical, in the rather narrow contemporary sense of 'exclusively mathematical'. And such ideas are often sustained and popularized by considerations that may look more metaphysical or physical than mathematical. This claim seems to apply equally to the ancient ∞-conception of infinity and to the Cantorian analysis of continuous magnitudes in terms of point-sets. How one conceives the opposition between the continuous and the discrete, as well as how one conceives the programme of overcoming that opposition, is as much a physical and a metaphysical matter as it is a mathematical matter.

[4] Aleksandrov, 'A General View of Mathematics', 34.

Select Bibliography

I have consulted all the following works, at some stage or other, in preparing the present study, although not all of them are cited in the text. Ancient works are not listed, except in cases where I have made use of notes or commentary accompanying the text or translations. Where I have made use of multiple papers from an anthology, I have cited both the anthology under the editor's name and the individual papers under the names of their authors. Where I have used but one paper from an anthology, a complete reference is given under the name of the author of the paper.

Aleksandrov, A. D., 'A General View of Mathematics', in Aleksandrov *et al.* (eds.), *Mathematics: Its Content, Methods, and Meaning*, i. 1–64.

Aleksandrov, A. D., Kolmogorov, A. N., and Lavrent'ev, M. A. (eds.), *Mathematics: Its Content, Methods, and Meaning*, trans. S. H. Gould and T. Bartha (3 vols., Cambridge, Mass., 1969).

Annas, J., 'Aristotle, Number and Time', *Philosophical Quarterly*, 25: 99 (1975), 97–113.

—— *Aristotle's Metaphysics: Books M and N* (Oxford, 1976).

Apostle, H. G., *Aristotle's Physics* (Grinnell, Ia., 1969).

—— 'Aristotle's Theory of Mathematics as a Science of Quantities', *Philosophia*, 8–9 (1978–9), 154–214.

Asmis, E., *Epicurus' Scientific Method*, Cornell Studies in Classical Philology, 42 (Ithaca, NY, 1984).

Bailey, C., *Epicurus: The Extent Remains* (Oxford, 1926).

—— *The Greek Atomists and Epicurus* (New York, 1964).

Bareuther, R., 'Aristoteles zum Problem des Unendlichen', in Irmscher and Müller (eds.), *Aristoteles als Wissenschafts-Theoretiker*, 127–30.

Barnes, J., Brunschwig, J., Burnyeat, M., and Schofield, M. (eds.), *Science and Speculation: Studies in Hellenistic Theory and Practice* (Cambridge, 1982).

Behnke, H., Bachmann, F., Fladt, K., and Süss, W. (eds.), *Fundamentals of Mathematics*, trans. S. H. Gould (3 vols., Cambridge, Mass., and London, 1974).

Behnke, H., and Grauert, H., 'Points at Infinity', in Behnke *et al.* (eds.), *Fundamentals of Mathematics*, iii. 252–75.

Bignone, E., *Epicuro* (Bari, 1920).

Bostock, D., *Logic and Arithmetic: Natural Numbers* (Oxford, 1974).
—— *Logic and Arithmetic: Rational and Irrational Numbers* (Oxford, 1979).
—— 'Aristotle's Account of Time', *Phronesis*, 25 (1980), 148–69.
—— 'Time and the Continuum: A Discussion of Richard Sorabji, *Time, Creation and the Continuum*', *Oxford Studies in Ancient Philosophy*, 6 (1988), 255–70.
Cantor, G., *Gesammelte Abhandlungen mathematischen und philosophischen Inhalts* (Berlin, 1932).
—— *Contributions to the Founding of the Theory of Transfinite Numbers* (*Beiträge sur Begründung der transfiniten Mengenlehre*, pts. i and ii), trans. P. E. B. Jourdain (New York, n.d.).
Charles, D., 'Aristotle on Hypothetical Necessity and Irreducibility', *Pacific Philosophical Quarterly*, 69: 1 (1988), 1–53.
Cherniss, H. (ed.), *Plutarch's Moralia, in Seventeen Volumes*, vol. xiii, pt. 2, Loeb Classical Library, 470 (London and Cambridge, Mass., 1976).
Cohen, R. S., and Lauden, L., *Physics, Philosophy and Psychology: Essays in Honor of A. Grünbaum* (Dordrecht and Boston, 1983).
Conen, P. F., *Die Zeittheorie des Aristoteles* (Munich, 1964).
Corish, D., 'Aristotle's Attempted Derivation of Temporal Order from That of Movement and Space', *Phronesis*, 3 (1976), 241–51.
—— 'Aristotle on Temporal Order: "Now," "Before," and "After"', *Isis*, 69: 246 (1978), 68–74.
Dauben, J. W., *Georg Cantor: His Mathematics and Philosophy of the Infinite* (Cambridge, Mass. and London, 1979).
Dedekind, R., *Essay on the Theory of Numbers*, trans. W. W. Beman (Chicago and London, 1924).
Denyer, N., 'The Atomism of Diodorus Cronus', *Prudentia*, 13 (1981), 33–45.
DeWitt, N. W., *Epicurus and His Philosophy* (Minneapolis, 1954).
Dijksterhuis, E. J., *Archimedes*, trans. C. Dikshoorn (Princeton, NJ, 1987).
Dillon, J., *The Middle Platonists* (London, 1977).
Drabkin, I. E., 'Notes on Epicurean Kinetics', *Transactions and Proceedings of the American Philological Association*, 69 (1938), 364–74.
—— 'Notes on the Laws of Motion in Aristotle', *American Journal of Philology*, 59 (1938), 60–84.
Düring, I. (ed.), *Naturphilosophie bei Aristoteles und Theophrast* (Heidelberg, 1969).
Edwards, P. (ed.), *The Encylopedia of Philosophy* (8 vols., London and New York, 1967).
Evans, M. G., *The Physical Philosophy of Aristotle* (Albuquerque, 1964).
Feyerabend, P., 'Some Observations on Aristotle's Theory of Mathematics and of the Continuum', *Midwest Studies in Philosophy*, 8 (1983), 67–88.
Fowler, D. H., *The Mathematics of Plato's Academy: A New Reconstruction* (Oxford, 1987).
Furley, D. J., 'Lucretius and the Stoics', *Bulletin of the Institute of Classical Studies*, 13 (1966), 13–33.

—— *Two Studies in the Greek Atomists* (Princeton, NJ, 1967).

—— 'Aristotle and the Atomists on Infinity', in Düring (ed.), *Naturphilosophie bei Aristoteles und Theophrast*, 85–96.

—— 'The Greek Commentators' Treatment of Aristotle's Theory of the Continuous', in Kretzmann (ed.), *Infinity and Continuity*, 17–36.

—— *The Greek Cosmologists*, i. *The Formation of the Atomic Theory and Its Earliest Critics* (Cambridge, 1987).

Galileo Galilei, *Dialogue Concerning Two New Sciences*, trans. H. Crew and A. De Salvio (New York, 1914).

Goldschmidt, V., *Le Système stoïcien et l'idée de temps* (Paris, 1953).

Graeser, A. (ed.), *Mathematik und Metaphysik bei Aristoteles* (Bern, 1987).

Graham, D. W., 'Aristotle's Definition of Motion', *Ancient Philosophy*, 8 (1988), 209–15.

Granger, H., 'The *scala naturae* and the Continuity of Kinds', *Phronesis*, 30 (1985), 181–200.

—— 'Aristotle and the Finitude of Natural Kinds', *Philosophy*, 62 (1987), 523–6.

Gray, J., *Ideas of Space: Euclidean, Non-Euclidean, and Relativistic*, 2nd edn. (Oxford, 1989).

Grünbaum, A., *Modern Science and Zeno's Paradoxes* (London, 1967).

—— *Philosophical Problems of Space and Time*, 2nd edn. (Dordrecht and Boston, 1973).

Hahm, D., 'Chrysippus' Solution to the Democritean Dilemma of the Cone', *Isis*, 63 (1972), 205–20.

Heath, T. L., *Aristarchus of Samos: The Ancient Copernicus* (Oxford, 1913).

—— *A History of Greek Mathematics* (2 vols., Oxford, 1921).

—— *Mathematics in Aristotle* (Oxford, 1949).

—— (ed.), *The Thirteen Books of Euclid's Elements*, with commentary (3 vols., New York, 1956).

Hintikka, J., 'Aristotelian Infinity', rep. in *Time and Necessity: Studies in Aristotle's Theory of Modality* (Oxford, 1973), 114–34.

—— Remes, U., and Knuuttila, S., *Aristotle on Modality and Determinism*, Acta Philosophica Fennica, 29: 1 (Amsterdam, 1977).

Hussey, E., *Aristotle's Physics: Books III and IV* (Oxford, 1983).

Inwood, B., 'The Origin of Epicurus' Concept of the Void', *Classical Philology*, 76: 4 (1981), 273–85.

Irmscher, J., and Müller, R. (eds.), *Aristoteles als Wissenschafts-Theoretiker* (Berlin, 1983).

Jammer, M., 'Energy', in Edwards (ed.), *The Encyclopedia of Philosophy*, ii. 511–17.

Jones, J. F., 'Intelligible Matter and Geometry in Aristotle', *Aperion*, 17 (1983), 94–102.

Kirk, G. S., Raven, J. E., and Schofield, M., *The Presocratic Philosophers: A Critical History with a Selection of Texts*, 2nd edn. (Cambridge, 1983).

Klein, J., *Greek Mathematical Thought and the Origin of Algebra*, trans. E. Brann (Cambridge, Mass., and London, 1968).

Kline, M., *Mathematics: The Loss of Certainty* (Oxford, 1980).

Knorr, W. R., *The Evolution of the Euclidean Elements* (Dordrecht, 1976).

—— 'Archimedes and the Pre-Euclidean Proportion Theory', *Archives Internationales d'Histoire des Sciences*, 28 (1978), 183–244.

—— 'Infinity and Continuity: The Interaction of Mathematics and Philosophy in Antiquity', in Kretzmann (ed.), *Infinity and Continuity*, 112–45.

Konstan, D., 'Problems in Epicurean Physics', *Isis*, 70: 253 (1979), 394–418.

Kosman, L. A., 'Aristotle's Definition of Motion', *Phronesis*, 14 (1969), 40–62.

Krämer, H.-J., *Platonismus und hellenistische Philosophie* (Berlin, 1971).

Kretzmann, N., 'Incipit/Desinit', in Machamer and Turnbull (eds.), *Motion and Time, Space and Matter*, 101–36.

—— 'Aristotle on the Instant of Change [Time Exists—But Hardly, or Obscurely (Physics IV, 10; 217^{b}69–218^{a}330)]', *Aristotelian Society*, supplementary vol. 50 (1976), 91–114.

—— (ed.), *Infinity and Continuity in Ancient and Medieval Thought* (Ithaca, NY, 1982).

Lear, J., 'Aristotle's Philosophy of Mathematics', *Philosophical Review*, 91: 2 (1982), 161–92.

—— *Aristotle: The Desire to Understand* (Cambridge, 1988).

Lee, E. N., Mourelatos, A. P. D., and Rorty, R. M. (eds.), *Exegesis and Argument: Studies in Greek Philosophy Presented to Gregory Vlastos* (Assen, 1973).

Lewis, F. A., 'Teleology and Material/Efficient Causes in Aristotle', *Pacific Philosophical Quarterly*, 69: 1 (1988), 54–98.

Lloyd, G. E. R., *Aristotle: The Growth and Structure of His Thought* (Cambridge, 1968).

—— *Greek Science after Aristotle* (London, 1973).

—— 'Observational Error in Later Greek Science', in Barnes (ed.), *Science and Speculation*, 128–64.

Long, A. A., *Hellenistic Philosophy* (London, 1974).

—— and Sedley, D. N. (eds.), *The Hellenistic Philosophers* (2 vols., Cambridge, 1986, 1987).

Luria, S. Y., 'Die Infinitesimaltheorie der antiken Atomisten', *Quellen und Studien zur Geschichte der Mathematik, Astronomie und Physik*, 2 (1932–3), 106–85.

Lyons, J., *Structural Semantics: An Analysis of Part of the Vocabulary of Plato* (Oxford, 1972).

Machamer, P. K., 'Aristotle on Natural Place and Natural Motion', *Isis*, 69: 248 (1978), 377–87.

—— and Turnbull, R. G. (eds.), *Motion and Time, Space and Matter* (Columbus, OH, 1976).

Mckay, K. L., *Greek Grammar for Students: A Concise Grammar of Classical Attic with Special Reference to Aspect in the Verb* (Canberra, 1977).

Makin, S., 'The Indivisibility of the Atom', *Archiv für Geschichte der Philosophie*, 71 (1989), 125–49.

Massey, G., 'Panel Discussion of Grünbaum's Philosophy of Science: Toward a Clarification of Grünbaum's Conception of an Intrinsic Metric', *Philosophy of Science*, 36: 4 (1969), 33–45.

Mau, J., *Zum Problem des Infinitesimalen bei den antiken Atomisten* (Berlin, 1954).

—— 'Was There a Special Epicurean Mathematics?', in Lee *et al.* (eds.), *Exegesis and Argument*, 421–30.

Mendell, H., 'Topoi on Topos: The Development of Aristotle's Concept of Place', *Phronesis*, 32: 2 (1987), 206–31.

Miller, F. D., Jr., 'Aristotle on the Reality of Time', *Archiv für Geschichte der Philosophie*, 56 (1974), 132–55.

—— 'Aristotle against the Atomists', in Kretzmann (ed.), *Infinity and Continuity*, 87–111.

Milne, E. A., *Kinematic Relativity* (Oxford, 1948).

Modrak, D. K. W., 'Aristotle on the Difference between Mathematics and Physics and First Philosophy', in T. Penner and R. Krant (eds.), *Nature, Knowledge, and Virtue: Essays in Memory of Joan Kung, Apeiron*, 22: 4 (1989), 121–39.

Morrow, G. R., 'Qualitative Change in Aristotle's *Physics*', in Düring (ed.), *Naturphilosophie bei Aristoteles und Theoprast*, 154–67.

Mueller, I., 'Aristotle on Geometrical Objects', *Archiv für Geschichte der Philosophie*, 52 (1970), 156–71.

—— 'Geometry and Scepticism', in Barnes *et al.* (eds.), *Science and Speculation*, 69–95.

—— 'On Some Academic Theories of Mathematical Objects', *Journal of Hellenic Studies*, 106 (1986), 111–20.

Newton, I., *Mathematical Principles of Natural Philosophy*, trans. A. Motte, ed. F. Cajori (Berkeley, Calif., 1946).

North, J. D., 'Finite and Otherwise: Aristotle and Some Seventeenth Century Views', in W. R. Shea (ed.), *Nature Mathematized: Historical and Philosophical Case Studies in Classical Modern Natural Philosophy*, Univ. of Western Ontario Series in the Philosophy of Science, 20 (Dordrecht and Boston, 1983), 113–48.

O'Reilly, P., 'What is Intelligible Matter?', *The Thomist*, 53: 1 (1989), 74–90.

Owen, G. E. L., 'Aristotelian Mechanics', repr. in *Logic, Science, and Dialectic*, 315–33.

—— *Logic, Science, and Dialectic: Collected Papers in Greek Philosophy*, ed. M. Nussbaum (Ithaca, NY, 1986).

—— 'The Platonism of Aristotle', repr. in *Logic, Science, and Dialectic*, 200–20.

—— 'Zeno and the Mathematicians', repr. in *Logic, Science, and Dialectic*, 45–61.

Pedersen, K. M., 'Techniques of the Calculus, 1630–1660', in I. Grattan-Guinness (ed.), *From Calculus to Set Theory, 1630–1910: An Introductory History* (London, 1980), 10–48.

Reichenbach, H., *The Philosophy of Space and Time*, trans. M. Reichenbach and J. Freund (New York, 1958).

Rist, J. M., *Stoic Philosophy* (Cambridge, 1969).

—— *Epicurus: An Introduction* (Cambridge, 1972).

—— (ed.), *The Stoics* (Berkeley, Calif., 1978).

Robinson, A., 'The Metaphysics of the Calculus', in J. Hintikka (ed.), *The Philosophy of Mathematics* (Oxford, 1969), 153–63.

Ross, W. D., *Aristotle's Physics: A Revised Text with Introduction and Commentary* (Oxford, 1936).

Russell, B., 'Mathematics and Metaphysicians', repr. in *Mysticism and Logic* (Totowa, NJ, 1981), 59–74.

Sambursky, S., *The Physical World of the Greeks* (Princeton, NJ, 1956).

—— *Physics of the Stoics* (New York, 1959).

—— *The Physical World of Late Antiquity* (Princeton, NJ, 1962).

Sambursky, S., and Pines, S. (eds.), *The Concept of Time in Late Neoplatonism* (Jerusalem, 1972).

—— *The Concept of Place in Late Neoplatonism* (Jerusalem, 1982).

Schoepsdau, K., 'Zur Tempuslehre des Apollonius Dyskolos', *Glotta*, 56 (1978), 273–94.

Schulz, P.-R., 'Das Verständnis des Raumes bei Lucrez', *Tijdschrift voor Filosofie*, 20 (1958), 17–56.

Scott, W., *Fragmenta Herculanensia* (Oxford, 1885).

Sedley, D., 'Epicurus and the Mathematicians of Cyzicus', *Chronache Ercolanesi*, 6 (1976), 23–54.

—— 'Diodorus Cronus and Hellenistic Philosophy', *Proceedings of the Cambridge Philological Society*, 207 (1977), 74–120.

Sherry, D., 'On Instantaneous Velocity', *History of Philosophy Quarterly*, 3: 4 (1986), 391–406.

Skyrms, B., 'Zeno's Paradox of Measure', in Cohen and Lauden (eds.), *Physics, Philosophy, and Psychology*, 223–54.

Smith, R., 'The Axiomatic Method and Aristotle's Logical Methodology', *Philosophia Naturalis*, 21 (1984), 590–7.

Solmsen, F., *Aristotle's System of the Physical World*, Cornell Studies in Classical Philology, 33 (Ithaca, NY, 1960).

—— 'Abdera's Arguments for the Atomic Theory', *Greek, Roman, and Byzantine Studies*, 29: 1 (1988), 59–73.

Sorabji, R., 'Aristotle on the Instant of Change', *Proceedings of the Aristotelian Society*, supplementary vol. 50 (1976), 69–89.

—— 'Atoms and Time Atoms', in Kretzmann (ed.), *Infinity and Continuity*, 59–65.

—— *Time, Creation and the Continuum* (London and Ithaca, NY, 1983).

Stenius, E., 'Foundations of Mathematics: Ancient Greek and Modern', *Dialectica*, 32: 3–4 (1978), 255–90.

Stroll, A., *Surfaces* (Minneapolis, 1988).

Swinburne, R., Review of A. Grünbaum, *Geometry and Chronometry in Philosophical Perspective*, British *Journal for the Philosophy of Science*, 21: 3 (1970), 308–11.

Szabo, A., *The Beginnings of Greek Mathematics*, trans. A. M. Ungar, Synthese Historical Library, 17 (Dordrecht and Boston, 1978).

Todd, R. B., *Alexander of Aphrodisias on Stoic Physics* (Leiden, 1976).

Treder, H.-J., 'Aristoteles und die Physik', in Irmscher and Müller (eds.), *Aristoteles als Wissenschafts-Theoretiker*, 150–8.

Verbeke, G., 'L'Argument du livre VII de la *Physique*: Une impasse philosophique', in Düring (ed.), *Naturphilosophie bei Aristoteles und Theophrast*, 250–67.

—— 'Ort und Raum nach Aristoteles und Simplikios: Eine philosophische Topologie', in Irmscher and Müller (eds.), *Aristoteles und Wissenschafts-Theoretiker*, 113–22.

Versteegh, C. H. M., 'The Stoic Verbal System', *Hermes*, 108 (1980), 333–57.

Vlastos, G., 'Minimal Parts in Epicurean Atomism', *Isis*, 56: 2 [184] (1965), 121–47.

—— 'Zeno of Sidon as a Critic of Euclid', in L. Wallach (ed.), *The Classical Tradition: Literary and Historical Studies in Honor of Harry Caplan* (Ithaca, NY, 1966), 148–59.

—— 'Zeno of Elea', in Edwards (ed.), *The Encyclopedia of Philosophy*, viii, 369–79.

Wallis, R. T., *Neoplatonism* (London, 1972).

Wang, P. P., and Chang, S. K. (eds.), *Fuzzy Sets: Theory and Applications to Policy Analysis and Information Systems* (New York and London, 1980).

Wasserstein, A., 'Some Early Greek Attempts to Square the Circle', *Phronesis*, 4 (1959), 92–100.

Waterlow, S., *Nature, Change, and Agency in Aristotle's 'Physics'* (Oxford, 1982).

—— 'Instants of Motion in Aristotle's *Physics VI*', *Archiv für Geschichte der Philosophie*, 65:2 (1983), 128–46.

—— 'Aristotle's Now', *Philosophical Quarterly*, 34: 135 (1984), 104–28.

Weyl, H., *Philosophy of Mathematics and Natural Science* (Princeton, NJ, 1949).

White, M. J., 'Necessity and Unactualized Potentialities in Aristotle', *Philosophical Studies*, 38 (1980), 287–98.

—— 'Fatalism and Causal Determinism: An Aristotelian Essay', *Philosophical Quarterly*, 31: 124 (1981), 231–41.

—— 'Zeno's Arrow, Divisible Infinitesimals, and Chrysippus', *Phronesis*, 27: 3 (1982), 239–54.

—— *Agency and Integrality: Philosophical Themes in the Ancient Discussion of Determinism and Responsibility*, Philosophical Studies Series in Philosophy, 32 (Dordrecht and Boston, 1985).

—— 'What Worried the Crows?', *Classical Quarterly*, 36: 2 (1986), 534–7.

—— 'On Continuity: Aristotle versus Topology?', *History and Philosophy of Logic*, 9: 1 (1988), 1–12.

Wolff, H., and Bauer, A., 'Absolute Geometry', in Behnke *et al.* (eds.), *Fundamentals of Mathematics*, ii. 129–73.

Zadeh, L. A., *Fuzzy Sets and Applications: Selected Papers by L. A. Zadeh*, ed. R. R. Yager, S. Ovshinnikov, R. M. Tong, and H. T. Nguyen (New York, 1987).

Zippin, L., *The Uses of Infinity* (New York, 1962).

Index